MW01641084

Reenacting the Enemy

In memory of my father

Contents

PART III. REENACTING THE ENEMY IN MEDIA AND IN THE MIND

Introduction

I started working on this book in spring 2019 while recovering from minor surgery that at the time felt like the biggest health scare to me. The writing of the first few theoretical chapters helped distract me from my health issue. I planned to continue my work on the book in the summer of 2020, which at that time I anticipated would be another quiet summer at home after my return from a planned trip to Europe. I did not know yet about the biggest world health scare that would coincide with the continuation of my work on the book: the COVID-19 pandemic. It slowly entered every corner of the world; made people socially distance from one another per national and state orders; and forced us to stay home, cancel all travel plans, wear masks, and get used to what the "new normal" might be while hoping for the miraculous return of the "old normal." For the second time in 2 years, I turned to the writing of my book as an escape—this time for a much-needed respite from the global madness and a rising death toll. It also made me think about all those petty ideological and political differences that separated countries in pre-pandemic times, such as Russia and the United States having grown so far apart in the past few years that they almost have reached the point of no return. I started wondering if a global health scare, such as the ongoing pandemic, could bring states and nations together in tackling the disease. I also wondered if the overused and therefore clichéd phrase "We are all in this together" could go beyond national borders and erase some of the differences that have prevented this "togetherness" from happening before.

This book represents a continuation of my growing interest in collective memory and how such memory is being shaped by official producers, media being one of those. A new angle taken in this project has allowed me to step into another territory that until recently had remained outside my academic interests—journalism and media. Although scholars of collective memory agree that media are one of the important official producers of memory and, as such, contribute to the formation and distortion of past memories, rarely do they examine the process of such memory formation as concerns the

Reenacting the Enemy. Ludmila Isurin, Oxford University Press. © Oxford University Press 2022.
DOI: 10.1093/oso/9780197605462.003.0001

coverage of recent political events, many of which have not found their place yet in the nation's memory. Moreover, media reports often are perceived as the first records of history. Knowing the specific techniques that journalists use to make their stories believable and consistent with the cognitive frames that exist in their target audiences allows us to investigate the emergence of a national narrative related to a specific event as memory formation, development, and—sometimes—distortion. We also can tap into the human mind, which ultimately is the targeted consumer of those stories. It is at the intersection of memory, media, and the mind that I attempt to capture how group memories are formed and how the image of the old rival, foe, or what is known in scholarship on collective memory as the *other* is reenacted and reinforced both by the official producers—media, in this case—and by the minds of the intended audience.

In this book, I have turned to memory construction of recent political events that were reflected widely in American and Russian media in the past 5 or 6 years. All these events involved Russia and, in some cases, the United States: the 2014 Winter Olympic Games in Sochi, the takeover of Crimea in 2014, the conflict in Eastern Ukraine, the downing of Malaysia Airlines flight MH17, the conflict in Syria, the 2016 US presidential election, and the poisoning of the Skripals. A large-scale media analysis based on American and Russian news reports in digital outlets of both countries provided the foundation for the survey conducted among Americans in the United States and Russian citizens in Russia. Through the analysis of media, it has been fascinating, yet unsettling, to see how the two countries clearly pushed against each other, thereby reenacting an image of the old Cold War enemy. By initially invoking not entirely forgotten stereotypes from the decades of the Cold War and later reinforcing those with new stories that perfectly fit old narrative frames, the two countries—via their respective media—became engaged in an information war that ultimately aimed at reaching the minds of people in those two countries. Those minds, however, while consciously questioning the trustworthiness of news coverage by their respective media, seem to have formed memories along the ideological lines provided by the very media that they claim they do not trust.

The current project is interdisciplinary and multifaceted; it bridges humanities and social sciences by utilizing methodologies from both. It examines three main domains of memory construction: (1) The effects of media (*producers*) on the construction of a group's memory, (2) media effects on the construction of the *other* through the dissemination of information about a political event involving the *other*, and (3) how information about a political event is consumed by members of the groups targeted by the respective media and how the *other* is reconstructed in individual minds.

The book opens with three theoretical chapters on collective memories, media, and the mind that prepare the reader for the main argument that I build in Chapter 4. These chapters give an overview of each field, with a specific focus on issues that are essential for the conceptualization of the framework. Having proposed a sociocognitive framework within which the current study was conducted, I take the reader to the second part of the book, which is entirely devoted to the results of the study. Chapter 5 explains the methodology used both in the media analysis and in the empirical part, and it provides the demographics of the survey's respondents. Chapters 6–9 discuss the results of the media analysis pertaining to the previously mentioned political events, and Chapter 10 discusses the results of the data analysis based on the survey conducted among Russians and Americans. Chapter 11 brings together all three components—collective memory, media, and the mind—and first reconceptualizes the framework in light of the major findings from the study by bringing the concept of the *other* into major focus and then discusses the results of the study within the original framework offered at the onset of this project.

Not all results revealed in this investigation are as straightforward as the reader might have expected; some can be viewed as controversial and challenging because they undermine well-established beliefs in the West that there is a clear-cut divide between the trustworthy free media in democratic states, such as the United States, and the state-censored—and hence, untrustworthy—media in authoritarian states such as contemporary Russia. As a scholar, I challenge such presuppositions by presenting evidence and providing my argument based on the analysis of the data. I strongly believe that only through the continuous dialogue across disciplines and national borders can we understand better the complexity of memory construction where media interact with the mind in order for the mind to consume the intended message, reinforce old stereotypes, reenact old enemies, and most likely form shared memories that inevitably fit the existent collective memories. In academia, we may never solve political crises and conflicts or make decision-makers and politicians smarter and more open-minded. Yet, we should not become messengers and oracles of the ever-shifting ideologies of those who are in power, no matter where we live or how much we want to be heard.

Having agreed to disagree, I am presenting the contents of this book for the readers to make their own judgment.

PART I
THEORETICAL BACKGROUND

1

Group Memory

Construction, Reconstruction, and Distortion

More than half a century separates us from the groundbreaking work of the French philosopher and sociologist Maurice Halbwachs, who undeniably is considered the father of contemporary research on collective memory. Numerous scholars in disciplines such as history, anthropology, literary studies, communication studies, and psychology explored the theme of collective memory using the methodology common to their respective fields. I am not attempting to provide an in-depth review of the research done in all those fields. Rather, in this chapter, I focus on a few phenomena related to collective memory that are essential for the conceptualization of the theoretical framework of the current study.

Although it is difficult to find clear definitions of collective memory in the burgeoning body of literature, before we proceed any further, we need to understand what collective memory is. The properties and boundaries of collective memory vary depending on the discipline and the domain of the analysis in which it is investigated (C. Harris et al., 2008), and as Wertsch (2002) noted, collective memory is a "term in search of meaning" (p. 30). In order to define the conceptual boundaries of collective memories, Wertsch and Roediger (2008) proposed three main oppositions along which research on collective memory is conducted: collective memory versus collective remembering (i.e., the relatively static nature of collective memory versus the dynamic process of collective remembering), history versus collective remembering, and individual versus collective remembering. Simply stated, every group of people—whether those are friends, family, classmates, or colleagues—and every nation forms some shared memories that are important for the sense of unity that a group strives to maintain as well as for the successful functioning of the group in the present time. Both shared memories of the distant past and memories of recent events are referred to as collective memories.

Reenacting the Enemy. Ludmila Isurin, Oxford University Press. © Oxford University Press 2022.
DOI: 10.1093/oso/9780197605462.003.0002

The underlying mechanisms of memory construction and reconstruction that we discuss more in depth are as follows. First, we need to understand to what extent collective memory is different from history. Second, the process of memory construction and memory distortion and the role of official *producers* of the collective memory, such as textbooks and media,[1] in memory construction and manipulation are central to the current study. Third, we must examine the role of the *other* in the construction of memory, a notion that takes center stage in the current project. Finally, we need to think about the contribution of the individual memory to the construction of collective memory. The main points discussed in this chapter will lead to our focus on the mechanisms—often similar to those I have just mentioned—responsible for how an individual mind constructs, absorbs, and distorts memory (see Chapter 3). The first three chapters of this book provide the foundation for the conceptualization of the framework within which I analyze the results of the current study.

Is History Always More Objective Than Collective Memory?

As mentioned previously, the opposition between collective memory and history serves as one of the boundaries within which collective memory is defined. Overall, there seems to be a consensus that collective memory is not history, although scholars agree that collective memory is grounded on historical facts, even if those facts are distorted and often turned into national myths.

The opposition between history and collective memory already was noted by Halbwachs (1950), who compared history with "a crowded cemetery, where room must constantly be made for new tombstones" (p. 52). Collective memory, in his view, focuses on the stability of events' representation, whereas history constitutes a record of changes. Moreover, collective memory does not exceed the boundaries of a group: "It is a current of continuous thought whose continuity is not at all artificial, for it retains from the past only what still lives or is capable of living in the consciousness of the

[1] See Chapter 2 for a more detailed discussion of media and its role in the construction and distortion of memory.

group keeping the memory alive" (Halbwachs, 1992, p. 80). The next point concerns the demarcation line drawn between present and past by historians, a line that never is found in the collective memory of a group. In collective memory, "the present . . . is not contrasted to the past in the way two neighboring historical periods are distinguished. Rather, the past no longer exists, whereas for historians, the two periods have equivalent reality" (Halbwachs, 1950, p. 82). As Kansteiner (2002) rightly notes, collective memory "can take hold of historically and socially remote events but *it often privileges the interests of the contemporary* [emphasis added]. It is as much a result of conscious manipulation as unconscious absorption and it is always mediated" (p. 180). This emphasis on the contemporary group's interests, which can provide new lenses to interpret the past as well as to construct a memory of an ongoing event (the latter being outside of historians' focus), is extremely important for the current study, in which we will examine the events of the past 5 years and how the memory of those events is being constructed through conscious manipulation of the representation of those events by media and how this memory is absorbed by the group members. If collective memory often privileges the interests of the contemporary while history requires a temporal distance in order to provide "objectivity," we may hypothesize that collective memory of the recent events precedes their conception in analytical history. Historians, however, are members of the group, and as they finally embark on exploring the event of the recent past, they already have been influenced by the shared collective memory of that event, which brings the notion of objectivity into further question.

Clearly, Halbwachs' formulation of how collective memory is different from formal history still presents a contested territory. In the view of Nora (1989), memory and history are not just different; they stand in fundamental opposition. As Novick (1999) asserts,

> To understand something historically is to be aware of its complexity, to have sufficient detachment to see it from multiple perspectives, to accept the ambiguities, including moral ambiguities, of protagonists' motives and behavior. Collective memory simplifies, sees events from a single, committed perspective; is impatient with ambiguities of any kind; reduces events to mythic archetypes. (pp. 3–4)

However, Winter (2009) maintains that the two should not be positioned as adversarial and separate concepts because

> they overlap in too many ways to be considered as pure categories, each living in majestic isolation on its separate peak. Historical remembrance is an analytical category of use here, in that it enables us to understand more fully both the field of force between history and memory and the people who fashion, appropriate, and pass on to us sites of memory. (pp. 256–257)

As Burke (1989) previously noted, history should be more appropriately defined as a particular type of cultural memory because "neither memories nor histories seem objective any longer. In both cases we are learning to take account of conscious or unconscious selection, interpretation and distortion. In both cases this selection, interpretation and distortion is socially conditioned" (p. 98).

Another area of contention concerning history versus collective memory relates to their susceptibility to change. Both history and collective memory undergo change. As Wertsch (2002) suggests, we should look into the reasons behind such changes in collective memory because their motivation often differs from those in historical analysis:

> At least in their idealized versions, historical accounts undergo change because the ongoing process of critical reflection reveals that one version of the past should be revised or replaced by another. In some cases, the need for such change may stem from the discovery of new evidence or archives, and in others it may stem from the use of new analytical tools or theoretical perspective. In all cases, however, the basic argument for why one account should replace another will be grounded in some notion of objective accuracy, completeness, and so forth. (p. 43)

However, the concept of accuracy that one expects to find in analytical history is not without its own problems. Histories are written by individuals belonging to a certain group or nation. Wertsch (2009, p. 125) further notes concerns raised by Mink (1978) and White (1987) regarding whether analytical history can be genuinely distanced and objective even in cases when it is presented by those who are mostly concerned with objectivity. In my previous work on collective memory (Isurin, 2017), I raised the question of which historical texts really are dispassionate and which texts are meant to build collective memory in a nation. Is scholarship always free of political bias or are scholars always free to express their honest interpretation of history? I illustrated my point with the case of the totalitarian regime of the former Union of Soviet Socialist Republics (USSR), where academia and media were controlled by the state ideology and where history textbooks did not differ in presenting official history from any academic scholarship published in those years.

It may take another half a century to resolve the ongoing debate of how collective memory differs from history and whether history is as objective as it often tends to present itself. Scholars coming from different fields of study may continue to promote their own ideas and their own agenda. In the meantime, collective memories—as biased as they always are—will be formed and consumed by individuals, whereas history—also often lacking objectivity—will be written and rewritten by those who are believed to maintain a dispassionate and objective interpretation of the event in question. Indeed, are historians—being, of course, human—immune to the forces of memories shared by the group to which they belong?

Are History Textbooks Real History?

Although many people may trust the account of historical events presented in school textbooks, scholars of collective memory argue that "histories [that] are taught in schools and presented in media are not impartial renderings of past events; rather, these histories reflect a bias to report the past in a way that confirms current preferences, goals, and beliefs" (Blatz & Ross, 2009, p. 224). Indeed, history textbooks present a committed perspective on the depicted event that does not tolerate any ambiguities or leave the door open for different interpretations. Because textbooks target a young generation, they should be considered the most powerful agents of the collective memory. As Ward (2006, as cited in Roediger et al., 2009) posits,

> Unlike independently authored historical accounts, textbooks are a quasi-official story, a sort of state-sanctioned version of history. In nearly all countries the government takes some role in setting the standards for an acceptable cultural, political, and social history—i.e., what the authorities want the next generation to learn about its own national heritage—enfolding them, as it were, into a collective national identity. The fundamental contribution of any textbook is, of course, the story, an account that reveals much about a nation's priorities and values. Because history textbooks contain national narratives written by national authors for a

national audience, they model the national identity in a very profound and unique way. (p. 143)

The profound effect of such narratives often contributed to the mobilization of the masses for war and for committing genocides, for those narratives often present biased tendentious myths or a distorted understanding of the past (Berger, 2007). As Bodnar (1992, as cited in Edy, 2014) suggests, such state-sponsored appeals to shared memory teach citizens patriotic lessons about sacrificing personal comforts, or even their lives, for the good of the nation.

It is not surprising that history textbook scholarship has a strong international research tradition (for a comprehensive review of the field, see Grever & van der Vlies, 2017). However, we should remember that the distortion of historical facts in history textbooks is not a phenomenon solely ascribed to non-democratic states. Loewen (1995), in his book *Lies My Teacher Told Me: Everything Your American History Textbook Got Wrong*, analyzed 12 high school history textbooks on a few important subjects, such as Christopher Columbus, Native Americans, and slavery, and concluded that the textbook authors propagate false Eurocentric views of American history.

Wertsch (2002) notes that "official history texts can be said to occupy a middle ground between religious texts, on the one hand, and other sorts of texts grounded in documentation and rational argument, on the other" (p. 28). However, I believe that the majority of people seeking answers or having a need to create myths about their collective past would travel this particular middle ground due to its availability, accessibility, or simply due to its inescapability in their life paths (Isurin, 2017).

Textbooks, like any educational materials, often are revised and rewritten. However, the rewriting of history textbooks never is a spontaneous process; it is driven by a change in the assessment of the national past or a change in the political regime. Textbooks are especially important in the period of nation building when both historical scholarship and history textbooks become major producers of national narratives (Grever & van der Vlies, 2017). If we take Russia as an example, we can see how throughout the entire 20th century, Soviet history textbooks reflected the current ideology that always supported the current communist leader. In history textbooks of the 1940s and 1950s that carried a portrait of Joseph Stalin, his name along with any visuals depicting him disappeared from subsequent history textbooks after his death and the subsequent denouncement of his cult of personality (Isurin, 2017). A more dramatic change happened after the collapse of the Soviet Union in 1991. History teachers faced the great challenge of presenting the national past to young Russians as the understanding of that past collapsed along with the country. Many young Russians who graduated from high school in the 1990s had a blank spot next to the grade for history on their diplomas (Wertsch, 2009). Indeed, this is a disturbing fact that illustrates the role that history textbooks play in the shaping of the national identity in the minds of young generations. Given the turbulent decade that Russia went through after the collapse of the USSR and the fact that history often was not taught in schools during that period, it is not surprising that as early as 2003—soon after he took office—Russian President Vladimir Putin met with members of the Russian Academy of Sciences to discuss the then-current senior-level history textbooks. It is worth mentioning that at that time, 82 history textbooks were recommended for schools by the Education Ministry, and some presented unverified facts and controversial concepts (Kuvaldin, 2013). Putin stated that history textbooks should instill pride in Russia's past and a sense of patriotism in young Russians (McDaniel, 2018). In 2014, he signed an act (Fundamentals of State Cultural Policy) that essentially aimed at developing a new "history curriculum that would produce a single history free 'from internal contradictions and ambiguities'" (Kovalyova, 2013). McDaniel (2018) provides a detailed analysis of a few historical facts that went through significant reinterpretation, compared to their treatment in the Soviet textbooks, in a newly produced Russian history textbook. The role of the Russian army in World War I, the significance of the Molotov–Ribbentrop pact, and the assessment of the German threat in 1941 were among a few themes that the author explored. It is noteworthy that already in 2014, right after the takeover[2] of Crimea, Putin suggested that history textbooks should include a section on Crimea, which indeed was added to a new textbook (McDaniel, 2018). Given the politically disputed actions concerning the events in Crimea in 2014 and persistent Western opposition to the takeover, the inclusion of this particular theme in a history textbook clearly serves an ideological goal. It cements Putin's action as rightful and irreversible in the minds of the young generation of Russians, as well as presents Crimea as an inherently Russian territory, once and for all. Despite

[2] Because Crimea is one of the themes in this book, I deliberately avoid using the word "annexation" so as not to invoke the Western perspective on this sensitive political issue contested by Russia and the West.

much outcry in Western media and scholarship concerning Putin's act of authoritarian control—this time, control over education—I may play devil's advocate by pointing out that Putin's sentiments that history textbooks should have no ambiguity in the interpretation of the past and that they should instill national pride in young Russians speak to the very fundamentals on which the collective memory of any nation is built. As scholars agree, history textbooks act as agents of the nation's collective memory and allow—if not necessitate a need for—a biased committed perspective on the nation's past. At a time when a political regime drastically changes and a country collapses—as happened in Russia in 1991—there is a need to develop a new history (read: collective memory) of the country. Would it be better to have a few more generations of young Russians graduating from high school without having any exposure to their country's past history or having learned about it from 82 different versions/interpretations of that historical past?

Construction and Reconstruction of Collective Memory

One of the major reasons why a group or a nation needs to have a memory of the shared past is because such memory promotes the integrity and consistency within the group. Without knowing the past, there is no movement forward because the past sustains progress in the present and defines the goals for the future. In other words, collective memory is motivated by social goals, such as promoting group cohesion, enhancing relationships, and negotiating the meaning of shared experiences (C. Harris et al., 2010). Collective memory often is viewed as the "useable past" because it provides the nation with the memory that makes sense for the successful functioning in the present. The most common reasons for developing a useable past have to do with individual or collective "identity claims that take many forms and are tied, among other things, to the need to mourn, the desire to foster patriotism, and the need to erase the sting of defeat and redeem a lost cause" (Wertsch, 2002, p. 31).

Moreover, memory is an inherently human faculty, and it is essential for survival at both the individual and the group level. It is driven by mechanisms—at the conscious and subconscious levels—that help individuals and groups to retain information about the past that serves the goals of the present and to forget the information that does not agree with the goals or identity claims of the present. Although there are many similarities between the way individuals and groups process and forget information, in this chapter, I focus on the construction, reconstruction, and distortion of collective memories (for a discussion of mechanisms of memory distortion in individual minds, see Chapter 3).

I start by stating that mechanisms underlying the construction of collective memory, at least at the production end of the continuum, function at the conscious, rather than the subconscious, level, and always there is some subtle or open control over what a nation constructs as its memory of the past. One of the major factors in the construction of collective memory is the current identity that a group strives to define. Thus, the selection of those historical events from the nation's past always would go toward the goals of the present identity. For example, if a nation wants to present itself as a powerful country whose might and power are defined by the presence of a strong leader, the nation's leaders who are perceived as strong would be resurrected from oblivion; conversely, weak leaders will be forgotten, if not erased, from the group's memory. I have illustrated this point using three Russian political leaders—Joseph Stalin, Mikhail Gorbachev, and Vladimir Putin—and put those three leaders in the context of the historical events (i.e., World War II, the collapse of the USSR, and the takeover of Crimea, respectively) that defined their tenure as leaders (Isurin, 2017). If Gorbachev's name is marred by the pain of the USSR's collapse that many Russians still feel, Putin's popularity has increased due to his decisive role in bringing Crimea back to Russia. At the same time, the collapse of the USSR destroyed the very foundation on which the Russian/Soviet identity was grounded for more than 70 years. Thus, the newly renegotiated identity of Russians—much influenced by the government's attempts to direct the process in the "right" direction—is heavily based on a few historical events of their past, with Russia's victorious role in World War II being reinforced and glorified in recent years. However, the remembrance of suffering during the war and the glory of victory seem to be disengaged from the name of Stalin, the most controversial leader in Russian history and the one who led Russia to victory in World War II. Banned and erased from the collective memory of Russians for three decades, only now can we see his name resurfacing in public discourse. However, I maintain that Russians reconstruct their memory of Stalin not in the vein of World War II; rather, they divorce his name from the event and perceive him as a strong leader who built a strong country. This reconstruction is taking place in light of the current leader who undeniably is viewed as a strong leader by Russians.

An interesting aspect of identity negotiation, both individual and collective, is the obvious desire that individuals and nations have to perceive themselves in the present as better and more accomplished selves than they were in the past. This strong drive toward positivity in self-perception and self-assessment is central to human survival. Without our constant drive to perceive ourselves as better selves in the present than we were in the past, there would not be progress in our development as humankind. Likewise, nations follow the same pattern of maintaining and reinforcing positive memories from their historical past, reconstructing that past in a more positive context, and erasing memories that do not agree with the current needs of the group. To add more to the previous argument, it was found that people who identified strongly with a particular ethnic group had more difficulty remembering events in which their ethnic group had committed violence compared to those who did not identify with that group (Sahdra & Ross, 2007).

As Pennebaker and Gonzales (2009) further suggested, "historical memories are reinterpreted and changed to match the needs of the culture. With time, the memories can often evolve into something mythlike, with positive outcomes emphasized and the costs forgotten. Interestingly, this phenomenon occurs across time and cultures" (p. 186). The strong reliance of political systems on important cultural and historical myths also is stressed by Etkind (2009), who suggested that

> for some political regimes, it is crucial to insist on their definitions of truth; when they fail to do so, they collapse. Having much at stake, various communities of memory either comply with claims of power, or ignore them, or reinterpret them according to their interests. (p. 190)

The favorable collective memories satisfy important group and individual needs, and the motivation of presenting a coherent identity may lead to sacrificing objectivity and accuracy (Wertsch, 2002). Entire communities can react to negative events by suppressing the memory thereof. Examples of the latter are discussed by Pennebaker and Banasik (1997) through showing how the entire community of Dallas, Texas, dealt with the John F. Kennedy (JFK) assassination and how the community of Memphis, Tennessee, reacted to the assassination of Martin Luther King, Jr. (MLK). When JFK was assassinated in Dallas, many Americans blamed the entire city for the tragic event. As a city, Dallas responded by pretending nothing had happened. Four years later, King was assassinated in Memphis, and a similar reaction was observed. As a result, unlike most cities in the United States, there were no schools, streets, or buildings named after Kennedy in Dallas; neither were there any commemorations of MLK in Memphis. However, Dallas had several buildings and streets named after MLK, and Memphis had schools and streets named after JFK. Such attitudes also are referred to as *collective self-deception*; the entire nation or a group of people will forget historical memories or certain details pertaining to those memories if they go against their current beliefs or threaten their positive self-image (Baumeister & Hastings, 1997). Conversely, some groups may focus on the accurate representation of the past no matter how threatening it is to identity commitments. This can be illustrated through the way Germany as a nation recently has gone through the painful process of asking public forgiveness for the horrible deeds committed by the Nazis in World War II.

The forgetting or suppression of historical memories is yet another important mechanism by which the reconstruction of collective memories operates. As Sigmund Freud argued, societies confront committed crimes with discrete monuments that allow people to forget those crimes (Marques et al., 1997). However, institutional repression of memories can explain collective forgetting only partially. Voluntary forgetfulness during the transition from repressive dictatorships to democratic states also can occur, especially if there is no sharp break from the past. Interestingly, a collective dynamic of silence and forgetting happens both among the defeated and among those who have won (Marques et al., 1997). The institutional response to forget and to neutralize what happened has been quite common in countries in which collective political catastrophes have taken place, including Germany, Italy, France, Spain, Chile, and Argentina (Marques et al., 1997).

Obviously, one of the important mechanisms underlying remembrance is social sharing (A. Brown et al., 2012). People need to actively talk about the event in order to solidify the memory of it. If the group is forbidden to talk about an emotionally charged event, the memory of the repressed event can still become very strong as the result of the intentional outside suppression of such memories. In my study of nine political events and figures in Russian history (Isurin, 2017), in which, among other things, I examined how individual memory contributes to the construction of the collective memory, I argued that the memory of Stalin silenced for three decades in Russia still lived in people's minds. In the absence of any official information related to Stalin's name in those decades, family stories shared with the young generation often became the cornerstones on which the memory of a disgraced—although currently risen out of the ashes—leader was built. Another example of memory reconstruction was based on the example of the Cuban missile crisis, which was not much mentioned in official Soviet publications while it was unfolding or thereafter. Despite a rather open discussion of the event in post-Soviet media that is very similar to how it is reflected on in the US media, Russians have not constructed a memory of the crisis and the majority still say they do not have any memory or knowledge of the event, which suggests that the event is perceived as insignificant, if not totally unnecessary, for building the useable past by contemporary Russians. I suggested that the reconstruction of any interpretation of the nation's past happens only when the initial construction took place at the time of the event and/or when it somewhat agrees with the collective memory already living in people's minds. Apparently, the Cuban missile crisis, never constructed as a national narrative, will not become part of the Russian collective memory.

Age and generational differences contribute to the reconstruction of collective memories as well. Political events that happened during the individual's adolescence and young adulthood may become the most impactful for the group identity; the collective memories maintained by the group will affect the way the people will express their opinions later in life. As Boyer and Wertsch (2009) stress, "Memories of youth are intrinsically normative—they tell us not just what happened but also to what extent it reflected what should have happened" (p. 31). Mannheim (1952, as cited in Wertsch, 2009, p. 133) further illustrates the impact of such memories by suggesting that each generation develops a distinctive picture of political and social reality depending on the experiences it has during the formative years of young adulthood. The impact of a significant event that happened during the formative years can be seen in how societies react to the event in terms of building monuments to commemorate it. It was found that usually it takes 20–30 years for the first national monuments honoring a past event to be erected: The timing can be explained by the general need of a society to distance itself from the event in order to acknowledge its impact, but also it takes exactly that many years for the generation of young participants/witnesses of the event to reach the necessary power and social standing in order to become the driving force behind such enterprises (Pennebaker & Banasik, 1997, p. 16).

As can be seen, the process of construction and reconstruction of collective memory is driven by a few fundamental factors: a need to remember the past in order to support the current identity, a constant internal push for remembering positive events over negative ones, a conscious attempt to forget or suppress memories that do not agree with the present identity, and an age factor favoring the construction of memories that affected a generation of group members during their formative years. However, it would be erroneous to assume that the process of memory reconstruction works in such a straightforward way: Remember and reinforce positive facts and forget/suppress negative ones. Collective memory can be distorted over time or, I argue, it can go through the process of distortion as a memory of the event is being constructed. Technically speaking, something that has not been constructed cannot be distorted. But what if we construct something that already is fundamentally wrong or incorrect? When incorrect information is presented at the time of the ongoing event, the construction of collective memory becomes distorted from the beginning. This argument rarely enters the academic debate; however, it becomes crucial for the conceptualization of the framework for the current research and brings a new angle to the discussion of distorted collective memories.

Distortion of Collective Memory

As Bourdon (2011) quite colorfully noted, "Memory is a 'double agent,' lying to all, and yet storing some genuine knowledge of the past even if it is the basis for lies" (p. 63). Baumeister and Hastings (1997), in their work with a self-explanatory title "Distortion of Collective Memory: How Groups Flatter and Deceive Themselves," examine collective self-deception in the construction of distorted memories. Because memories are not perfect and always there is room for error, the authors argue that

> errors that systematically make an individual's own group look worse are relatively rare. The asymmetry in errors, that is the tendency for the majority of errors to enhance rather than diminish the group's positive image—suggests that they are motivated. (p. 278)

However, later the authors conclude that "the line between deliberate and unintentional distortion is inevitably a fuzzy one, because self-deception cannot succeed if it is recognized as such, by definition" (p. 292). They further argue that if one finds any distortion of collective memory in such a country as the United States—a country that enjoys a long-standing tradition of free speech, free press, and the right to criticize any public official—this must support the idea that collective memories often are distorted. Indeed, they provide a few examples of distorted collective memories of the American past. One such example is the purchase of Manhattan Island for $24, which is mentioned in school textbooks and makes students laugh at the naivete of the Indigenous population. The textbooks fail to mention that the $24 was paid, perhaps deliberately, to the wrong tribe that did not care about the value of another tribe's land. Other examples concern the deliberate omission of any mention of slavery when it comes to the founding fathers of the country: Thomas Jefferson, who wrote in the *Declaration of Independence* that "all men are created equal," owned many slaves and advocated the expansion of slavery into the Western territories; and the omission of the ugly historical fact of the first settlers giving the so-called "Indian blankets" infected with smallpox to the Indigenous population while at the same time exaggerating the origins of the Thanksgiving holiday that until the end of the 19th century was not associated with Pilgrims being invited by the Indians to a festive dinner. According to Baumeister and Hastings (1997), there are a few distinct strategies and mechanisms by which the collective memory of a group can be distorted: selective omission, fabrication, exaggeration and embellishment, linking versus detaching, blaming the enemy, blaming circumstances, and contextual framing. One of the examples of exaggeration and embellishment concerned the role of the Soviet and US forces in World War II, which resonates with my findings from the Russian side of the story (Isurin, 2017). As Baumeister and Hastings (1997) note, whereas Russians believe that the victory in the war was due to the heroic efforts of the Russian people and the Red Army and do not consider the contribution of the Allies significant enough for the ultimate victory,

> in the American collective memory—especially as sustained in movies, television shows, and other mass media—the war was fought and won mainly by American soldiers. . . .
>
> Although British and American troops did certainly make important contributions to the victory, the revisionists generally point out that the Red Army bore the brunt of the war and were by far the most important force in bringing about the victory. Germany's best forces were on the Russian front, and it was there that the war was decided. The *Economist* recently concluded that the Normandy invasion and the American attack into Germany was "almost a sideshow" in comparison with the eastern conflict. (p. 282)

I will not repeat all the examples that the authors provide in what I find one of the most fascinating articles on collective memory distortion; I will only add two more important points. First, among all the strategies listed previously, pure fabrication of collective memories happens quite rarely (Baumeister & Hastings, 1997):

> The implication may be that collective memories to some extent are constrained by the facts. Facts may be deleted, altered, shaded, reinterpreted, exaggerated, and placed in favorable contexts, but wholesale fabrication seems to lie beyond what most groups can accomplish. (p. 282).

Second,

> the very tradition of free speech allows people to speak falsehoods as well. Many informed Americans have probably been exposed to speakers and writers who deny that 6 million Jews were murdered by the Nazi Germany system during World War II. People are free to express such views even if they are demonstrably false. . . . In contrast, other countries sometimes have passed laws prohibiting people from denying such facts. (p. 279)

Schwartz (2014) provides another example of collective memory distortion, namely the reinterpretation of Abraham Lincoln's *Gettysburg Address*. Intended originally to honor the casualties of the battle put to rest at the Gettysburg cemetery and to reassure the families of the fallen that their loved ones did not die in vain, the speech has gone through major reinterpretations throughout the past century and a half due to the only phrase that implied equality ("all men are created equal") and was reinterpreted by civil rights activists as a call for racial equality. The example of Barack Obama choosing to talk to journalists in 2007 (before he was elected President) at the same spot where Lincoln had spoken 150 years before (Berkowitz, 2011), or choosing Lincoln's Bible to take his presidential oath and paying tribute to Lincoln's monument the night before his inauguration, signifies the profound effect of the historical inaccuracy on the minds of contemporary Americans, including their first Black President. As Schwartz (2014) argues,

> Lincoln had no reason to torment his listeners by expressing a conviction they did not share. He was not prepared to tell them, in the midst of thousands of fresh graves, that they had been tricked, that the purpose

> of the war was different from what they believed it to be. Most soldiers believed they were fighting to save the Union, and the last thing Lincoln wanted to do, especially in south-central Pennsylvania, a stronghold of rebel sympathizers . . . was to give the impression to bereaved families that he had manipulated their young men into dying to free blacks, for whom they had no interest, let alone compassion. (p. 221)

Memory distortion requires the contextualization of the past event so that the event from the nation's past is reinterpreted in such a way that it serves the goals of the present day. Yet, the idea that collective memory is malleable regardless of the political system and that democracy does not prevent falsehood in the construction of collective memories may seem counterintuitive to scholars educated in Western academia. This becomes important for building my argument in the conceptualization of this book.

Official Producers and the Role of the *Other* in the Construction of Memory

There is a consensus in the scholarship that collective memory is inherently selective (A. Brown et al., 2012) and that memories are malleable in the first place. However, we need to understand how they are shaped and by whom, as well as the limits to this malleability (Burke, 1989).

As discussed previously, the official history presented in history textbooks can be viewed as one of the major state-controlled producers of collective memory. Textbooks target the minds of young members of a society and as such are supposed to deliver the narrative of the national past in the most unambiguous way, without leaving the door open for differing interpretations. The selection, as well as the construction, of national narratives changes over time, as the state decides what memories of the past are crucial for the present national identity and the formation of that identity in the young citizens of the state. Although there are a few exceptions—for example, the Netherlands, where the central government does not screen textbooks and allows for the development of historical thinking rather than the prescribed interpretation of the historical past (Grever & van der Vlies, 2017)—most states exercise some form of control over history textbooks.

However, history textbooks—as important as they are—serve to educate young members of the group. Media can be viewed as the next biggest producer of collective memory that targets all adolescent and adult members of the group. Here, it is difficult to disagree that people living in the age of digital media are bombarded by information that often is difficult to filter. Although we talk more in depth about the role of mainstream media in the construction of collective memories later (see Chapter 2), I emphasize here that media, as another agent of collective memory, often are as biased as history textbooks. Moreover, the construction of national narratives in all texts often is tilted against other groups, which allows a group to show its superiority and instill pride in in-group members. Blatz and Ross (2009) note that

> people's memories of the histories of the national, ethnic, or religious groups to which they belong (ingroups) are often tilted in favor of their ingroups and against other groups . . . historical memories are skewed, in part, because children and adults are presented with selective and biased depictions of the past. Educators, religious leaders, politicians, and media all play an important role by influencing the knowledge available. (p. 223)

Through media, members of the group are exposed not only to the reinterpretation of the historical facts but also to the coverage of ongoing events, which contributes to the construction of collective memories, even if some of those memories will be less stable in the public consciousness than others. Also, media introduce the audience to public officials, who often invoke historical facts to win the hearts and minds of their respective audiences. In general, politicians deliberately influence the public's memory through the use of propaganda, speeches, and other types of political techniques (Lambert et al., 2009).

In the previous section, I discussed democratic states enjoying free speech and how nevertheless those societies are prone to present falsehoods in the interpretation of historical facts. I argue it can affect also the coverage of ongoing political events. Let us examine the fate of the so-called Fairness Doctrine in the United States (Pickard, 2020, p. 137). Formally adopted in 1949, the doctrine required broadcasters to devote some of their airtime to discussing controversial matters of public interest and always to have two different views on the matter in question. This seems to be the most logical way to discuss ongoing political events, especially those that involve other countries. However, the doctrine had as many proponents as it had opponents, and after almost 40 years of exercising some sort of control over media, it was repealed in 1987 under President Ronald Reagan: "Indeed, when it was in place, citizen groups used the Fairness Doctrine as a tool to expand speech and debate" (Rendall, 2005). More than 20 years later, the coverage of world news by mainstream television channels and news outlets in the United States rarely differs in its content and represents one committed perspective, without leaving room for any doubt in the truthfulness and correctness of the presented facts in the minds of the targeted audience.

In other words, the construction of collective memory by official producers can be viewed as biased and tilted in favor of their own group by using the *other* in order to show their own superiority. The examples of such deliberate distortion of collective memory in favor of one group can be found in how their participation in World War II is exaggerated by some countries or how Hiroshima is linked to Pearl Harbor but is not viewed as a relevant response to Pearl Harbor by the Japanese (Pearl Harbor had few civilian casualties, whereas Hiroshima did), or how the German air force mistakenly bombed the German city of Freiburg and in order to save face blamed the bombing on the French (Baumeister & Hastings, 1997).

In my book on collective memory (Isurin, 2017), I specifically examined how the same event/historical figure from the recent Russian past was reflected in the Soviet, post-Soviet, and US media. One of the findings concerned the memory of the last Soviet leader, Mikhail Gorbachev, and its opposite interpretation in the media outlets of the two countries. The Russian media rarely turn to Gorbachev due to his rather controversial legacy in Russian collective memory, yet not incidentally he was brought into the spotlight after his open support of the current Russian policy in Ukraine. At the same time, the US media that once heavily praised Gorbachev occasionally reminisce about their "fallen star," and when there was a need to report about Gorbachev's "unfavorable behavior," such as his support of the Crimea takeover, after a delay of only a few days an appropriate American media article emerged (Fasick & Balsamini, 2016). Although it started with an opening statement about Gorbachev's support of the Crimea takeover, the major part of the article aimed to distract the reader's attention from such disgraceful behavior by someone who used to be the darling of the West. The report was done in such a skillful way that by the end of the text, the reader was expected to remember one thing and one thing only—Gorbachev's dislike of Putin. Another finding concerned the Chechen wars conducted by post-Soviet Russia in the late 1990s and early 2000s. If the post-Soviet media show the brutality of Chechens and equate the Chechen fighters committing acts of terrorism against civilians with terrorists, the US media are reluctant to apply the same term to the Chechen rebels whose cause they justify (note that hundreds of those fighters joined ISIS; Hauer, 2018). Moreover, when a major terrorist act, recognized by all US outlets as such, gets linked to the Chechen mastermind, he is referred to as a "Chechen warlord" rather than a terrorist (Stelnbuch, 2016). Those examples show how official *producers* in both countries target their respective groups and present the information in such a way that this information will affect the minds of people most efficiently. In other words (Isurin, 2017),

> the official producers, regardless of what group they represent and how much freedom the "free media" actually possess, tend to tilt the information about past and current political events toward the needs and goals of their respective groups, often pushing against the *other*. (p. 278)

My reference to the media representation of events in the Russian past and present is not accidental. Not only does it serve the purpose of preparing the reader for the case study that becomes the main focus of the book but also it demonstrates that the two countries, the biggest former Cold War foes, can be viewed as the best exemplars of how the *other* is constructed in the public discourse and, as a result, in the collective memory of both countries.

Collective Memory and Language

According to Halbwachs (1950), memory is social because it is based on language and on an external or internal linguistic communication with significant others. Indeed, one of the major tools by which collective memory is presented by official producers is language. As Pennebaker and Banasik (1997) note, the social mechanism underlying memories is language—"the primary symbol system that defines the framework for individuals' memories" (p. 4). They go on to state,

> Translating events or images into language affects the ways they are thought about and recalled in multiple ways. . . . When an event is discussed, its perception and understanding is likely to be affected by others in the conversation. On a more psychological level, talking about an event is a form

> of rehearsal. Further, the act of rehearsing the event through language can influence the way the event is organized in memory and, perhaps, recalled in the future. (p. 7)

Later, Kansteiner (2002) supported this claim by suggesting that "the very language and narrative patterns that we use to express memories, even autobiographical memories, are inseparable from the social standards of plausibility and authenticity that they embody" (p. 185).

Wertsch (2009) developed the idea of linguistic forms and embodied practices in constructing collective memories further by noting that in studies on collective remembering, one can observe a clear "divide between explicit linguistic forms, especially narratives, that represent the past, on the one hand, and forms of mediation that rely less on explicit linguistic representation and more on embodied practices, on the other" (p. 120). The role of schemata[3] or culturally based templates in which a memory reconstruction takes place was originally suggested by Halbwachs. Being critical of Halbwachs' conceptualization of group memory, Bartlett (1967), the founder of modern memories studies in psychology, argued that

> social organization gives a persistent framework into which all detailed recall must fit, and it very powerfully influences both the manner and the matter of recall. Moreover, this persistent framework helps to provide those "schemata" which are a basis for the imaginative reconstruction called memory. It is equally probable that the social creation and clash of interests aid in the development of the specific images which . . . may be present in individual recall. But we need to go far beyond this if we are to show that the social group itself possesses a capacity to retain and recall its own past. (p. 296)

In his work *Voices of Collective Remembering*, Wertsch (2002) promotes the idea of using narrative templates as a linguistic tool in the analysis of collective memory. He takes the example of Russian interpretation of historical memory—the role of the USSR in World War II in particular—through Soviet and post-Soviet texts to illustrate culturally embedded schemata in Russian war narratives. He argues that "schematic narrative templates function to exert a conservative, yet often unrecognized force

[3] The role of schemata is discussed in more detail in Chapters 2 and 3.

on collective memory, making it quite resistant to change" (p. 130). He maintains that the Russian understanding of crucial historical episodes can be illustrated through a basic plot structure that he calls "expulsion of foreign enemies," a schematic narrative template that includes the following elements:

1. An initial situation in which Russia is peaceful and not interfering with others.
2. The initiation of trouble in which a foreign enemy viciously and wantonly attacks Russia without provocation.
3. Russia almost loses everything in total defeat as it suffers from the enemy's attempts to destroy it as a civilization.
4. Through heroism and exceptionalism, and against all odds, Russia, acting alone, triumphs and succeeds in expelling the foreign enemy. (p. 93)

Wertsch's idea was further explored by Garagozov (2002), who went even deeper into Russian historical narratives in order to demonstrate that a schematic narrative template is the product of the interaction of numerous factors—political, religious, sociocultural, historical, and psychological. I argue that not only narrative templates but also the very language and the structure of the text are used by official producers of memory to deliver the intended message, which is somewhat underinvestigated in the field of collective memory. I previously presented one example from the US media report on Gorbachev's support of the takeover of Crimea. The opening line—factual information—that Gorbachev supported Putin's action in taking over Crimea may be overwritten in the individual's mind by the rest of the text presenting Gorbachev's poor health (indeed, can we expect clear thinking in someone who is old and sick?) and his admitted dislike of Putin—which are also factual information (Isurin, 2017). Another example is a repeated reference to Russian soldiers or "Russian boots" being on Ukrainian soil when a referendum in Crimea and the subsequent takeover of Crimea by Putin were taking place. What was missing—or I suggest deliberately omitted—in most reports was the fact that a large Russian Black Sea fleet is harbored in Sevastopol, a port city in Crimea; it never left Crimea after the collapse of the USSR. So technically Russian "boots" *always* were in Crimea. However, an uninformed reader/listener would assume that the Russian army indeed invaded Crimea. Five years after the takeover, there is hardly any mention of the referendum in which the people of Crimea overwhelmingly voted for joining Russia. Instead, the distorted reference to Russian troops that annexed Crimea in 2014 prevails in US media outlets (Hodge, 2019). As Putin is criticized for bringing the takeover of Crimea as a justified act based on people's will into history textbooks (McDaniel, 2018), the US mainstream media seem to have written off the entire historical fact of the referendum in Crimea. Thus, the clichéd "Russian boots" and "Russian troops" represent a linguistic manipulation of the information that aims to reflect only part of a true story.

Chapter 3 discusses how the mind perceives the information and constructs a distorted memory. For now, readers just need to keep in mind that linguistic forms are powerful tools in how official producers of memory—whether this memory relates to past or present events—manipulate the minds of the intended audience.

Collective Memory and the Mind

Producers of collective memory would not succeed if the collective memory delivered through their numerous channels were not somehow consumed by the in-group members. The continuum between production and consumption of collective memory, in my view, is one of the most fascinating—albeit still rather illusive—ideas in the field of collective memory research. It was the topic that I explored in the case of Russian collective memory (Isurin, 2017), and I intend to investigate it further in this book.

The study of collective memory mostly has been appropriated by historians and anthropologists, whereas the study of individual memory has fallen into the domain of psychology. Despite the fact that both types of memory originally came from the field of philosophy, the separate treatment of these two phenomena by scholars from different disciplines that recognize distinctly different methodologies pushed the research on collective and individual memory more apart than it was at the time when Halbwachs conceptualized the idea of collective memory. For Halbwachs, collective and individual memories seem to represent unity rather than disparity; the remembrance of personal memories is viewed from the perspective of a group whose presence is essential for triggering and validating such instances of remembrance; and the removal of an individual from a group results in forgetting or distortion of shared memories. Halbwachs (1950) states,

> From the moment when we and . . . other witnesses belong to the same group and think in common about . . . matters, we maintain contact with this group and remain capable of identifying ourselves with it and merging our past with it. Putting it another way, we must from this moment on never have lost the habit and capacity to think and remember as a member of the group to which we all belonged, to place ourselves in its viewpoint and employ the conceptions shared by its members. (pp. 25–26)

Although the precise relation between the individual and collective memories remains one of the unsettled areas of collective memory (Kansteiner, 2002), in recent decades there have been growing calls to merge the two fields of research—collective and individual memory. As Hirst and Manier (2008) state, "We can treat collective memories as 'shared individual memories,' but locate them, not in 'the head' or 'in the world,' but in the interaction between what is out in the world and what is in the head" (p. 189). Bourdon (2011) further criticizes the lack of the human component in the study of collective memory. As he rightly notes,

> Many contemporary historians who want to tackle "collective memory" head-on do not, for the most part, ask people what they remember. Collective memory researchers tend to use widely diffused cultural texts, notably popular media, but also ceremonies and monuments: Just about anything, any "medium" in the widest sense, can serve to document "collective memory." To be blunter, collective memory research seems to have little to do with actual memories of actual people. (p. 66)

Also, Boyer and Wertsch (2009) made a strong call for a merger of the two types of research because

> it makes little sense to think of memory as "individual" (for psychologists) or "cultural" (for historians and anthropologists), as the most fascinating phenomena occur in the individual creation of cultural and historical representations. To understand those phenomena, one should not be "interdisciplinary," if that means concocting a witches' brew of disparate results. Rather, one should ignore disciplines altogether and forge ahead. (p. 1)

The idea of ignoring disciplines, promoted by Boyer and Wertsch (2009), and a call to find the collective memory at the intersection of "what is in the head" and "what is in the mind," made by Hirst and Manier (2012), were liberating indeed. In my recent book (Isurin, 2017), I brought together methodologies both from humanities (textual analysis) and from social sciences (empirical data from human participants) to study the way collective memory gets reconstructed over time in group members, such as Russians in Russia, and those who left the group, such as Russian immigrants in the United States. My interest in determining how group members might be different from former group members in the reconstruction of the past was triggered by Halbwachs' (1950) statement that as group members who never lost contact with the group, we maintain the ability to think and remember as group members. But what happens when an individual no longer belongs to the original group and has moved to another group that for some reason has a vested interest in presenting the history of the *other* group in a light that serves its own purposes? That interest in seeing how the possible consumption of information related to the group's shared past via outlets of the two countries that for decades remained the biggest rivals may influence how memories of the nation's past are reconstructed in group members versus former group members was boosted by Boyer (2009), who noted that

> the appropriation of an event requires complex individual processes whereby people locate historical events in relation to their own life stories. . . . Also the ways people think of themselves as parts of groups is strongly constrained by individual cognition, in particular by people's essentialist assumptions about communities. (p. 10)

In other words, I wanted to see to what extent the efforts of official "producers" of collective memory in both countries reach the minds of "consumers" and how individual memory of a political event contributes to the construction of collective memory. Because, to the best of my knowledge, there was no other empirical work that bridged those two lines of research in collective memory in such a way, I allow myself to share here a few findings from that study.

A clear difference in the interpretation of the shared past between Russians in Russia and Russian immigrants in the United States signaled the role of identity and affiliation with the group as the major factors in the way the two groups remember their nation's past. To illustrate, despite the fact that World War II was the only event that remained equally important for the generational transmission for both groups, the glorification of the war and a belief in the decisive role of the Soviet army in the ultimate victory persist and are reinforced in the Russian consciousness, whereas Russian immigrants present a more critical take on the war and credit both the USSR and the Allies in the victory. Also, whereas the immigrants maintain a very negative view of Stalin, contemporary Russians are more willing to forgive him for the Great Terror and view him as a more complex leader rather than just a mass murderer. Another important event, the USSR's collapse, and the role of another political leader, Mikhail Gorbachev, also showed differing attitudes between the two groups. Whereas Russians regret the disintegration of their country and put much blame on Gorbachev, immigrants view the collapse as the end of the "empire of evil" and are less critical of Gorbachev's role. These trends resembled the findings in the analysis of the media texts from the outlets of the two countries related to the previously mentioned events and suggested that the consumption of the official history indeed may influence how individuals reconstruct their collective past to fit it into their new identities. Although I acknowledged that immigrants' memories of the past as well as their attitude toward Russia may have been different from the start and this could have affected the way immigrants reconstructed memories of their pre-immigration past, we cannot deny the role of the official producers in the new host country that often push against the *other*—the Russian past, in this case—in order to present their own superiority. Another factor concerned the recency effect and lived-in experiences. The recent immigrants in my study, those who lived through the collapse and the subsequent dark years of the economic crash, tended to associate Gorbachev's name with that period more than did immigrants who viewed the event from the other side of the Atlantic Ocean. Similarly, the assessment of the Chechen wars by the recent immigrants who lived in Russia during that period was different from that of the old-timers and much closer to the assessment given by Russians. This trend was observed for almost all events analyzed in my work (Isurin, 2017), suggesting that not only the time separating the former group members from their group (recent immigrants versus old-timers) but also the personal lived-in experience and the context in which the collective memories were formed and later reconstructed (the USSR versus post-Soviet Russia) affect the collective memory in people's minds.

The most fascinating differences in how the two groups constructed their memory concerned the then ongoing political event, the takeover of Crimea in 2014. There was no other event central to the project that would show such divisive opinions expressed by Russians living in Russia versus Russian immigrants in the United States, which led to the following conclusion (Isurin, 2017):

> If both groups of participants, former and current members of the same group, often reconcile their differences and agree—although to a different extent—on what makes certain memories from their shared past important, the "memory in construction"—the ongoing Ukrainian crisis—has divided the two groups into opposite camps where each represents an ideological stance clearly articulated by each respective society, Russia and the U.S. There is no longer a need or attempt to look back and revisit those events that defined the lives of both groups. As their countries are brought to the brink of a Cold War following the takeover of Crimea, Russians who shared the same country and same memories but who now live in "enemies'" lands become consumers of the official information and history produced by those lands. This is no longer about the shared past; Russians actively are constructing their own collective memory, this time not shared with their former compatriots, whereas the latter, often torn between their two identities, gradually are becoming loyal *consumers* of the official history presented to them by their new host country. (p. 234)

In addition to my investigation of the production–consumption continuum, I attempted to take a broader perspective on individual memory and suggested that this type of memory includes the memory of lived experiences as well as what are known as communicative memories (Isurin, 2017). Such communicative memories are transmitted among generations within the same family (Paez et al., 1997) and become appropriated by the younger generations as their own memory of the event. The power of such family stories in the construction of collective memories is not always appreciated by historians. As Blight (2009) passionately states,

> We [historians] might wish the public would demonstrate a more critical sense of history, that they would listen to their professors and teachers and read good history; but shutting off antiquarianism is like stopping Niagara. And often a grandparent simply carries far more authority than we do, and a feel-good story can trump our tragedies and contradictions any day of the week on the History Channel. (p. 242)

The idea of autobiographical memories being part of collective memories indeed is not novel, although it had not been tested empirically prior to my recent investigation. As A. Brown et al. (2012) propose,

> Autobiographical memories are simultaneously reconstructed to be distinct from that of another person and converge with it as a result of social interactions. Through this convergence, emerges collective memory that will in turn establish a collective identity and promote sociality. (p. 1)

The content analysis of personal memories shared by my participants, often transmitted from grandfathers to grandchildren, revealed some common trends that are not typically found in the analysis of texts. To illustrate, a 20-year-long silence surrounding the commemoration of World War II in the USSR could be detected only through personal memories of the participants. Another example—already mentioned in this chapter—is how Russians only now construct the collective memory of Stalin. As I suggested, when collective memory is being constructed and there is little official information available, or when the information has been silenced for decades, the individual memory becomes the primary source for the construction of the collective memory. In the case of the memory of Stalin, depending on the personal impact that the Great Terror had on the family and how the memory of Stalin was remembered or negotiated within each family, the resulting individual memories indeed contribute to the construction of the collective memory. On the other hand, the analysis of the individual memories also indicated why Russians do not align with the interpretation of the Chernobyl disaster by the official producers of the collective memory that, in the aftermath of the disaster, insisted that all necessary measures were taken and that Chernobyl should be put to rest or become the problem of Ukraine, where it is located. It was only through the individual recollections of the effects of the nuclear fallout personally felt by many participants that it became clear why the consumers are not yet "buying" the producers' side of the story.

Having reinterpreted the role of the individual memory in the construction of collective memories, I went even further and suggested a provocative idea that flashbulb memories (i.e., almost photographic memories of a major or often traumatic event; the term was first introduced by R. Brown and Kulick, 1977), such as the launch of the first Russian astronaut into space, could remain uniquely personal and, when combined together, could become a shared "flashbulb" memory of the group (Isurin, 2017). This further supports the notion of social contagion: Over time, individual distinct memories can become shared collective memories—the collective variant of autobiographical memories—either through discussing such memories with other group members or through the intergenerational transmission of individual memories. As in the case of official producers of collective memory that may distort the factual information related to the remembered event, cognitive mechanisms underlying individual memories often involve memory distortions, and these distortions often are shared across community members and, as a result, lead to distorted shared memories (A. Brown et al., 2012).

Altogether, the idea of examining how official history is produced and how it is consumed by individual minds is fascinating indeed. As previously mentioned, the production–consumption continuum in the research on collective memory and the role of an individual in the construction of such memories are as important as the role of official producers of collective memories. After all, the latter act as agents of collective memory while they still remain human beings, with their own cognitions and beliefs, who belong to their own group. By actively constructing the memory of their group through those means that they have hold of—whether it is through writing a history textbook or reporting on an ongoing political event via media outlets—official producers of collective memory inherently remain members of the group. Such belonging makes any individual author involved in the process of memory construction among the members of their group potentially biased in presenting a true story. It is through such a biased committed and tilted against the *other* perspective that we learn about the historical past of nations and learn about those events that still are making their way into history.

Summary

In this rather brief discussion of how collective memories are constructed, a few points have been identified. First, collective memories are not history, as the latter is supposed to be more or less objective in presenting the factual information, whereas the former always presents only one committed—and often biased—perspective on the past event. Second, collective memory focuses only on historical events that serve the goals and identity claims of the group, thus turning some positive events into national myths and downplaying or simply omitting less pleasant facts from the nation's past. Third, because collective memories are biased, they allow for distortion, which may be done via different mechanisms, such as omission, exaggeration, and fabrication. What is even more important is that distortion of memory happens across the board, and both democratic states with freedom of speech and authoritarian systems with tight state control over any information related to the past and present events provide equally good conditions for memory distortion. The next point that should be noted is the role of official producers of collective memory, among which we focus on media that rightly can be considered the second largest agent of collective memory—after history textbooks—and a first recorder of history. A major difference between history textbooks and media in the construction of collective memory is that textbooks cover important events from the nation's past in order to create what is known as a "useable past," whereas media contribute to both the reconstruction of past memories and the construction of new memories. I also argue that media play an even larger role in the construction and reconstruction of collective memories, as exposure to textbook information ceases with the individual's graduation from high school or college. From then on, media will take a major part in providing the individual with the information related to the past events as well as in presenting an interpretation of the ongoing political events—or writing the first draft of history, as some may argue—that have yet to find their place in what Halbwachs (1950) called "a crowded cemetery, where room must constantly be made for new tombstones" (p. 52). Although an in-depth discussion of the role of media in the construction of collective memory is presented in Chapter 2, suffice it to say that the proliferation of media reports has intensified in the past two decades due to the technological advance of digital media.

Moreover, because official producers of collective memory often deliberately tilt the memory construction in such a way that they emphasize their group's superiority at the expense of presenting an inferior group in a negative light, I may go even further by arguing that the media coverage of ongoing political events aims at creating the *other*, if that *other* does not already exist in the minds of the targeted audience. The manipulation of those minds can be achieved through emphasizing certain facts and omitting other information, which I call the content manipulation of the delivered information. However, any information is delivered through some sort of medium, with language remaining the most powerful and effective tool used by official producers of collective memory. In other words, simultaneously examining *what* was said and *how* it was said may give us a better glimpse into the construction of collective memory and the construction or reenactment of the *other* in the age of digital media. However, media production is at the opposite end of media consumption in the production–consumption continuum. Without looking into the minds of the consumers, we will not be able to understand fully whether the efforts of official producers succeeded in making their targeted audience believe in the delivered—and often carefully distorted—information. This brings us closer to the next major question: How does an individual's mind process information, especially if the information is deliberately distorted? Before we answer this question, let us examine the role of media in the construction of collective memory about ongoing political events and the reconstruction of collective memory about past events.

2
Collective Memory, Journalism, and News Making

Collective memory is constructed by the group and lives within the group: "In today's society, collective memory is increasingly shaped by specialized institutions: schools, courts, museums and the mass media" (Misztal, 2003, p. 19). Although much has been said about the way collective memory is constructed and reconstructed due to various sociocultural and political reasons and about various forces—mostly those representing power in the group—that determine the direction in which such reconstruction would go, only in the past two or three decades were there attempts to examine the role of media as one of those "specialized institutions" through which such reconstructive processes operate. Moreover, scholars working at the intersection of the two fields—collective memory and media studies—call for bringing them together in order to get a deeper understanding of each. As Neiger et al. (2011) note,

> The fundamental role of mediation and the dominance of social construction lie at the heart of these two fields and tie them together. As a result, both fields are demarcated by similar themes regarding issues of representation, sociocultural power relations, and the role of narrativity in the process of the social construction of meaning. This fundamental interconnectivity between the two fields enables us to point at key concepts, questions, and characteristics that bind these two realms of inquiry in order to look at each of them through the prism of the other. (p. 4)

The role of media and journalism in the construction of collective memory is undeniable. If history textbooks, as discussed in Chapter 1, serve the goal of educating the young generation about the nation's past, mass media target a much larger audience and have the capability of producing a daily impact on the minds of the intended group. From this point of view, media's role in the construction of collective memory goes beyond the representation

Reenacting the Enemy. Ludmila Isurin, Oxford University Press. © Oxford University Press 2022.
DOI: 10.1093/oso/9780197605462.003.0003

of past events: Journalism is on the front line of recording history and constructing new memories. However, memory studies and journalism have gone through strikingly different paths in academia. As Zelizer (2014) pointedly notes, the past few decades have

> displayed a battleground for competing academic disciplines, each of which produces its own vision of what memory looks like. In sturdier times, such a focus might have certain advantages, but the uncertainty and instability of the current academic environment have positioned collective memory front and center in localized struggles to fortify disciplinary boundaries and enhance topicality. And though collective memory now regularly appears in curricula in literature, psychology, sociology, history, communication, anthropology and education, no discipline offers a sufficiently inclusive vantage point on memory's trappings. (p. 42)

On the other hand, journalism has turned into an autonomous and self-contained discipline. To illustrate, most large US universities have departments of journalism and departments of communication studies, whereas there are no separate academic units devoted to memory studies (Olick, 2014).[1] Such isolation of journalism, in addition to the already existent compartmentalization of numerous disciplines dealing with collective memory, calls for an interdisciplinary approach to memory studies. Moreover, by ignoring the importance of media as the first-hand recorder of collective memory, we miss an important perspective in its study. Conversely, journalism, and more precisely media studies, as "such an autonomous discipline does not keep abreast with highly relevant developments in other disciplines and might soon lag behind the development of its own theoretical frameworks" (van Dijk, 1988, p. 3).

In this chapter, we examine the role of media and journalism (I use both terms interchangeably) in the construction of collective memory, especially in the post-broadcast era. We discuss the role of institutions and power organizations standing behind journalists[2] and influencing how news stories are reported. Then, we discuss various techniques used by journalists to make such stories believable, relevant, and accessible to the target audience,

[1] Washington University in St. Louis has an interdisciplinary program in memory studies but not a department.

[2] Throughout this chapter, I use the word "journalist" not only to refer to individual reporters but also as a collective term referring to editors, agencies, etc.

as well as techniques that intend to manipulate the minds of the group. All these elements are important for the conceptualization of the framework within which the study central to this project was conducted.

Journalism and Memory Studies

Although, in literature, there are repeated references to journalism as the first draft of history, "historians are very clearly invested in the claim that they are *not* journalists, and journalists are at least somewhat careful about this distinction and usually recognize what it entails" (Olick, 2014, p. 21). Olick (2014) identifies one of the reasons why journalism has been neglected in memory studies—the limited intellectual position of journalism—which he explains as follows:

> Because it is a mere "first draft," it is prone to error without revision. Journalism, like memory but in distinction to history, is fallible and ephemeral, and hence not corrected as carefully as historians would like. Journalism is, indeed, temporary by design. After all, who but a historian would read an old newspaper? At the same time, from the perspective of memory studies, journalism looks a lot like history: It is a professional enterprise, it is public, it values sources and rules of confirmation, and its residues are relatively permanent. (p. 23)

It would be an overgeneralization to state, however, that journalism has been involved in recording all historical events on which the nation's collective memory is built, simply because journalism, as a distinct field, is a relatively modern entity and its wide reach to the community has become possible only due to technological advances in the past century and a half. However, media have contributed much to the construction of memories related to at least those events that took place in recent times: Collective memories often have their origins in news events (Edy, 2014), and our memory of public events "often incorporates the journalistic images of the events that journalism itself framed. Memory of public events is thus ultimately inseparable from their journalistic coverage and constitution" (Olick, 2014, p. 28). As Zelizer (1992) writes, "The story of American past [or of any other contemporary past] will remain in part a story of what the media have chosen to remember, a story of how the media's memories have in turn become America's [or any other country's] own" (p. 214). By extension, Bird (2011) adds, "If the media have *not* chosen to remember—indeed, have not told the story in the first place—the official memory is also erased" (p. 90). The latter can be supported by my recent findings on collective memory of the Cuban missile crisis among Russians. Because the Soviet media provided very limited, if any, information about the crisis as it was unfolding and never mentioned it after it was resolved, the majority of college-educated Russians, including those who lived during the crisis, admitted having no knowledge or memory of the event (Isurin, 2017).

Although often originated in news stories, collective memory, if strictly defined as memory of the shared past living in the present life of the group, rarely becomes a focus of journalism. Scholars agree that journalism hardly is concerned with non-commemorative memory because journalistic work is routine and non-commemorative by nature (Neiger et al., 2011). To illustrate, in the United States, there are annual media segments devoted to national celebrations, such as Independence Day, D-Day, or MLK Day (although the latter is not wholly a celebration because it is observed in memory of the assassinated leader, it does signify a positive change or hope for change in American society), as well as segments commemorating the nation's tragedies, such as 9/11 or Pearl Harbor. In other words, when it comes to past events, journalism "is more inclined to the coverage of events than conditions, especially old conditions: That Holocaust survivors suffered long-term trauma is hardly 'news,' in any sense of the word" (Olick, 2014, p. 22).

Despite a clear trend to devote full-length articles to commemorative rather than non-commemorative events, journalists often refer to past events to bring awareness to what they are reporting about present happenings. For example, Barnhurst (2011, cited in Schudson, 2011, p. 87) sampled a few major US newspapers at 20-year intervals from 1894 to 1994 and found a steady increase in the percentage of articles that made some reference to past events while reporting on current happenings (i.e., from 25% in 1894 to almost 50% in 1994). Schudson (2011) suggests that one of the reasons why journalists increasingly refer to the past is "that the world is complex beyond measure and that part of the journalist's job is not just to report the latest happenings but to fit them into some kind of coherent framework for the audience" (p. 88). Or as Berkowitz (2011) adds,

> Collective memory allows news to gain a semblance of the familiar—journalists are able to tell their stories in a way that seems resonant to

> both news organizations and news audiences. In essence, through collective memory, their version gains authority as *the* version. (p. 201)

Regardless of whether this is what journalists indeed intend to do by referencing the past in their reports on the present, this practice does serve as an additional reinforcement of the collective memory in the minds of the audience.

Furthermore, I suggest that such construction of news stories that would fit the existent sociocultural framework in the targeted community resonates with how collective memories are reconstructed always to serve the present goals of the group, thereby making both fields—memory studies and journalism—socially and culturally grounded in the particular group of people, be it a local community of a newspaper's readers or the entire nation. Like any recorder of history or producer of collective memory, journalists inherently remain members of the group and they write for the group whose interests, expectations, and current needs they understand. Both journalists and the organizations for which they work "use and are shaped by *social* memory—that is, by an awareness of history, of what is important to the group, and of where various events and themes came from and how they have developed over time" (Olick, 2014, p. 25).

Moreover, as we know, any reconstruction of collective memory is a process devoid of objectivity and historical accuracy; it is also biased against the other group, which is perceived as inconsonant with the values of the present group. The same partially may hold true for journalism. As van Dijk (1988) asserts, journalism, as "any transformation of source texts into news texts must involve subjective or group-based (professional as well as ideological) norms and values" (p. 118) because

> news is not produced by isolated individuals. . . . Journalistic activities and interactions, as well as the actual writing and rewriting of news texts, are also inherently social. . . . Journalists participate in news encounters and write news articles as social members. This fact also affects their knowledge, beliefs, attitudes, goals, plans or ideologies, all of which are also partly shared by a professional or wider social group. (p. 99)

However, the failure to contextualize properly the events on which journalists report was named as one of journalism's shortcomings (Schwartz, 2014), which indicates that certain expectations to see journalism as a discipline closer to history (meaning: objective) than to collective memory (meaning: subjective) are not always met. Furthermore, scholars acknowledge the existence of "what is traditionally called the bias of the news" (e.g., van Dijk, 1988, p. 111), which seems to be a logical outcome of a subjective transformation of any original source, be it the news information gathered by a journalist in the field where the event just happened or a historical fact that often is distorted by "official producers" of collective memory—journalists being one of those—to form a collective memory.

Another interesting angle that ties collective memory and media studies together concerns the role of personal memories in the construction of collective memories. As discussed in Chapter 1, individual memories often shape the direction in which the process of memory reconstruction will go, especially in cases in which the official producers of collective memory kept silent on a particular event while the memory of the event still continued living in the minds of the group members. Edy (2014) suggests that when "the past is beyond personal memory, the media's power over collective memory likely expands" (p. 75). To illustrate, the ongoing reconstruction—or as I argued, construction—of memory of Stalin in contemporary Russia would support this point. Young Russians who have no personal memory of Stalin's atrocities are more likely to align with the representation of Stalin as a strong leader in contemporary Russian media and to vote for the rehabilitation of his legacy (Isurin, 2017).

Having established a few points that bring collective memory and media studies closer together, we may want to see how media report on ongoing events. Ultimately, such first drafts of history—even if not recognized by historians as such—will build the foundation for the construction of a new collective memory of the group. It may take historians years to establish a sufficient distance from the current event in order to study it in depth with all the accumulated methodological acumen, and by then they may or may not consider such "first drafts of history" credible, whereas the construction of memory in the individual minds will be going on due to such drafts to which, as humans in the 21st century, we are exposed on a daily basis. This brings us to the following question: How have media and, as a result, their influence on the construction of memory, changed in what is known as the post-broadcast era?

Media and Memory in the Post-Broadcast Era

The rapid technological advances at the end of the 20th century that in full force galloped into the 21st century have left few people unaffected by such changes. Long gone are the times when TV news and morning newspapers were the only sources through which we learned about the latest events, both domestic and international. Pickard (2020) predicts that in the near future, reduced home deliveries of newspapers, newspapers going online, and bankruptcies in the media world will increase. Also, there is a clear generational divide in what kind of media formats certain audiences prefer. Nowadays, a local newspaper spotted early in the morning in someone's driveway probably suggests that the home's residents are people of the older generation. Numerous internet sites, including those representing major newspapers and TV channels, have become an integral part of our lives and have attracted the younger generations of readers. As Gans (2003) notes, "The fact that young people, who have a well-earned reputation for ignoring the news, are paying some attention to it on the web is seen as a good omen for the future" (p. 42).

With such obvious changes that happened in the post-broadcast era, journalism—and its role in the construction of memory in particular—is changing, too. In the past two decades, the term "media memory" instead of "collective memory" has come into focus (Neiger et al., 2011); another term, "globital memory," referring to "the synergetic combination of the social and political dynamic of globalization with digitalization" (Reading, 2011, p. 242), was even offered as an alternative. There are increasingly more voices in academia suggesting that digital media technologies are changing human memory practices both individually and collectively (e.g., Marsh & Rajaram, 2019; Reading, 2011). As Hoskins (2011) says, "None of the 'what,' 'how,' 'why,' and 'when' of remembering and forgetting are untouched by the advent of digital media" (p. 279).

As a result of such technological advances, the commercial model of news production, predominant for more than a century, is said to be rapidly collapsing. As Edy (2014) explains, "In the case of commercial media, the assumption is that mediated messages reach a mass audience or are at least intended to appeal to a mass audience in order to maximize profit and influence" (p. 67). Thus, news organizations sought money coming from large audiences.

> Moreover, a growing number of scholars were finding the news looked essentially the same, regardless of the specific outlet. From the late 1980s until the new millennium, a number of prominent U.S. scholars of media and politics repeatedly documented the hegemonic nature of journalism. They pointed out that no matter which specific news source one chose, the news generally served as an amplifier of the government. (Edy, 2014, p. 68)

In the last few decades of the 20th century, however, as Edy points out, news audiences in the United States were becoming more concentrated. To illustrate, during US presidential elections, major national—and often local—newspapers choose to endorse a candidate, which likely reinforces the readership of those who support that particular candidate and turns away those who root for a rival candidate. As an anecdotal observation, *Columbus Dispatch*, a major newspaper in the capital of Ohio where I live, has endorsed Republican presidential candidates for the past few elections. Incidentally, this newspaper was more likely than not to be seen in the driveways of houses that also had a lawn sign with the name of a Republican candidate during the election campaign.

However, the fast change in the American news industry at the turn of the century was somewhat masked by keeping the same high-profile anchors—greatly familiar faces for the American TV audience from the last two decades of the 20th century—at the desks of major TV news channels. Thus, the time of great instability in journalism was covered up by keeping in place legacy news anchors who were supposed to symbolize stability (Kitch, 2014). Moreover, despite the abundance of digital news outlets, most Americans still could access online news through the websites of the legacy news institutions. The propagation of cable TV networks that started with 24-hour news coverage by CNN has created, however, partisan division in the viewers, and assumedly readers of those respective sites, with, for example, Fox News appealing to conservatives and MSNBC and ABC to liberals.

> Audiences could now select news sources they found ideologically congenial, and in recent years, interest in theory of selective exposure has come roaring back as scholars have begun to consider the social consequences of the high choice media environment . . . . Virtually . . . selective exposure to media content, particularly news content, leads to a public that has less common ground than it did in the broadcast era and brings into question previous assumptions about the mass audience and about mediated collective memory. (Edy, 2014, p. 69)

In light of such dramatic changes that have led to a collapse of what traditionally has been known as "mass audience" in media studies or a "collective" in memory studies, Edy (2014) questions the very term "collective" as it is applied to memories, arguing that scholars need to redefine what it means to "share" memories. Bella et al. (1996, cited in Edy, 2014) proposed an interesting concept of redefined communities. In their view, communities can be described as communities of place—those people who live in close proximity to each other—and communities of interest—those people who are united by the same interest or concern. Living in the same area, however, does not guarantee that all people have the same political interests and convictions, despite being served by the same local newspaper that likely endorses one political party over another and delivers ideologically biased news. In the post-broadcast era, communities of interest have gained power. People no longer need to change their place of residence in order to reach out to like-minded citizens: The internet has allowed for individual niches where one can find the information that appeals to their interests. Such selective exposure—not yet well studied by scholars—can turn controversial collective memories (e.g., the Vietnam War for Americans or the atomic bombing of Hiroshima and Nagasaki, Japan) into consensual ones in a social process mediated by journalism. Moreover, incompatible collective memories, such as American and Japanese views on the end of World War II, may be fostered by social groups using rival media sources (Edy, 2014). In other words, one of the detrimental consequences of selective exposure to media is that it can lead to historical ignorance: People may choose not to read or watch the news altogether or be committed to a particular outlet that will be promoting one side of the story. Giving two different viewpoints on why the United States erred in the Vietnam War, one being the lack of military commitment from the US government and another being the United States' involvement in the internal affairs of another country in the first place, Edy (2014) raises a critical question:

> What if political conservatives selected media that only offered one version of the story while political liberals selected media that only told the other? And what if analogies to Vietnam continue to be used to make sense of military conflicts, as they have been for the US military undertakings from the 1980s until now . . . ? Could such memory silos undermine the potential for political compromise? (p. 75)

Nevertheless, one of the unchanged aspects of journalism in the post-broadcast era seems to be its claimed authority in reporting on current events that are supposed to lay the foundation for the nation's collective memory (Edy, 2014). Here, I argue that the media coverage of political events that are taking place on foreign soil, where the nation's military is not involved and where the nation's sons are not dying for a questionable political goal, is unlikely to differ from one media outlet to another. When the nation has little at stake, such news coverage may become just another government-supported version of the story. Moreover, the audience understandably finds national news much closer to home than international affairs unless foreign events cause a tangible impact on the local society (Gans, 2003); thus, international stories are less memorable to local audiences than reports on major domestic events.

Institutions as Power Players Behind News Making

There is no disagreement among scholars that media, especially news outlets, function at the service of organizations and power groups that promote their own—most of the time government supported—ideologies. To illustrate the increasing power of corporate control over media, Pickard (2020) points out the growing monopolies in the information industry, such as two massive conglomerates Comcast and Charter, and states that at the very least, the news organizations have an incentive to protect their owners' economic interests.

Indeed, the notion of "free media" in the West can be as ephemeral as the notion of "a free country" without law enforcement agencies. As van Dijk (1988) notes,

> Unlike advertising in the press, news does not primarily aim at promoting goods or services coming from a special firm or institution. Of course, economically, news is also a market commodity that must be promoted and sold. Ideologically news implicitly promotes the dominant beliefs and opinions of elite groups in the society. (p. 83)

The promotion of such beliefs becomes essential when journalists try to convey a message about a political event that may not be easily accessible to the audience. Thus, contextualizing and structuring it in familiar frameworks based on the intended ideological goal set by the elite groups becomes crucial for the reporters. Media are said to "echo" or "index" public officials. Edy (2014) remarks that "when officials are united, media are said to be incapable of generating a challenge to the official perspective" and later admits that "for communication to qualify as democratic, there must be a genuine diversity of perspectives in public discussion, and groups not in power must be able to break into the discussion" (p. 37). However, this is not the case in most instances of the coverage of foreign affairs in the US media. As discussed the Chapter 1, after almost four decades the US Fairness Doctrine that mandated the presence of diverse opinions on the same public matter in a broadcast was repealed in 1987, which makes major US news outlets very similar in their coverage of, at least, foreign affairs. For the most part, political news comes to the audience from the top down and journalists in general "follow the power" (Gans, 2003, pp. 46–47).

One should not forget, however, that although journalists work at the mercy of elite groups and report their stories through the lenses imposed on them by those groups, they remain human beings who are prone to their own errors, misinterpretations, speculations, and the subsequent misinformation that is fed to their audience. Myths, propaganda delivered to them by their unreliable sources, stereotypes, and biases that are prevalent in their social circles and in the country's newsrooms all creep into the reported news. In other words, bias and distortion of the presented information can be as intentional as they are accidental. Although journalists may automatically be assumed to be capable of informing citizens due to their somewhat better knowledge of the reported facts and "they are surely better informed than their audience," as Gans (2003) writes, "most are generalists who sometimes know little about the subjects of their stories before they report them, and who do not always get enough time to educate themselves properly" (p. 57).

However, whereas Gans (2003) equates the reporting of the inaccurate or factual information with bias, van Dijk (1988) argues against the notion that news should be seen as ideologically biased or distorted:

> Such a view presupposes that the distorted image can simply be compared to some kind of objective reality or with some kind of neutral or correct image. Yet, this reality represented in or through the news is itself an ideological construct, based on the definitions given by the accredited sources of journalists, such as the government or the union leaders. In other words, the media are not a neutral, common-sensed, or rational mediator of social events, but essentially help reproduce preformulated ideologies. (p. 11)

Furthermore, Zelizer (2011) discusses the phenomenon of the cannibalization of memory via news coverage by the West. Essentially, she refers to the impact that Western journalism has had on the construction of the collective memory in other—often underdeveloped—nations. She gives the example of the devastating tsunami in Asia in 2004: Western journalists immediately turned to Western tourists or high-profile visitors who happened to be in the area as eyewitnesses of the catastrophe. Those stories were widely televised, and the names of those people were given, whereas the multiple local victims shown in news reports remained anonymous. As Zelizer (2011) notes, "The dissonance between local experience and global interpretations of that experience was so great that one Indian journalist proclaimed that 'southeast Asia's biggest tragedy [had] become every American network's Disneyland party.' Disaster, he said grimly, had finally found its paparazzi" (p. 30). Zelizer (2011) provides her interpretation of such widespread memory cannibalization by Western journalism:

> The West's central role as a key player in the global news media environment is instrumental in cannibalizing local mnemonic impulses. In part it stems from the difficulties among those from afar in grasping the often contradictory, tentative, partial, and multiple interpretations that produce mnemonic hesitation among those who experience trauma, crisis, or catastrophe. At the same time, the Western media need immediate mnemonic certainty so as to make their news stories accessible, understandable, and formulaic. Because the mediated platforms of news are most often driven by the West, the memories they invoke thus tend to reflect this need for immediate clarity to explain what happened. They also reflect a Western perspective on events, which easily fills mnemonic pauses with definitive interpretations of what transpired on the local plane, regardless of whether or not they reflect local experience. (p. 29)

Gans (2003) compares news production with factory line manufacturing where the process of news making starts with assignment editors choosing events, statements, and other phenomena that deserve to be reported. Then reporters do legwork to obtain the raw materials they synthesize. Subsequently, stories are put on a metaphoric "peg" on which usable news can be hung, which helps journalists choose between the alternative stories usually available to them. Knowing about such techniques and especially working on this book have made me more attentive when watching and reading the US national news, especially stories related to Russia. In this respect, I was deeply puzzled by one such supposedly "pegged" news story. On January 15, 2020, CNN's internet site posted a brief report about a major event in Russia, the resignation of the entire Russian government. The headline, "The Entire Russian Government Resigns as Putin Proposes Reforms That Will Weaken His Successor and Shift Power to the Prime Minister and the Parliament" (Ilyushina & McKenzie, 2020), was short-lived. A few hours later, the same story appeared under a different headline by the same authors: "Russian Government Resigns as Putin Proposes Reforms That Could Extend His Grip on Power." One does not need to be a political analyst to understand that the two headlines present a directly opposite interpretation of the event, whose reinterpretation probably happened from top down to ensure that the evil image of the Russian President is not softened by whatever reforms his government opposed. Ironically, this major event in a rival/"enemy" country remained largely ignored in the broadcasting of the national nightly news. The ongoing impeachment of Trump, a deadly collision on a highway, winter storms threatening the United States, and a baseball scandal filled the 30-minute slot of NBC news that night. I wonder if the story is still pegged in news agencies or whether the power groups are uncertain about the appropriate reaction to this major political event so that it becomes accepted as usable news by the American public.

If organizations behind journalists' work establish the ideological direction in which news reports should go, how much freedom do journalists have in providing their subjective opinion that may clash with that of the power group for which they work?

> When the integrity of the journalistic institution is threatened by an individual journalist or news organization that has violated professional principles, the broader institution comes together to show how the aberration was isolated to one person or organization—the institution as a whole is thus not represented as flawed, with the blame placed solely on those who have deviated. (Berkowitz, 2011, p. 202)

In other words, constrained by the ideologies of the power groups for which they work and by professional principles—partially established by those groups—that define their job, journalists have to navigate multiple loopholes in making their story believable, accessible, and timely. In the next section, we discuss a few techniques that journalists use in reporting a news story.

Journalists' Techniques in Delivering News Stories

Van Dijk (1988), in his still highly relevant book, *News as Discourse*, summarized a few major approaches that journalists use in reporting the news:

> These devices include the remarkable use of numbers; a selective use of sources; specific modifications in relevance relations (incompatible propositions are played down or ignored); ideologically coherent perspectives in the description of events; the uses of specific scripts or attitude schemata; the selective uses of reliable, official, well-known, and especially credible persons and institutions; the description of close, concrete details; the quotation of eyewitnesses or direct participants; and the reference or appeal to emotion. (p. 94)

Obviously, it is beyond the scope of this chapter to discuss in detail all these devices. So I limit our discussion to a few most pertinent to the current study.

Selective Choice of Sources, Eyewitnesses, and Visuals

Van Dijk's (1988) earlier mention of the selective choice of eyewitnesses in reporting the news has been echoed by numerous other scholars a few decades later (e.g., Andén-Papadopoulos, 2014; Olick, 2014; Reading, 2014). In this regard, Olick (2014) raises an important question of memory fallibility in the journalistic practice:

> Understanding how memory, and in particular misremembering (memory distortion), work is thus essential to the journalist's professional practice. It is also essential to the scholar who studies that work: for instance in evaluating whether a journalist is presenting a biased account or whether journalism as a whole is biased, as well as in investigating the relationship between the elite, institutionalized versions of history's first draft and the immediate accounts on which such versions are based. (p. 26)

Indeed, a selective choice of interviewees and the journalist's reliance on the credibility of those accounts make news reports highly subjective, albeit accessible to the audience that tends to believe those who "were there" and "saw what happened." The fact that eyewitnesses may be wrong in their testimony, however, is not that important: "It is not so much the real truth as the illusion of truth that is at stake in the rhetoric of news" (van Dijk, 1988, p. 86). To illustrate, a high-profile NBC correspondent, Richard Engel, was reporting from a detention camp for ISIS fighters and their families (September 20, 2019).[3] Because ISIS members come from different countries, understandably those countries do not welcome back their families. The journalist chose to interview a woman by asking her where her home was and got the answer "Russia." To make sure that the viewers in the United States heard it correctly, he repeated the country of her origin again. It is not a secret that hundreds of Chechens—a small Muslim minority in the south of Russia—joined ISIS, but the reporter's choice of this particular interviewee among thousands of others at the time of a strained relationship between Russia and the United States was not accidental. The unsuspecting viewer was intended to take away from the TV broadcast that Russians not only meddle in US elections but also were part of ISIS.

In order to increase the credibility of sources, reporters often turn to high-profile officials who often are perceived as more trustworthy. The social hierarchy is essential in the choice of eyewitnesses as well as in the choice of direct quotations (van Dijk, 1988):

> Quotations are the reporter's protection against slander or libel, and the rhetorical illusion of truthfulness here finds its social and legal correlate in the veracity of representation. . . . Quotations not only make the news report livelier but are direct indications of what was actually said and hence true-as-verbal acts. . . . That quotations are seldom fully correct contextually is irrelevant. They should merely suggest that they are true, hence their rhetorical function and effect. (p. 87)

Recently, a new term, "media witnessing," emerged to reflect the high position of journalists in the immediate witnessing of related events (Reading, 2014). Here, not only the use of appropriate—albeit subjectively selected—eyewitnesses is involved. Photojournalism, as a subfield in journalism, has remained as important as ever. It is noteworthy, however, that the advent of technology in the 21st century and anyone's ability to take immediate pictures of the event or even record a video with the help of a cell phone well before

[3] NBC, retrieved September 22, 2019, from https://www.nbc.com/nightly-news/video/nbc-nightly-news-sep-20-2019/4029164.

the news crews arrive at the scene take some control over the news coverage out of the hands of the news organization. Termed "crowd-sourced photojournalism" (Andén-Papadopoulos, 2014), this type of witness testimony has become a new but widespread phenomenon. From school shootings with disturbing pictures taken by students inside the classroom to police patrol car cameras reporting live high-speed pursuits or bystanders filming a person being beaten by cops, such images become a new "reality show" of the news broadcasts. Whereas professional photojournalism has been criticized for its complicity in the reproduction of oppressive global powers and its almost trivial representation of suffering in distant lands, crowd-sourced journalism or "citizen journalists" fill the void by providing their instant evidence of what happened (Andén-Papadopoulos, 2014). Whether this trend will change the face of journalism in the near future or whether such amateurish contributions to news coverage will affect the news' credibility, I argue that the choice of which "crowd-sourced" images to select, if any at all, to show to the audience or publish in the report remains solely the journalist's decision. That decision, in turn, needs to comply with the ideology and professional practice of the organization that the journalist represents.

Although video reports from the scene where the event is happening remain a common technique in broadcasting news on TV, journalists are constrained by space in posting relevant pictures in print or digital versions of their reports. Here, especially in the coverage of national and international politics, they often resort to rather symbolic—if not clichéd—visuals, such as showing feet or hands to illustrate anonymous masses, often in suffering (e.g., hands reaching out for food delivered by humanitarian aid workers, or boots, such as "Russian boots on Ukrainian soil"), or full-size bodies to represent the political elite. To illustrate, during Barack Obama's tenure as the US President, there were numerous images of him playing volleyball or vacationing on the beach in Hawaii. Clearly, such images were supposed to appeal to an audience that admires a healthy and fit-looking leader. Similarly—if not to a larger extent—Russian media portray their President, Vladimir Putin, often engaged in sports, hunting, or other outdoor activities. Although in Western scholarship and media, such exhibitionism on the part of Putin is criticized heavily (e.g., Goscilo, 2012), I believe his behavior, at least partly, is intended to appeal to his own people rather than to the West. In this vein, Hariman and Lucaites (2014) warn that images are partial records that can mislead or be reinterpreted for memory, history, and political accountability. I add that by choosing a particular symbolic, rather than a regular, image to illustrate the news report, journalists act as subjective and biased agents of memory construction in their targeted audience.

Typification of Newsworthiness, Media Templates, and Reinforcement of Stereotypes

When journalists—or rather the organizations for which they work—choose what news story to cover, they often are driven by what is known in sociology as "typification" (Tuchman, 1980) or in cognitive psychology as "schemata": habits, routines, assumptions, or events with which individuals approach any new situation.

> Typifications of newsworthiness—which are based on memory of what was considered newsworthy in the past—shape the routines not only of individual journalists, but of the organizations in and for which journalists work. News editors (who are individual workers in journalism), for instance, prefer predictable events to unpredictable ones because they are easier to prepare for. In turn, news organizations are structured in ways that depend on such typifications. (Olick, 2014, p. 25)

Another way to view such journalistic approaches is through the prism of media templates that provide contextualization of any new political event covered by journalists.

> Media templates are the frames, images and, more broadly, discourses (presumed by journalists, news editors and producers to be familiar to their audiences) that are routinely employed as sometimes near-instantaneous prisms through which current and unfolding events are described, presented and contextualized. (Hoskins, 2014, p. 183)

But such templates, as Kitzinger (2000) warns, often broadly summed up as a set of fears (e.g., "another Vietnam," "another Chernobyl," or "another Hitler") are not always benign; they act, however, as a crucial tool of media power. To illustrate, in the past few years when the US media were almost daily reporting on political affairs involving Russia (e.g., the takeover of Crimea, a conflict in Eastern Ukraine, the downing of Malaysia Airlines flight MH17, or the alleged Russian meddling in the 2016 US presidential election), such repeatedly made references to the "menace" nation were easily understood by an American audience that still has a fresh memory of Russia as the biggest US foe in the relatively recent Cold War. Because the public discourse related to Russia hardly has changed since the collapse of the USSR in 1991, the existent template to fit the new event already was available and accessible to the American audience. By complying with such templates and using typification as a major tool in reporting on unfolding events, journalists also contribute to the reinforcement of old stereotypes on which such templates were built in the first place. As van Dijk (1988) emphasizes,

> The media, along with the authorities (the control structure), work with a model of deviancy amplification. That is, the media account of an initial problem—through various stages of misperception, sensitization, dramatization and escalation—contributes to increased deviance and hence to the confirmation of stereotypes. (p. 10)

A well-known technique in the reinforcement of stereotypes and in the articulation of an ideologically charged opinion in news reports is the choice of words. For example, the Istanbul Airport shooting and suicide bombings of 2016 claimed the lives of 45 people and left hundreds injured. The mastermind behind those attacks was identified as a Chechen, Akhmed Chatayev, who had been wanted by Russia for his terror acts there and nevertheless was granted political asylum in Austria. The US media, having acknowledged the bombing as a terrorist act, were cautious not to call the Chechen a terrorist and used the word *warlord* instead (Isurin, 2017). Van Dijk (1988) offers a similar example of selecting the words *freedom fighter* or *terrorist* to refer to the same person:

> Whether the newspaper selects *terrorist* or *freedom fighter* to denote the same person is not so much a question of semantics as an indirect expression of implied but associated values incorporated in shared-word meanings. Besides this standard example of ideologically based lexical variation in the news media, such opinion-controlled lexical choices abound, although many are more subtle. (p. 81)

In addition, the use of specific syntactic structures, such as deleting agents from typical subject positions and using passive constructions instead, may be employed to dissimulate the negative actions of elite or powerful groups (van Dijk, 1988).

How Persuasion Works in News

One of the journalist's major goals is to make the audience believe their story and make the story accessible, informative, and interesting. The first task—to make the audience believe the story—can be seen as the easiest or the most difficult, depending on how we look at it. If the journalist presents the report in the outlet whose audience is in alliance with what the new story is about (e.g., their opinion coincides with that of the journalist), then the journalist has accomplished the goal of making the story believable and persuasive. However, if the audience does not share the opinion presented in the report or the story does not fit the framework already built by previous reports on a similar topic, then the story is dismissed as untrustworthy. Van Dijk (1988) notes, "Assertive persuasion is the zero level of persuasive processes: Without at least believing what the other says, it can hardly be expected that we change our opinions based on such beliefs" (p. 83).

Van Dijk (1988, pp. 84–85) lists a few basic strategies that journalists usually employ to make their stories persuasive:

(A) Emphasize the factual nature of events, e.g. by
   1. Direct descriptions of ongoing events.
   2. Using evidence from close eyewitnesses.
   3. Using evidence from other reliable sources (authorities, respectable people, and professionals).
   4. Signals that indicate precision and exactness such as numbers for persons, time, events, etc.
   5. Using direct quotes from sources, especially when opinions are involved.

(B) Build a strong relational structure for facts, e.g. by
   1. Mentioning previous events as conditions or causes and describing or predicting next events as possible or real consequences.
   2. Inserting facts into well-known situation models that make them relatively familiar even when they are new.
   3. Using well-known scripts and concepts that belong to that script.
   4. Trying to further organize facts in well-known specific structures, e.g. narratives.

(C) Provide information that also has an attitudinal and emotional dimension:
   1. Facts are better represented and memorized if they involve or arouse strong emotions (if too strong emotions are involved,

however, there may be disregard, suppression and hence disbelief of the facts).

2. The truthfulness of events is enhanced when opinions of different backgrounds or ideologies are quoted about such events, but in general those who are ideologically close will be given primary attention as possible sources of opinions.

Having followed all or some of these strategies in preparing a news report, journalists now have to put their narratives in the structure that pertains to news texts and that fundamentally is different from any academic text.

Structure of the News Text

Much research has been done on the analysis of media texts using the linguistic tools of discourse analysis (see van Dijk, 1988). Basically, any news discourse can be studied from the perspective of macrostructure (e.g., text structure and content) and microstructure (e.g., use of different linguistic means to deliver the message). Because the current study does not aim at providing a multifaceted analysis of the media reports, and focuses on macrostructure and a few linguistic features, such as discussed in the previous section, I limit our discussion here to a few basic characteristics of the text structure in news reports that are relevant for this book.

Each news text has a headline, which roughly can be compared to a title in any other text. However, the difference between a regular text title and a headline lies in the information that is embodied in each. To illustrate, the hypothetical article title "The Analysis of Trump's Involvement in Dealings with Russia" does not reveal the content or the results of such analysis, whereas a media text with the headline "Democrats Accuse Trump of Dealings with Russia" not only gives away what the report is about but also shows the major players in this particular political scandal—that is, the House and the Senate Democrats against the US Republican President. In addition to the headline, which is mandatory for news texts, there may or may not be a lead. Both the headline and the lead are marked off by larger or simply different fonts separating those two structural parts from the main text. Together they serve to signal what the report is going to be about (headline) and to provide some summary of the main content of the text (lead). Here, however, we have to beware of thinking of a lead as a summary similar to what we find at the end of an academic text. Not only does the lead precede the main text but also it does not necessarily act as a summary of the actual content of the text. Ironically, the lead can be rather *misleading* because it expresses the journalist's intended message and subjective opinion that often are not supported by the facts provided in the main body of the text. This major manipulative technique used by journalists aims at catching the attention of the reader and implanting the information—or misinformation—in case the person does not read the entire text or does not read it carefully enough to detect such manipulation. Thus, through the adherence to a strict structure into which the news narrative is embedded and though the use of different other techniques, discussed here, news makers, as the producers of first drafts of history and as true agents of constructing collective memories of the ongoing political event, target the minds of the intended audience. In Chapter 3, we discuss whether their attempts reach the minds of the audience and construct the memory in the "right" direction.

Summary

The question of journalism as the first draft of history and collective memory having its roots in journalism still may present a disputed argument for some scholars. However, through reading the literature on the deep interconnected nature of the two fields—memory and journalism—and joining the voices of those who call for bridging the two together, I provide a few points that will lay the groundwork for the major argument presented in this book.

Not all political events happening in the world will enter the collective memory of the group, yet those that will form a long-lasting memory are impacted, to a great extent, by how media, as the first-hand messengers in reporting on those events, deliver it to the intended audience. So, from this point of view, collective memory and media are not two separate fields functioning in parallel worlds; rather, they are part and parcel of the same process that is rooted deeply in the sociocultural construct of the group. Collective memories are constructed in the world and in the mind, with official producers of memory—journalists being one—playing a crucial role in how a particular historical event will be represented and subsequently remembered. However, as with any official producer of collective memory, journalists are not merely ephemeral forces: They are real people whose ideologies, beliefs, attitudes, and values are formed by the group within which they live and whose members they inform through their reports. Moreover, journalists—despite being individual people with their own personalities and life stories—do not articulate their own independent opinions in their professional lives; their reporting is constrained by the ideologies and the expectations of the power groups that stand behind them. In other words, the idea of *free media* not controlled by such ideological organizations even in democratic societies, such as the United States, is rather misleading. Journalists act at the mercy of the elite groups that control them and that will abandon reporters who go rogue against the prevailing ideologies and well-established rules of engagement.

Although scholars of collective memory agree that official producers of memory always are subjective and always commit to only one nonambiguous perspective in the interpretation of the past event—the perspective that serves the present goal and the identity claim of the group—it is not always easy to identify the exact steps of how such reconstruction, if not distortion, of memory occurs. In contrast, we clearly can see those specific techniques that journalists use in delivering the coverage of ongoing events and—by extension—constructing the first drafts of collective memories, if not history. Among those techniques, a few resonate with how collective memories are formed. First, journalists tend to incorporate any new political event into a familiar framework in order to make a new event understandable and accessible to their audience. By invoking such preexistent frameworks, they unavoidably reinforce old stereotypes, especially when their reports concern the *other group*—an old foe or simply a group that is perceived as inconsonant with the values and ideologies of their own group. Second, the structure of the news reports, in print or digital media, is rather rigid, with headlines and summaries preceding the main text and not necessarily reflecting the content of that text. Rather, such information placed upfront in the news reports reflects the subjective opinion of the journalist and—we may add—the ideological power group behind the journalist. The structure of news reports at many levels conditions the readers to develop specific interpretation frameworks based on the pervasively dominant knowledge and attitude structures that make such models intelligible rather than alternative ones, in which other goals, norms, values, and ideologies are used to provide counterinterpretation of news events (van Dijk, 1988). Third, by subjectively selecting eyewitnesses, accompanying images, or particular linguistic tools in order to transform the source information into the report, journalists choose *what* side of the story to present and *how* to do this. This particular side of the story, furthermore, should comply with the perspective established by the power group or—often—by the government. Moreover, I argue that the role of the government in reports about foreign affairs will be decisive, whether we talk about "free media" in the United States or state-controlled media in Russia. Finally, journalistic work is intended for a targeted audience and thus cannot be realized without the appropriate consumption of the story by that audience. Similar to collective memory, the production–consumption continuum remains one of the most important constructs in journalism, the study of which clearly requires an interdisciplinary approach.

Van Dijk (1988) was among the first scholars who called for the interdisciplinary approach to the study of news making by stressing the importance of combining social cognitions with cognitive accounts of understanding the news. "Only in this way," he pleaded, "are we able to relate cognitive processes with their social context, that is, with social practices of social members, groups and institutions, and with class, power, and ideology" (p. 99). In other words, production of news reports, and by extension, construction of group memories, cannot be fully understood without looking into the consumption part of this construct. In Chapter 3, we will be looking into how the mind perceives news reports and in particular how the mind processes misinformation, which assumedly abounds in news reports.

3

How the Mind Processes Text, Media News, and Misinformation

In the previous two chapters, we discussed how collective memory is being constructed by official producers and we specifically looked at the role of media in the construction of memory. Different mechanisms are employed by the official producers of memory: From a deliberate distortion of the representation of past events to providing an ideologically biased shift in reporting on ongoing events, producers of memory, as true agents of collective memory of the group, ultimately target the minds of their respective groups. The question that we aim to answer in this chapter concerns the mind that consumes such information supplied by official producers of memory. How does the mind process the text in general and information from media news in particular, and how does the mind process misinformation?

In this chapter, we first discuss the general existent evidence on text and discourse processing as it relates to the scope of this book. Then we specifically look into how individual minds process and consume media news. Finally, we discuss how deliberately distorted information is processed by the individual's mind. The surveyed findings come from a few fields, such as psycholinguistics, cognitive psychology, and social psychology. Although I do not attempt to provide an in-depth review of the evidence obtained in each of those fields, I humbly hope not to do disservice to any of those fields by bringing into the spotlight only the knowledge that is central to the current investigation. Where possible, I refer the reader to additional resources. Moreover, the goal of this review is not to test any of the previous findings further; rather, we proceed on the assumption that scholars in the previously mentioned respective fields have accumulated reliable evidence on how the mind processes the text, media news, and false information. This, in turn, will build the foundation for the conceptualization of the framework for the current investigation.

Reenacting the Enemy. Ludmila Isurin, Oxford University Press. © Oxford University Press 2022.
DOI: 10.1093/oso/9780197605462.003.0004

Text Comprehension

Unless we open a text from a highly specialized field that we are not familiar with, comprehension of most texts that we read in our daily life involves the same basic processes. To illustrate, when we read a new text on World War II, we already have some background knowledge about the event: when it happened, what parties were involved, key battles of the war, the aftermath of the war, and so forth. In other words, the new information that we learn from the text is grounded in our preexistent knowledge about World War II. Often, we do not remember where we first learned about the event and whether it was a history teacher, a grandfather, or a film director who has created in our minds a concrete picture of this historical event. In cognitive psychology, the latter is known as schemata or scripts.

Role of Schemata in Text Comprehension

Psychological models of discourse date back to the pioneering work of Bartlett (1932), who proposed that text understanding is not just a passive registration of information but an active, reconstructive process. His fundamental notion of a schema, in which previous experiences and knowledge about a text are organized, has been influential in later works on discourse processing (van Dijk, 1988, p. 101). However, most of the research on the role of schemata in text comprehension or the role of frames and scripts, as they are called—often interchangeably—by different authors, happened in the 1980s (e.g., Reynolds et al., 1982; Rumelhart, 1980). It is a consensus now that certain scripts are evoked the minute we start reading a new text. Those scripts guide the reader through the text and assist in comprehending the content of the text in the absence of numerous unnecessary details that already exist in the mental script. In other words, schemata can be perceived as a set of background knowledge that, as humans, we acquire throughout our entire life. Returning to the example of a new text on World War II, the reader will evoke the World War II script but will only be focusing on the new information related to the event. This new information will be negotiated against the existent knowledge and may or may not modify the script that exists in the reader's mind. This makes schemata a fluid concept that is never static in its entirety, yet its basic frame remains more or less stable.

The idea of schemata is not a new concept. A German philosopher and psychologist of the 19th century, Johann Friedrich Herbart (cited in Mandl & Ballstaedt, 1982, p. 482), for example, described the process of acquiring new knowledge as the process of integration of new ideas into the mass already available. In this respect, the text activates schemata or schemata can be activated by other schemata that had been evoked during the reading process, which allows the reader to make inferences. There are two types of inferences, although it is not always easy to draw a clear line separating the two. One type of inference is based on schemata that have been activated by the text itself. This process is obligatory for any text comprehension, and it accounts for the so-called slot-filling inferences (Mandl & Ballstaedt, 1982). To illustrate, while reading a text on World War II and coming across a phrase such as "a Holocaust survivor," the reader fills in the slot for the omitted information: (1) who were victims of the Holocaust and (2) who committed such atrocities during World War II. It is presupposed that the knowledge necessary for filling in such slots exists in the schema of an individual reader. Other inferences, however, are not obligatory and go beyond slot-filling. If the text contains information that requires the activation of an additional script, this new schemata may have the effect of enlarging and supplementing the text, which can be viewed as an elaborative inference (Mandl & Ballstaedt, 1982). For example, an American reader, well familiar with the basic facts concerning the Holocaust, comes across a mention of the ship *St. Louis* that in 1939, amid the beginning of the slaughter of Jews in Europe, carried more than 900 German refugees, mostly Jewish, to the US coast. The asylum seekers were rejected by the US government and sent back to Europe, where later many died in concentration camps. This fact still remains part of the US history that haunts many Americans; however, it remains a subject not widely discussed and, as a result, not known to some Americans. Thus, the reader may not know this fact, and through reading this new piece of information the reader may elaborate on the new knowledge by thinking more about immigration laws in the pre-war United States, the United States' reluctance to get involved in World War II until much later, and a change in the attitude toward refugees in the post-war United States. The role of inferences in discourse processing never is underestimated. Actually, they are considered the cement of discourse (Wender, 1982).

I suggest we view schemata from a different angle. What does it mean that an individual has background knowledge of a certain matter? We cannot assume that the background knowledge that forms schemata is some sort of solid objective knowledge formed through the acquisition of undisputable facts and concepts. It might be true if we think about some solid factual information that individuals acquire through formal education, such as the fact that the Earth is round or that 2 × 2 = 4. Yet, where does an individual get the knowledge about historical facts? We may suggest that historical facts are learned first in school and later they are supplemented by additional knowledge acquired through readings, films, public debates, and so forth. Schemata are socially grounded, culturally specific, and ideologically biased. If we take the example of a historical event such as World War II, we may argue that readers in the United States and in Russia would evoke different scripts while reading the same text on World War II in which both Russia and the United States figure. Moreover, there are individual variations within the same sociocultural group, and the schemata activated by one reader will not necessarily be the same as the schemata activated by another reader. Moreover, the amount of knowledge on the topic will result in a different number of slots that need to be filled by inferences during the reading process. Conversely, we would not be able to progress with research involving a large group of participants from the same sociocultural background if we did not make assumptions—as erroneous as they might be—that there exist more or less general schemata for the interpretation of a text on a particular topic by a particular group of participants. One of the leading scholars in the field of discourse processing and news as discourse, van Dijk (1988), asserts that cognition is deeply and fundamentally social:

> Memory, therefore, is cognitively designed to serve social needs. It involves information but also social communication. The acquisition of knowledge and beliefs through discourse in the lives of people has continually taken place in contexts of socialization, interpersonal and intergroup perception, and interaction. (p. 107)

He extends this notion to the shared understanding of public discourse forms, such as mass media, and suggests that "it allows large groups of people to have similar models of the same situations. These models may be used again and again as input for the communication about new events" (p. 107).

Updating the Knowledge

One line of research that does not necessarily invoke the term schemata—despite going hand in hand with that concept—deals with the process of updating the knowledge of the world through reading a new text. When we read a new text for the first time, it rarely is an entirely new piece of information that is not based on some knowledge that we already have about the discussed topic. What happens in such instances is that we may modify our prior knowledge with the new information or we may maintain our out-of-date knowledge due to the bias existing in our minds. According to Larsen (1982), "The cognitive process of knowledge updating owes its existence to the fact that a vast number of phenomena in the world are not static but rather change over time" (p. 205). Larsen further makes a valid point that

> the study of memory and learning has focused almost exclusively on the acquisition of knowledge about the invariant properties of the world, or, at the most, knowledge about events that have already been concluded so that no further changes will take place. In contrast, updating is concerned with knowledge about ongoing events in real time where it is a basic problem that one's knowledge may at any moment be rendered out-of-date by subsequent events. (p. 205)

Larsen (1982) proposes four distinct characteristics of the updating process. First, readers should believe that the received piece of information reflects the true state of affairs. Second, they need to relate this new information to what they already have acquired as knowledge about this particular event. Third, they need to correct the previously formed knowledge for the new information. Fourth, they need to decide what to do with the information that now may be considered outdated: to retain it at the risk of running into two conflicting pieces of evidence or to dispose of it? One of the most important questions is how additional details and facts are integrated into the general knowledge about ongoing historical events. Besides a theoretical assumption that scripts of a very high order may be invoked to account for this development of knowledge of contemporary history, as Larsen (1982) concedes, the process seems to be too complex to investigate experimentally. However, the argument that our knowledge is updated by new information about an ongoing event is important for the current book, which largely focuses on the representation of political events in media texts and the construction of memory related to those events in group members.

Text Manipulation: Changing the Reader's Perspective

One of the major issues in memory studies concerns retention and forgetting. Why do we tend to remember certain episodes and facts better than others, and why do we forget certain things easier and faster than others? Although this issue relates to a range of phenomena studied by cognitive psychologists, we look at a narrower line of research that deals with remembering details from a text. There seems to be a consensus in the field of memory studies that the importance/unimportance distinction has strong implications for the memory processes. This is not counterintuitive to most individuals outside academia. Why would we remember something that is not going to be useful for our survival or well-being? (Kazanas & Altarriba, 2015).

Based on the previous research on text encoding and its subsequent recall, Flammer and Tauber (1982) conducted an experiment on text recall under different conditions, such as a shift in the reader's perspective or no shift condition. Namely, the participants were supposed to read a text about a boy giving a tour of his parents' house to a friend while nobody was in the house. The text contained numerous descriptive details. The participants were instructed to read the text from the perspective of either a homebuyer or a burglar. Then there was an immediate recall and a delayed recall, with the reading encoding either matching (text was read from a homebuyer's perspective and recalled from the same perspective) or mismatching (text was read from a homebuyer's perspective but recalled from the burglar's perspective) the recall condition. The results showed that when the reading perspective was incongruent with the recall perspective, recall was worse than in the congruent condition. The authors concluded that

> ideas unimportant to the reading perspective had a smaller probability to be recalled, even if they had become important from the recall perspectives. This can be taken as a consequence of the encoding ceiling which was biased by the encoding perspectives. Some of the formerly unimportant material just might not have been encoded in some permanent way. (p. 386)

If we extend these experimental findings to our everyday life in which our encoding perspective is not enforced on us by an experimenter, we may ask the following question: Does the reader have an encoding bias based on their preexistent beliefs when exposed to a text with new information related to the old knowledge? We may never get scientific evidence to answer this question, but the fact that encoding bias exists and can be manipulated, whether by an experimenter or the text's author, is important for the sake of the argument presented in this book.

Do We Tend to Remember the End of the Text Better Than the Beginning?

Throughout our lifetime, we read numerous texts, including works of fiction. We do not need to have a cutting-edge experiment to prove to us that the end of a detective story that we have just read is remembered better than the beginning. Often, we even struggle not to look up what happens at the end of the book while being engulfed in its dramatic action. This anecdotal evidence suggesting that the end of the text is remembered better than the beginning has found significant support in laboratory studies on word lists and paired numbers learning. Even the earliest experiments on the learning of meaningless lists of numbers or random words showed that participants could immediately recall approximately six or seven words, mostly from the very end of the list (Murdock, 1962). However, it appears that memory research has mostly been concerned with lists of items (words, nonsense syllables, and even sentences) and not with texts (Kintsch, 1982). In order to avoid any sweeping overgeneralizations not substantiated by laboratory findings—from better remembering the end of a word list to better remembering the end of a text—we put this issue to rest until we discuss some findings on news comprehension later in this chapter.

Role of Titles and Illustrations in the Memory for a Text

While attending professional conferences and deciding what talks to attend—in the absence of familiar authors' names that could determine my pick—I often choose either talks that clearly describe the theme of the presentation or those that have an interesting, catchy title. Aside from such anecdotal evidence on the role of titles, there are studies which suggest that indeed titles play a role in better remembering and recalling the text. Numerous studies were conducted in the 1970s that show the effect of titles and summaries on text comprehension (for references, see León, 1997). A common feature in those studies was the use of titles whose brief contents represent the essential macrostructural information. As León (1997) notes, there are different theories that account for such an effect: (1) Titles activate mental schemas to direct the reader's previous knowledge, (2) titles accentuate the links between concepts, (3) titles provide a core content that promotes the retrieval of the information that they represent, and (4) titles can provide additional interest and greater motivation to read texts that especially are long and difficult to understand. However, Kozminsky (1977) raised a provocative question:

> If a title assumes the role of an anchoring point or superordinate context around which the text is organized, then biasing titles may alter the comprehension of the text. They may provide different interpretations to context elements in the text, or alternative organizations of the ideas in the text. Ideas that were central for one title may be less important when another title is used, and information that does not fit a biased organization of the text may be overlooked. (p. 482)

Indeed, in his study, three texts were assigned titles: Two had biasing titles, and the third had a combined version of the two. Texts with biasing titles were used to demonstrate that immediate free recall is biased toward the theme emphasized in the title. Although the direct effect of titles on overall recall was not significant, the interaction of titles and theme-relevant propositions (i.e., semantic units) reached significance. Kozminsky (1977) took this finding to demonstrate how the text organization together with the text title guides the reader's comprehension and allows the reader to extract the most important thematic information. Despite the fact that no significant effect of titles on recall was registered in the study, the author concluded that "text comprehension is in part a selection process which is guided by advance information about the text in the form of title" (p. 487).

Niegemann (1982) applied the same idea to the study of the effects of titles on the comprehension and recall of instructional texts. In his experiment, three instructional texts, with two different titles each, were used as stimuli. The results supported those in Kozminsky's (1977) study that titles may influence recall of texts but only in a qualitative manner. The author also agreed that recall of texts is widely influenced by much more important variables than just their titles, such as macrostructure of the text, the degree and specificity of individual interest in the content area of the text, as well as a primacy effect that may also bias what is remembered from a text. We should keep in mind, however, that the cited studies examined the immediate recall of the texts. In real life, an individual is not expected to report immediately what they just read or whether the title of the text has biased the comprehension of it. Yet, the suggested evidence that the text titles may bias reading comprehension and lead to the extraction of information that is more relevant to the title is important for our discussion. Later in this chapter, we will see that titles might play a much larger role in news reports.

Not only titles but also illustrations accompanying a written text have been the focus of academic inquiry. Do pictorial images enhance reading comprehension and the subsequent recall? Hinder (1982) reported that pictorial illustrations improved free recall and affected not only the amount of retention but also its organization. It was suggested that pictorial illustrations provided a context within which the text information could be more deeply processed.

Interim Summary

So what do we take away from the research on text comprehension that might be relevant for the current investigation? Undeniably, the role of schemata—or background knowledge—remains essential for text comprehension. However, schemata should not be viewed as a stable or universal concept. Each person will develop and further update their worldview through individual experiences, which makes schemata a fluid concept. However, schemata also can be perceived as a sociocultural phenomenon, thereby allowing us to assume that a group of people coming from the same sociocultural and educational background may have more or less similar worldviews. Schemata are the first element that is evoked in reading comprehension; they allow the reader to fill in empty slots in the text, activate additional schemata, and make necessary inferences. Another perspective on schemata can be taken through the negotiation of new knowledge against the preexistent knowledge. What happens in our minds when we come across information that contradicts our previous beliefs and knowledge? One of the most important assumptions is that readers have to believe in the source and content of the new information in order to integrate it into their long-term memory. The existent bias in the individual mind can become a deciding factor in how new information is processed: If a person firmly believes in a fact encoded in their mind, new information contradicting that knowledge may automatically be rejected as false. However, once the information is perceived as trustworthy, it can either rewrite the previous information or face the risk of becoming a piece of conflicting information in the reader's mind if it is kept along with the old information. Unfortunately, science does not know yet what exactly happens in the mind of the individual when reading new information about an ongoing political event: Memory for such events is being constructed on a daily basis, and the process of updating the information that might be just a week old is different from how new information about a distant historical fact enters the individual mind.

Another important aspect of reading comprehension concerns a possible encoding bias that can be manipulated through different mechanisms, as experimental studies showed. Those can range from changing the reader's perspective to using biasing titles that can shift the comprehension process. Also, despite the convincing evidence that the last items in the lists of words, numbers, and syllables always are remembered better than the first items, it is not clear if the end of the text is remembered better than the beginning.

In the next section, we specifically look into media texts—or news reports—and how comprehension of those texts and their encoding in the reader's mind are similar to or different from the underlying reading comprehension processes discussed previously.

Comprehension of News Discourse

After two decades of the 21st century, we safely can conclude that digital media—and not just the old-fashioned print media and TV—have secured their place in our lives. We often browse internet news while having a cup of coffee in the morning or check the news headlines on our cell phones as we go through the day. Very little research, however, has been done on the news media or on how people remember the news. As Gans (2003) suggests, most informative studies on news effects come from laboratory experiments. Yet, "laboratory studies systematically overestimate the effects of the news, because people participating in the experiments concentrate far more on the news in the laboratory than they do at home" (p. 71). It is important to keep this notion in mind while discussing the evidence from such experimental studies.

It is noteworthy that no difference in consumption, reading patterns, or quality of news recall between the print and online version of news texts was found, suggesting that the presentation of news in digital media is not inherently different from that in a more traditional paper version (D'Haenens et al., 2010). For now, this allows us to extend any findings on comprehension of news in print to comprehension of news in digital media. Yet, at the end of this section, we take a look at the emerging debate about the mind and the digital media.

The question of how the individual mind processes news discourse and how different it may be from processing a basic text became a focus of investigation at the end of the 20th century and has continued in the early 21st century. In order to keep the structure of this section similar to that of the previous section, we discuss mechanisms that news processing shares with text processing while also trying to identify some of its distinctive features. Although we discussed the production side of news reports in Chapter 2, often it is difficult to talk about news processing separate from news production because the two represent the opposite ends of the same continuum. News reports are constructed and produced with one goal—to make them believable and make the consumer acquire the information. In other words, the processes of production and comprehension interlock with news discourse structure (van Dijk, 1988). Thus, occasionally I make brief detours into the production side of the process and hope to avoid much repetition of what was discussed at great length in Chapter 2. As in our discussion of news production and news structure, I rely greatly on the groundbreaking work of van Dijk.

Schemata and the Role of the *Other* in News Comprehension

As in the comprehension of a basic text, the understanding of the news requires the activation of particular schemata related to the described event. However, because news reports often concern events and conflicts taking place outside the group's boundaries and involve out-of-group members, the evoked schemata acquire a strong sociocultural meaning. Van Dijk (1988) notes,

> Group members have a self-schema about one's own group and schemata about other social or ethnic groups. This is also the way group stereotypes and prejudices can be represented. Such schemata may be thought of as general information about the basic distinctive features of the group (appearance, social position, etc.), as well as about their shared norms, values, goals, and interests. Personal and group schemata also explain how

social members perceive and interpret the actions of other social members and how such information is stored. Various types of biases thus can be explained. (p. 109)

According to van Dijk (1988), prejudices are formed because they are relevant and useful in the enactment of social domination. To illustrate, a group may create a certain bias about another group because this bias will boost the sense of their own superiority. This argument is not new and finds much reflection in the field of construction of collective memory: In the process of memory construction, a group will strive to push against the *other*, thereby reinforcing its own positive—and, in their view, much superior—image and memory of the past. In other words, schemata activated while the reader comprehends the news text always will be much more biased against other social groups than the schemata evoked by the reading of a text about a political event not related to the *other*. The sociocognitive approach to the study of discourse and communication is grounded heavily in the notion that the speakers/readers enact the norms and values, interests, power relations, or ideologies of their own group. This becomes the major mechanism underlying news production and news comprehension because both journalists and media consumers are members of the same group. Moreover, van Dijk (1988) stresses the importance of consonance—that is, news should be consonant with socially shared norms, values, and attitudes:

> It is easier to understand and certainly easier to accept and, hence, to integrate news that is consonant with the attitude of journalists and readers, that is, with the ideological consensus in a given society or culture. . . . News is also about persons, countries, or actions that are dissonant with our dominant attitudes, but (1) such news has less chance to be covered unless (2) it confirms our negative schemata about such persons or countries, and (3) the perspective of description is consonant with these schemata. (p. 122)

Information Updating

Reading a news report requires the activation of the other knowledge and beliefs that we already have. As discussed previously, knowledge updating is not a straightforward process, and it becomes even more complex when we consider the understanding of the news discourse. The acceptance of new knowledge presupposes some minimal coherence, if not consistency, with our old beliefs. "Without good reasons and evidence, we do not discard fundamental beliefs constructed from years of understanding, experiences, and actions" (van Dijk, 1988, p. 83). People remember best what they already know, regardless of getting new information about major developments in the ongoing event; they remember better the information that retrieves old schemata or that can be fitted in the old schemata. Conversely, knowing the most about a situation leads to better comprehension and recall of details related to that matter. However, as van Dijk notes,

> causes, consequences, context, and history of many issues, especially foreign ones . . . as well as most details about places and numbers, tend to be forgotten. In other words, only repeated and concurrent information about certain issues may lead to a modest change or construction of current situation models. (p. 173)

One of the recent studies on the correction efficacy in news misinformation investigated the timing of correction feedback for an unfolding news event (Rich & Zaragoza, 2020). First, the authors assessed whether receiving a correction minutes after reading a mistaken news story was more effective than receiving the correction 2 days later. Second, they examined whether corrected beliefs persisted over time. It was found that although initially corrections successfully reduced people's belief in the mistaken news story, people started falling back on the mistaken information a few days later, despite remembering the content of the correction. Rich and Zaragoza (2020) conclude, "These findings raise concerns that corrections provided by journalists . . . may not lead to lasting changes in beliefs even if they lead to lasting changes in knowledge" (pp. 310–311), which further illustrates how the mind is biased to process the news information according to people's preconceived notions and convictions.

Larsen (1982) compares knowledge updating from reading a scientific text and reading a news report and concludes that new information in a scientific text revises or increases the individual's knowledge about the subject matter, whereas news reports illustrate the opposite of scientific reports. Their goal rarely is to increase the reader's knowledge because the production side of such reports often presupposes manipulation of the factual information and—we can add—of the reader's mind. This again brings the interconnected nature of news production and consumption to the forefront of our discussion.

Role of Headlines and Text Structure for News Comprehension

Research conducted by cognitive psychologists has provided much evidence on what affects the comprehension of written material—its structure, summaries, and titles being among other factors. It was found that the initial summary assists the memory by operating like a retrieval program (van Dijk & Kintsch, 1983), which becomes even more important for understanding the news report. As discussed in Chapter 2, the macrostructure of most formal media texts will have the following components: headline (sometimes followed by a sub-headline), lead (i.e., summary), and the main text. Headlines usually are presented in large bold type, whereas leads may be expressed separately in bold print or may coincide with the first, thematical sentence of the text. These two components of a media text are crucial because often this is all that the individual will read and take away from the news report. Thus, newsmakers pay much attention to these structural components of their reports. We may ask the following question: Does the mind fall into a trap set up by official news producers? In two separate experiments, León (1997) manipulated the presentation of media text. In the first experiment, the same news article was offered to randomly assigned participants as (1) the complete original article, including the headline, an initial summary, and the basic text; (2) the basic text preceded by an initial summary; and (3) the basic text only. Two groups of participants took part in the experiment: high school students and journalism majors. Contrary to expectations, there were no differences with regard to the type of text, and only a between-group difference emerged. León concluded that

> the previous reading of the headline and/or the summary of a newspaper article . . . does not necessarily bring about an improvement in the comprehension and retention of the contents. Rather, from the point of view of macrostructural theory, the headline and summary prove to be ineffective in better organizing the information processes in the memory. (p. 93)

León, however, acknowledged that his participants—especially those in the group of high school students—may be more accustomed to reading academic texts whose structure is different from that of news reports. To test this hypothesis further, in his second experiment, the title and summary of the original text were modified to resemble those of a basic scientific text. The results of that experiment did show a significant effect for the title and summary. This led León to suggest that

> the criteria followed by journalists in creating a headline or a summary do not necessarily correspond to the organizational structure in scientific texts . . . some journalists regard an introductory paragraph not as a content-based summary but as an *interpretive* summary. The difference lies in the fact that a content-based summary depends solely on the contents of the text whereas the initial summary of a newspaper article contextualizes the news item in question according to the journalist's preferences. (p. 99)

León (1997) later discusses in depth the fundamental differences between content-based summaries in scientific texts that guide the reader's comprehension and quite arbitrary summaries, based on the journalist's biased perspective and intentions, in news articles that often mislead the reader and make it challenging for the reader to build correct inferences. The lack of consistency in the introduction of a summary that actually captures the content of the news articles leaves only good readers capable of detecting the important points in the news report, whereas less able readers—and we may suggest that there are many of those in the targeted audience—tend to find such important points by pure chance.

Other Factors Affecting News Comprehension

As discussed in Chapter 2, the structure and rhetoric of news reports target readers' minds to make the information believable and consumable. Different mechanisms are employed by newsmakers to reach the minds of their target audiences. One such mechanism involves presenting an eyewitness testimony or introducing quotations or quasi-quotations to make the report more believable. When readers come across such testimonies—as semi-truthful as often they are—they can relate to those ordinary people sharing their personal (and subjective, we may add) opinion about the situation. Introducing participants as interviewees or eyewitnesses conveys both the human and the dramatic dimensions of news reports. The reader may not question the subjective selection of such participants by a journalist; neither would the reader question the veracity of such testimonies. After all, those "random" participants are perceived as more trustworthy than the journalist behind the report who *chose* those interviewees.

Unsurprisingly, prior studies found that the educational level of media users influences news comprehension and recall, with more uneducated than educated people not understanding key notions from the news. Also, it was reported that domestic news is recalled better than foreign news (van Dijk, 1988, p. 154), which is not surprising because most people would relate more to their own immediate context than to some faraway lands where they never have been and may not even know where on the map those lands are situated. Bringing back the notion of schemata, we may suggest that readers may not have adequate schemata to fit in the information about an event taking place in a different country.

There is also a gender factor that comes into play when the reader processes the news discourse. Grabe and Kamhawi (2006) examined the emotional valence of news reports and found that women show signs of an avoidance response to negatively framed news; men, in contrast, are associated with a negativity bias, reporting the highest arousal levels and producing the best recognition memory and comprehension scores for negatively valenced messages. Finally, it was found that people in general understand the TV news better than written news. TV news discourse is less complex than press news. Oral discourse, such as the one used in TV news reports, is simpler linguistically and structurally, and TV news relies greatly on different types of visuals, from photographs to live coverage. Visual representation plays a secondary role in printed news due to the limited space allowed for the report, in the first place, but it facilitates the comprehension of TV news (van Dijk, 1988, p. 141).

News Comprehension in the Digital Age

Although the major research on news comprehension was conducted in the 1970s and 1980s—in the pre-internet age—recently cognitive psychologists have raised legitimate questions about the broad consequences of frequent internet use for human cognition. Marsh and Rajaram (2019) published a highly provocative article on the digital expansion of the mind. They outlined 10 properties of the internet that may influence cognition. Among other things, the authors were specifically interested in understanding whether the internet (1) encourages superficial processing of information, (2) is a powerful source of misinformation, and (3) inflates people's beliefs about what they believe they know. Although much of their argument goes beyond the issue of news processing—central to the current investigation—it is worth mentioning a few of the concerns that are relevant to the current book. First, the social nature of the internet increases the spread of misinformation, which, as the authors state, makes it the "wild west" of media. Second, the information's source often is obscure because "entire websites are sponsored by political or other organizations with agendas, and yet the involvement of that organization is difficult to spot" (p. 5). Third, frequent internet use may change metacognitive awareness. In other words, the very act of searching for answers may change one's beliefs about what one knows. By citing the evidence from experimental studies, the authors assert that it is the act of searching that inflates confidence in one's own knowledge. Unsurprisingly, this publication attracted much scholarly attention, which resulted in half of the journal issue[1] devoted to multiple responses from the academic community. Having acknowledged unanimously the importance of the raised questions and having praised the publication as a "timely stepping-stone for advancing the area of research" (Storm, 2019, p. 29), some scholars (e.g., Yamashiro & Roediger, 2019) were critical of the strong stand that Marsh and Rajaram (2019) took in their argument about the negative impact that internet use might have on the human mind and advocated numerous positive consequences that the internet has brought into our lives. Yet, others expanded the original argument by bringing in new perspectives. Wang (2019) elaborates on the veracity of the information found online and the selectivity of the individuals' information processing:

> The seemingly indefinite information online and the anonymity of many of the information sources intensify the uncertainty about the truthfulness of the information. As a result, individuals often tune into sources that are familiar to them and sources that tell them what they *want* [emphasis added] to hear. . . . They frequent internet sites that meet their personal interests and align with their ideologies. . . . In the process of information dissemination in our digital age, the power of selectivity is no longer only in the hand

[1] *Journal of Applied Research in Memory and Cognition*, 8, 2019.

of the information producer; much of it rests in the personal choice of the information consumer. (p. 26)

Wang illustrates the previous point using the findings from an earlier study (Wang et al., 2009) in which middle-aged adults from five countries (the United States, United Kingdom, Germany, Turkey, and China) were asked to recall public news events that took place in any period of their lives. The recalled memories did not correspond with the news coverage in the respective countries. For example, the most frequent memory concerned disaster events (16.3% of memories across the sample), although news about disasters accounted only for 2.3% of global news coverage. Also, memories related to foreign countries were disproportionally high about the United States in the non-US participants (e.g., United Kingdom: 54.8%; Germany: 61.4%; Turkey: 53.2%; and China: 75.2%), whereas the US-related media coverage in those countries constituted only approximately 17.7% of news. This indeed suggests that memory for news is largely influenced by the individual's selective information processing rather than by media coverage alone.

The issue of misinformation in internet news was discussed and reinforced further by Hamilton and Benjamin (2019). These authors illustrated the notion of "fake news" (first promoted by US President Trump and his supporters) on the example of a provocative claim made by an article in *The Political Insider* during the 2016 US presidential election. The article reported that Democrat candidate Hillary Clinton sold weapons to the militant group ISIS. Although the story was quickly identified as false and removed from the site, it generated much reaction from internet users. Once removed from a site, does false information remain accessible to the reader? In 2018, 2 years after the original report emerged and was subsequently removed from the site, simply by Googling the information about the reported incident the authors came across multiple articles, with 10 headlines suggesting that the claim is true and only two headlines directly stating that the message is false. Hamilton and Benjamin (2019) argue that in contrast to human memory that tends to forget and discard irrelevant or outdated information, the internet does not "forget," which can promote the proliferation of misinformation even after it is proven to be false.

The superficiality of news processing in the digital age also was addressed by a study on news' viewers checking the information on second screens (e.g., checking the information—relevant or irrelevant to the news coverage—on cell phones while viewing the news on TV). Van Cauwenberge et al. (2014) predicted that searching for information not relevant to the news coverage could be disruptive to the processing and recall of the news content, whereas searching for relevant information on a second screen could be less disruptive or even beneficial for the news recall. Although this prediction was not supported statistically, the study did confirm that

> second-screen viewing led to lower factual recall and comprehension of news content than single-screen viewing. These effects were mediated by cognitive load: Second-screen viewing led to a higher cognitive load than single-screen viewing, with higher cognitive load, in turn, leading towards lower factual recall and comprehension of news content. (p. 100)

There is another interesting question: Do people read differently online and in print? Although D'Haenens et al. (2010) found no difference in consumption, reading patterns, or quality of news recall between the print and online version of news, suggesting that the presentation of news in digital media is not inherently different from that in a more traditional paper version, in later years evidence was found that points to the opposite conclusion. Reading on-screen increases eye fatigue, and people tend to read more slowly when reading online texts compared to hard copy. People may also read in different orders: Whereas print texts are linear in their structure, online texts are filled with hyperlinks that the reader may be tempted to open while reading the target text, thus becoming distracted from the original text, which in general leads to impaired comprehension. As Marsh and Rajaram (2019) note, the

> internet typically offers *more* information at once and requires more choices than other forms of communication. A single choice offers us dozens of links to articles and blogs, and once we choose an article to read it will likely be littered with advertisements and "related" hyperlinks to other sources of information. As a result, no single link or article may be processed with enough depth to matter in the long run. (pp. 7–8)

In other words, we may suggest that reading articles—and news articles in particular—on-screen depletes our attentional resources, which, as discussed in the next section, makes the reader more susceptible to misinformation.

Interim Summary

Understanding the news discourse is a complex process that should be studied from the scientific perspective and accumulated knowledge in more than one discipline. Processing media information is not a purely cognitive act. News comprehension is a deeply social phenomenon, which involves the reader in the process of active construction of the news representation. As in the process of comprehending a basic text, in order to understand news reports the reader needs to evoke schemata that would assist them in processing the information. However, unlike schemata activated during the comprehension of a scientific text, schemata evoked while reading news already are biased against the other group that is reported on in the news. The sociocultural feature of schemata becomes more crucial for understanding the news than for understanding a basic text. News is read and understood in social situations defined by norms, values, interests, and ideologies shared by a group. Thus, the sociocognitive approach to the study of news processing appears to be the most appropriate, given the complexity of the phenomenon. Van Dijk (1988) states,

> People usually do not read news just to update their personal models of the world but also because such models may be relevant for further social interaction, if only for daily talk about topics in the news. This means that, just as for theory of news production, a psychological approach to news comprehension involves a theory of social cognition and a theory of the social contexts of news reading, representations, and use. (p. 140)

If the evoked schemata already are deeply biased in the mind of the reader and if knowledge updating while reading news is even more modest than in the process of reading an ordinary text, why are we bombarded by news reports on a daily basis? As van Dijk (1988) notes, only repeated and concurrent information is likely to update our knowledge and beliefs about an ongoing situation reflected in the news. Hence, media producers, who might be aware of the reluctance of the human mind to simply believe in any new piece of information provided in news reports, use their own mechanisms—some obvious and some more subtle—of mind manipulation. As we often quickly browse through news headlines without taking the time to read the full text, headlines and opening summaries catch our eyes. We quickly read those, wrongly assuming that headlines and leads capture the essence and the truthfulness of the described political event. However, unlike summaries of a scientific text, news summaries often are misleading and ideologically biased. By being exposed to such distorted pieces of information, the unsuspecting reader may boost the old, biased knowledge existing in the activated schemata without reading through the entire report. Even if the individual does go carefully through the whole text, only more educated and able readers can discern the manipulation embedded in the news text by a journalist and the ideological organization that stands behind the process of news production. Unlike academic writing, in which authors always are pushed to be consistent so as not to "lose the reader," the point of most news reports actually is to "lose the reader" and make the reader's mind process, absorb, and retain the information presented in the text in one way and one way only.

The age of digital media exacerbated the wide spread of misinformation and bias in news coverage. Although the research on how the internet affects the human mind and information processing is still in its infancy, with more questions raised than answers found, a recent debate started by Marsh and Rajaram (2019) invoked fascinating issues, some of which are not new in the field of text and news processing (distorted information, knowledge updating, encoding bias, selective processing, etc.) and some that relate directly to how the mind processes digital media (e.g., the obscured nature of the information source or the persistent nature of false information that never can be deleted entirely from the internet's "memory"). Currently, science is just entering the field of digital media and human cognition, thereby leaving us with rather scanty—albeit intriguing—evidence of the impact that digital media have on individuals' minds and memory.

How the Mind Processes False or Distorted Information

A more prominent and well-established line of research in cognitive psychology that deals with false information and memory distortion comes from psychology labs. In this section, we first discuss memory fallibility that allows for misinformation to be absorbed by the human mind. Then we look at the substantial accumulated evidence on how misinformation implanted in the human mind leads to the retrieval of false memories. Finally, we discuss what factors, such as individual differences and personality traits, might make some people more susceptible to misinformation and whether people pay attention to subtle linguistic traps while encoding and later retrieving inaccurate information.

Memory Fallibility

Schacter (1999) rightly reminds the reader about a bitter controversy that raged throughout the 1990s—and we may add, well into the 2000s—that concerned the accuracy of recovered memories of childhood sexual abuse. Some of those memories were corroborated and seem to be accurate, but many are believed to be false memories that are associated with devastating psychological and legal consequences for the alleged accusers. Given the serious consequences of these recovered false memories, psychologists increasingly have been working on developing and testing experimental paradigms to investigate illusory memories in which people confidently claim to remember events that never happened. In his review of multiple studies from psychology labs (cognitive, social, and clinical), Schacter (1999)[2] suggested that memory fallibility can be classified into seven sins, three of which might be of interest for our discussion.

First, misattribution may account for situations in which some form of memory is present but it is misattributed to an incorrect time, place, or person. If applied to memory for a political event, we may present a hypothetical scenario in which an individual may remember that Russia, for example, was involved in a proxy war with the United States in a recent conflict in Syria but may misattribute this information to the recent military actions in the US-led operation in Iraq.

Second, false memories may occur in response to suggestions that are made when one is attempting to recall an experience that may or may not have occurred. Suggestibility in memory refers to the tendency to incorporate information provided by others, such as misleading questions. "When people are asked suggestive and misleading questions about a previous event, their recollections of the original event may be altered by the provision of erroneous postevent information" (Schacter, 1999, p. 191). Returning to the hypothetical example about a proxy war in Syria in which a researcher surveys the participants' memory of the event with a true/false question, we may expect the following situation. The question, "In Syria, like in Iraq before then, was the Russian military on the ground engaged in a proxy war with the United States?" may receive a positive answer, although the retrieved information about Russia's involvement in Iraq is incorrect and was suggested

[2] For more information on the reviewed experimental studies, see the original publication.

by a misleading question. The latter is highly important for any social scientist who polls participants outside the laboratory context. The issue of suggestibility becomes central to studies on eyewitness testimony, where even the subtlest suggestions can produce astonishingly false witness reports. A few studies showed how participants simply are asked if they have seen video footage of a well-known news event when in fact there was no such footage. In one study (Ost et al., 2008, cited in Frenda et al., 2011), 40% of participants reported seeing nonexistent footage of a bus exploding in the 2005 London terrorist attacks when they were asked if they saw such news coverage. Of those who claimed that they have seen the footage, 35% offered detailed memories of what they could not have seen. Also, it was found that conversations can serve as a mechanism enabling the spread of a memory from one person to another: What was not mentioned at the beginning of a conversation is less likely to be included in the final shared memory (Brown et al., 2012). By extension—if we go back to the issue of news discourse and how the mind processes news reports—omitting details in the initial media reports on an event may prevent the individual from remembering the facts correctly at later stages.

Finally, memory encoding and retrieval are highly dependent on the preexistent knowledge, beliefs, and expectations that influence—and often distort—what one will recollect about a particular event or experience (e.g., Jalbert et al., 2020). Schema or the preexistent knowledge have been discussed at great length in this chapter. What we can add here is that bias also can manifest itself in mood congruency—that is, an individual may be more inclined to remember negative events from the past if the person is in a negative mood at the time of recollection. Moreover, people's recollections tend to adjust the recovered memories about their past selves to their present attitudes and beliefs. However, here it must be mentioned that individuals who believe that they have changed and are different from their past selves tend to overestimate a change in their attitude on a particular issue. This is known as retrospective bias and has been well established in studies by cognitive and social psychologists. To illustrate, someone who opposed gay marriage 20 years ago but now supports it may recover a false memory of a more drastically exaggerated change in their personal beliefs about this issue. Conversely, one who believes that their attitude to gay marriage always has been stable may be influenced by consistency bias and also will present the unchanged state of personal beliefs in an exaggerated form.

Implanting Misinformation in the Human Mind

One of the leading scholars in the field of false memories, Elizabeth Loftus, significantly has contributed to the field of false memory research through conducting numerous experimental studies on false memory and eyewitness testimony as well as representing the strong collective voice of scholars working in the field of false memory. As early as 1992, she summarized the major findings on the misinformation effect in human memory in a publication with the self-explanatory title, "When a Lie Becomes Memory's Truth," and in 2005, she expanded on the accumulated body of research with another review, "Planting Misinformation in the Human Mind: A 30-Year Investigation of the Malleability of Memory." So what do we know after 30 years of extensive research on false memory? What follows here is a brief recap of major findings, as discussed by Loftus (2005). Those findings form possible answers to a few major questions. First, under what conditions are people particularly susceptible to the negative impact of misinformation? People are more prone to accept misinformation as truth with a longer passage of time since the event when the original memory weakens. However, there is a possibility that when faced with misinformation that sounds credible, people may suspect that their original memory is not accurate. Second, can people be warned about misinformation and successfully resist its damaging consequences? It has been shown that pre-misinformation warnings might help one resist the misinformation. However, warnings about misinformation after it was processed and incorporated into memory are unlikely to change the individual's memory of the event. Also, it was suggested that the accessibility of misinformation can be enhanced by presenting it multiple times versus a single time. Third, when misinformation has been embraced by individuals, what happens to their original memory? Here there is no straightforward answer to the question because scholars are split in their opinions. What remains clear is that some people come to believe in misinformation and report it as their true memory; others had no original memory of the event and accept misinformation as their only memory; and yet others may have their original memories impaired in the process of deliberating misinformation. As Loftus (2005) concludes, "The idea that you can plant an item into someone's memory (apart from whether you have impaired any previous traces) was downright interesting in its own right" (p. 363). This raises an ethical question faced by experimenters on false memory: How far can one go with people in terms of the misinformation one can plant in memory? Indeed, such manipulation of the human mind without any clear evidence of possible consequences of the implanted misinformation can be perceived as problematic, to say the least. Loftus (2005) brings in the evidence of "rich false memories" from studies performed in the 1990s in which, in corroboration with family members, participants were led to believe in a made-up story going back to their childhood; one of these was conducted by Loftus (1993), and this became known as the "lost-in-the-mall" technique. In this scenario, an adult, is convinced by their relatives, in collaboration with the researcher, that as a child the person was lost in a shopping mall and later was rescued by an elderly person. Even if initially participants may reject such a story as their own memory, later they report that they clearly recalled the details of this situation. In another study (Bernstein et al., 2005), participants were falsely convinced that as children they got sick from eating dill pickles. A week later, participants returned for a delayed post-test to complete a Food History Inventory—the same as they did during the first trial—and those who received false feedback on the first trial reported less preference for and willingness to eat dill pickles as adults. As Bernstein and Loftus (2009) note,

> Once implanted, these false memories have consequences: They affect what someone thinks and feels about that experience, they can endure, they have repercussions for later intentions and actions, and they can be virtually indistinguishable from true memories of childhood experiences. (p. 138)

Apart from a rather unethical, in my view, intrusion into the human mind and tampering with human cognition, the results of such studies are fascinating indeed and support the power of strong forms of suggestion. Loftus (2005) emphasizes the significant practical implications from research on misinformation:

> In the real world, misinformation comes in many forms. When witnesses to an event talk with one another, when they are interrogated with leading questions or suggestive techniques, when they see media coverage about an event, misinformation can enter consciousness and can cause contamination of memory. These are not, of course, the only source of distortion in memory. As we retrieve and reconstruct memories, distortions can creep in without explicit external influence, and these can become pieces of misinformation. (p. 365)

Who Is More Susceptible to False Memory?

One of the questions raised by cognitive psychologists is whether some types of people are particularly susceptible to misinformation. Age is an important factor, with younger children and older adults being more prone than older children and younger adults to accept misinformation as truth. However, Kersten and Earles (2017), in their study on eyewitness testimony based on mugshot viewing accompanied by questions about an action, found that participants who chose a particular mugshot tended to associate the pictured person and the queried action and later were more prone to falsely recall that indeed they had seen the person perform that action. Moreover, emotional content may sometimes lead to increased rather than reduced likelihood in participants to falsely remember later how they have seen an action carried out by someone who actually had been seen doing something else (Earles et al., 2016).

Also, some personality traits, such as empathy, absorption, self-monitoring, and attention control, have been associated with the response to misinformation. To illustrate, it is known that misinformation effects are stronger when attentional resources are limited, which makes the age factor important, yet that is not sufficient to explain why people of all ages are subject to false memories (Loftus, 2005). A recent study on personality traits in those who tend to believe misinformation (Bronstein et al., 2019) found that delusion-prone individuals displayed an increased belief in "fake news." The study also reported that dogmatic individuals and religious fundamentalists were also more likely to believe false (but not true) news. A practical implication drawn from the study was that two related forms of thinking may protect against the belief in fake news: open-minded thinking and analytic thinking, both of which involve the search for alternative explanations and the use of evidence to revise beliefs.

Other Factors Affecting Susceptibility to Misinformation

We may ask another question: Do people tend to construct false memories as a result of sharing their thoughts with in-group members? This may have an interesting implication for the process of construction and reconstruction of collective memories that we discussed in Chapter 1. Indeed, there is a paradigm in cognitive psychology that tests exactly this phenomenon, which is known as collaborative memory contamination through the co-witness suggestibility effect. In one such scenario, two participants watch two different versions of the same movie while believing that they watch the same one. Later, participant pairs answer questions collaboratively, which guide them to discuss conflicting details, after which they take a recognition test individually. It was found that on the final test, participants often reported a non-witnessed answer that their co-witness had expressed during the discussion phase (Garry et al., 2008, cited in Ito et al., 2019). Furthermore, a large-scale study replicating Garry et al.'s (2008) experiment was conducted in 10 different countries (Brazil, Canada, Colombia, India, Japan, Malaysia, Poland, Portugal, Turkey, and the United Kingdom), and a significant effect in each country was found (Ito et al., 2019). What is even more intriguing is that the selected countries represent both individualist and collectivist cultures, where, according to Hofstede (2001), people's behavioral norms are different: They either heavily rely on in-group norms and opinions (collectivist countries) or value independence and individuality (individualist countries). The absence of a significant difference between the samples in the study shows that the suggestibility effect—that is, the implanting of misinformation by someone with whom a person discusses an event—is a universal phenomenon that supersedes the sociocultural makeup of the society.

Another factor that may contribute to higher susceptibility to believing in misinformation relates to reading speed. Participants instructed to read slowly were reported to be more careful in identifying misinformation implanted in the text (Tousignant et al., 1986, cited in Ito et al., 2019), which is quite logical. However, as Marsh and Rajaram (2019) note, reading onscreen involves a more superficial and much more distracted reading of the text than reading a hard copy, which may put the previous findings to test.

Less studied—although important nevertheless—is a linguistic factor that elaborately is used by authors to implant misinformation in the individual's long-term memory. Consider the following example. When the reader comes across a sentence in a news report, such as "The *alleged* mastermind behind the terrorist attack was X," the information encoded by the reader's mind might well be that it was X who committed the terrorist act and the qualifier "alleged" may not be remembered upon the subsequent retrieval of that particular memory. In a study that specifically examined what the researchers called "qualifying language," Stanley et al. (2019) investigated how epistemic qualifiers (e.g., positive, such as *certain*, *probable*, and *likely*, vs. negative, such as *uncertain*, *improbable*, and *unlikely*) might affect the encoding of false information that later might be retrieved as true information. The results revealed that 2 days later, the qualifiers had no impact on truth ratings. The authors concluded that this finding

> highlights a unique way in which false beliefs and misconceptions can enter one's knowledge base with potentially serious, negative consequences. Decision makers in high-stakes contexts—including those operating in medicine, law, finance, and intelligence—rely on epistemic qualifiers to communicate and comprehend critical information. If qualifying information no longer informs truth judgments after two days have passed, then individuals may not possess the requisite information to make informed, accurate decisions. These shortcomings in high-stakes decision making could have serious negative ramifications for the well-being of the decision-maker and others. (p. 127)

Interim Summary

Human memory is as malleable as it is fallible. The latter accounts for the retrieval of inaccurate memories that often are reconstructed due to external forces. However, the reconstruction of memories can occur without any outside influence: One recollects a memory that already carries elements of misinformation, even if this misinformation was not implanted deliberately into the person's mind. The complexity of human memory and our inability to tap into it with the required scientific precision leaves us with many questions unanswered but nevertheless allows us to rely on some evidence that suggests how memory reconstruction works and how the mind processes false information.

Among the "seven sins" of memory discussed by Schacter (1999), misattribution and suggestibility appear to be the most relevant to our investigation. The very fact that the individual may retrieve a memory where certain facts are attributed to the wrong place, time, face, or event is intriguing. However, we do not know how often it happens and whether some people are more susceptible to this particular "sin," yet I want to believe that such incidents do not define how our memory works in general. In mentally healthy individuals, such lapses of memory retrieval are assumed to be occasional, unless that memory relates to another land and another group. Another fallibility of memory is known as suggestibility, meaning that a person can alter the original memory due to an open or subtle suggestion by a peer, a relative, or the journalist behind a news report.

The idea of suggestibility as one of the major reasons why people recollect false memories was further explored experimentally by cognitive psychologists. Thirty years of accumulated research on implanting misinformation into the human mind have provided us with the undisputable evidence that (1) such misinformation indeed can be implanted into one's memory and (2) it is difficult to undo the effect of such implantation after inaccurate information was encoded in memory. The suggestibility effect leading to the acceptance of false information as truth—whether through reading a text or discussing an event with someone else—depends on a few factors, such as age, open-mindedness, ability to think analytically, and attention control. If we disregard a somewhat morally questionable intrusion into the human mind—especially in the case of implanting "rich false memories" related to the individual's personal life—experimental manipulation of misinformation has allowed us to understand better how the mind encodes, processes, and retrieves a memory of something that one has never witnessed.

Summary

In this chapter, we discussed how the mind processes a text, news discourse, and misinformation, and we identified a few common notions that emerged in these fields of study.

Probably the most remarkable idea is schemata, or background knowledge acquired by individuals throughout their entire life. Schemata are activated when we start reading a text, thereby helping us evoke a script within which the comprehension of new material will occur; schemata will be helping us make inferences because a new text will not necessarily have all the details that already exist in our mental schemata; likewise, new information that we learn from reading a new text will expand our background knowledge. Schemata allow us to avoid redundancies and the overloading of our cognitive resources. Moreover, understanding a text is an active reconstructive process and it happens within a sociocultural context, which makes schemata socially grounded, culturally specific, and ideologically biased. This bias becomes much stronger when we turn to processing news in general, and news reports about foreign affairs in particular. In the latter case, the activated schemata often will be biased about the other group and will stereotype that group. Such bias and the prejudice against the *other* are rooted in the group's desire to project as superior in its beliefs, attitudes, and values. The acceptance of negative information about the *other* most likely will happen if that *other* is presented as dissonant with the group's beliefs and values. If we keep in mind that domestic news is understood better than news about a foreign country, we may suggest that (1) there is no strong schemata about a foreign country covered by the media report in the individual's mind; and (2) any negative information supplied by media will be accepted more readily by the individual's mind due to the lack of such a strong and clear script, in the first place, and due to the dissonance of the presented foreign group's values with those of the in-group's values. Schemata help us understand how social members perceive and interpret the actions of other social members, especially if the latter are presented as dissonant with the group's dominant attitudes. Furthermore, the notion of schemata largely is invoked in research on misinformation and false memories. The extent to which misinformation is capable of entering one's mind and being encoded as true information depends on the preexistent knowledge, beliefs, and expectations of the individual.

If schemata represent the knowledge acquired throughout one's life and heavily rely on the sociocultural context within which they are built and against which new information is negotiated, is it possible to change that knowledge and possibly intrude into the individual's mind with deliberately distorted information? The question raised by scholars in all three fields of research discussed in this chapter (i.e., text processing, news processing, and processing of misinformation) is whether preexistent knowledge can be updated easily by the new incoming information. As evidence shows, the process of updating such information is not straightforward. Indeed, our life would lose much of the needed stability if we easily dropped our fundamental values when coming across a new piece of information that contradicts our previous knowledge. As prior research on text comprehension suggests, foremost, we need to trust the source of information. However, as scholars working on the interconnection between the internet and cognition assert, such trust is put to the test: The source of information in digital media often is vague and ideologically biased due to the journalist's subjective opinion and the agenda of an organization that stands behind the report. Also, it was stated that the human mind has an encoding bias and people tend to remember best what they already know; they also turn to those sources and sites where they get the information that they *want* to hear. This selective and biased processing of information—especially in the digital age—makes knowledge updating very complex. The same was suggested by cognitive psychologists working on false memory and misinformation. The only way that new—and especially false—information can be embedded in the individual's mind is through the repeated exposure of the reader or listener to the intended message; scholars in all three fields agree on this. Yet, we may ask whether a simple warning about misinformation prevents its absorption by the mind. Unfortunately, it was found that such a warning can work only at the pre-information stage; conversely, once the information is processed and encoded by the mind, a warning that the information was false is not likely to change the individual's beliefs in its accuracy.

The idea of the experimental manipulation of the human mind can be as fascinating as it is disturbing. Nevertheless, the results of numerous studies in all three fields have demonstrated that the reader's mind can be manipulated through a change of the reading perspective or through the use of biasing titles. The reader's attention to details or ability to detect misinformation can easily be manipulated. Such mind manipulation becomes crucial for media producers who macrostructure their texts in such a way that headlines and summaries become the main focus of the report, neither accurately reflecting the content nor representing an objective statement. This stands in stark contrast with, for example, the structure of a scientific text in which a summary reflects the content of the text and is consistent with the major claims made within it. If we add that online texts have numerous hyperlinks and distracting advertisements that interfere with the reading process and render it more superficial, it becomes clear that the attentional resources of the internet consumer already are limited, which makes readers of digital media more susceptible to misinformation. Only good readers—educated ones, in the first place—are capable of detecting inconsistencies and misinformation in such digital texts. The same was reported in the field of false memory: People with poor attentional resources are more prone to misinformation.

Another shared notion is that of suggestibility, or the influence provided by someone—a co-witness, peer, or journalist—on the individual's mind. From subtle suggestions made by a detective during a witness interrogation and from a specific choice of interviewees in a news report to the elaborate, though innocent on the surface, use of linguistic devices by a reporter, suggestibility remains one of the most powerful tools in the implantation of misinformation. The power of the suggestibility effect found across cultures makes it a universal phenomenon, and the ease with which inaccurate information enters someone's mind and 2 days later is believed to be true makes suggestibility one of the major memory "sins." Probably the strongest evidence of the suggestibility effect comes from studies on "rich false memories"—as unethical as they are and as beneficial for practical implementation in legal matters as they appear to be.

In conclusion, as humans in the 21st century, we are bombarded by new information on a daily basis. But our mind is biased to absorb only information that fits easily into our preexistent knowledge and beliefs. We select to read those texts and news reports that we believe will tell us what we want to hear. We stereotype and show prejudice against other social groups whose values and beliefs are dissonant with ours. Thus, browsing internet sites and reading the headlines and a few opening statements in the articles often suffice to update our knowledge about ongoing world events. However, by doing so, we are falling into the very trap carefully prepared for our fallible minds by media producers. Often what we read as the summary of a news article will guide us to absorb the inaccurate information implanted in the report. Furthermore, even if originally we may question some facts discussed in the news article, after coming across the same misinformation again and again, we finally may accept it as accurate. After all, rarely would we want to admit—or realize—that our mind, the most valuable part of who we are, easily can be manipulated.

4

Sociocognitive Approach to the Construction of Memory

At the Intersection of Media, Mind, and Memory

Human memory is one of the most important faculties that allows for our survival, progress, and sociality. The fallibility and malleability of memory, however, account for the constant process of reconstruction where inaccuracies and distortions abound. Such distortions often are within the volition of an individual; yet they can be implanted deliberately into an individual's mind by outside agents, such as official producers of memory. In this book, the main focus is on media as one such producer. By targeting individual minds of the group, media aim at constructing the memory of ongoing events—truly acting as the first history recorder—and reconstructing old memories. The active engagement of media reports and individual minds that process the delivered news information can be viewed as two agents involved in the process of memory construction. From this point of view, collective memory, mind, and media are not three independent units; rather, they represent the intricate phenomenon of memory construction. In the previous three chapters, we took a separate look at each of the three entities under investigation—collective memory, mind, and media—which brought multiple disciplines to the forefront of our discussion. In this chapter, I attempt to bring all three together within the same sociocognitive framework, which I hope will allow us to understand better how and why certain memories are constructed and reinforced by social groups.

It has become clear that a few similar trends emerge in the study of collective memory, media, and mind. First, one of the best understood mechanisms behind the construction of shared memories is schema or schemata. The role of schemata in the construction of shared memories widely has been discussed in the field of collective memory. All newly constructed memories should fit the sociocultural script as well as the previously formed memories. Thus, media agents need to report all new information about an ongoing

Reenacting the Enemy. Ludmila Isurin, Oxford University Press. © Oxford University Press 2022.
DOI: 10.1093/oso/9780197605462.003.0005

event in such a way that it will fit the schemata existent in their target sociocultural group and in the minds of individual group members. The latter will process any new information by trying to fit it into the familiar scripts. Second, the reconstructed memories of the shared past, as well as the newly constructed memories, tend to push against another group—often referred to as the *other*—whose values are perceived as dissonant with and inferior to those of the present group. Reporting new media information about the *other* invokes certain schemata as well as reinforces old stereotypes in the individual minds, which makes the processing of such information easier and the information more believable and more likely to be accepted as accurate. Third, bias—closely linked to the representation of the *other*—has been reported in all three fields of study: collective memory, media, and mind. Collective memories always are biased in presenting the group's past in a more positive light and dismissing those memories that do not serve the present goals of the group. Neither are media reports—even in the most democratic societies—free of ideological bias. There are power groups and ideological institutions behind any news agency that dictate what news reports should be delivered and how they should be delivered. Moreover, individual minds also are biased in how they process the news reports. The overwriting of old beliefs and values against which the new information is negotiated rarely happens unless the same—often inaccurate—information repeatedly is implanted into the minds of the group members. Fourth, collective memories never are objective, and gross inaccuracies occur in memories shared by a group. Such distortion of memory results from numerous sociocultural and political factors that tend to tailor the group's memory toward its current needs. However, the construction of collective memory intentionally can be influenced by media that do not necessarily present accurate information. To complicate the process further, the individual mind is fallible and tends to distort the information while processing news reports. Conversely, it is susceptible to accepting misinformation as accurate. Finally, there is a constant interaction between the media and the mind, the mind and memory construction, and a direct interaction between media and memory construction, as witnessed in media contributions to history records where the mind of an individual group member may or may not directly be involved. In order to grasp the complexity of the proposed theoretical framework, we first discuss the previously listed issues and see how the dichotomy of each phenomenon contributes to the integrity of the entire process of memory construction.

Mechanisms of Memory Construction

Schemata

One of the most accepted and discussed phenomena across disciplines—albeit originating from cognitive psychology (first introduced by Bartlett, 1932)—is the notion of schemata. Our knowledge of the world is believed to represent a set of scripts that are acquired throughout our lifetime. Those scripts help us make sense of new information that we will try to fit into the preexistent framework in our mind. As has been emphasized before, schemata are socially grounded, culturally specific, and ideologically biased. Moreover, they act as a major mechanism in the construction of shared memories.

Media agents are well aware of this fundamental mechanism behind information processing. They also are members of the community and, as such, share the sociocultural framework with their group; they understand what script is available in the community and how to deliver the message to the audience so that it will fit that script. While covering a new event, the reporters often refer to a past event with which the audience is familiar; they invoke the script that will provide a coherent framework for understanding new information, and by doing so they often invoke and reinforce old stereotypes. The more familiar the script is to the viewer/reader, the better new information will be accepted as believable, regardless of how inaccurate it actually might be. This is known as typification in news making, which may be equated with the notion of schemata in cognitive psychology. The prevalence of typification in news coverage accounts for what is known as media templates—frames, images, and linguistic means through which new events are discussed and contextualized. Indeed, a few basic strategies that journalists use aim at the activation of schemata by, for example, mentioning previous events as a precursor for the present event, if not as a predictor of a future one; inserting facts into well-known situation models to make them relatively familiar; or using well-known scripts and concepts that belong to that script (van Dijk, 1988).

Yet media attempts to invoke certain scripts in the minds of their group members would be fruitless if those minds did not have such scripts in the first place. The way the mind processes regular texts and news articles, as discussed in Chapter 3, heavily relies on the frames available for understanding the content of new information pieces. What we have to remember, however, is that the human mind is capable of filling in some slots in the schemata with the new information from the texts; conversely, the existent script helps make inferences about the new information. This dichotomy often results in the construction of false memories because the existent script in the individual's mind might interpret new information by making wrong inferences (e.g., remembering a bus explosion from the footage of a terror attack when such an explosion did not occur). The interplay between the media attempts to invoke particular scripts in the minds of their community and the availability of those scripts in the minds of the group members—as fallible as those minds might be in interpreting the new information—leads to the construction of new memories shared by the community.

Such shared memories, however, when distanced from the moment when they were first recorded, go through the process of finding their own place in the complex canvas of the group's collective memories. The contextualization of such memories often involves their framing within the existent templates or schemes. Some elements of those schemes partly will be cross-cultural, such as the group's effort to remember those events from their past that fit their current needs and identity claims, yet those templates partly will be tailored to a specific sociocultural script, such as narrative templates for discussing major wars in Russia, as demonstrated by Wertsch (2002).

As can be seen, schemata are the underlying mechanism behind the construction of shared memories. With time, every group will decide what shared memories fit the sociocultural script and are deemed important for the present well-being of the group and what memories will be forgotten. Those memories that will stay with the group, in turn, will provide interpretive tools and scripts for understanding new events and constructing memories thereof. Then again, those memories of the past events that have stayed with the group were first recorded by individual minds through whatever means of information available in that time period. Although we cannot go back in time to see how initially the first-hand information that later turned into a shared group's memory was processed by individual group members, we can look into media effects in recording history on individual minds in our time. In the 21st century, news coverage in all possible formats (newspapers, digital media, or broadcast) continues to rely on the schemata that are present in the targeted group as a whole and in individual minds in particular.

The *Other*

As mentioned previously, media agents attempt to activate specific scripts in their community, and often this involves the invoking of past memories about an old foe and reinforcing old stereotypes. Playing on such old stereotypes serves two goals. First, it helps the reporter fit the information about a new event into the framework that would make the story believable. Second, it resonates well with ideological organizations that stand behind any news reporter. Previously, I illustrated this point with the example of a high-profile journalist, NBC chief foreign correspondent Richard Engel, who often uses statements such as "Ukraine is involved in a war with Russia" (cf.: officially Russia is not involved in a military conflict) or "Russian boots are on the Ukrainian soil" (cf.: officially those "boots" never left Crimea because the Russian Black Sea Fleet is harbored in Crimea) in order to convince the audience that Russian aggression has not changed since the Cold War, the memory of which still is fresh among Americans. Actually, it is fascinating to watch how effortlessly Russia has reemerged as an enemy in the American public discourse and how media have contributed to the reinforcement of an old stereotype.

According to van Dijk (1988), media accounts of a new event contribute to increased deviance and, as a result, to the confirmation of stereotypes. The more the *other* is presented as deviant from and inferior to the values and beliefs of the present group, the more the audience will be convinced of the accuracy of an often inaccurate presentation of the *other* in the news coverage. One of the techniques for achieving this goal is ideologically motivated lexical choices, such as the use of the term *freedom fighters* or even *warlords* instead of *terrorists*.

If we turn to the mind that processes the information about the *other*, we have to go back to our previous discussion of schemata. Each group has a self-schema about one's own group and schemata about other social or ethnic groups. The latter often provides ground for group stereotypes and prejudices, both at the group and at the individual level. Such prejudices are persistent because they are useful in the reenactment of social dominance (van Dijk, 1988). So, news that confirms negative schemata existent in the minds of the group members or portrays a social group whose values and actions are dissonant with the dominant attitudes of the target audience is easier to process for individual minds, as in the former case the negative schemata simply will be reinforced and the accuracy of the report will not be questioned, whereas in the latter case a new schemata negotiated against the already existent self-schema will be built. However, van Dijk (1988) contends that events about a new *other* for which there is no preexistent negative schemata in the group have less chance to be covered. In other words, media always will favor the reenactment of an old *other* that already has well-established schemata in the mind of a group member over creating a new *other*, which would require more work and not necessarily be in line with the ideology of the power group behind the news agency.

The role of the *other* in the construction and reconstruction of shared memories has received much attention in the field of collective memory. People's memories of their national or group past indeed are tilted in favor of their in-groups and against other groups (Blatz & Ross, 2009). All official producers of memory, including media, contribute to pushing memories of their group's glorious past against the *other* that often played an important role in past events remembered by the group. Scholars of collective memories demonstrate how nations renegotiate a past event that involved both groups and how each group tries to embellish its role and show its righteousness compared to the other group (e.g., Hiroshima and Pearl Harbor as viewed by Americans and Japanese or the exaggerated role that countries claim to have played in bringing victory in World War II, as discussed in Baumeister & Hastings, 1997 and in Abel et al., 2019).

To summarize briefly, the indisputable role of schemata in comprehending the new information is recognized by media agents who tend to frame their news reports in such a way that they easily fit such very familiar scripts. When providing coverage of domestic or international affairs, the image of the *other*—an old enemy or any other group perceived as inferior to the target audience—may be reenacted. Because the human mind operates by utilizing cognitive scripts on which media heavily rely, such reenactment of the *other* is accepted as a believable story: After all, why would that notorious *other* become less dissonant with the beliefs and attitudes of the present group? Thus, the interplay between reporters' techniques and the nature of the mind accounts for the reinforcement of stereotypes and invoking of negative scripts related to the "other." If we also remember that the press is ideologically controlled by power institutions and that the construction of collective memories of the group that often are tilted toward emphasizing positive self-image and painting a more negative image of the *other* is influenced greatly by official producers of memory (i.e., media), we can argue that media and the mind equally are biased in presenting (media) and processing (mind) the information about the *other* or old enemy, such as the case under investigation in the current study. In the next section, we address a major issue of bias that goes beyond just the tilted representation of the *other*: How are the media and the mind biased in constructing new memories, and why are collective memories, as the outcome of such co-construction, biased?

Bias

The very nature of memory and its tendency constantly to be reconstructed suggests that it is not a precise recorder of what happened; rather, it is a subjective representation and interpretation of past events. Memory subjectivity, at both the production and the consumption ends of the continuum, translates into memory bias.

If we look at the production end of memory construction, such as media in our case, we hardly can escape an extensive debate in the field of media studies concerning the ideological power that stands behind any news reporter and any news agency. Media are not a neutral mediator of social events; instead, they promote preformulated ideologies of the accredited groups, such as the government (van Dijk, 1988). Olick (2014) goes even further by suggesting that often it is challenging to understand whether a journalist is presenting a biased account or whether journalism as a whole is biased. Selectivity in presenting particular facts and omitting or misrepresenting other facts has been recognized as one of the major techniques used by journalists. Such selectivity has become even more important in the post-broadcast era when journalists target a community of interest rather than a geographically situated community, thereby delivering the information that their audience expects to receive (Edy, 2014). Also, the internet allows journalists to make the information source obscure by hiding the actual power players whose agenda and ideology control the report, yet whose presence is difficult to spot (Marsh & Rajaram, 2019). The subjective selection of interviewers and eyewitnesses, the specific choice of linguistic means to deliver the message, the reenactment of old frameworks within which old stereotypes are reinforced, or even memory cannibalization by Western journalism, as illustrated by Zelizer (2011)—all these techniques discussed previously in this book provide a rich illustration of media bias. Free media hardly is a concept that one can accept at face value: No media, regardless of how much democracy the society entertains, are free of the ideological bias and the agenda of the elite groups for which a reporter works. As discussed in Chapter 2, a reporter's disobedience and the refusal to play by the rules result in the power organization distancing itself from the reporter.

If media are so fundamentally biased, why does the human mind consume the biased information without processing it through better filters? The most intriguing aspect of interaction between media and the mind is that both media that deliver inaccurate information and the mind that processes this information are defined by bias. The human mind is biased against accepting any new information that does not agree with the preexistent knowledge, beliefs, and values of an individual. Updating the knowledge through reading a new text or a new media report is not a straightforward process. Individual minds are biased to overwrite the previous knowledge firmly established in memory; the acceptance of new knowledge presupposes some basic coherence with old beliefs. However, repeated reexposure to the new information can help overwrite the previous knowledge; this is well known to journalists who attempt to redeliver the same message again and again until it is consumed by the imagined community. In addition, the encoding specificity of human memory that explains why unimportant information is not recorded in any permanent way provides another example of memory selectivity. Such selectivity bias has been reinforced as a result of the media proliferation into numerous internet platforms that unite people with the same interests and ideologies. The lack of exposure to differing opinions or simply different information about the same issue contributes to the boost of memory bias. As gloomy as the presented picture of the imperfect mind is, it becomes even more disturbing if we remember a recent debate in the field of cognitive psychology about the damaging effect of the internet. The post-broadcast age has expanded the scope of media and made them more accessible to the audience. However, it also has limited our ability to read any news article in depth due to the distracting force of commercials and additional hyperlinks incorporated into the text that the reader comes across and is tempted to open. As Marsh and Rajaram (2019) speculate further, the habit of superficial reading of digital texts can translate into a lack of in-depth reading of print texts as well. Also, the internet has allowed individuals to select what they want to read and what information sources to believe. As Edy (2014) cautions, such selectivity of what individuals' minds want to accept as accurate knowledge can lead to historical ignorance.

The bias of the human memory also explains how and why the information about out-of-group members or what we call the *other*, the group whose values and beliefs are perceived as inferior to ours, is processed easily and stereotypes about those whom we do not like as a community are so quick to resurface in our cognition. It is the bias of the human memory, not incidentally interacting with the bias of the officially produced information, such as media reports, that is a major mechanism underlying the process of construction of shared or collective memories.

The subjectivity or bias of collective memories is a notion agreed on by scholars who study this broad multidisciplinary—and unfortunately, rarely interdisciplinary—phenomenon. A clear shift toward presenting a better self in the shared memories of the past events undeniably involves the biased reassessment of that past. By exaggerating and embellishing supposedly glorious facts of the nation's history and omitting or suppressing unfavorable memories, groups strive to progress toward better and more accomplished selves. Moreover, the newly constructed memories that already are subjective and inaccurate in their nature feed into and are defined by the existent shared memories. Thus, the bias not only infiltrates the construction of new memories but also is the driving force behind the reconstruction process involving old memories; this reconstruction process evolves within specific frameworks that allow old memories to better serve the present goals of the community as well as facilitate the accommodation of new memories. The perpetual reconstruction process defined by subjectivity, inaccuracy, and ideological bias leads to the formation and persistent presence of distorted memories.

Distortion

Distortion of information or, simply, omission of accurate information has been a widely discussed phenomenon in media studies (e.g., van Dijk, 1988). A few of the regular techniques used by news reporters inadvertently or intentionally result in inaccuracies. As discussed in Chapter 2, journalists can present the coverage of the ongoing event by framing it within a story that previously has been discussed extensively; by doing so, they allow themselves to distort the facts in order to paint the ongoing event in a certain color. Their subjective choice of interviewees or accompanying images makes the coverage more believable to their target audiences, albeit sometimes at the cost of accuracy. The use of titles and leads in news articles is different from the use of titles in academic publications and aims at catching the reader's attention with the most important—yet subjective and often inaccurate—message that may not capture the content of the report.

This brings us to the following question: How does the mind process misinformation? One of the most disturbing findings reported in the previous chapters, in my view, is the susceptibility of the human mind to believing misinformation. From the studies on text manipulation in which the reader remembered the content of the text based on the perspective imposed by the experimenter to studies on false memories that can be implanted into the individual's mind and later accepted by the individual as actual true memories of an event directly experienced by the person, cognitive psychologists have provided ample evidence of the fallibility of the human mind. Suggestibility or subtle imposition of the inaccurate information has been found to be one of the mechanisms leading to distorted memories. This effect becomes stronger with shared memories where people tend to believe in false memories due to what is known as collaborative memory contamination. Social interaction between community members enhances the construction of collective memories. "Through acts of social remembering individuals become vulnerable to incorporating details about the past that they did not actually experience" (A. Brown et al., 2012, p. 2), and this may also account for the spread of the often distorted information learned through the media reports. Also, our minds can carry misinformation or misattribute the information even without any obvious outside influence. As can be seen, the interaction between media reports in which the delivery of inaccurate information is a regular occurrence and our malleable minds that are capable of accepting inaccuracies as true facts makes distortion one of the mechanisms on which the construction of shared memories heavily operates.

Now if we look at collective memories of the group—whether those memories resulted from the previously mentioned interaction of the mind and media or not—we can see numerous instances of distorted historical facts in the memories shared by the group. Because such incidences were reported for the most democratic and, arguably, most open societies, such as the United States, we can expect similar occurrences in the collective memories of other groups that lack the tradition of free press and free speech. However, as Baumeister and Hastings (1997) contend, self-deception indeed is a notoriously difficult topic to study.

To bring the three entities—collective memory, media, and mind—together and look at their engagement through the single mechanism of distortion, we can argue that the news coverage of an ongoing political event intentionally or unintentionally will deliver factual inaccuracies. These inaccuracies often are framed within the already existent memories shared by the group, which also are not an accurate record of the historical past. The goal of each news delivery, in turn, is to be accepted by the intended audience as believable. Conversely, the intended audience is represented by individual people who share memories of the group's past and have come to believe in the historical but often distorted facts that most likely they learned in school. So the new information links to their beliefs in the truthfulness of what they already know—as untrue as that knowledge might be—and is fed to their minds, which are susceptible to processing the distorted information as accurate.

Sociocognitive Framework in the Study of Media, Memory, and the Mind

Conceptualizing the Main Framework

The constant flux in which old shared memories, newly constructed memories, and the mind interact accounts for the complexity of the phenomenon known as collective memories. Neither objective in their nature nor randomly constructed, these shared memories serve the present goals and identity of the group. However, because the group's goals and identity claims change over time, so do collective memories. The process of memory reconstruction—as complex as it is on its own—does not happen overnight. Moreover, newly constructed memories need to fit the framework that already exists in the group and comply with those memories that are shared by the group at the present historical moment. "Official producers" of a new memory, such as media agents in our case, carefully structure the information related to a new event so that this new information will fit the framework of the existent memories and be accepted as believable by individual minds. The interaction between media and individual minds presents a fascinating process that has the similar underlying mechanisms and notions. As discussed above, the role of schemata, the reenactment of the *other*, the persistent bias that exists both in the mind and in the media industry, the mind's tendency to accept false information as accurate, on one hand, and the ideologically biased misinformation that often drives news reports, on the other, and the resultant distortion of a newly constructed memory—all this is shared by the main agents of memory construction, such as official producers and individual consumers.

In this book, I am taking a sociocognitive approach to the construction of shared memories and attempting to illustrate it with a specific case study: recently constructed memories related to the same events in the past few years and widely covered both in Russia and the United States.

The idea of using a sociocognitive approach for the study of complex phenomena is not new. Van Dijk (2018) has offered such an approach to the study of discourse analysis and to the study of news reports in particular. Sociocognitive discourse studies describe and explain discourse in terms of its social and political contexts but also include a cognitive interface between discourse and society. Van Dijk asserts that social and political structures can affect text only through the minds of language users, as group members represent both social structures and discourse structures in their minds. Yet his holistic approach is deeply rooted in text analysis, in which the mind is viewed as a major player in text construction and text comprehension but is not looked at from the empirical point of view.

My proposed framework has three major components that can be considered independent of each other but can be understood fully only when viewed as a whole entity. In addition, it focuses on memory construction rather than on the close critical analysis of discourse, even if discourse contributes greatly to the construction process (Figure 4.1).

First, we can look at the media coverage of an ongoing political event. As the first recorder of history, media play an undisputedly important role in the construction of shared memories. By applying a few methodological approaches to the news analysis (van Dijk, 1988) and relying on the substantially large data set, we can examine titles, leads, accompanying illustrations, choice of linguistic means, selection of quotes or interviewees, representation of the *other*, and so forth. Second, based on the results of the analysis, we turn to the second major component—the mind. In order to understand how the mind processed and comprehended the information delivered by media and how this information fit the existent cognitive frameworks, we need to survey a representative sample of the group members who serve as the recipients of the news information in question. Third, any newly constructed memory feeds into the previously formed collective memories of the group. Media agents, being members of the same group as their target audience, tailor their reports in such a way that they will fit schematic representations in the already existent shared memories or directly invoke such memories in

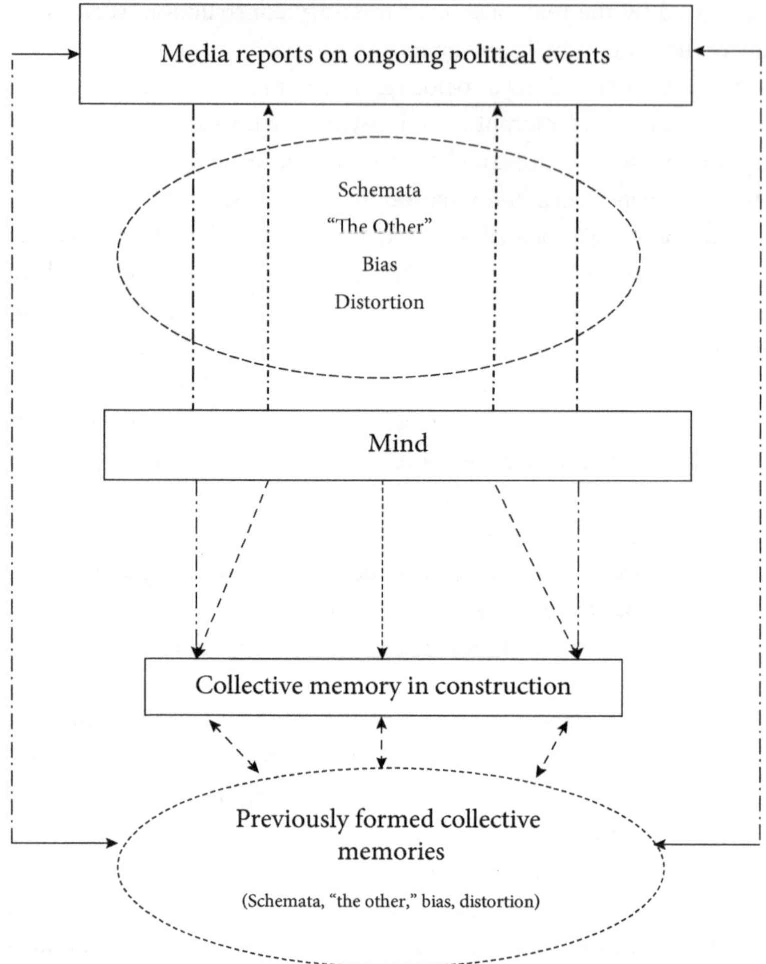

Figure 4.1 Media effects in memory construction: sociocognitive framework.

order to make their reports more accessible and believable. Thus, the process of memory construction can be studied at the interface of social structures (media, society, ideology, etc.) and cognitive structures (mind, text processing, bias, cognitive scripts, etc.).

If we look at the schematic representation of the framework (see Figure 4.1), we can see how media coverage aimed at delivering accessible and believable new information targets the minds of the audience by also relying on the previously formed collective memories that had built the groundwork both for the creation of new reports by media and by making the cognitive scripts available in the minds of the individual group members. Conversely, both media and individual minds are driven by the same cognitive mechanisms that are presented here as schemata, the representation of the *other*, bias, and distortion. The individual mind processes the delivered information, no matter how much the mind is constrained by the previously mentioned forces and contributes to the construction of a new memory. However, this new memory is negotiated against the existent, previously formed collective memories that were constructed and reconstructed as a result of—but not limited to—the same four mechanisms.

The Cross-Cultural Component in the Sociocognitive Framework

What may add an interesting twist to this already complex sociocognitive framework is a cross-cultural comparison of how shared memories related to the same event—not necessarily an event experienced by both groups but one covered by both group's media—are being construed in the minds of the respective group members. This becomes even more intriguing if each of the two groups is being figured as the canonical *other* for another group, thereby providing grounds for the reemergence and reinforcement of old stereotypes. This cross-cultural comparison is presented schematically in Figure 4.2.

The underpinning mechanisms behind memory construction would remain the same, with only the sociocultural scripts within which each group interprets a new event being specific to that group. Such scripts, in turn, reactivate old memories that had been constructed and reconstructed within similar schematic frameworks. The most interesting component, however, would be the reenactment of the notion of the *other*, which becomes the major player in the negotiation of newly constructed memories. Because each of these two hypothetical groups represents the *other* for another group and that *other* already is established firmly in the frameworks of memories related to the group's past, we can see an interesting angle through which we may look at the construction of new memories in two separate groups. Even if the event under investigation does not affect both groups directly, its interpretation would be different in the media of the two groups as well as in the minds of the respective group members. In the attempt to use

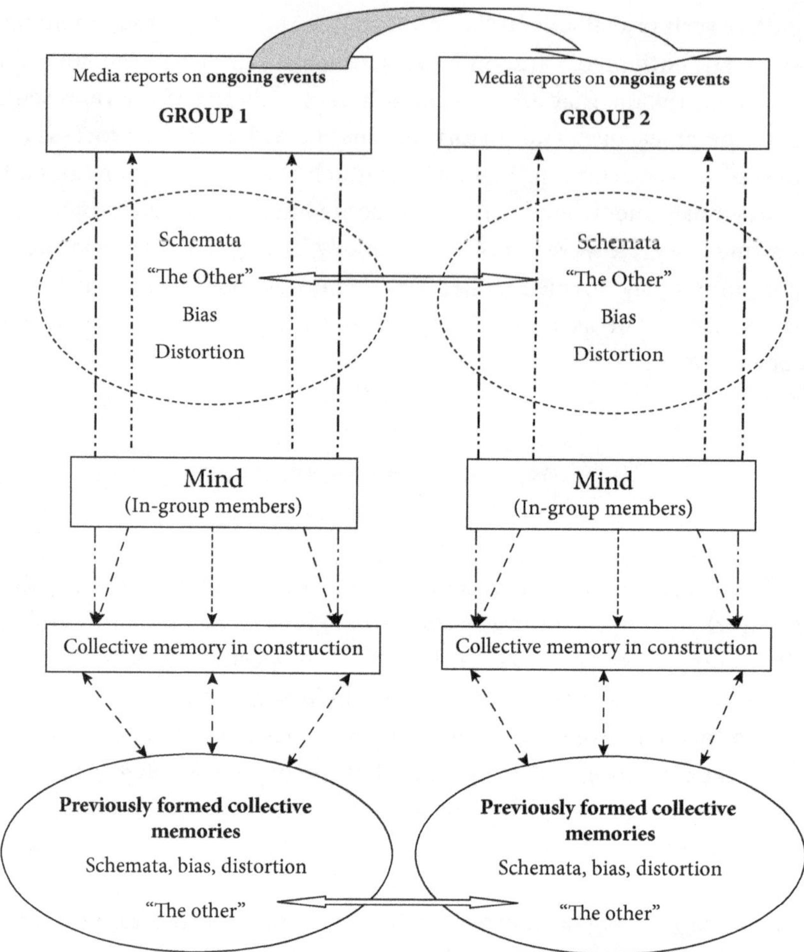

Figure 4.2 Media effects in memory construction: cross-cultural component in the sociocognitive framework.

the reported event as an opportunity to present the group's superiority and dominance, a contrast against the group that is perceived as deviant and dissonant with the present group's beliefs and attitudes is needed. So the reactivation and reinforcement of old stereotypes and the old foe become crucial parts in the negotiation of a new memory. Media—as ideologically biased as they are—would become the main agent in bringing back that old *other*, as its reenactment makes their stories more believable, acceptable, and legitimate. As discussed previously, news about a new *other* for which there is no preexistent negative schemata in the group is less likely to be covered (van Dijk, 1988).

Summary

I have attempted to conceptualize a sociocognitive framework within which the case study central to this book will be discussed. My goal is not to test the findings from numerous disciplines to which the first three chapters of the book were devoted; neither is it to confine myself within the boundaries of a particular discipline that would dictate the choice of methodology and analyses undertaken in the current study. Rather, by ignoring the disciplinary boundaries and breaching into some familiar and some new areas of investigation, I will rely on the accumulated knowledge in those areas of scholarship. I follow Boyer and Wertsch's (2009) call for an interdisciplinary approach to the study of collective memory, which plainly stated that "to understand those phenomena [collective memory], one should not be 'interdisciplinary,' if that means concocting a witches' brew of disparate results. Rather, one should ignore disciplines altogether and forge ahead" (p. 1).

I have called my framework sociocognitive, hoping that it would capture the interface between cognitive psychology and the social sciences. Moreover, I have expanded it by showing how it can be applied to different scenarios and different research interests. The three major components of the framework—media, the mind, and the previously constructed collective memories—and the interaction between them can be viewed in their entirety as well as in their duality. To illustrate the duality, one can choose to look closely into the media's engagement in the construction of new memories and investigate the effect that the media produce on how such memories are being constructed by individual minds—the angle that was chosen for the current study. Conversely, we may look at a bigger picture and include the analysis of old collective memories that provided the script within which a new memory in the making is being negotiated. Or we can look at the media effects on the reconstruction of old memories and how the individual mind processes such reconstruction. Regarding the mind component in this framework, one can look into one particular group or simultaneously look into two groups. The latter also will involve the expansion of media analysis beyond the media produced by a single group—what the current study aimed to accomplish.

Whatever combination of the above strategies and scenarios the researcher chooses, I hope the presented framework will serve as an analytical tool in future investigations of memory construction. As Hirst and Manier (2008) maintain, we "can treat collective memories as 'shared individual memories,' but locate them, not in 'the head' or 'in the world,' but in the interaction between what is out in the world and what is in the head" (p. 189).

PART II

COLLECTIVE MEMORY CONSTRUCTION IN RUSSIAN AND US MEDIA

5

Media, the Mind, and the Reenactment of the Enemy

Methodology

The previous four chapters outlined the major issues that one can find at the intersection of the three entities—collective memory, media, and the mind. Based on the accumulated scholarship in all three areas, I have built an argument—and, as a result, the framework—of how we can explore this intricate interconnection empirically.

The following five chapters focus on the analysis and discussion of the findings from a study conducted within the proposed framework. As mentioned previously, I have become increasingly interested in how media contribute to the creation of collective memories about ongoing political events and how they contribute to bringing back the *other*, against which the coverage of those events and the construction of a national narrative are being shaped. Furthermore, if we think about any major political foes—or the *other*, the term used throughout this book—in the recent history of the world, probably the Soviet Union, and its official successor, Russia, on the one hand, and the West, with the United States being the major player, on the other hand, come to the forefront of the discussion.

Indeed, the decades of the Cold War that started soon after the end of World War II reinforced the negative perception of the two countries in the eyes of their leading politicians, which was passed on to the ordinary public through ideologically biased media channels. The role of media in the creation of the *other* during the Cold War remains outside of my interests in this book. Yet, as an individual who has lived in both countries and grew up during the Cold War in the Soviet Union, I suggest that the media effect on the minds of people must have been much stronger in the United States than it was in the USSR due to the distrust that educated Russians had toward any official press conveying the government ideology. To reiterate, what follows in this section of the chapter is based on my observations, first-hand

Reenacting the Enemy. Ludmila Isurin, Oxford University Press. © Oxford University Press 2022.
DOI: 10.1093/oso/9780197605462.003.0006

experience of living in the Soviet Union until the early 1990, and my previous research on the Russian past, as it was reflected in the Soviet/Russian texts and the contemporary US media as well as in the minds of college-educated Russians (Isurin, 2017).

The end of the Cold War in the mid-1980s is credited to two presidents—Ronald Reagan, on the American side, and Mikhail Gorbachev, on the Soviet side. The infatuation with Gorbachev in the West and the growing disappointment with his leadership in the USSR, coupled with the freedom of speech that Russians finally could enjoy as a result of Gorbachev's *glasnost*, gradually have marred a rather idealistic image that educated Russians had formed about the United States during the Cold War years. The collapse of the USSR in 1991 and the subsequent decade of economic downfall, lawlessness, and chaos under a dysfunctional alcoholic president, Boris Yeltsin, removed Russia from the front pages of the US media as an old enemy. Instead, Russian borders had opened for American and other Western businesses that saw great opportunities in the vast new market, lenient financial policies, and murky waters of the crumbling and falling apart country. Not surprisingly, many Russians, as my research has shown, blame Gorbachev for "selling out" their country to the West and in particular to the United States (Isurin, 2017).

In 2000, Vladimir Putin came to power and has been the president—legitimate or de facto—ever since. Initially, he was embraced by US President George W. Bush, who "looked into Putin's eyes and saw his good soul." Even Hollywood was charmed by Putin, as the BBC documentary *The Power of Putin* (2017)[1] demonstrates.

However, the period of relatively normal relations between Russia and the United States was short-lived. The Cold War rhetoric gradually was coming back and a standoff between the two countries was becoming a new—or not yet forgotten—normal. The political situation has deteriorated seriously since 2014 when Russia took over Crimea.

Political Events at the Center of the Project

In this book, I focus on seven major events that happened between 2014 and 2018 and were heavily covered in the media of the two countries (Table 5.1).

[1] Retrieved March 25, 2020, from https://www.youtube.com/watch?v=ZZ-Kwr0VFUE.

Table 5.1 Major Political Events

Political Event	Date/Year
Olympic Games in Sochi	February 2014
Takeover of Crimea	March 2014
Conflict in Eastern Ukraine	2014—present (major events in 2014–2015)
Downing of Malaysia Airlines flight MH17	July 2014
Proxy war in Syria	2015–2018
US presidential election	2016
Poisoning of the Skripals	March 2018

Without taking any particular stance on these events—as opposite as they are in American and Russian narratives—I briefly outline them for the reader.

In 2014, the Ukrainian Parliament voted to force President Yanukovych to resign, which led to riots in Kiev, armed nationalists taking over government buildings, and people in Crimea, as well as in Eastern Ukraine—two major enclaves of the ethnic Russian population—not recognizing the new government in Kiev as legitimate. This resulted in two outcomes, both heavily criticized in the United States. The referendum in Crimea in 2014 showed that people overwhelmingly voted to join Russia, an outcome that was quickly acknowledged by the Russian government and applauded by Russians. Crimea had been part of the Russian Federation until 1954 when Nikita Khrushchev, a Soviet leader of Ukrainian origin, added it to Ukraine within the big map of the Soviet Union. Similarly, the rebellious population in Eastern Ukraine did not recognize the new government in Kiev as legitimate and demanded its autonomy, which soon led to a direct military conflict between the opposition forces and the Ukrainian government army. Since then, Russia has been accused by the United States of being involved in the conflict on the side of the rebels, which Russia has been denying while at the same time offering Russian passports to anyone from that territory. The horrific downing of Malaysia Airlines flight MH17 over the conflict-ridden airspace in Eastern Ukraine in July 2014 was blamed on rebels allegedly supported by the Russian military; however, the results of the international investigation of the tragedy remain inconclusive. The takeover of Crimea—unanimously termed as annexation in the West—served as a justification to impose multiple sanctions, both political and economic, on Russia. The sanctions have not been lifted since then.

In winter 2014, a month prior to the events in Ukraine and the takeover of Crimea, a nonpolitical event—although it is no longer possible to keep such large-scale events nonpolitical—the Winter Olympic Games in Sochi, took place. The US coverage of the games demonstrated the growing negative attitude of the United States toward Russia. Thus, it was decided to include this major event in world athletics on the list of other political affairs.

In 2011, a wave of unrest in the Arab world, known as the "Arab spring protests" and heavily supported by the White House administration, resulted in the overturning of a few governments across the Middle East and Africa and a prolonged civil war in Syria. Having started as the fight of Syrian rebels against the Syrian army forces representing the government of Assad, the war soon escalated into a wide-ranging conflict against Islamic State (ISIS) fighters. Unsurprisingly, in this military conflict, Russia and the United States happened to be on opposite sides: Russia supported Assad, with whom it had a long history of good relations, in addition to having a military base in Syria, and the United States supported the rebels; however, both countries agreed on one shared goal of eliminating ISIS. This makes the civil war in Syria the perfect example of a proxy war between the United States and Russia, even if the term rarely, if at all, is used in media to describe this confrontation.

Probably the largest political standoff between Russia and the United States happened during the 2016 US presidential election when Russia was accused of interfering in the American election in order to bring victory to Donald Trump. Indeed, Russian social media clearly showed their jubilation over Trump's victory, and a few Russian social media outlets were identified as having influenced the course of the election. The Russian government, however, consistently has denied its involvement in the alleged meddling.

The last event that attracted much attention from the media of the two countries was the poisoning of Sergei Skripal, a former Russian military officer and double agent for the UK intelligence services, and his daughter, Yuliya Skripal, in London in March 2018. The actual "assassins" have never been found, but the nerve agent used in the poisoning immediately was linked to Russians, which Russia has denied.

As can be seen, all but two events (the Olympic Games in Sochi and the 2016 US presidential election) that provided the contested territory for Russia and the United States in the past 6 years have happened elsewhere and not on the soil of either of the two countries. However, it was those seven major events that served as a perfect background for the reenactment of the *enemy* and a return to the Cold War rhetoric both in Russia and in the United States.

Media Data Collection

During the past few years, a large number of digital media texts ($n = 307$), both from Russian ($n = 168$) and American ($n = 139$) outlets, were collected (Table 5.2). Altogether, 50 internet sites representing major newspapers and other news outlets were surveyed (US = 28; Russia = 22). The largest focus was on three major events—the takeover of Crimea ($n = 114$), the conflict in Eastern Ukraine ($n = 51$), and the downing of Malaysia flight MH17 ($n = 37$)—with the rest of the events receiving relatively equal attention. Every attempt possible was made to keep the representation of Russian and American texts equal for each event. Moreover, wherever possible, reports related to the same fact and/or the same day in the development of the event were gathered from the media of the two countries.

As noted in Chapter 2, in a Western country such as the United States, it is unlikely to see much difference in the coverage of a foreign affair where the nation's military is not directly involved or where the nation's interests are not at stake. Thus, the US outlets were treated in a nonpartisan way, not dividing the outlets into liberal versus conservative, although Table 5.3 shows the

Table 5.2 Media Data Collection

Political Event	Country	No. of Texts	Subtotal
Takeover of Crimea	Russia	65	114
	United States	49	
Conflict in Eastern Ukraine	Russia	27	51
	United States	24	
Olympic Games in Sochi	Russia	10	20
	United States	10	
Downing of Malaysia Airlines flight MH17	Russia	22	37
	United States	15	
Proxy war in Syria	Russia	11	25
	United States	14	
US presidential election	Russia	19	36
	United States	17	
Poisoning of the Skripals	Russia	14	24
	United States	10	
Total			307

approximate breakdown of the internet sites into left liberal, center, and right conservative.[2] Conversely, the Russian media sources were chosen both from the state-controlled media, heavily criticized in the United States, and the liberal media, whose existence rarely is acknowledged in the United States[3] (see Table 5.3).

Table 5.3 Media Outlets

Country	Media Outlet	Hyperlink
United States (28)	Left liberal	
	CNN	http://www.cnn.com
	The New York Times	http://www.nytimes.com
	NPR	http://www.npr.org
	Huffington Post	http://www.huffingtonpost.com
	Atlantic Council	http://www.atlanticcouncil.org
	Politico	http://www.politico.com
	The Washington Post	http://www.washingtonpost.com
	CBS News	http://www.cbsnews.com
	NBC News	http://www.nbcnews.com
	TIME	http://time.com
	Business Insider	http://www.businessinsider.com
	CNBC	http://www.cnbc.com
	Vox	http://www.vox.com
	Brookings Institution	http://www.brookings.edu
	Newsweek	http://www.newsweek.com
	International Business Times	http://www.ibtimes.com
	The Nation	http://www.thenation.com
	Center	
	USA Today	http://www.usatoday.com
	Bloomberg News	http://www.bloomberg.com
	The Hill	http://thehill.com

[2] Classification of the US outlets was based on information retrieved May 18, 2020, from https://www.allsides.com/sites/default/files/AllSidesMediaBiasChart_Version1.1_11.18.19.jpg and https://mediabiasfactcheck.com. Classification of Russian outlets was verified by a Moscow-based journalist working for independent media outlets.

[3] As presented in the West, Putin's control over media leaves no doubt in the reader's mind that *all* Russian media are state-censored. However, there are quite a few liberal independent outlets available to the Russian audience. I have received a long list of those from a liberal Moscow-based journalist, Nadezda Azhgikhina, and many of those indeed were frequented by the participants who provided the data for the empirical part of this project.

Table 5.3 *Continued*

Country	Media Outlet	Hyperlink
	Foreign Affairs	http://www.foreignaffairs.com
	Voice of America	http://www.voa.com
	The Christian Science Monitor	http://www.csmonitor.com
	Right conservative	
	The New York Post	http://nypost.org
	Fox News	http://www.foxnews.com
	Forbes	http://www.forbes.com
	Chicago Tribune	http://www.chicagotribune.com
	The Daily Signal	http://www.dailysignal.com
Russia (22)	State-controlled	
	RIA	http://ria.ru
	Nasledie Pravda	http://nasledie.pravda.ru
	Pravda	http://www.pravda.ru
	Lenta	http://lenta.ru
	Izvestia	http://iz.ru
	Novye Izvestia	http://newizv.ru
	R93	www.r93.ru
	Komsomol'skaya Pravda	www.kp.ru
	Tass	http://tass.ru
	NTV	http://www.ntv.ru
	Vesti	http://www.vesti.ru
	Interfax	http://www.interfax.ru
	1 TV	http://www.1tv.ru
	Polit.ru	http://Polit.ru
	Independent/liberal	
	Novaya Gazeta	http://novayagazeta.ru
	RBC	http://www.rbc.ru
	Rosbalt	http://www.rosbalt.ru
	Vedomosti	http://www.vedomosti.ru
	Gazeta	http://www.gazeta.ru
	Meduza	http://medusa.io
	Tvrain	http://tvrain.ru
	Kommersant	http://www.kommersant.ru

Classification of the U.S. outlets was based on information accessed May 18, 2020, from https://www.allsides.com/sites/default/files/AllSidesMediaBiasChart_Version1.1_11.18.19.jpg and https://mediabiasfactcheck.com. Classification of Russian outlets was verified by a Moscow-based journalist working for independent media outlets.

Media Analysis

As discussed in Chapter 2, van Dijk (1988) has developed a detailed approach to the analysis of news discourse, and a few of his main ideas were incorporated into the analysis of media texts in this book. However, the current analysis mainly was based on the framework built in Chapter 4. Here, I outline the direction in which the analysis of texts within this project was conducted.

According to van Dijk (1988), any news report should be studied from two perspectives: macrostructure and microstructure. Macrostructure concerns the organization of the text (e.g., headlines, leads, and content), whereas microstructure involves different techniques used by a reporter in delivering the story (selection of visuals, eyewitnesses, linguistic devices, etc.). Thus, in the analysis of media texts, headlines and content were scrutinized closely. Keeping in mind the four major concepts around which the framework was built—schemata, the *other*, bias, and distortion—the content analysis and the analysis of headlines specifically targeted those underlying principles. For starters, headlines could address bias or distortion by simply misrepresenting or exaggerating the factual information reported in the text, whereas the content could illustrate the representation of the *other*, a use of scripts that are familiar to the audience, and references to prior events in order to contextualize a new happening. From the perspective of microstructure, the media data were analyzed in terms of accompanying visuals, the use of quotations, selection of sources or eyewitnesses, and the use of linguistic means.

In order to provide consistency, separate analyses within each political event and within each country's outlets were conducted, and then a more general analysis of the texts as a whole was done. Here, the attention shifted to showing how the outlets of the two countries reflected on the same fact or the development of the event related to the same date. Given a large data set that would not allow for the inclusion of more than 300 individual text analyses, it was decided to present the major findings and illustrate those by giving concrete evidence from individual texts. For all but one event (the conflict in Eastern Ukraine), all analyses followed the same structure: First, the US media analysis was presented with a more in-depth analysis of one selected representative text, then it was followed by the same procedure within Russian media, and a general summary concluded the discussion of the event. However, for the conflict in Eastern Ukraine, it was decided to focus on a few key points and provide a parallel analysis of the two sets of media. The next four chapters are devoted to the analysis of the media coverage of the events central to this book.

Empirical Part: The Mind

Based on the results of the media analysis, a survey related to how the media in each country reflected on a particular event was designed. Although most of the questions remained the same across both surveys, some questions were specific to each group and reflected differing stances taken by the media in each country in their coverage of the event. Moreover, for all but one event (Russia's alleged interference in the 2016 US presidential election), Americans were offered the option to assess the extent to which they remembered the event (e.g., remember very well, remember relatively well, have a vague memory of the event, and do not have any memory of the event). The instructions urged the participants, however, not to choose the last option—"no memory of the event"—if they had at least some vague recollection. In case the participants chose that answer anyway, they were asked to skip all the questions related to that event and to proceed to another event. The analysis was based only on the data from those who claimed at least some memory of the event. Because most of the events discussed in this project literally were close to home for Russians, such an option of skipping the event was not offered. The latter resulted in an unequal number of participants responding to certain event-related questions across the two groups, which it is hoped was resolved by using percentile comparisons.

Americans in the United States and Russian citizens residing in Russia were surveyed via the internet using my personal contacts and relying on the snowball effect. The survey offered to Russian respondents was in Russian, whereas the survey for Americans was in English. In addition to questions pertaining to the events central to the current study, basic demographic information was gathered (age, gender, education, political affiliation, main media outlets frequented, etc.). The data collection in this part of the project took place in August and September 2020. Because one of the questions in the US survey concerned the 2020 US presidential election, it was important to conclude the data collection before election day.

Not unexpectedly, the nature of the questions that pertained to political events was perceived as threatening by some potential respondents who initially agreed to participate and later refused to, with the effect being stronger among Russians. As anecdotal evidence, a middle-aged Russian approached by my contact in St. Petersburg aggressively refused to participate by saying that he knows *who* stands behind such an investigation and is not willing to help Americans. A similar reaction occurred from one of my American contacts, who first asked about the type of questions she would have to answer and then immediately refused to participate for fear of repercussions that might result from her responses. This suggests that there may be a fear of government surveillance among both Americans and Russians, which makes data collection related to politics, even via an anonymous online survey, challenging. Regardless of all the difficulties involved in this part of the investigation, two representative samples were surveyed in both countries.

Due to the exclusion criteria applied to the US pool, the data on two participants were discarded (only those who were born in the United States or came to the country as children could participate), which resulted in two equal-sized participant groups on both sides (n = 103 for each country; n = 206 total).

The basic demographic information for the surveyed samples is presented next.

Demographic Background

The gender was relatively balanced across the two groups, with almost equal numbers of male and female participants in the Russian pool (male, 50.5%; female, 49.5%) and slightly more female than male participants in the US pool (male, 44.7%; female, 55.3%).[4] The age distribution, although similar in terms of the mean age (United States, 42.7 years; Russia, 39.5 years), showed a much higher concentration of people in the 30–49 age range for Russia (67.3%, total), whereas the highest numbers for the US group fell in the younger group, the 19–39 age range (53.9%), and the older group, those aged 50 years or older (36.5%). Such discrepancy in the groups' age is not surprising because it was registered in prior studies involving Russia (e.g., Isurin, 2017). Older Russians are more reluctant to participate in any studies,

[4] One participant in each group preferred not to reveal their gender and was excluded from this analysis.

especially those initiated by an American researcher, due to the deep-seated caution inherited from the Soviet times and also due to the lack of sufficient internet skills that are necessary to complete such a survey (e.g., some of my older contacts were willing to participate, but they did not have email accounts to receive the survey link). Thus, the youngest participants in both groups were aged 19 years, whereas the oldest participant in the Russian sample was aged 73 years and the oldest participant in the US sample was aged 91 years (Table 5.4).

The majority of participants in both groups came from large cities (United States, 75%; Russia, 84.6%), with some residing in small towns (United States, 16.4%; Russia, 12.5%), and just a few representing rural areas (United States, 8.6%; Russia, 2.9%). In terms of educational background, although the overwhelming majority in both groups were college educated (United States, 75%; Russia, 85.6%), the Russian sample consisted of more people with postgraduate degrees, Master's and PhD's, combined (67.3%), compared to the American group (27.9%). Note that due to cultural difference, a choice of the response "some college" was offered only to the US group. In Russia, people usually would report their terminal degree, whether they attended some more advanced educational institution or not. Thus, the data on "some college" for the Russian sample were based on the reports of associate degrees or some other post-secondary educational credentials (Table 5.5).

Regarding the participants' current occupation, there is a wide range of employment venues. To illustrate, apart from 13.5% retired individuals in the US sample, the rest represent all walks of life granted by the educational background reported previously, such as government workers, medical doctors, college professors, law enforcement officers, educators, speech pathologists, scientists, engineers, service workers, lawyers, real estate agents, musicians, finance consultants, business owners, military personnel, and even an Episcopal priest. On the Russian side, with only 2.9% retired participants and no clergy representatives, we also can see a variety of professions that require advanced

Table 5.4 Major Demographics of Participants: Age

Group (*n* = 103 each)	Age, Years (%)			
	19–29	30–39	40–49	50+
United States (mean = 43.3 years)	27.9	26	9.6	36.5
Russia (mean = 39.5 years)	16.35	43.26	24.04	16.35

Table 5.5 Major Demographics of Participants: Education

Group (n = 103 each)	Education (%)				
	Bachelor's	Master's	PhD	Some College	High School
United States	47.1	15.4	12.5	25	0
Russia	18.3	52.9	14.4	10.6	3.8

education, such as college professors and school teachers, lawyers and film producers, psychotherapists and playwrights, business managers and communication experts, engineers and entrepreneurs, medical doctors and designers, scientists and customs officers. Moreover, in both groups, there were a few participants with blue collar jobs, such as factory workers, drivers, and construction workers, as well as a few homemakers or stay-at-home mothers.

Because the study investigated political events that happened in the second decade of the 21st century, it was important to look into the respondents' political affiliation and voting choice in the last presidential election. In the US sample, 10.6% preferred not to reveal their political affiliation. Having removed those from the pool, Democrats represented the majority (44.1%), followed by independents (35.5%) and Republicans (20.4%). When asked for whom they voted in the 2016 US presidential election and by excluding those who preferred not to answer (13.3%) and a few participants who were not eligible to vote due to their young age at the time of the election (7.7%), the distribution of other choices somewhat aligned with the previously mentioned political affiliations and showed many more votes for the Democratic ticket (57.8%) than for the Republican one (28.9%), with 13.3% of the respondents having voted for someone else. Although Russian respondents could not be asked a similar question concerning their political affiliation due to a complex multiparty political system in Russia, a question of whether they voted for Vladimir Putin in the last presidential election (2018) was asked. Having excluded 13.5% of those who preferred not to answer this question and those who were not eligible to vote due to their young age (1.9%), it showed that only 23.3% voted for Putin, whereas 76.7% did not. Because most of the respondents in both samples came from large cities that tend to produce more liberal votes than from rural areas or small towns, both in Russia and the United States, the finding hardly was surprising. In other words, although the data on these particular samples do not seem to represent the current political makeup in either the United States or Russia, where the sitting presidents at the time of writing of this book were not those whom the majority of the respondents preferred, it is noteworthy that both samples lean toward a liberal platform, thereby being comparable for the purpose of this project.

When asked how well-informed the participants were about world affairs, strikingly similar results were revealed by both groups: The majority reported being relatively informed (United States, 60.6%; Russia, 58.7%), followed by being poorly informed (United States, 28.8%; Russia, 29.8%) and well-informed (United States, 10.6%; Russia, 11.5%).

Because the focus of the media analysis in this project was on digital news sources, it was important to know where the participants routinely got their daily news. The overwhelming majority in both groups were receiving their daily news either solely via the internet (United States, 45.2%; Russia, 72.2%) or some other sources (e.g., TV, radio, or printed newspaper) and the internet (United States, 41.3%; Russia, 21.2%), with just a few relying solely on a printed newspaper (United States, 2.9%) or on TV coverage of the news (Russia, 2.9%). This finding further supported the choice of digital media for the analysis of the events selected for this book.

However, when asked how often the participants discussed world affairs with friends or family, there was a clear trend among Americans to discuss such things more often than do Russians (United States, 48.1%; Russia, 26.9%), and almost twice as many Russians reported avoiding the discussion of this topic altogether (United States, 9.6%; Russia, 18.3%). This finding suggests some level of weariness that Russians may feel toward politics due to numerous economic and political repercussions that happened after the collapse of the Soviet Union, although the latter is a speculative suggestion partially based on my prior research (Isurin, 2017).

Procedure and the Data Analysis

The number of questions in the survey slightly differed between the two groups (United States, 50; Russia, 47) due to a few additional questions asked of the American sample (e.g., the upcoming 2020 US presidential election, political affiliation of participants, and more questions related to Russia's alleged interference in the 2016 US presidential election), fewer questions related to other events asked of the American group (e.g., the 2014 Sochi Olympics) and more questions asked of the Russian sample (e.g., the West accusation of Russia's wrongdoing even before the evidence is found). The survey was administered online, which protected the respondents' anonymity. The survey started with the consent form, which explained the purpose of the study and the participants' right to discontinue participation at any point if they chose to do so. The data were gathered online and later underwent both quantitative and qualitative analyses. Each political event was analyzed as a between-group analysis against the results of the media analysis of each of those events in each respective country. Moreover, participants were encouraged to share any additional thoughts and comments at the end of the survey. The latter, in addition to multiple cases in which the participants chose to elaborate on a given question by providing their own opinion (i.e., the response option "other" allowed for such deviations from the prefabricated responses), were analyzed qualitatively.

The results of the study are discussed in the remaining part of the book, with Chapters 6–9 devoted to the content analysis of media related to the political events central to this project, and Chapter 10 based on the results of the empirical data gathered through the survey. Chapter 11 offers the main discussion, where we connect the dots and reexamine all the findings in light of the proposed framework that formed the basis for the current study as well as reconceptualize the framework due to the emerged findings.

6
Takeover of Crimea

One of the most significant events that detrimentally changed the relationship between Russia and the United States in the 21st century was the takeover of Crimea in March 2014. Although this once heavily discussed event is no longer a focus of the US media, it was perhaps the most important point in the tenure of Vladimir Putin and the most powerful event for the construction of Russian collective memory related to its current leader.

We can identify a few key events surrounding the takeover of Crimea, although not all of them were covered equally by the media of the two countries. Those events can be recapped briefly as follows: First, Ukraine turned away from trade with the European Union (EU) and instead opted to revive its relationship with Moscow, thus fueling significant public outcry and protests. Second, Yanukovich, the Ukrainian President, and Putin met to discuss an economic partnership, resulting in Russia buying $15 billion worth of debt from Ukraine and significantly cutting the price of their gas supplied to Ukraine. Third, protests resulting in deaths erupted in Ukraine, and tension between the West and Russia culminated in the Ukrainian Parliament voting to remove Yanukovich from office and later issuing a warrant for his arrest due to the mass deaths of protesters. Yanukovich refused to resign and allegedly fled the country. Fourth, soon after Putin won government approval to deploy the army in Crimea, armed protesters began to overrun airports and the parliament building in Crimea, an area predominantly populated by ethnic Russians. Soon after that, Russian forces taking part in military training in central and western Russia were called back to their barracks, putting an end to the "war games," as Putin called them. Finally, a Crimean referendum to join Russia passed, yet its legitimacy was scrutinized by the West. Two days later, Putin signed a bill to return Crimea to Russia. A year or two later, the US and Russian media returned to the topic of Crimea to cover its current state after it joined Russia—using the Russian terminology—or was annexed by Russia—as the United States describes it.

Reenacting the Enemy. Ludmila Isurin, Oxford University Press. © Oxford University Press 2022.
DOI: 10.1093/oso/9780197605462.003.0007

US Media

In two separate articles, *The New York Times* journalist Herszenhorn (2013a, 2013b) outlines the events of late 2013 when Ukraine turned away from a deal with the EU. "An ambitious effort to draw in former Soviet Republics and lock them on a trajectory of changes based on Western political and economic sensibilities" failed (Herszenhorn, 2013a), and Russia was blamed for threatening to impose economic sanctions on Ukraine if it signed an agreement with the EU. Ukraine's decision not to sign the deal and instead to strengthen their ties with Russia was met with "fury and regret directed at Kiev and Moscow" (Herszenhorn, 2013a). Note that such negative reaction of the West toward Ukraine soon would change dramatically. Also, the author briefly acknowledges Russia's unwillingness to accept the expansion of the North Atlantic Treaty Organization (NATO) eastward in case Ukraine enters the EU, a reason that was soon forgotten once the conflict in the region erupted. Already in these early publications, the possibility of unrest in the southeastern parts of Ukraine is mentioned subtly (Herszenhorn, 2013a):

> The mostly Russian-speaking and Russian Orthodox eastern and southern sections of the country tend to favor close ties with Moscow. In the West, Ukrainian speakers predominate, the Ukrainian Catholic Church has many adherents and Russia is regarded with suspicion or even hostility.

In other words, here the American reader is being educated briefly on linguistic, religious, and political differences between Eastern and Western Ukraine that will become central to understanding the further development of the conflict. Also, the use of the modifier "Russian-speaking" to describe the population in Eastern Ukraine can be considered relatively accurate. Ironically, soon it will be replaced entirely with "Russian" in most media texts related to the conflict in Ukraine. If we look at the headlines of these two articles, the first publication can be viewed as simply biased, presenting Russia as a villain threatening poor Ukraine ("Facing Russian Threat, Ukraine Halts Plans for Deals with E.U."), whereas the headline in the second article is misleading. The author describes small-scale protests in Ukrainian cities, whereas the headline "Ukraine *in Turmoil* [emphasis here and throughout all media-based chapters added unless specified otherwise] After Leaders Reject Major E.U. Deal" suggests a much grimmer picture.

Ukraine's "desperate" need for money and the EU's refusal to bail it out was answered by Putin, who "opened his wallet in the battle with the European Union over Ukraine's future" and agreed to purchase $15 billion worth of Ukraine's Eurobonds. The move received negative reaction in the United States and was perceived as "a clear jab at the International Monetary Fund" (Isachenkov & Danilova, 2013). Also, "some in Europe [not clear who] have accused Moscow of using strong-arm tactics to try to influence Ukraine's course," but Russia denied it (Smith-Spark et al., 2014). Although these early publications express concern about the possibility of unrest in Ukraine and portray both Putin and the Ukrainian President Yanukovich as villains—or as a "traitor," in the case of the latter—they so far lack the aggressively negative attitude toward Russia. Whatever ulterior motives they attempt to ascribe to Putin's move and no matter how much they regret that Ukraine chose Russia over the West, one fact remains undisputable: Russia offered to bail out Ukraine while the West turned away from such a request.

In February 2014, in the midst of the growing protests in Kiev, the Ukrainian parliament voted to dismiss Yanukovich from office despite his objections: "I am not planning to leave the country," he announced, "I am the legitimate president, and I am not going to resign" (Booth, 2014). However, "the White House released a statement that praised the 'constructive work' done by the Ukrainian parliament and urged 'the prompt formation of a broad, technocratic government of national unity,'" despite not having the official resignation of the legitimate president. As an unidentified State Department official added, the United States had been advocating "a de-escalation of violence, constitutional change . . . and early elections. The developments we are seeing on the ground are . . . moving us closer to those goals" (Booth, 2014). Such fast acceptance of the parliament's decision, even in the absence of Yanukovich's resignation, by the White House further supported the side that the US had taken in the conflict. American journalists, for their part, went on glorifying what was happening "on the ground" and in particular the role of protesters in removing Yanukovich from office. The repeated references to the "more or less peaceful" overturn of the government and the "orderly and polite" crowds contradict, however, the description of "self-defense" militias "whose members . . . continued to march in military columns, brandishing homemade metal shields and carrying wooden clubs and axes on their shoulders" or police "that surrendered the center of Kiev to protesters, who commandeered water cannon trucks and personnel carriers from retreating security forces and claimed full control of the city." Even looting can be presented as an innocent act, if needed. To illustrate, an elderly man finally entering Yanukovich's mansion that until now had remained closed to the public "shouted 'What a thief [referring to Yanukovich]!' as he took in the marble statuary" (Booth, 2014).

Another event that seems to have overshadowed the ouster of Yanukovich was the release from prison of his political opponent. Neuman and Ritchie (2014) devote an opening statement to Yanukovich who was voted out and spend the rest of the article praising his opponent, citing her words about Yanukovich as a dictator, and presenting protesters as people simply fighting for what morally is right. Although Russia's position on Yanukovich's ouster as a "violent 'neo-fascist' coup supported and even choreographed by the West and dressed up as a popular uprising" is acknowledged, the American reader quickly is reassured that "Few outside the Russian propaganda bubble ever seriously entertained the Kremlin line," suggesting that ideological propaganda can be found only in Russian, but not in the US, media (Higgins & Kramer, 2015;). After all, would the American reader seriously believe that the US is capable of changing governments in sovereign nations?

Shortly after Yanukovich was ousted, protests in Ukraine intensified and the government of Crimea turned to Russia with a request for assistance in keeping order. President Putin received permission from Russia's parliament to send troops to Ukraine to protect the lives of Russian citizens and "the Crimean population from lawlessness and violence" as well as the nation's military interests in the region, Russia's Black Sea Fleet harbored in the capital of Crimea, Sevastopol. It was decided to "send a limited contingent there to provide security." Moreover, the chairman of the Russian Federation Council asserted that "while Russia was justified in approving the use of troops in Ukraine, neither NATO nor the United States had that right" (Lally et al., 2014). This decision was met with outcry from the interim Ukrainian government and calls for full mobilization from the militant Ukrainian nationalist group. The presence of such "far-right ultra-nationalist groups" in protests, dubbed "fascists" by Russians, rarely is mentioned in the US media (Fisher, 2014).

In the meantime, Putin ended military exercises—or "war games," as he called them—in the central and western regions of Russia and the troops were sent back to their barracks (CNBC[1]). What follows next was called

[1] "Putin Ends Army Exercise, Russian Markets Rally." (2014, March 3). CNBC. Retrieved September 3, 2018, from https://www.cnbc.com/2014/03/03/us-halts-military-engagements-with-russia-over-ukraine-crisis.html.

the "low-key" invasion of Crimea (Landau et al., 2014). From reading different original reports from those days in early March 2014, it is not clear how many troops were involved or whether they were the Russian military. As Landau et al. write, "The standoff in Ukraine's Crimea region is a strange one, where soldiers appear to be standing around amid an air of calm. They wear no military insignia, but there is little doubt about who they are." Later they cite the words of another CNN correspondent that "In Crimea's capital, Simferopol, soldiers were circling government buildings and patrolling some streets, but their presence did not feel invasive," which, as they say, contradicts the Ukrainian statement that their border post was attacked by ten heavily armed troops from the Russian Black Fleet. According to the authors, "three six wheeled military trucks used for transporting troops, had black license plates *indicative* of Russian forces based in Crimea, per the agreement between Ukraine and Russia". All in all, this CNN report coming from the days preceding the takeover of Crimea seems to focus on the presentation of the observed facts without instilling any ideological hysteria. Not much was known at the time, the troops were not easily identifiable, and the presence of the Black Sea Fleet made it impossible even to estimate the number of soldiers on the ground. To illustrate, Landau et al. refer to the estimate provided by a senior US administration official that the total of Russian ground and naval forces in the region was 6,000, whereas a quick check on the size of the Black Sea Fleet alone shows a much larger number of 20,000.[2]

What followed next was a referendum held in Crimea with the overwhelming majority of people voting in favor of seceding from Ukraine and joining Russia (Figure 6.1). Immediately after that Putin signed a bill officially adding Crimea to Russia. Without a single shot fired the peninsula that had been part of Russia until 1954 was annexed. The swiftness of this bloodless act took many by surprise. As Fridman (2018) later noted, Russians outsmarted the West: " . . . Western experts were surprised not only by the effectiveness of the Russian military performance but also by its successful coordination of different simultaneous activities in different dimensions: military (covert and overt), political, informational, economic, and others" (p. 108), and this effectiveness has been "raised at the level of art" (p. 111). The surprise effect clearly is seen in the immediate reaction of the US media to the takeover of Crimea. As Myersand and Barry (2014) noted, "The speed of Mr. Putin's annexation of Crimea, redrawing an international border that has

[2] Retrieved May 23, 2020, from https://fas.org/nuke/guide/russia/agency/mf-black.htm.

Figure 6.1 Members of a Crimean self-defense patrol near a referendum poster in Simferopol (poster reads "Together with Russia. March 16–Referendum"). March 17, 2014. Reuters.
Credit: Sergei Karpukhin.

been recognized as part of an independent Ukraine for 23 years, has been breathtaking and so far apparently unstoppable" and the "world remained on edge" to see if Russia would go one step further and invade Eastern Ukraine (CBS[3]). All major outlets initially acknowledged the referendum, the peaceful nature of the act, the huge support that Putin received from his base for bringing Crimea back to Russia, and the new economic sanctions imposed on the country, and yet refrained from bluntly attacking Russia for the "stealthy takeover of Crimea" or "invasion of Ukraine" (e.g., Morello & Constable, 2014; Myersand & Barry, 2014; M. Smith & Eshchenko, 2014). American reporters also covered Putin's announcement and his "ominous" reference to the United States and Europe "that had crossed 'a red line' on Ukraine by throwing support to the new government," which Russia as well as the Russian-speaking populations in Crimea and southeastern parts of Ukraine refused to recognize as legitimate. "He denounced what he called

[3] "Russia Officially Annexes Crimea Away from Ukraine with Signature from Vladimir Putin." (2014, March 21). CBS. Retrieved May 25, 2020, from https://www.cbsnews.com/news/russia-annexes-crimea-away-from-ukraine-with-signature-from-vladimir-putin.

the global domination of one superpower [i.e., the US] and its allies that emerged. 'They cheated us again and again, made decisions behind our back, presenting us with completed facts,' he said. 'That's the way it was with the expansion of NATO in the East, with the deployment of military infrastructure at our borders. They always told us the same thing: 'Well, this doesn't involve you' " (Myersand & Barry, 2014). Without making any comments, the authors acknowledge Putin's criticism of NATO and the US for NATO's expansion to Russia's borders, the US-led war in Kosovo in 1999, their direct involvement in the toppling of the Libya's leader on the false pretense of humanitarian intervention, and their support of uprisings known as the Arab Spring. None of those accusations thrown into the face of the West easily can be dismissed as inaccurate, no matter how inconvenient they may be for American reporters. However, by including these quotes in their coverage they preserve professional integrity. Except for one CNN article, "Ukraine Cries 'Robbery' as Russia Annexes Crimea" (M. Smith & Eshchenko, 2014), headlines cannot be considered biased in this dataset.

In the next few years, due to other events that took place in the region (i.e., the downing of Malaysia Airlines flight MH17 and a conflict in Eastern Ukraine), attention shifted away from Crimea. However, in order to keep the story alive and continue framing other stories within the context of annexation, reporters occasionally returned to Crimea. The tone of all subsequent publications also has become more aggressive and demonstrated irreconcilable positions held by the United States and Russia. Now the takeover is described as annexation, Russian invasion, intervention, or occupation, whereas Ukraine's government is dubbed "Western-allied," thereby drawing a solid line between good and bad, allies and enemies. Whatever the topic of those post-annexation reports, the reader is reintroduced to what happened back in 2014 with a reference to the referendum that expressed the free will of the people entirely omitted. Instead, a typical narrative would contain a distorted fact that "Russia seized Crimea by force" (Fisher, 2014). It must be quite inconvenient for American journalists to counterargue the fact of the referendum in Crimea: The free will of the people is one of the most fundamental values that is ingrained in the American psyche and often has served as justification for the US government to intervene in the affairs of sovereign states.

The attempt of the International Criminal Court (ICC) to call on Russia regarding charges of human rights violations and war crimes failed as Russia formally withdrew. Here again, the criticism of Russia for such a move does not sit well with American reporters: The United States never became a member of the ICC, fearing that if it did, its soldiers might be charged with war crimes (B. Murphy, 2016). The United States firmly refused to recognize Crimea as part of Russia and pointedly said that it would never accept the Crimea annexation and that sanctions imposed on Russia would not be lifted until Russia left Crimea (Gaouette & Roth, 2017; G. Harris, 2017). One of the major issues addressed by the US media in the post-annexation period was the fate of Crimean Tatars who did not support the takeover and whose human rights allegedly were violated after the annexation (Birnbaum, 2014; Nechepurenko, 2016; Paschyn, 2016). The American media took up the Tatars' cause in order to attack Russia and essentially accuse it of genocide. Usually, those reports were based on a few select witnesses or the fact that the Tatars' legislature was recognized as extremist and banned by Russia.

On the first anniversary of the takeover, Putin publicly indicated that the decision to reclaim Crimea was made soon after Yanukovich was deposed as the president of Ukraine. Although Putin confirmed that he "had delayed a decision while awaiting the referendum results" (MacFarquhar, 2015), for the first time he admitted that there were Russian servicemen on the ground to support "local self-defense units." Such testimony contradicted the assertion maintained by Russian officials that the takeover was a spontaneous act and that there were no Russian troops surrounding Ukrainian military bases in Crimea, and it gave reporters another hot story, which further painted a dark portrait of the Russian president and, by extension, corrupt Russia. This new information also revealed how the Kremlin media are ideologically biased and misleading (Shuster, 2015).

For this particular theme, it was decided to take a closer look at two similar reports on the Russian and the US sides. Both discussed Crimea a year after it was taken over by Russia. If we take an article from *USA Today* (Peleschuk, 2015), titled "What's Happening to Crimea a Year After Russia Annexation," we can consider the title unbiased despite the use of the term "annexation," which is contested by the Russian side. The report starts by putting the takeover into a familiar script of Russian President Vladimir Putin sending troops to secure a referendum in Crimea. The reference to troops and Putin already is enough to activate both a prior event and a script within which the *other* reemerges in the reader's mind. Later, the *other* is seen in multiple references, such as "Ukrainian government forces are still battling *Moscow-backed rebels*" or that "only a handful of countries—among them

Syria, North Korea and Afghanistan—believe Crimea belongs to Russia."[4] The choice of the three countries that are mentioned here is not accidental due to the political tension between the United States and North Korea or the lack of trust in the conflict-ridden states, such as Afghanistan and Syria. The statement that "most locals that apparently still approve (publicly at least) of their new master" equally can fit the macrostructure [the content where the factual information can be considered questionable due to words such as "apparently" and "approve (*publicly at least*)"] and the microstructure, where the use of the previously mentioned lexical devices along with the word "master" (a word used twice in the article) referencing a slave or dog owner rather than the president of the country casts a negative tone over the report. The report focuses on the economic situation in Crimea a year after it was annexed by Russia and paints a rather gloomy economic and political picture by providing some factual evidence, such as Visa, MasterCard, PayPal, Apple, and McDonald's pulling out of Crimea, while its dependence on Ukrainian gas and water supplies puts its future in jeopardy. Although the author acknowledges that the "state of affairs in mainland Ukraine is less than stellar," he also is quick to explain why the Ukrainian situation is not bright: "Ukrainian government forces are still battling Moscow-backed rebels, while officials are relying on Western creditors to bail out their ailing economy" (Peleschuk, 2015). Therefore, it becomes clear where the author's allegiance lies and who should be blamed for the poor situation both in Crimea and in mainland Ukraine. To underscore the point further, the author presents a few examples of persecutions conducted by the Russian government, such as the forceful removal of some members of the Muslim minority group, the Tatars.

Returning to the microanalysis, a further illustration of the lexical measures in painting the picture in ideologically biased colors would be the reference to the referendum in Crimea as a "sham referendum" or to Russia "formally *absorbing* the region," or saying that a Russian airline was forced to suspend flights "*thanks to* Western sanctions" (instead of using the more neutral phrase "due to"). Thus, the lexical measures in delivering the report should be considered biased. The article provides only one direct quotation from Amnesty International—without giving a concrete reference—and mentions reports in the British newspaper *The Guardian* and

[4] A total of 89 countries voted against, 24 voted absent, 11 countries recognized that Crimea belongs to Russia, and four abstained. Retrieved March 28, 2020, from https://en.wikipedia.org/wiki/Republic_of_Crimea.

the Organization for Security and Co-operation in Europe, again without giving a concrete reference. Interestingly, the visual accompanying the report presents a picture of fireworks and two Russian naval flags. The latter may be considered iconic for Crimea, as it continued harboring the large Russian Black Sea Fleet even after the collapse of the Soviet Union—a fact that often is omitted in the US media—making the everyday presence of official Russian navy forces normal for the peninsula. Whether or not the choice of the picture was accidental on the part of the journalist, it stands out in sharp contrast to the content of the text: Jubilation and the iconic Russian navy flag hardly symbolize the dark picture of Crimea presented by the author.

Although there was a much larger data set for the theme of Crimea than for any other events central to this project, it is impossible to discuss all publications without unnecessarily expanding the size of this chapter. Many are repetitive, as different outlets usually cover the same story; nevertheless, regardless of the outlet, all constitute a unanimous collective voice of angry disapproval of Russia's act and, not incidentally, such disapproval represents the official stand that Washington took on Crimea. Moreover, the analysis of the media texts suggested not only that news agencies presented the story in a similar way but also that the narrative did not change when the occupant of the White House did: The takeover of Crimea happened under President Barack Obama, and its coverage continued through the presidency of Donald Trump. Russians reportedly celebrated Trump's victory in the 2016 election with champagne; however, President Trump did not change the tone of the media discourse on Crimea nor did he lift any sanctions imposed on Russia for the annexation of the peninsula.

Russian Media

While reading and analyzing multiple media publications surrounding the events of late 2013 and early 2014 in Russian media, one is struck by the absence of Putin's name prior to the takeover of Crimea in March 2014. Instead, the official public discourse seems to revolve around issues that ultimately led to the referendum and the subsequent takeover of Crimea, which became a star moment of Putin's presidency in the eyes of his nation, if not in the eyes of the West.

Earlier publications related to the Ukrainian conflict seem to serve the goal of educating the reader about the events preceding and directly following the change of power in Kiev and the legal side of the referendum in Crimea. To illustrate, already in 2013, Russian independent media (Shvejc et al., 2013) warned that Ukraine would follow Russia's lead because of Russia's pressure and especially because it potentially would face problems if it joined the EU. Such concerns seemed to coincide with similar ones expressed by the Ukrainian government of President Yanukovich. As a high-level Ukrainian government official stated, the renewal of negotiations about entering the EU were possible only if the benefits of such membership would be much higher than the losses resulting from the worsened relationship with Russia. To emphasize the lack of any benefits for Ukrainian citizens if the deal with the EU materialized, another article discusses Ukraine's exit and stresses that the deal only would have benefited their oligarchs and that Ukraine should rebuild relations with Russia.[5] The article then goes on to state that the trade deal with the EU more likely than not would have put a lot of undue strain on the average Ukrainian citizen, while the rich mostly would be the ones to profit.

The state media continued to prepare the reader for the unfolding events in Ukraine by explaining the agreement between Russia and Ukraine, according to which Russia would invest $15 billion in the Ukrainian economy and reduce the price of gas.[6] Compared to the preceding event, here we clearly can see how the discourse is framed firmly around Putin and his report on the decision of the Russian government. However, the deal seems also to be criticized heavily by Putin's critics, such as his fierce opponent Latynina (2013), a journalist representing independent media, who draws comparisons between the actions of Putin in this trade deal and those of Leonid Brezhnev during his leadership, in that Brezhnev made bad investments just as the author believes Putin currently does. She claims that whereas Brezhnev sank money into spreading communism rather than ensuring food for his own people, Putin is wasting money on Ukraine which it can never hope to pay back. The author then goes on to ask why Putin decided to do this. His plan, according to the author, is to back Ukraine into a corner, where its only option would be to work with Russia and then take on a loan that it cannot afford so that Russia eventually could obtain different Ukrainian enterprises. Note

5 "Ukraina ne Budet Podpisyvat' Soglashenie s ES, Schitajut v Gosdume" ["Ukraine Will Not Sign a Deal with the EU, Says the State Duma"]. (2013, November 29). RIA. Retrieved October 11, 2018, from https://ria.ru/world/20131129/980687891.html.

6 "Rossija Investiruet v Ukrainu $15 mlrd i Snizit Cenu na Gaz" ["Russia Will Invest $15 billion in Ukraine and Cuts/Reduces Gas Prices"]. (2013, December 17). RIA. Retrieved October 11, 2018, from https://ria.ru/world/20131217/984720312.html.

that the tone of this article is different from that in most other Russian media publications, including those in the independent media outlets, because the author clearly is way too passionate for a political analyst, which results in some ill-conceived and "politically incorrect," from the Western perspective at least, references. For example, she implies that the leaders[7] of underdeveloped African countries supported by the Soviet Union were a step away from cannibals: "Leaders, *not picking human meat out of their teeth* [emphasis added] silently laughed at the craziness of idiot communists but claimed to love Leonid Il'ich Brezhnev forever. . . . And right away they ran to *damn* [emphasis added] capitalists to ask for more money."[8] Unfortunately, such openly racist comments, had they been made by Putin, would have created an outcry in the West, but when made by a Putin critic, they are overlooked entirely by the US government, with the latter presenting Latynina with the Freedom Defenders Award.[9]

In late 2013 when protests against the deal with Russia were gaining power in Kiev and when Yanukovich still remained in office, there was one particular event that made headlines in most Russian news outlets. Victoria Nuland, a Career Ambassador (the highest diplomatic rank in the US Foreign Service) representing the US State Department in Ukraine, accompanied by the US Ambassador, came out to the central square in Kiev to feed protesters sandwiches and cookies.[10,11] Because such open support of the protesters demanding the removal of their legitimate president can be viewed as unacceptable—especially when performed by the highest-ranking American diplomat—Nuland with her cookies and, by extension, the country she officially represented became a target of mockery from Russians, and her actions once and for all demonstrated who was behind the change of the government in Kiev (Figure 6.2). The accompanying images and video clips proved the authenticity of this incident. Ironically, the US media ignored the outrageous fact of a high-ranking diplomat feeding protestors in their coverage of

[7] There are two words for "leader" in Russian: *lider* and *vozhd'*. The latter, chosen by Latynina, also can apply to the chief of a tribe.

[8] All translations from Russian media sources were made by the author and are treated as direct quotations henceforth.

[9] Latynina received the Freedom Defenders Award from the U.S. State Department. Retrieved October 11, 2018 from https://2001-2009.state.gov/secretary/rm/2008/12/112974.htm.

[10] "Viktorija Nuland Razdala Mitingujushhim na Majdane Pechen'e" ["Victoria Nuland Was Giving Maidan Protesters Cookies"]. (2013, December 11). RIA. Retrieved May 28, 2020, from https://polit.ru/news/2013/12/11/nuland.

[11] "Zamgossekretarja SShA Nuland Razdala Mitingujushhim na Majdane Pechen'e" ["U.S. Assistant Secretary Nuland Was Giving Maidan Protesters Cookies"]. (2013, December 11). RIA. Retrieved May 28, 2020, from https://ria.ru/20131211/983404951.html.

Figure 6.2 US State Department Diplomat Nuland accompanied by US Ambassador to Ukraine Pyatt distributes sandwiches to anti-government protestors in Kiev. December 11, 2013. Reuters.
Credit: *Reuters*

Ukraine, although Nuland's "highly symbolic appearance" in the square was acknowledged in some news outlets.[12] Because Nuland did not feature much in the US media, it would be appropriate to mention here another moment, a few months after the "cookies scene," that has become embarrassing for the US government, as a report by D. Murphy (2014)indicates: An audio conversation between Nuland and the US Ambassador to Ukraine, Jeffrey Pyatt, leaked and was posted anonymously on Twitter and then YouTube. In that conversation, Nuland openly discussed the makeup of the next Ukrainian government and suggested the names of people she thought would be the best fit. The United States did not deny the authenticity of the tape but the State Department spokesperson Jen Psaki called the leak "a new low in Russian tradecraft," although, as the reporter adds, Nuland's "strong preference for

[12] "Top U.S. Official Visits Protesters in Kiev as Obama Administration Ups Pressure on Ukraine President Yanukovich." (2013, December 11). CBS. Retrieved May 28, 2020, from https://www.cbsnews.com/news/us-victoria-nuland-wades-into-ukraine-turmoil-over-yanukovich.

how Ukraine's government should be formed—and apparent confidence that the US has major influence over that—is a reminder of the disconnect between the US government assurances that it does not meddle in nations' internal politics and its actual behavior." In other words, a clear photo of the US State Department official feeding protesters in Kiev and an audio tape revealing US plans to create a new Ukrainian government according to its vision hardly could convince the Russian reader that the United States was not orchestrating the change of government in Ukraine. Although this conviction was acknowledged in the US press, too, there was a clear attempt to dismiss such suggestions as an absurd ideological stunt by the Kremlin. As Fisher (2014) sarcastically notes, "When the Ukraine crisis started, Putin's state media spun up a narrative that the Ukrainian protests were an American conspiracy to isolate Russia."

The state media[13] acknowledged the Ukrainian parliament's vote to force President Yanukovich to resign from office; however, they focused mostly on the turbulent events in Kiev as a means of questioning the legitimacy of Yanukovich's resignation, which would be crucial for any Russian claims concerning his replacement. However, this claim was challenged by the West, as discussed in the same outlet.[14] This article explains that the European Commission along with the United States fully recognized the removal as legitimate and refused to call it a coup. The article cites the statement made by the official representative of the European Commission that they "respect the decision made by the Ukrainian government" and accepted the appointment of opposition leader Alexander Turchinov as temporary president. Despite this acceptance by the West, the article maintains that Yanukovich's removal did not follow proper impeachment procedure under Ukrainian law, which calls for an investigation and court involvement. This turning point, totally dismissed by the US media, is essential for our understanding of the Russian perception of all the events preceding and following the takeover of Crimea. Years later, the official state media would turn again and again to Yanukovich's

[13] "Verhovnaja Rada Progolosovala za Otstavku Yanukovicha" ["The Verkhovna Rada Voted for the Resignation of Yanukovich"]. (2014, February 22). *Lenta*. Retrieved October 11, 2018, from https://lenta.ru/news/2014/02/22/elections.

[14] "Evrokomissija Priznala Otstranenie Janukovicha" ["The European Commission Recognized the Removal of Yanukovich"]. (2014, February 24). *Lenta*. Retrieved October 11, 2018, from https://lenta.ru/news/2014/02/24/eu.

ouster to support their original claim that it was unconstitutional and therefore illegitimate.[15]

Contrary to U.S reports, Russian media closely covered Crimea in the weeks before the referendum and the subsequent takeover. Here the situation is described as growing tension between the Russian-speaking population that opposed the new Ukrainian government supported by the ultranationalist forces that were dominant in the protests and the ethnic Tatar minority that opposed reunification with Russia. Although the protests are described as almost peaceful in the state media, occasional attacks by Tatars, who threw water bottles at Russians, did not escape the attention of reporters (Azar, 2014). Journalists from the independent outlets reporting from the ground took a closer look at the situation and did present two opposite perspectives expressed by Russian-speaking residents of Crimea who supported reunification with Russia and Tatars who opposed it (Dergachev & Zinchenko, 2014). However, their coverage—albeit more detailed than what one can find in the state media—still shows a similar picture of relatively peaceful street protests and overwhelming support for Putin taking over Crimea and bringing in the military to defend Crimea against the Ukrainian nationalist "fascist" units. A quote from one of the interviewees, "If Russia does not take up Crimea, the United States will do it," became a catchy headline of the independent media report and reflected the opinion of the ethnic Russian population in Crimea who believed that the West had brought the new government in Kiev. The accompanying images show protesters holding signs such as "Thanks to Putin" and "No to Fascism."

Subsequent to the ouster of the Ukrainian president, the Russian government approved moving armed forces into Crimea in the wake of the unrest there.[16] The independent media article starts by stating that the deployment of troops was requested by Putin and approved by the Russian government. However, a few paragraphs later it states that earlier it was the government that requested Putin's approval to use all available means to protect the people of Crimea. Such reiteration underlines the legitimacy of the approved deployment, showing the reader that it was not an authoritarian decision

[15] "Otstranenie Janukovicha ot Vlasti Bylo Antikonstitucionnym, Schitaet Azarov" ["Removing Yanukovich from Power Was Unconstitutional, Azarov Said"]. (2016, December 16). RIA. Retrieved May 27, 2020, from https://ria.ru/world/20161216/1483786240.html.

[16] "Sovet Federacii Odobril Vvod Vojsk na Ukrainu" ["The Federal Council Approved the Deployment of Troops into Ukraine"]. (2014, March 1). *Vedomosti*. Retrieved October 11, 2018, from https://www.vedomosti.ru/politics/articles/2014/03/01/sovet-federacii-edinoglasno-odobril-vvod-vojsk-na-ukrainu.

made by the president. The article also informs the reader about the planned referendum in Crimea where the only presented question would be if "the autonomous[17] republic of Crimea has state independence based on decrees and agreements." Although the initial reaction of the Russian government was to keep silent on the fact that Russian troops were involved in Crimea, indirectly the state media suggested their presence there (Turchinov, 2014). A year later when Putin admitted having sent Russian troops to Crimea, the state media framed this story into an almost innocent picture of "polite and quiet" soldiers securing peace in Crimea.[18]

Compared to the US media that did not focus on the results of the referendum, the Russian press covered it widely and emphasized the overwhelmingly positive vote (96%) that the people of Crimea cast in favor of returning to Russia. To show its legitimacy, the state media provided multiple direct quotes from international observers who confirmed that the referendum was democratic and transparent,[19] despite the US press maintaining that the referendum was conducted without international monitors (Fisher, 2014). Since this moment of a major victory for Russia has become a star moment of Putin's presidency, the government outlets published almost identical reports that showed a portrait of Putin giving his speech to the people of Crimea and included multiple quotes invoking such concepts as "love for Russia," "return to the home harbor after a long and exhausting sail," "Russian heart and soul welcoming Crimea," or the sacred concept in Russian culture, "the motherland."[20] In Russia, the news of the reunification with Crimea was received with a sense of euphoria and gratitude to their strong and decisive leader. In the next few days after the referendum, Russian media had a heavy focus on the legal procedures of incorporating Crimea and Sevastopol (the port that harbors the Russian Black Sea Fleet), with a portrait of Putin signing the bill omnipresent in media outlets.[21]

[17] It is noteworthy that the U.S. media refer to Crimea as a "semi-autonomous" republic.

[18] "Vezhlivo i Tiho: Voennyj Aspekt 'Russkoj Vesny' 2014 Goda v Krymu" ["Polite and Quiet: The Military Aspect of the 'Russian Spring' of 2014 in Crimea"]. (2015, March 14). *Lenta*. Retrieved November 1, 2018, from https://lenta.ru/articles/2015/03/14/crimea.

[19] "Mezhdunarodnye Nabljudateli: Referendum v Krymu Otvechal Demokraticheskim Proceduram" ["International Observers: Crimean Referendum Was Democratic"] (2014, March 17). *TASS*. Retrieved May 27, 2020, from http://tass.ru/mezhdunarodnaya-panorama/1051375.

[20] "Putin: Krym i Sevastopol' Vozvrashhajutsja v Rodnuju Gavan'—v Rossiju" ["Putin: Crimea and Sevastopol Return to Their Native Harbor—in Russia"]. (2014, March 18). RIA. Retrieved October 12, 2018, from https://ria.ru/politics/20140318/1000079137.html.

[21] "Putin Podpisal Zakony o Prisoedinenii Kryma i Sevastopolja k Rossii" ["Putin Signed a Bill on Adding Crimea and Sevastopol to Russia"]. (2014, March 21). RIA. Retrieved October 12, 2018, from https://ria.ru/politics/20140321/1000544230.html.

As can be seen, the presentation of the events surrounding the takeover of Crimea was orchestrated carefully by Russian media sources. Putin was kept totally out of the picture while the reports concerned the turmoil in Ukraine and then, in all his knightly armor, was ushered onto the stage to mark the victory and triumph of his leadership. To fast forward from the events in Crimea to 2018, we can see how Putin took center stage again by driving the first heavy truck across the newly built bridge connecting the Crimean Peninsula with mainland Russia.[22] Every year since Crimea joined Russia, the anniversary of the "reunification" has been acknowledged widely by all state media, and the legitimacy of how Russia redrew the national and international borders has not been questioned.[23] Moreover, celebrating the first anniversary since the takeover of Crimea, Putin made it clear that the Ukrainian opposition that brought the new government to Kiev was supported, first of all, by Europe. And then he pointedly added, "We know quite well that the real puppet masters were Americans and their allies."[24] Later, to remind the reader about the West and the United States in particular, the state media released occasional reports on new sanctions[25] and how Ukraine and the West refused to recognize the free will of the people and, in turn, how Ukraine expects Western allies to support the Ukraine's supposedly planned war for Crimea.[26] The White House's position on Crimea has not changed since Donald Trump took office. Using his favorite social media platform, Twitter, Trump stated that Crimea *was taken* by Russia. What made this statement interesting, nevertheless, is how—deliberately or not—it was "lost in translation," with the neutral word "taken" replaced with the Russian word "captured."[27] The article concludes with a quick history

[22] "Poehali! Putin za Rulem KamAZa Otkryl Dvizhenie po Krymskomu Mostu" ["Let's Go! Putin at the Wheel of KAMAZ Opened the Crimean Bridge"]. (2018, May 15). *Vesti* Retrieved October 12, 2018, from https://www.vesti.ru/doc.html?id=3017491.

[23] "Vecher Edinenija s Krymom: k Prazdnovaniju Prisoedinilis' Desjatki Gorodov" ["The Evening of Unity with Crimea: Dozens of Cities Joined the Celebration"]. (2015, March 18). RIA. Retrieved November 1, 2018, from https://ria.ru/society/20150318/1053289256.html.

[24] "'Put' na Rodinu'"—Putin Raskryl Podrobnosti Vossoedinenija Kryma s RF" ["'Path to the Motherland'—Putin Revealed the Details of the Reunification of Crimea with the Russian Federation"]. (2015, March 15). RIA. Retrieved November 1, 2018, from https://ria.ru/politics/20150315/1052668652.html.

[25] "SShA Rasshirili Sankcii Protiv Rossii" ["US Expanded Sanctions Against Russia"]. (2016, December 20). RIA. Retrieved December 2, 2018, from https://ria.ru/economy/20161220/1484167781.html.

[26] "Sovetnik Poroshenko Predrek Skoruju Vojnu za Krym" ["Poroshenko's Adviser Predicts War Soon for Crimea"]. (2016, February 15). *Lenta*. Retrieved May 27, 2020, from https://lenta.ru/news/2016/02/15/sovetnik.

[27] "Tramp Zajavil, chto Rossija 'Zahvatila' Krym" ["Trump Said That Russia 'captured' Crimea"]. (2017, February 15). NTV. Retrieved February 28, 2019, from https://www.ntv.ru/novosti/1764018.

lesson on how Russia acquired Crimea and how it was all done legally. The same narrative can be found in some independent media, too. When covering a recent meeting between the US State Department Secretary, Pompeo, and the current President of Ukraine, Zelensky, a few questions related to the relationship between the two countries were discussed. However, not incidentally, Pompeo's words regarding one of those issues, the "annexation" of Crimea—"we will never recognize Crimea"—made the headline of this independent media publication (Poplavsky, 2020). Such a repeated unchanged discourse on Crimea can serve as a great example of how persuasion works in news reports.

If we take a separate look at Russian independent media, we can see how the initially restrained coverage of the unfolding events and a rather unbiased discussion of the legal side of the takeover (e.g., Galimova, 2014), or an attempt to grasp the upcoming burden of sanctions imposed on Russia for its "occupation" of the Ukrainian territory (Mineev, 2014), or the coverage of the first problems faced by people in Crimea as a result of their return to their "motherland" (Romanova, 2014), or a focus on individual lives affected by the takeover, both positively and negatively, a year after the takeover,[28] later were replaced by the sad acceptance of the reunification as something that cannot be undone. Fahrutdinov (2018) quotes Western politicians who assert that unfortunately, there is no more Crimea: Ukraine cannot get it back without a major war, which neither NATO nor the EU needs. However, liberal journalists also express much sadness regarding the moral side of the takeover. Martinov (2019) contemplates what happened in 2014 and how it has affected life in Russia and in Crimea. Although the majority of Russians still believe that bringing Crimea back to Russia was a positive act and 90% of people in Crimea are still happy about joining Russia, the economic sanctions that were placed on Russia by the West have a price tag that hardly can justify the reunification. As he writes, "The carnival has ended with a question: Well, we have taken Crimea and now what?"

Similar to the US article chosen for closer analysis, a Russian article describes the situation in Crimea a year and a half after its takeover (Lashov, 2015). Its title, "Crimea Under Sanctions: What Has Changed in a Year and a Half" signals that the sanctions imposed on Russia—and, by extension,

[28] "Krymovaja Gora Vladimira Putina. Itogi Pervogo Goda Kryma v Sostave Rossii" ["Crimean Mountain of Vladimir Putin. The Results of the First Year of Crimea as Part of Russia"]. (2014, December 18). *Tvrain*. Retrieved April 1, 2020, from https://tvrain.ru/teleshow/reportazh/krymovaja_gora_vladimira_putina_itogi_pervogo_goda_kryma_v_sostave_rossii-379550.

on Crimea—by the West and the United States will be the focus of the report. The lead following a picturesque panorama of the peninsula (the largest visual out of the six presented in the report) captures the main content of the article: "Ban on public transportation and import, spotty telecommunication, and problems with the use of international credit cards"—just a few restrictions that people in Crimea face as a result of their referendum in March 2014. Clearly, Russia as a player behind the takeover is removed from the scene, which makes the content somewhat biased. Instead, both the title and the lead shift the focus to the innocent population of Crimea that was punished for holding the referendum. As a matter of fact, the referendum is referred to four times throughout the text and sanctions are mentioned 13 times. Thus, the picture of deprivations faced by the people of Crimea is contextualized within the unjust measures taken by the West (i.e., the United States, which is mentioned four times total) for the referendum. It is noteworthy that all eight subtitles in the article incorporate negative lexical or grammatical devices, such as "blockade," "stopped the import," "isolation," and "closed" (lexical); or "are *not* welcome," "there is *no*," "do *not* come," "are *not* able," and "are *not* in a hurry" (grammatical).

The factual information, such as the withdrawal of credit cards, eBay, Adobe, and others from Crimea, as well as bans imposed by the Ukrainian government, partly resembles the information mentioned in the US source. However, the tone of this narrative is drastically different: The author is sympathetic toward the people in Crimea and presents them as survivors of the strenuous conditions imposed on them for the expression of their free will during the referendum. Without making direct references to Russia being behind the takeover, the author shows the supportive role of the Russian government that allowed the residents of Crimea to travel abroad using Russian passports and Russian airlines and provided 1.4 thousand diesel generators to ensure electricity transmission in case the Ukrainian side—as had happened in the past—would cut the electricity supply to the peninsula. Similar to the US source, Tatars are mentioned in this article too, yet from a different perspective. The author describes an attempt by leaders of the "unregistered organization of Crimean Tatars" to block food delivery from Ukraine to Crimea but reassures the reader that the food deficit predicted by the Ukrainian government did not happen because Crimea switched to Russian and local products. In general, the tone of the report is optimistic and presents Crimea as a place unfairly punished by the sanctions but resilient in its spirit and having undeniable Russian support. The language of the narrative is rather reserved compared to the analyzed article from the *USA Today*. No specific terms or modifiers that qualify as biased—except for the repeated use of the word "sanctions" and the previously mentioned negative terms in the subtitles—were detected in the report. The visuals illustrate certain points made in the article, such as ATMs and the food blockade. As in the US article, quotations—in quotation marks—are used without providing any direct reference to the quoted source.

In general, the analysis of the Russian media related to Crimea has shown the meticulous preparation of the reader for the upcoming event; the detailed explanation of the legality of the reunification process; the emphasis on the free will of the people expressed at the referendum; and the continuous reminder, years later, of how it all happened and why the takeover was legitimate. At the same time, the image of the United States as a puppet master of Europe in the orchestration of the government change in Kiev and the major force in imposing unjust sanctions on Russia has been reinforced. Six years later, Russians, still supporting the takeover and quietly suffering under the burden of economic sanctions, have been helped by their media to reenact the United States as an old enemy. Surprisingly, there is little difference in how this event has been reflected in the state and independent press, with the latter remaining more critical and inquisitive, albeit accepting the takeover as a political act that cannot be reversed.

Summary

The events in Ukraine in late 2013 and early 2014 have become the major turning point in the relationship between Russia and the United States. For many Americans, Crimea was not a part of the world they had heard of until 2014. For Russians, on the other hand, Crimea always has been perceived as Russian, and its "temporary" assignment to Ukraine in the 1950s did not matter much during Soviet times because it was still within the scope of the Soviet Union. This difference in perception has been crucial in framing the public discourse in both countries.

Through the analysis of the large media data set on both sides, it was fascinating to see how each country has developed its own narrative, which remained unchanged throughout the years following the 2014 takeover. Moreover, media, as an obedient servant of the government ideology, repeated the story with the emphasis on those specific details—often distorted—that promoted the political ideology of power groups—the two respective governments, in this case. Russian media have created a narrative in which the Ukrainian president was removed from his post in violation of constitutional laws, thereby making the decisions of the new government illegitimate. The growing tension in Crimea, which is populated by ethnic Russians, and the call of the Crimean government for help against the attacks of Ukrainian nationalist groups have justified the decision of the Russian government to send some limited military contingent, whose presence on the ground was acknowledged only a year later. The results of the referendum in Crimea that showed the overwhelming support of people in Crimea for joining Russia and the legal status of Crimea as an autonomous region in Ukraine (a fact omitted in the US press) have allowed Russia to present a bill of Crimea's reunification with Russia as legally sound. At the same time, the United States' adamant refusal to accept the legality of the takeover and the clear evidence of its role in supporting—if not orchestrating—the turnover of power in Kiev, in addition to numerous economic sanctions that it placed on Russia as a result of Crimea's "annexation," have turned into a continuous reminder to Russians, both in media reports and in their daily lives, that the United States actually is the old enemy, no different from how it was depicted by the Soviet propaganda.

As for the American press, it has created an almost idyllic picture of a Ukraine that was trying to escape the sphere of Russia's influence in favor of joining the Western orbit. The Ukrainian president who chose stronger ties with Russia instead of entering the EU was removed from office without his formal resignation or any impeachment procedure required by the Ukrainian constitution. The legitimacy of the removal was not questioned by the United States, which quickly recognized the new interim government and showed much support for street protests. Although some evidence of US involvement in the government change leaked into the American press as an embarrassing fact, it was not covered widely. On the contrary, Russia was blamed for making such evidence public. The United States, undeniably representing democracy and Western values (i.e., the best values in the world), took a strong stance on supporting Ukraine and opposing Russia in this conflict. As expected, the takeover of Crimea received negative reflection in the US media, and not incidentally, the results of the referendum that expressed the "free will of the people" were dismissed as "sham" and later were not even mentioned. The story of Crimea has been woven firmly into a much larger picture of a resurgent Russia fighting for its sphere of influence.

One cannot disagree that land-grabbing and the redrawing of international borders is not an acceptable practice in the 21st century; neither is an attempt to install governments in sovereign states in order to promote one's seemingly superior values.

Interestingly enough, the annexation of Crimea, as it is called in the West, took both politicians and media by surprise, as Russian President Putin was not perceived yet as a game player that one should reckon with. The clichéd phrase "Putin's Russia" would enter the public and academic discourse later. As for now, Crimea was taken by Russia; the Russian people, contrary to expectations in the West, did not bow down under the US sanctions to turn against their president. So just like this, the two countries came to the brink of a new Cold War phase in their relationship, and the media covering the development of the events and promoting the official ideology of the Kremlin and the White House, respectively, contributed to this outcome.

7
Conflict in Eastern Ukraine and the Downing of Malaysia Airlines Flight MH17

Two events discussed in this chapter are connected intrinsically to the takeover of Crimea. The civil war in Ukraine that started with protests in southeastern regions of the country in spring 2014 and the crash of the Malaysia Airlines flight MH17 in the territory controlled by the separatists in summer 2014 are major events contested by the US and Russian governments and, by extension, the respective media of the two countries.

Conflict in Eastern Ukraine

In spring 2014, the protests opposing the new Ukrainian government spread over the southeastern regions of Ukraine that are predominantly populated by Russian-speaking people. This area of Ukraine, known as Donbass, is the richest in natural resources, such as coal and iron, and has the most fertile farmlands. However, contrary to the situation in Crimea where people expressed their free will to join Russia, the separatist movement in those regions never has been about joining Russia. The conflict has escalated into a civil war between separatist fighters and government forces, with the separatists demanding their independence from Ukraine and recognition of their self-declared states of Donetsk and Luhansk. Multiple ceasefire agreements were violated by both sides and fighting between the two camps intensified in 2014 and 2015. The West accused Russia of supporting the rebels and being militarily involved in the conflict; Russia, however, contested this accusation. The official Russian position has been to deny that its military is involved in the war and to contend that if Russian citizens choose to join the opposition forces, they do so on their own and their participation is not sanctioned by the government. However, the West and the

Reenacting the Enemy. Ludmila Isurin, Oxford University Press. © Oxford University Press 2022.
DOI: 10.1093/oso/9780197605462.003.0008

United States have put much pressure on Russia to broker a ceasefire, and its failure to do so has been criticized heavily by the United States. Thus, the information war that started with the takeover of Crimea raged over the ongoing conflict in Ukraine.

The analysis of media related to this conflict focused mostly on the events in 2014 and 2015 when the largest offensives took place. However, often it was difficult to find texts that solely addressed this particular conflict, at least in its earlier stages, without referencing the takeover of Crimea that seems to be an intrinsic part of the entire Ukraine crisis. Therefore, occasionally Crimea will be brought back into the discussion of publications in this data set. In addition, the analysis of all other events discussed in this book followed the same pattern, with the analysis of the US press followed by the analysis of Russian media. However, for the conflict in Eastern Ukraine, it was decided to take a parallel look—wherever possible—at how both media sources reflect on the same issues within this conflict. It is hoped that such an additional angle will not undermine the consistency of the data analysis in this project.

Comparative Analysis of Russian and US Media

What Do We Know About the Conflict?

Already in 2014, Fisher (2014) provided a detailed background of the Ukrainian conflict. At times, the coverage reads like a 101 in the history/geography of Ukraine, much of which represents basic facts probably unknown to the reader, but also there is much bias in how the current situation is described. By the time of this publication, Crimea had been annexed, so I am not repeating the information that was discussed in depth in the previous chapter and which is not presented differently in this text. Although only a year later Putin admitted that there was some limited military presence in Crimea during the takeover and there was no clear evidence to identify troops in unmarked uniforms as Russian, as reported by US journalists, the author claims that Putin used the Russian military during the takeover of Crimea to "seize Crimea by force" and now asserts that "the Russian military is one of the largest in the world and is pushing back the Ukrainian forces fairly quickly. It is not clear whether they plan to occupy and annex eastern Ukraine as they did in Crimea." This description contradicts some facts presented earlier in the article, such as that "Russia started arming the rebels with high-tech surface-to-air missiles" (a fact not proven yet) that were used by the rebels to shoot down a civilian airliner (the investigation into that incident was still going on in 2014, as discussed later) or that the rebels "are widely thought" to include unmarked Russian special forces. So, a few paragraphs later, those "*widely thought*" to be Russian special forces are folded into the collective term "the Russian military troops" that invaded Ukraine. It is intriguing that, in this article, the word "invade" and its derivatives are used 24 times and, in five of those instances, the modifier *overt/overtly* was used to describe the invasion of the Russian military. Such excessive use of the word that in military terms means a massive entry of one country's army into the territory of another with the goal of occupying it is inaccurate as far as the scale of this conflict, and the absence of solid evidence that the "overtly invading military" indeed were Russian troops serves a clear ideological goal of painting Russia as an aggressor fighting Ukrainian government forces in what the author calls "outright-if-undeclared war between Russia and Ukraine." The US position on the conflict is presented as the White House being clearly outraged and punishing Russia with economic sanctions while having no plans to intervene. The latter would put Western troops into direct combat with Russian troops and could lead to World War III. A similar article about the early days of the conflict, including the Crimea takeover, and the reluctance to directly oppose Russia's action uses the same rhetoric of Russia's *invading* Ukraine (Zinets & Carbonnel, 2014).

If the previously discussed texts aimed at ideologically educating the American reader and painted Russia as an aggressor invading sovereign states, the self-explanatory title of a publication in the Russian state outlet, "Seven Myths the West Has About Events in Ukraine,"[1] presents the Russian perspective on what the West supposedly misconceives about the crisis in Ukraine. With its major reliance on the opinions of British and Norwegian political scientists, the article supports the main idea behind the takeover of Crimea, such as the illegitimacy of Yanukovich's removal, the turnover of power in Kiev viewed as a coup, the need to protect Russians from the ultra-right militant groups in Ukraine, and the fascist makeup of the new government in Ukraine. In at least two instances, the authors argue that the

[1] "Sem' Mifov Zapada o Sobytijah na Ukraine" ["Seven Myths the West Has About the Events in Ukraine"]. (2014, March 7). *Pravda*. Retrieved March 20, 2020, from https://www.pravda.ru/world/1197564-ukrain.

accusations against Russia by the West are wrong or demonstrate double standards that exist in their politics. To illustrate, first, the text brings up the Western perspective on Russia's action in Crimea as an "occupation" and denies any presence of the Russian military, except for a limited contingent present there—a fact soon to be admitted by Putin himself. Second, based on the direct quotes by a Norwegian political scientist, the authors argue that although the West maintains that "the international law does not allow the use of force in response to the call of regional governments," it is "a bit strange that when the West goes against such international laws [probably hinting at the war in Kosovo], then it is good and O.K. When Russia does the same—this is an unlawful aggression." Unfortunately, such a response, especially when coming from a Western political scientist, sounds a bit childish and could have been substantiated by concrete examples, which I believe one easily can find. The article wraps up with the assertion that so far Russia has not used any force and if it has to do so, it will do this not at the request of the regional governments but, rather, at that of the legitimate President Yanukovich. Ironically, a few days earlier, the Russian government approved the use of the military in response to the call of the local government in Crimea and not the ousted President Yanukovich. To be fair, the force was not used, as the earlier US reports claimed, even if the troops bearing no insignia on their uniforms were peacefully present (see Chapter 6). Yet, whether the authors meant any future military assistance that Russia could provide in Ukraine due to the call of the "legitimate" president, they clearly demonstrated how facts can be distorted. This report seems to serve two goals: to justify the Russian mission in Ukraine by overturning the Western claims with the help of a few Western—thus more "weighted," in the eyes of the Russian reader—political analysts, which adds more power to the argument; and to reinforce a negative image of the West in doing so. In other words, both American and Russian texts show the ideologically biased representation of the facts and the depiction of the *other*.

Demonstrations in Eastern Ukraine

In spring 2014, demonstrations widely spread over the southeastern regions of Ukraine. The protestors demanded a referendum to recognize their region as autonomous and to separate themselves from the new "fascist" government in Kiev. Those protests were covered both in Russian and in US media. Despite mentioning almost the same facts, the reports remarkably differed in the presentation of those facts. For example, a Russian state

Figure 7.1 Participants hold signs during protest against Ukrainian military action held in the center of the Eastern Ukrainian city of Donetsk (signs read "No to fascism, "Save people of Donbass from the Ukrainian military," "Ukraine, do not kill us," "We want peace," etc.). July 6, 2014. Reuters.
Credit: Maxim Zmeyev.

media outlet,[2] when covering such a demonstration in two of the 11 cities where the protests took place, emphasizes Russian and Soviet Union flags that people were carrying, chants such as "Russia," "Donetzk is a Russian city," and banners carried by the demonstrators calling for Russia's help ("Russia, save us!" and "Our language—Russian") and opposing the ultra-right group ("Right sector—murderers") (Figure 7.1). The latter is reinforced by the accompanying visual with a banner "Fascism will not come through even if I am the only one left." Not incidentally, the article wraps up with a brief history of how Crimea was legalized as part of Russia. As mentioned in Chapter 6, repetitive reminders of how Crimea was taken over by Russia are common in all texts related to Crimea in the years after it joined Russia; however, such a detour into the very recent past where Russia "saved"

[2] "Zhiteli Donecka i Har'kova Vyshli na Mitingi s Trebovaniem Referenduma" ["Residents of Donetsk and Kharkiv Rallied to Demand a Referendum"]. (2014, March 30). RIA. Retrieved June 3, 2020, from https://ria.ru/20140330/1001635874.html.

another Ukrainian region is not accidental. At this point, the reader does not know yet what Russia's action will be as far as the growing discontent in the southeastern areas of Ukraine, and journalists playing the Crimea card, highly popular among Russians at that time, seem to serve the goal of preparing the reader for whatever other legally justified "help" Russia can offer.

Compared to a Russian article with a neutral headline, a biased headline in a similar report in *The New York Times* (Roth, 2014), "From Russia, 'Tourists' Stir the Protests," promises another implication of Russia in the conflict, which indeed becomes the focus of this publication. In the opening paragraph, the author states that demonstrators demanded "a wider invasion of their country by Moscow." The choice of words in this statement is not incidental as far as the intended message and the obvious adherence to the negative word "invasion" among American reporters, yet it sounds bizarre that any demonstrators would ever call for their country to be "invaded" by a neighboring state (Figure 7.2). In order to support the idea that "Russian intervention" is called for not by the residents of those Ukrainian cities but

Figure 7.2 Participant holds a sign during a rally supporting the pro-Russian people living in Ukraine's eastern regions and the self-proclaimed Peoples Republics of Donbass and Lugansk (sign reads "Putin, bring in troops!"). June 11, 2014. Reuters.
Credit: Sergei Karpukhin.

by Russians themselves, vague references to "*some* of the people" who are Russians and to some "*reports* of busloads of activists arriving from Russia itself" serve to support the unverified fact that Russia is behind another disturbance in Ukraine. By giving the name of one of the alleged Russian tourists, citing the words of a former seamstress who "is sure that those activists are paid," or the words of a member of a legislature who believes that "this is the hand of Russia" as well as referring to the demonstrators as a "crowd" or "militia" (cf.: "pro-West or pro-Kiev demonstrators"), or providing the visuals that depict stern-looking male protestors, the author delivers a very biased report on a demonstration. Yet he later contends that the protests did not have "outright violence" and acknowledges that clearly "in this part of Ukraine, many ethnic Russians distrust the fledging government, and some would indeed welcome Russian troops." However, those few remarks are lost in the intended negative message to the reader that Russia is stirring up another conflict in Ukraine.

Ceasefire Talks in Minsk

The initially peaceful protests soon escalated into a full-fledged war between the separatists and the Ukrainian government forces that resulted in huge civilian and military personnel losses. By September 2014, it was clear that the separatists' advancement threatened the deteriorating Ukrainian army, so it was decided to hold negotiation talks between Russia, Ukraine, and the separatists in Minsk, Belarus. The *New York Post* article with the neutral headline stating the fact of the ceasefire talks[3] devotes only the first sentence to confirming the outcome of the talks and when the ceasefire is supposed to start. The rest of the article concerns the conflict itself, the losses of the Ukrainian forces (i.e., 846 out of the total losses of 2,600, including both civilians and separatist fighters), and one particular battle for gaining control of the seaport of Mariupol. According to the report, "The rebel offensive follows two weeks of gains that have turned the tide of the war against Ukrainian forces, who until recently appeared close to crushing the five-month rebellion in the east." Probably to justify such embarrassing losses of government forces, it was important to add that "Ukraine and the West say the rebel counterattack was spearheaded by regular Russian army units, a

[3] "Ukraine Signs Ceasefire with Pro-Russia Rebels." (2014, September 5). *New York Post*. Retrieved June 3, 2020, from https://nypost.com/2014/09/05/pro-russia-rebels-say-theyve-signed-cease-fire-deal-with-ukraine.

charge the Kremlin has denied." Such hearsay about Russian involvement in the conflict—despite being plausible—never is supported by solid evidence but seems to be sufficient to establish the narrative framework and identify the real "enemy" behind the conflict. The content of the entire report is irrelevant to the headline that promised more than one sentence of information about the ceasefire agreement.

The Russian state media released their take on the outcome of the talks: The main message was that Russia is not involved in the conflict, which remains Ukraine's internal affair, and that it cannot provide any guarantees of the ceasefire. Instead, the conversation between Putin and Ukrainian President Poroshenko, held behind closed doors, reportedly concerned the relations and economic cooperation between the two countries. When the question was raised about 10 Russian troops detained by the Ukrainian forces not far from the Russian border, Putin replied that it could have been a case of accidental trespassing, as the border is not marked, and recalled that recently 450 Ukrainian troops on military trucks crossed the border into Russia and that it was no big deal (Vernitzky, 2014).

Conversely, a report in one of the independent Russian media outlets (Dergachev, 2014) takes an in-depth look at the underlying motives of each side participating in the ceasefire negotiation. The parties agreed to open pathways to get humanitarian aid and food into the region. However, the author acknowledges that

> the negotiating parties do not fully control the situation. And in case of failure of the agreements, they will accuse the other side of not fulfilling them. In principle, the fire can be stopped, but local fighting is likely to continue.

In this report, the author equally is critical of Putin, the leaders of the separatist forces, and Ukrainian President Poroshenko in the discussion of their hidden agendas and respective goals in the conflict. It is noteworthy that the major disagreement between the separatists' agenda and Putin's plan seems to lie in the final outcome: Moscow has been insisting on the increase of the autonomous status of the southeastern regions while the separatists intend to gain their full independence from Ukraine. The latter illustrates that the separatists' goals by far exceed what Moscow would like to accept as the outcome of the conflict. Yet the author contends that "the major statements made by the separatists anyway are coordinated with Russia, so it could have been just a diplomatic game in order to get preferable conditions from Kiev." And then he adds that "Moscow has been stressing repeatedly its non-involvement in the conflict." Such an objective and very critical look at their own government, at the groups in the neighboring state that claim to be Russian and allegedly calling for Russia's help, and at Ukraine—majorly perceived as a negative party by Russians—illustrate professional and unbiased, at least on the surface, journalism.

The United States Arming Ukraine

Despite Putin's assertion that Russia, as a party not involved in the conflict, could not guarantee the continuation of the ceasefire, when it was broken—with each side blaming the other—and the advance of the separatist forces threatened the integrity of Ukraine's government army, the US government reached a quick and rare bipartisan agreement on arming Ukraine with lethal weapons (Wong, 2015). By clearly presenting their alliance with Ukraine (e.g., calling it a "friend") and praising the Ukrainian forces that "have fought courageously" against Russian-backed separatists, by blaming Putin for a violation of a ceasefire agreement and outright calling him a "thug," as well as acknowledging that economic sanctions imposed on Russia are not working and that the United States must "change Russia's behavior" using other means, both the House and the Senate, "in an unusual display of bipartisan agreement," concluded that the United States "cannot let Vladimir Putin get away with invading another sovereign country." By then, the term "invasion" solidly had secured its place in the American public discourse; likewise, the conviction—often unsubstantiated with clear evidence—that Russia "has continued to arm and train pro-Russian rebels in Eastern Ukraine" is repeated in most American reports on this topic.

However, not all US media were unanimously supportive of such a move to provide Ukraine with lethal weapons. The Brookings Institute, for example, offered a very cautious warning about such blatant military help that could result in the escalation of the conflict and the bringing of the United States into direct combat with the Russian military (Shapiro, 2015). The author quite accurately outlines the situation in Russian politics as anti-American:

> The Russian regime has defined the struggle in Ukraine as part of an existential battle against American imperialism, in which the United States eventually seeks to impose its will on Russia itself. American provision of arms would lend credence to that view and increase the Russian government's freedom of action at home.

When comparing Ukraine's civil war with similar recent conflicts in Bosnia, Chechnya, and Syria, the author contends that the Ukrainian conflict appears rather tame. Furthermore, he argues that the US goal to stand up to Russia in Ukraine in order to oppose an emboldened Putin "is the familiar credibility argument that gave [the country] the war in Vietnam, among other misadventures." Without any ideological fervor related to the conflict or any justification of Russia's actions in the region, this publication provides a deep analytical look and a rather far-sighted perspective on the US move of supplying Ukraine with lethal weapons to fight the separatists. Indeed, it is quite rare in contemporary US politics to reach bipartisan agreement on any issue. However, when it comes to Russia, it appears that the anger and hatred of an old enemy unite American politicians, as they say, "across the aisle," more than anything else does.

The Russian state media reacted to the US plans to provide Ukraine with lethal weapons partly in line with Shapiro's (2015) argument: Such an action may lead to a point of no return as far as peace in Ukraine and may escalate the war outside Ukraine's border (i.e., in Europe), which would benefit the United States (Hrolenko, 2015). However, the similarity between the two arguments ends there. The author continues with outlining what he calls a rather transparent plan:

> The U.S. will produce and supply the weapons, Europe will pay for it, and Ukraine will fight with its geopolitical enemy. Thus, the new market will provide both the goal and the means, whereas peace talks will remain just goodwill intentions.

To emphasize the far-reaching plans of the United States and its role in the creation of the "global craziness," the author states that "the European weather is being cooked across the ocean." Later he reminds the reader why the relationship between Russia and the West has deteriorated to such an extent: "The NATO forces cannot enter the territory of Ukraine or Georgia. Ukraine should not be part of the NATO bloc—this is best for all of Europe."

The independent Russian media covered the United States' decision to supply lethal weapons to Ukraine, too (Bratersky & Telmanov, 2015). Having outlined the facts related to the decision, the authors remain sharply critical of such military assistance and align with the official Russian side that such an act would be perceived as the United States interfering directly in the conflict.

Moreover, based on the words of a high-profile expert—without naming the person—they note that already there is direct contact and coordination between the US military attaché and the head of the Ukrainian military in Kiev. However, they sadly acknowledge that even if the official decision to supply lethal weapons to Ukraine does not come through, "Americans have a rich experience of supplying weapons in secret." What follows after this opening statement is factual information of numerous instances in recent history when the United States backed militant groups (i.e., the CIA funded mujahedeen during the Soviet war in Afghanistan), sold weapons to the late dictator Saddam Hussein in Iraq, secretly sold weapons to Iran with the help of Iran's biggest enemy—Israel, or signed a secret order to send weapons to the opposition groups in Libya in order to overturn the government of Gaddafi. Moreover, the authors compare such tactics with similar ones widely used by the Soviet Union. None of those facts easily can be challenged by the US side, and none of them ever resurfaces in the US media as a justification for yet another American attempt to arm a foreign country. The statement that "the West, in turn, accuses Russia of backing the separatists and providing them with weapons, which Russia denies" establishes a parallel between the actions of both countries without explicitly drawing such a parallel. In other words, coverage of the event in the Russian independent media once again demonstrated the journalists' ability to rise above the national interest and the ideology promoted by their own country and to provide criticism of a political issue, even if their stance—once in a while—aligns with the official one taken by their government.

Putin's Amendment of a Decree to Keep Military Losses a National Secret

In May 2015, Vladimir Putin added changes to a decree that has been in effect since 1995. The decree concerned the nondisclosure of the number and identifying information of military losses unless family members requested such information. Now he has expanded the decree to include military losses that resulted from special operations during peacetime. The representatives of Russian independent media filed a complaint that was dismissed by the Supreme Court, thereby legalizing such a change in the decree.

The state media acknowledged the Supreme Court decision, explained the legality of such a change and, as before, refrained from providing any criticism of such an action or pointing out the "incidental" timing of such a change when the conflict in Eastern Ukraine was raging and Russia was accused of sending its military to the region.[4] Conversely, the independent media were very critical of the change in the decree and noted that "the least amount of information about the causes of Russian military casualties is in the second half of 2014, when, according to media reports, soldiers and officers participated in the fighting in Donbass" (Aptekar, 2015b). The concern about the persecution of journalists who may reveal such information is discussed in yet another independent media report (Gorjashko, 2015).

An article in *The New York Times* (Kramer, 2015) is relatively similar to the previous ones released by the Russian independent press and views the amended law as "a tacit acknowledgement of covert action by the Russian military." The major difference, however, is in the dramatization of the facts not substantiated by any identified witnesses or other solid evidence: "Witnesses have described secret nighttime burials illuminated by truck headlights. Relatives of dead soldiers have told journalists about confusion over whether their loved ones died in training accidents in southern Russia or in combat in Ukraine." Another US report released by CNN (Schoichet, 2015), albeit less dramatic than the one previously mentioned, delivers the same sentiment that "not only is this decree a blatant attack on freedom of expression, it also has sinister undertones that will intensify speculation President Putin has something to hide—specifically losses incurred by Russia's military in Ukraine." But all in all, the analysis of the media related to this event has shown an agreement between the US and Russian independent journalists on a sudden change in the Russian law that does point a finger at Russia as one of the powers behind the conflict in Eastern Ukraine.

Should Russia Be Added to the State Sponsors of Terrorism List?

What is interesting about this particular issue is that until Ukraine decided to file a suit against Russia in the International Criminal Court demanding that Russia be added to the list of other states sponsoring terrorism, separatists fighting for the independence of a few southeastern regions from Ukraine were called just this—separatists—or the modifier "Russian-/Russia-backed" was added to indicate Moscow's involvement, or they would be called "militia" and "rebels." However, the news about Kiev's intention to accuse

[4] "Sud Priznal Konstitucionnym Ukaz Putina o Zasekrechivanii Poter' Voennyh" ["The Court Recognized the Constitutional Decree of Putin to Classify Losses of the Military"]. (2015, August 14). *Lenta*. Retrieved June 5, 2020, from https://lenta.ru/news/2015/08/13/court.

Russia of terrorism ignited a wave of ideological hysteria among American journalists, causing a new, much more sinister term, "terrorist," to replace the previous terms that by then were common in media discourse. Moreover, such obvious "excitement" about a new perspective on fighters in Ukraine was short-lived because the case did not make it through the court and the West, including the United States, viewed the further escalation of tensions with Russia as unwise. Nevertheless, it is intriguing to see how quickly the new terms "terrorist/terrorism" were embraced by reporters, only to be dropped a few weeks later. To illustrate, an article in *Foreign Affairs* (Kuzio, 2015) goes beyond outlining why Ukraine claims that Russia is a state sponsor of terrorism, as the author himself asserts that it is true: "Ukraine's demands for justice should not be ignored. The Donbas separatist groups do, indeed, fit the definition of terrorist groups, especially after the Mariupol rocket attack." The description of the military acts by the separatist forces, which until now were qualified as advances or attacks, now are classified as terrorist acts. It is almost amusing to read the report from a reputable outlet in which the words "terrorism" and "terrorist" are used 29 times total.

In contrast, coverage of the same event in an independent media outlet, *Novaya Gazeta*,[5] that was released the same day as the previously mentioned US article, describes the Ukrainian government's plan to file a lawsuit in the Hague Tribunal for crimes against humanity—against Ukrainians in Donbass. Ukraine's national security and defense council also has declared the Donetsk National Republic and Lugansk National Republic to be terrorist organizations. The article notes that this comes at the same time as international governments are deciding to tighten sanctions on Russia in hopes that Russia will stop supporting self-declared republics and destabilizing the region. The report simply states charges without going into any details or taking any sides in the international lawsuit that has yet to be resolved. The word "terrorist" is used only once, as in the above charge from Ukraine, and there is no mention of Russia as a state sought to be named as a sponsor of terrorism. The same is true about the state-sponsored outlet RIA,[6]

[5] "Kiev Podast v Gaagskij Tribunal Isk po Prestuplenijam Protiv Chelovechnosti" ["Kiev Will File a Lawsuit in the Hague Tribunal for Crimes Against Humanity"]. (2015, January 25). *Novaya Gazeta*. Retrieved June 5, 2020, from https://novayagazeta.ru/news/2015/01/25/109574-kiev-podast-v-gaagskiy-tribunal-isk-po-prestupleniyam-protiv-chelovechnosti.

[6] "SNBO Poruchil Podat' Isk v Gaagskij Sud po Prestuplenijam v Donbasse" ["The National Security and Defense Council Instructed to File a Lawsuit in the Hague Court for Crimes in the Donbass"]. (2015, January 25). RIA. Retrieved June 5, 2020, from https://ria.ru/20150125/1044204663.html.

which published an almost identical report on the same day the two articles previously mentioned appeared.

Summary

The conflict in Eastern Ukraine soon followed the takeover of Crimea. However, compared to the quick and somewhat surprisingly bloodless act of adding Crimea to Russia, the civil war in Ukraine has been raging for a few years and has caused much destruction and much human loss on both sides of the conflict. Also, if the presence of Russian troops in the first event originally was suspected by the West and only later confirmed by Putin, the second event was framed in the US media discourse as a result of direct Russian interference. The terms "Russian invasion" and "Russian separatists" firmly have entered the narrative related to the conflict. Moreover, what makes this narrative different from that of Crimea's takeover is that Russia has been reduced to—or embodied by—one person, President Vladimir Putin. The image of a powerful, sinister leader—sometimes unceremoniously referred to as a "thug" capable of sending troops to a neighboring state and grabbing land without any direct military response from the West—was reinforced in US media publications in the first 2 years of Ukraine's crisis. Putin was held responsible for a violation of the ceasefire by whichever side—separatists or the Ukrainian government forces—and for allegedly "overtly" participating in the conflict. This, in turn, led to the quick bipartisan decision of the US government to send lethal weapons to Ukraine, which now was perceived as a "friend" that was eager to accept Western values. The fight by the Ukrainian forces is described with much sympathy, as is the reference to pro-Kiev demonstrators who are contrasted to the "crowd" of pro-Russian protestors calling for Russia to invade their country. Such a ridiculous choice of words to deliver an ideologically biased message to the readers at home is not incidental. When a slim chance to add Russia to the list of terrorism sponsor states arose—the act not openly supported by the US government—American media quickly and enthusiastically reframed the entire conflict as terrorist acts committed by terrorist groups, if not by a state sponsoring terrorism.

Russian media, on the other hand, distinctively followed two directions in reflecting on Ukraine's crisis. The state-controlled outlets promoted the government's position of Russia's non-involvement in the conflict or reported basic facts representing the official stance on a particular issue.

In order to support such a stance, Ukraine's crisis is framed by repetitive references to the legality of Crimea's takeover. The US opposition to Russia's actions in Ukraine builds up a strong argument of Russia being surrounded by enemies that intend to circle it with NATO bases and isolate Russia from the rest of the world. The reference to the United States as the major force behind the tightening sanctions imposed on Russia and as the orchestrator of major European responses against Russia contributes to the growing anti-American sentiments. However, the independent media, while generally being very critical of the Russian government and of Putin in particular, do not necessarily deviate from Russia's official position on some issues, such as the danger of the United States arming Ukraine with lethal weapons. Yet, when it comes to the change in the decree classifying military losses during peacetime, as pushed through by Putin, the position of independent journalists is the same as that of American ones. However, they also remind readers about facts from relatively recent American history where the United States sold weapons to enemy states and overturned governments in sovereign nations. By bringing up such arguments and making parallels between the Soviet Union's actions and American ones, liberal Russian reporters attempt to keep a healthy balance between attacking the decisions of their own country and completely aligning with the similarly biased stance taken by American media. Surprisingly, this type of journalism is more likely to be found in Russian media that the West often perceives as entirely state- (i.e., Putin-) controlled.

The Downing of Malaysia Airlines Flight MH17

On July 17, 2014, Malaysia Airlines flight MH17 on route from Amsterdam to Kuala Lumpur, Malaysia, was shot down while flying over the war zone in Eastern Ukraine. All 298 people on board were killed. The West put the immediate blame for the crash on separatists, allegedly backed by Russia, whereas Russia denied any involvement in the incident. The investigation of the crash was led by the Dutch Safety Board, which refused to include Russian experts on their team. The conclusion of the investigation remained uncertain, suggesting that the airplane was hit by small, high-velocity fragments that entered the plane externally and the only weaponry in the area that was capable of doing this was identified as the Soviet-made surface-to-air Buk missile system that allegedly was spotted on the separatist-controlled territory. The Russian government denied involvement in the shooting down of the plane and held the Ukrainian government at fault for allowing civilian flights in a war zone. The accident led to another battle in the information war between the United States and Russia.

US Media

The coverage of the MH17 crash roughly can be broken down into three themes: immediate reports on the incident, pondering the key question of who should be blamed for the tragedy in the 2 years after the crash, and the reports on the investigation results.

The analysis of the articles released by three outlets—Huffington Post, CNN, and Fox News—the day when the crash took place and in the aftermath of the next 2 days has shown that all presses report the facts known at that time but slightly differ in the delivery of the information. The tragedy triggered an obvious question: Who hit the plane? The finger-pointing

Figure 7.3 A pro-Russian separatist standing at the crash site of Malaysia Airlines flight MH17, near the settlement of Grabovo in the Donetsk region. July 18, 2014. Reuters.
Credit: Maxim Zmeyev.

between Russia and Ukraine did not answer this question. However, the immediate accusation—well before any evidence was obtained—targeted the separatists who are defined as "Russian-backed separatists" or simply "Russian separatists" in all articles (Figure 7.3). Although both Cohen (2014), writing for CNN, and Griffin (2014), writing for Fox News, acknowledge that the suggested evidence was not independently verified by their presses, a Huffington Post journalist, Hart (2014), who reported on the accident a few hours after it occurred, proceeds with the presentation of unverified facts in such a manner that the reader may process them as accurate information. He mentions in passing that "U.S. officials"—without naming any—said that "the plane was shot down by a surface-to-air missile" and that "they were trying to determine who fired the missile." However, the very next sentence states that "Russian separatists have shot down several Ukrainian military planes in recent months," thereby implying that MH17 also was shot down by the separatists. To support the unverified accusation further, the author cites Vice-President Joe Biden's conclusion that "the crash was not an accident." To make the report more sensational, he adds gruesome details describing body parts scattered around the crash site. Incidentally, Griffin (2014) also frames the crash within the previously shot down Ukrainian military planes, but here the responsibility directly is placed on the Russian military that "has been shooting down Ukrainian military aircraft in recent weeks, and most likely mistook the airliner for a Ukrainian military aircraft." Whether it was the Russian military, as Fox News reports, or Russian separatists, as Huffington Post maintains, the American reader who vaguely can picture a border between Russia and Ukraine or the line separating opposition forces in Eastern Ukraine from "Russian separatists" will be convinced that it was again notorious Russia that shot down a plane with hundreds of innocent civilians on board.

Interestingly, although Putin's words blaming Ukraine for allowing passenger planes over the war zone and for not ending the conflict in the first place are well acknowledged in all publications, the attention is shifted toward building an argument that separatists by themselves would not be able to shoot the plane out of the sky and that the Russian military was involved in the training of the separatists and supplying them with missiles, if not conducting the actual shooting of the plane. So a call for more sanctions to be imposed on Russia for its failure to take steps to stop the conflict, as reported by Cohen (2014), sounds like a highly expected and logical punishment for the crash: After all, the American reader needs to know *how* the accused is going to be punished even before the investigation is over. Because little information was known in the aftermath of the crash, it is not surprising to see much qualifying language throughout the reports, such as "it is believed," "highly likely/unlikely," "reportedly," "appeared to be," and so forth.

This type of language continued throughout the ongoing investigation and even when the results of the investigation became public. To illustrate, the headline of *The New York Times* article, "Malaysian Airlines Flight 17 *Most Likely* Hit by Russian-Made Missile" (Clark & Kramer, 2015), clearly suggests that the evidence obtained a year after the crash is not conclusive. Yet the authors, albeit showing that the shrapnel found in the victims' bodies is consistent with weaponry present in both Russian and Ukrainian arsenals, still lean toward the earlier accusation of Russian separatists being behind the attack. They cite a statement made by a Dutch investigator, "There is no *plausible military reason* why this aircraft . . . *would have been considered* a threat by Kiev." Although such a statement is rather logical, it would not be admissible in any court as proof of innocence of one party over another. The authors further state that "while the findings stop short of assigning responsibility for the crash . . . they *appear* consistent with a theory *widely promoted* by the authorities in the United States and Ukraine: that the plane, a Boeing 777, was shot down by Russian-backed separatists." Not only do we see a strong unity between the United States and Ukraine in widely promoting a "theory" that originated before any evidence was obtained but also we can suggest that no evidence in the world pointing in another direction could have changed the position of the two countries blindly united by their hatred of a common enemy. Jansen (2015) delivers the same type of report with the upfront blame assigned to Russia. By having stated in the first sentence that "Russian Buk missile shot down" MH17, the author acknowledges that the Dutch-led joint investigation "did not specify *who* launched the missile and *where* it had come [from]." In order to answer those questions, right away the author brings in a quote from a former Ukrainian official who calls for putting more pressure on Russia for that crime and cites a Dutch official—not part of the investigation board—who says that "the overall picture is conclusive"—that a Buk missile was fired from the separatist territory. Clearly, the reporter is not willing to wait another year to find out who exactly was behind the crash: His readership expects some fast answers and straightforward messages, and playing the old broken record that Russia is to blame serves the purpose.

Incidentally, an article in the *Chicago Tribune*[7] covering the same Dutch report appears 2 weeks before the previously mentioned report in *USA Today* (Jansen, 2015). A slight change in the headline's wording, from "Russian-Made Missile," as used in Clark and Kramer's (2015) text, to "Buk Missile *from* Russia," seems to provide a long-anticipated answer of where the missile was fired. Indeed, citing the same Dutch report that presumably could not specify who launched the missile or where it originated (see Jansen, 2015), the authors state that "Dutch-led criminal investigators said . . . they have *solid evidence* that a Malaysian jet was shot down in 2014 by a Buk missile that was moved into eastern Ukraine from Russia." Although the entire article later gives some evidence contradicting this opening statement, it is not incidental that the headline and the opening sentence in the text make the reader believe where the missile was fired. What is puzzling here is that the two reputable media sources, *USA Today* and *Chicago Tribune*, provide coverage of the same Dutch report and deliver contradictory information. Thus, driven by a desire to reach conclusive answers based on inconclusive evidence, the information delivered to the reader is distorted.

A much-anticipated answer also was delivered by a UK-based organization, which bills itself as a group of citizen investigative journalists that conducted its own investigation based on open media sources and social media. The organization's sensational finding that the Russian military was involved in shooting down MH17 made headlines in the US media (Flintoff, 2016). Unsurprisingly, the spokesperson for the Russian Ministry of Foreign Affairs, as cited in this publication, dismissed such an amateurish report by saying that the whole campaign is "an attempt by certain destructive forces to demonize Russia by creating an image in the mass consciousness that's very far from reality." Nevertheless, 2 years later, the investigative team (supposedly the same official Dutch-led team) implicated a Russian military brigade in owning the particular missile launcher used to shoot down the plane (Smith-Spark & Masters, 2018). Although the team's conclusion was based on "extensive comparative research," the investigators could not confirm whether the brigade itself was involved actively in downing MH17.

[7] "Investigators: Malaysia Airlines MH17 Downed by Buk Missile from Russia." (2016, September 28). *Chicago Tribune*. Retrieved January 15, 2019, from https://www.chicagotribune.com/news/nationworld/nationalsecurity/ct-mh17-probe-malaysia-airlines-20160928-story.html.

In addition to covering the crash and the subsequent investigation, the US media brought some personal testimonies from victims' families to the reader (Smith-Spark, 2015). Understandably, through much grief caused by the horrific loss of the loved ones, family members sought closure in seeking the punishment of those who were responsible for the tragedy. In contrast to the obvious US media bias toward blaming Russia or Russian separatists for the crash, grief-stricken relatives refrained from finger-pointing. As one of them noted,

> It could be Russia, it could be Ukraine, it could be the separatists. I think it is important that [investigators] find out who did it, who was responsible for it. I'm not very interested in who pushed the button, but who was responsible, which organization, which country.

The identification of the country responsible for the crash, however, was not appealing to the United States: If the Russian-speaking separatists—Ukrainian citizens—in Eastern Ukraine were found guilty, would Ukraine be blamed for the crash? The question of whether victims' families would ever see justice resurfaced a year later (Jamieson, 2016). It is noteworthy that here again we can see some testimonies not necessarily falling in line with the official US position on whom to blame. As one family member admits, it is unlikely "that anyone intended to bring down a passenger plane. Nobody benefited except possibly the Ukrainian government as an excuse to escalate the war." The latter repeatedly has been maintained by Moscow in denial of its involvement in the crash. Jamieson (2016) also points out that it may take years and would be a monumental challenge to bring any particular individuals to trial.

The anticipation of bringing real people and not just a hypothetical entity to trial filtered into news coverage in 2017. In the absence of any new developments in the investigation but with the obvious need to keep the story alive 3 years after the crash, reporters repeated the details of the event; the alleged suspects (i.e., Russia); and the possibility that even if identified and charged with the crime, the defendants would be tried in absentia (Almasy & Gray, 2017; Corcoran, 2017). When finally, after almost 5 years of the investigation, four people were announced as suspects in allegedly transporting the missile from Russia to Ukraine, the US news quickly revived the story by reminding the reader what the facts were—albeit those were still contested by Russia—and the identities of the four accused, even if they would never be brought to court in person (Britton, 2019; P. Smith, 2019).[8] Moreover, as Smith (2019) reports, there was "high-level collaboration" between Russia and the separatist fighters. This note can be viewed as evidence of Russia's involvement in the crash.

All publications in this set of media data are accompanied by the same repetitive images of the plane's wreckage, the horrific crash site, and armed separatists guarding the site. The latter often are described as "unfriendly militiamen." What is interesting to observe in these selected media reports is the way the words Russia and Russian loosely are used to mislead the reader to some extent. Opposition forces in Eastern Ukraine are interchangeably called "Russian separatists" or "Russian-backed separatists." Although the former technically may be correct, as the majority of the population in Eastern Ukraine are ethnic Russians, for the American reader the concepts of ethnicity, nationality, and citizenship somewhat are blurred and different from how such terms are conceptualized in Russia. In other words, for Americans, "Russian" is perceived as anyone who comes from Russia (Isurin, 2014) and "Russian separatists" may sound like Russian citizens fighting against the government forces in Ukraine. Technically, it would be correct to call those separatists opposition forces, as they remain Ukrainian citizens fighting within the territory of Ukraine. The use of another label, "Russian-backed separatists," is not accurate either, as Russia has denied all accusations that it militarily or financially supports the opposition forces in Ukraine and no hard evidence was ever presented to legitimize such accusations. The deliberate confusion continues throughout the entire process of the investigation, where indeed it was found that the origin of the missile was the Soviet Union, yet Russia claimed that it discontinued the manufacturing of those missiles in 1999. So, by saying "Russian-made missile," Ukraine, as a former member of the USSR where such missiles were manufactured, incidentally is excluded from the argument, although at least one report does state that both Russia and Ukraine possess those missiles in their arsenals (Clark & Kramer, 2015). The Dutch-led investigation could not identify who fired the missile and from where. But there was an observation-based report that suggested that the missile launcher traveled across the Russian–Ukrainian border and was pulled back into Russia. In other words, by saying that the plane was

[8] "MH17 Crash: 3 Russians, 1 Ukrainian Face Murder Charges for Downing of Malaysia Airlines Flight 17." (2019, July 19). CBS. Retrieved May 15, 2020, from https://www.cbsnews.com/news/mh17-crash-murder-charges-russian-ukrainian-nationals-malaysia-airlines-flight-17.

"downed by a Buk from Russia,"[9] the author provides distorted information that can be processed as the fact that the missile itself was fired from Russia. The world may never know who exactly pulled the trigger to down flight MH17 and the goal of my analysis was not to find the guilty party or to blame the journalists for their deliberately misleading use of certain lexical terms. Instead, through the close analysis of the media texts, it is fascinating to see how language is manipulated to provide inaccurate and biased information.

What was intriguing to see in this analysis is the almost total absence of Putin in the discussion of the crash. Indeed, it is strikingly different from how the later events discussed in this chapter will shift the focus to a single person symbolizing the entire country, Russian President Vladimir Putin. From this point of view, an article published in *Forbes*, "Is Putin Preparing to Admit Guilt for MH17?" (Gregory, 2017), presents additional interest and is discussed in more detail. The author reports on Ukraine's suit against Russia at the International Court of Justice (ICJ). Because Russia does not recognize the jurisdiction of the International Criminal Court, the ICJ remains the only venue for adjudicating Russia's responsibility for the MH17 downing. Among numerous indictments, the Ukrainian accusation of Russia having deliberately supplied the separatists with the missile launcher that shot down the plane seems to be inadmissible in court because the intent to down the plane never has been proven. As the London lawyer representing Russia stated, "There is no evidence before the court, plausible or otherwise, that Russia provided weaponry to any party with the intent or knowledge that such weaponry be used to shoot down civilian aircraft." Here the author speculates that Russia's British lawyer is probably not drafting the case all on his own, thereby discrediting the counselor's professionalism. Then Gregory asserts that there is "conclusive" evidence that it was a Russian crew that fired the missile and references findings of the Dutch investigation as well as the group of journalists from the United Kingdom that were mentioned earlier in this section. In other words, the information reported by other journalists (e.g., Jansen, 2015) in the same year as when this article was published and based on the same Dutch report is distorted by stating that the Dutch investigation found *who* fired the missile and from *where* it was fired. Presumably, if such solid evidence implicating the Russian military in the crash indeed existed, we would not see so much uncertainty expressed through the qualifying language

[9] "Investigators: Malaysia Airlines MH17 Downed by Buk Missile from Russia." (2016, September 28). *Chicago Tribune*. Retrieved January 15, 2019, from https://www.chicagotribune.com/news/nationworld/nationalsecurity/ct-mh17-probe-malaysia-airlines-20160928-story.html.

and the ICJ would render a verdict on Russia's case. Ironically, the author also contrasts the Russian people, apparently brainwashed by Putin's propaganda machine and believing in conspiracy theories, to the much smarter American public that "*instinctively* knows the truth. They know *exactly* that Russian-supplied rebels shot down MH17." One may wonder where those *healthy instincts* in the Western and American public come from, if not from the equally ideologically biased media that have convinced their readership of the only truth of who was behind the MH17 crash. The article then ends by speculating why Putin may decide to admit guilt; although they all are very good and plausible reasons, there is no hard evidence to support him doing so and therefore the author's argument strays into the territory of pure speculation, which does not make it good reporting.

Throughout the analysis of the US media on the MH17 crash, we can see how the immediate intention to blame Russia or Russian separatists in the crash and the support of the Ukrainian side in whatever arguments it provided have not changed over the 5 years of the investigation. Whether there was any undisputable evidence provided, American journalists unanimously accused Russia in the horrific crash in 2014. This blind belief that the guilty party is found prevented most of the reporters from questioning the often-unsubstantiated accusations. The American reader once again has received the news, highly expected and unquestionable now (because American readers have good *instincts* to know that it is true!), that the Cold War enemy repackaged slightly as Russia remains the same evil *other*. The biased headlines, manipulation of language, and simple distortion of facts—all those techniques were widely used in the analyzed texts.

Russian Media

The analysis of Russian media followed the same temporal line as the analysis of the US media: immediate reaction about the crash, reports a year later, and coverage of the results of the Dutch-led investigation.

Publications from two state-controlled outlets, *Pravda* (Bukker, 2014b) and *Lenta* (Sychev, 2014), the day after the crash operate on the facts that were available at the time. From this point of view, Sychev (2014) provides a large technical overview of what happened to MH17, what weapons were used, and which party is in possession of the missile launcher. The author does acknowledge the instantaneous finger-pointing among the separatists, the Ukrainian government, and Russia but stays away from taking any sides or bringing up the US–Russia standoff over the crash. Yet, he acknowledges that the day after the crash there was not sufficient information available in order to draw even preliminary conclusions and it will be impossible to find out who fired the missile and from where. Incidentally, this relatively unbiased report is titled "Beyond the Responsibility Zone," with the lead posing a hypothetical question of whether the plane was hit by *Ukrainian* Buks. Because the article does not defend any of the possible suspects, one may suggest that a somewhat misleading headline and lead were needed to have this text published in a state-censored outlet. If a less careful reader browses the site and comes across this report, the reader may read it through the angle of Russia's innocence regardless of whether the author built such an argument: The headline and lead served the purpose of suggesting such an interpretation. Moreover, by using the generalized modifier "Ukrainian" in the lead to refer to the missile launcher, the reporter puts the blame either on the Ukrainian forces or the Ukrainian separatists but takes Russia out of the equation.

Conversely, Bukker (2014b) takes an aggressive and straightforward stance and goes after the Western—and specifically, US—media that less than 24 hours after the crash blamed Russia for the accident. The headline, "Flight MH17: Instead of the Truth—The Game of Intelligence Agencies" promises the reader exactly what it delivers: The United States had led other countries to blame Russia in the crash even before any evidence was presented. In the lead, the author sarcastically adds that right now Russia only is blamed for this plane's crash and not another Malaysian Boeing that had disappeared a few months earlier, but it could be blamed for this as well. The entire point of this ideologically biased piece is to discredit the United States by showing how its accusations operate without evidence. However, the author seems to fall into the same trap by insinuating—also without evidence– that the United States might be behind the crash because it is in American interests to strengthen the Ukrainian government by portraying the rebels as terrorists.

Equally aggressive but ideologically opposite to Bukker's (2014b) report is one in a liberal media outlet, *Novaya Gazeta* (Yavlinsky, 2014), which uses the MH17 cause to criticize the Russian "leadership" (i.e., Putin) for supporting the so-called "separatists" (quotation marks original), for arming those fighters and bringing destabilization to the region. Although all three reports discussed here appeared a day after the MH17 crash, surprisingly this piece mentions the crash in the opening sentence only and does not get into any of the details or possible theories of who is behind the crash that were abundant at the time. Clearly, this horrific incident serves the author's goal to criticize his own government and shift the reader's attention to something larger than the fate of the passenger plane downed in Eastern Ukraine—the ongoing conflict in the region that led to one disaster and promises many more to come.

The liberal Russian media continued its very critical position on the Russian government in the years following the crash. They questioned why Moscow and the Kremlin—two names that are consistently used in these articles to differentiate Russia as a country from its leadership—opposed the international call for the tribunal (Aptekar, 2015a; Artemjev, 2015). Instead, as Aptekar (2015a) notes,

> Moscow, which constantly is spreading more and more new versions of the causes of the tragedy, does not care about their credibility, but only about in advance sowing distrust in the conclusions of investigators and judges. This game is quite understandable, but it does not fit a great power that is convinced of its own truth.

The official position of Russia on the idea of the tribunal was stated by Putin and defended by the leading state press outlet, *Pravda*,[10] which argued that

> such tribunals are held when the guilty parties already are identified, whereas the investigation on the crash is not over yet. Thus, the call for such a tribunal is politically motivated as part of a campaign that aims at discriminating against Russia and the internationally unrecognized republics of Donbass.

However, when the initial results of the investigation were announced, the liberal Russian media did not align immediately with the findings of the Dutch-led team (Figure 7.4). In contrast, they either reported both Russian and Dutch results without criticizing either (Petelin & Gromov, 2015; Sokolov, 2015), thereby allowing the readers to see the facts for themselves, or looked deeper into discrepancies between the Dutch, Russian, and Ukrainian reports (Vaschenko et al., 2015). To illustrate the latter, they investigated the type of missile reportedly involved in the downing of MH17. As

[10] "London Trebuet Sozdat' Tribunal dlja Suda po Krusheniju Malajzijskogo Boeing" ["London Demands to Form the Tribunal on the Crash of the Malaysian Boeing"]. (2015, July 17). Retrieved May 19, 2020, from https://www.pravda.ru/news/world/1267464-boeing.

Figure 7.4 In Gilze Rijen, the Netherlands, Tjibbe Joustra, Chairman of the Dutch Safety Board, presents the final report on the July 2014 crash of Malaysia Airlines flight MH17 in Ukraine. October 13, 2015. Reuters.
Credit: Michael Kooren.

the Russian side claimed, it was an older model than the Dutch investigators found, and that model has not been used by Russia since 2011. Another example of the discrepancies among all three reports was the place from where the missile was launched. Ukrainians claim it came from a separatist controlled area, Russians claim it came from an area controlled by Ukraine, and the Dutch report suggests it came from an area where the two sides were clashing. In other words, by pointing out such discrepancies, Vaschenko et al. (2015) cast doubt on the conclusiveness of the Dutch investigation without necessarily whitewashing Russia's possible involvement in the crash. The state-controlled media, in turn, bring in the third party to defend Russia against any accusations. To illustrate, *Izvestia* cites the Malaysian Minister of Transportation who said that the Dutch report does not have any accusations against Russia or separatists: "This report," in his words, "is important for finding out *what* happened to the plane and not *who* did it."[11]

[11] "Malajzija ne Vidit Obvinenij Protiv Rossii v Doklade po Krusheniju Boeing" ["Malaysia Does Not See Any Accusations Against Russia in the Report on the Crash of Boeing"]. (2015, October 17). Retrieved May 19, 2020, from https://iz.ru/news/593400.

During the following few years, Russian media released numerous publications related to MH17. The state-controlled press mostly provided different theories of who might be behind the crash, and those were substantiated by some references to Western sources, such as a BBC documentary suggesting that the plane could have been shot by a Ukrainian fighter jet.[12] Or they would report about a German private investigator, hired by an unspecified individual to conduct an investigation into the crash, and how the Dutch team refused to take his findings into consideration.[13] Also, Russia's disagreement with the conclusions of the Dutch-led investigation repeatedly appeared in the state outlets. And here the authors openly blame the United States that "for two years has not been showing satellite images that they allegedly had to prove that the plane was shot from the territory of the separatists" and Ukraine that "does not present their data about the aircrafts that were in the air at the time of the tragedy" (Levin, 2016).

If the state-controlled press was unanimous in presenting the investigation as inconsistent in its methodology and findings and discriminatory against Russia, journalists from independent media outlets were more diverse in their coverage. Some report on the results of the official Dutch investigation without taking any stance (Balandra, 2018; Dergachev, 2016)[14] or on the attempts of the lawyer representing victims' families to sue Russia (Dzhordzhevich, 2020), whereas others discuss the findings of the UK-based group Bellingcat, already mentioned in relation to the US texts, and provide a detailed explanation of the findings without supporting or refuting any of those either (Sidorkova, 2017). However, one also can find publications with sharp criticism of the official Russian position on the issue. Apple and Sinitzyn (2016), for example, in their article "Politics of Denial," warn that Russia's tendency to deny its involvement leads to the building of a dossier against the Kremlin in the West. Contrary to Moscow's claim that the

[12] "Britanskie SMI: MH17 Mog Byt' Sbit Ukrainskim Istrebitelem" ["British Media: MH17 Could Have Been Shot Down by a Ukrainian Fighter Jet"]. (2016, April 24). NTV. Retrieved February 26, 2019, from https://www.ntv.ru/novosti/1624301.

[13] "Niderlandy ne Hotjat Prinimat' Novye Dannye o Krushenii MH17" ["The Netherlands Do Not Want to Accept New Data About the MH17 Wreck"]. (2019, July 30). *Pravda*. Retrieved May 19, 2020, from https://www.pravda.ru/world/1427667-boeing.

[14] "Putin: Rossija Priznaet Vyvody Sledstvija po Krusheniju MH17 Tol'ko pri Uuslovii Dopuska k Rassledovaniju" ["Putin: Russia Will Recognize the Findings of the Investigation Into the Crash of MH17 Only If Allowed to Participate in the Investigation"]. (2018, May 24). *Meduza*. Retrieved April 11, 2020, from https://meduza.io/news/2018/05/24/putin-rossiya-priznaet-vyvody-sledstviya-po-krusheniyu-mh17-tolko-pri-uslovii-dopuska-k-rassledovaniyu.

Dutch-led team did not consider its evidence, the investigators said that Russia did not respond to all of the inquiries and did not present the initial data from its radars. Finally, Russia did so, but, as the authors note, why not do this right away or at least in August or September of 2014? However, as the authors explain, back then there was a dominant Kremlin version that the plane was shot by a Ukrainian fighter jet. "Any new theory worked more and more against Russia and was perceived as an intentional attempt to mislead the investigation" (Apple & Sinitzyn, 2016). To illustrate this point further, they refer to the hybrid war in Ukraine and Russia's claim that it does not have a military presence in the region, and if there are some, those officers are on leave. Strikingly, this article, albeit critical of the Russian government, shows the authors' concern that "soon Russia will be isolated from the rest of the world and nobody will talk to us."

In the barrage of reports on the crash of Malaysia Airline flight MH17, one publication from the independent media outlet *Meduza* stands out. Baklanov (2018) presents the reader with the constantly changing positions of the Russian government in the 4 years since the tragedy. By giving dates, concrete facts, and quotes from government officials, Putin included, the article shows how one version of who is behind the crash is replaced with another, just to be forgotten a year later. The suggestion that a Ukrainian fighter jet was detected next to MH17 shortly before the crash was maintained by the Russian government for at least 1 year. It was replaced with a new theory—in light of the findings of the Dutch investigation—that the missile allegedly involved in the attack was produced by Ukraine and not Russia. One particular soft spot—and rightly so, in my view—that Russians found and used in blaming Ukraine for the crash was that Ukraine did not close its airspace for civilian flights over the war zone. To make Ukraine look like a suspect, Putin reminded the nation of other "tragic incidents," such as the unintentional downing of a passenger plane with 78 people on board by the Ukrainian military in 2001. In contrast to other texts, this coverage presents dry facts and dates that are not cohesively connected into any kind of narrative. The journalist's position here is to put together facts and let the readers see for themselves how the Russian government's official presentation of the MH17 story evolved. The absence of the author's voice and his deliberate reliance on the reader's interpretation of the information can be viewed as very refreshing and unbiased, unless we ask the following question: Was the selection of the presented facts biased? However, the goal of this book is not to find the real truth behind any of the events discussed here but, rather, to look into *how* the *truth* is delivered. So it will suffice to say that such presentation of simple facts—as biased as they may be in their selection—still is much welcomed coverage of a contested political event. After all, instead of ideologically brainwashing the readers or trusting their *instincts* to know the truth, journalists once in a while should allow their audience to make up their minds on how to understand the complexity of an event that has happened in the world.

Summary

The tragic downing of Malaysia Airlines flight MH17 in the war-ridden territory in Eastern Ukraine has become part of history for most people except for those who lost their loved ones in the crash and who may never learn who fired that fatal shot in 2014. Six years later, a story that made major headlines both in the United States and in Russia has been replaced by new ones, big and small. In this section, we have examined the development of this event in media coverage over 6 years. If American journalists seem to have convinced their audience that Russia and Russian separatists—two concepts often presented and perceived as interchangeable—were behind the attack, Russian media continued their quest to find answers and fire back at the United States and Ukraine with denial of any involvement in the crash. The immediate accusations of Russia by the US press hours after the incident and even before any evidence was presented or any investigation was complete has not changed throughout the years. Russia, in turn, has maintained its position of innocence and produced its own theories of who downed the plane. Finger-pointing and blame assignment have characterized this event. Although not directly involved in the incident, the United States explicitly sided with Ukraine in blaming Russia, whereas Russia had to defend its position, often by blaming the other two parties. The American reader, impatient to get fast answers and not to wait years until the investigation is over, was served by journalists who delivered almost identical stories, regardless of the political affiliation of their outlets or who occupied the White House at the time of the event: Russia, as an enemy, is an easy sell for the American audience. Indeed, such bipartisan adherence to the immediate reenactment of the *other* is remarkable when we read American reports on the MH17 crash. In this respect, Russian state-controlled media are not different from the US media. They too produce ideologically biased reports that present innocent Russia once again being blamed by the West for a crime it did not commit. What makes Russian media different from the American media, at least in their coverage of the MH17 crash, is how the independent liberal press reacted. Those outlets strikingly differ both from the Russian state-controlled press and from the US media. Instead of offering immediate blame assignment or denial of accusations, journalists in those agencies try to uncover the truth by presenting facts for their readers to interpret while remaining critical of their own government. As previously mentioned, in the West and in the United States in particular, there is a firm belief that there is no press in Russia that is not censored by the government. As demonstrated here, such media exist and can be an example of good journalism to many American reporters who seem to be more ideologically biased in covering foreign affairs and who rarely divert from the official US stance on a particular political event.

8

Civil War in Syria and the 2016 US Presidential Election

Two events in the second decade of the 21st century brought Russia and the United States to another standoff: the engagement of both countries in Syria's civil war and Russia's alleged meddling in the 2016 US presidential election. What makes these two events more similar than different is that both took place in an area not necessarily controlled by either of the two sides: the Middle East and cyberspace. Moreover, in both instances, Russia was accused by the United States of interference in the affairs of another state, which Russia strongly denied.

Civil War in Syria

The ongoing civil war in Syria broke out as a result of the wider wave of Arab Spring protests in 2011, which were openly welcomed and backed by the US government. Since its beginning, the war has turned into a multisided conflict, involving the government forces of Syrian President Bashar al-Assad supported by domestic and foreign allies and different groups—both domestic and foreign—that oppose the Syrian government and each other in various combinations. The Arab Spring movement and the civil war in Syria in particular also have led to the worst refugee crisis in Europe. Moreover, the Arab Spring protests happened during Barack Obama's presidency, whereas the withdrawal of US troops from Syria was done under Donald Trump's leadership, which also is reflected in how the two administrations and, as a result, media reacted to different events within the war. Russia's engagement in the war, however, did not start until 2015 when Russian President Vladimir Putin pledged his support of an old ally, Assad, and entered the Russian military into the conflict under the official justification of fighting the militant Islamic group ISIS, in which allegedly more than 2,500 Russian militants—predominantly from the Russian southern republic of Chechnya

Reenacting the Enemy. Ludmila Isurin, Oxford University Press. © Oxford University Press 2022.
DOI: 10.1093/oso/9780197605462.003.0009

as well as some former Soviet states in Central Asia—were involved. In other words, although siding with two opposite forces—the Syrian government army and the government opposition groups—both the United States and Russia seemed to have a shared interest in fighting ISIS in Syria.

US Media

In order not to overload this part of the analysis with numerous military confrontations that have happened during the almost 10 years since the beginning of the civil war in Syria, we discuss a few events that may present particular interest within the scope of this project.

First, the very fact of Russia—the name interchangeably used with Putin, as a sole power representing the country—entering the conflict stirred the American media. From a single opinion expressed by Snyder (2015) in the liberal outlet *TIME* to the arguments made by 14 "Kremlinologists," Snyder included, in the conservative *Politico*,[1] American journalists and experts pondered the *real* reason why Putin entered the game. The most discussed and agreed on motive is him taking advantage of the power vacuum in the Middle East and asserting more dominance in the region and on the global stage. Other experts argue that Putin planned to use Syria as a bargaining chip

> to open some cracks in the wall of economic and diplomatic isolation around Russia. In a signature Putin move, he stirs up greater chaos and then offers the West a choice: deal with him in the hope he can and will help fix the problem or watch him stir up even greater chaos.

Some argue that Putin's involvement in Syria is a diversion from the failing intervention in Ukraine. Therefore, in order to garner public support and boost his approval ratings, the war on ISIS is meant to be a new popular TV series in which Russia again bravely fights terrorists and outwits the West. As one expert sarcastically notes,

> The soap opera in Ukraine is over. The heroic separatists, their evil fascist foes, and the cynical Western meddlers have been retired. The new

[1] "What Is Putin Really Up to in Syria?" (2015, October 1). *Politico*. Retrieved May 5, 2020, from https://www.politico.com/magazine/story/2015/10/russia-putin-syria-invasion-experts-strategy-213213.

entertainment is a thrilling and exotic epic set in Syria, with the Assad regime as the heroic defenders of civilized values, Russia their valiant allies and the West as the defenders of jihadist barbarians.

At this point, the reference to Ukraine has become an almost constant in the authors' contemplation of Russia's role in Syria. One sarcastically points out that in Putin's view, "the United States caused the current bloodshed in Syria by supporting the protesters—the same way the United States caused the current 'civil war' in Ukraine by supporting the protests there."[2]

What is surprising about the *Politico* article is that for once Putin's power is recognized, and the fact that Putin is winning the battle while the United States is losing it is acknowledged. However, while admitting that the peace deal in Syria is possible but "the only country which *could* conceivably make that happen is the United States," the article sends a strong message that the wrong leadership (i.e., Obama, who "was at his waffly worst: a leader who treats rhetoric as a substitute for policy") has led the United States to the point where it may be on the losing side of the game against Putin, who "once again proved the pundits wrong when they said he was crippled by Western sanctions and failing oil prices."[3] And because "the United States has no clear policy, and Europe cannot even think of a policy while being flooded with Syrian refugees . . . Putin can thus push the United States and Europe to closer interaction with Russia." After all, for Putin, "it is pleasant to foil the United States' poorly laid plans." Being unable to defend their country's "poorly laid plans" in Syria, the authors still attack Putin relentlessly and do not shy away from reminding the reader of his KGB past (e.g., "claiming to fight ISIL while actually bombing US-supported rebels and other rivals is classic Putin, whose taunting subterfuge represents a KGB officer's vision of foreign policy"); labeling the entire country as Putin—or even Putinist—Russia, a clichéd phrase that firmly, although quite sadly, has entered the public and academic discourse in the past decade; or blaming Putin for restoring "Moscow's Cold War power."

The second event that caused a heated outcry in the US media concerned a series of chemical attacks committed during the civil war in Syria

[2] "What Is Putin Really Up to in Syria?" (2015, October 1). *Politico Magazine*. Retrieved May 5, 2020, from https://www.politico.com/magazine/story/2015/10/russia-putin-syria-invasion-experts-strategy-213213.

[3] "What Is Putin Really Up to in Syria?" (2015, October 1). *Politico Magazine*. Retrieved May 5, 2020, from https://www.politico.com/magazine/story/2015/10/russia-putin-syria-invasion-experts-strategy-213213.

(Figure 8.1). After one of the chemical assaults in 2013—before Russia got involved in the conflict—Assad agreed to a Russian–American deal to eliminate his country's chemical weapons program and to join an international treaty banning chemical weapons. However, in the next few years there were at least two more attacks allegedly committed by Syrian government forces. In both instances, the United States unequivocally accused Syria and—by extension—Russia of the attacks, while Assad denied any role, with Russia backing its ally's claim and suggesting that, for example, in the 2017 attack Syrian warplanes had struck an insurgent storehouse containing toxic substances to be used in chemical weapons. Although the initial media reaction to the 2017 attack did not leave any doubt in the reader's mind that once again Assad had used a chemical weapon against his own people, there was a subtle question posed at the end of one report (Barnard & Gordon, 2017):

> A chemical weapons attack, if carried out by the government, would be a brazen statement of impunity, coming during a major international meeting in Brussels where officials are debating whether the European Union and

Figure 8.1 A man carries the body of a dead child, after what rescue workers described as a suspected gas attack in the town of Khan Sheikhoun. April 4, 2017. Reuters.
Credit: Ammar Abdullah.

> other countries will contribute billions of dollars for reconstructing Syria if it is presided over by a government run by Mr. Assad.

The US response to the attack was rather swift. A few days after the attack, *The New York Times* (Davis & Cooper, 2017) outlined a declassified report that denied Moscow's claims and presented the evidence of the Syrian government's involvement. The report further urged international condemnation of Syria's use of chemical weapons while harshly criticizing Russia for "shielding" an ally that has used weapons of mass destruction. In turn, Putin denied any accusations and requested a formal examination. His argument that the US allegations cannot be trustworthy is difficult to dispute for American journalists who are well aware of the falsified statements that led to a post-September 11, 2001, war in Iraq: Putin compared the recent allegations to the United States' claim that Iraq had weapons of mass destruction in 2003. As he said,

> This strongly resembles what happened in 2003 when representatives of the United States showed in the Security Council what was supposed to be chemical weapons found in Iraq. A military campaign in Iraq ensued, and it ended in devastation of the country, growth of the terror threat and emergence of ISIL on the international scene.

It should be acknowledged, however, that although the United States maintained Syria's responsibility and defended targeting Assad's forces in missile strikes, it did not provide any evidence of Russia's involvement in the attack.

The blame game between the United States and Russia continued into 2018 when another alleged chemical attack took place. In the absence of any information from the ground and without even knowing what chemical was used, an article with the self-explanatory title "Suspected Chemical Attack in Syria" (Victor, 2018) lists the facts available in the aftermath of the attack. The narrative almost repeats what we know from the year before: Syria denied that the government used chemical weapons and accused rebels of fabricating the videos showing the gruesome aftermath of the attack to drum up international support. Russia, along with Syria's other allies, backed up this claim, whereas the United States believed chemical weapons were used but was not sure yet whether the attack was committed by government forces or by Syria's allies.

Victor (2018) provides a cautionary note about a possible US response to the attack by pointing out that the US missile strike as a punitive measure in 2017 did not have much of an effect and that any strike could result in escalation of the war, which "could invite a direct military confrontation with Russia" because the Kremlin warned that it would shoot down any missile. Nevertheless, the US-led coalition did respond to the attack by bombing three Syrian sites allegedly linked to a chemical weapons program, thereby angering Moscow even more and prompting it indeed to shoot down American missiles. As one article states, "In the days leading up to the US attack, Russia had warned that it would defend its troops in Syria. This has raised fears of a possible direct clash of U.S. and Russian forces" (Katkov & Myre, 2018). It is noteworthy that the US media reporting on US airstrikes do not provide any hard evidence clearly pointing to who was behind the two chemical attacks. However, this did not prevent the US military from conducting response airstrikes against Syrian sites, with media giving a very vague idea of the number of casualties or amount of damage, which leaves the reader with the Pentagon's assurances that "the sites were chosen to minimize [but not to prevent] civilian loss of life and possible release of chemical agents." What we learn from another report (Dorell, 2018) is that Russians claimed to have shot down most of the missiles that were launched to destroy Assad's chemical sites and that Putin reaffirmed his position on the alleged chemical attack as a fake, warned of unspecified "consequences," and called for an emergency meeting of the United Nations Security Council. He further maintained that the US response was "a pre-designed scenario" against Russia and Syria. A Russian official is cited as blaming the US and its allies:

> Again, we are being threatened. We warned that such actions will not be left without consequences. All responsibility for them rests with Washington, London, and Paris. Insulting the president of Russia is unacceptable and inadmissible. The U.S.—the possessor of the biggest arsenal of chemical weapons—has no moral right to blame other countries.

The article does not specify, however, the nature of the insult to the Russian president.

The coverage of both chemical attacks in Syria also has revealed the growing dissatisfaction of the US media with President Trump and identified a third direction in which the current data set was analyzed. Concerns about Trump's lack of commitment to the Syrian conflict or his possible response that could provoke Russia percolate through most of the reports analyzed here. As Blake (2017) notes, there is a blame game—although not directed at Russia this time—within the United States, with President Trump blaming President Obama's administration for his weakness on Syria in "not holding to its 'red line' policy on Syrian President Bashar al_Assad using chemical weapons." Then Blake sarcastically notes that the Trump administration does not seem to have any real strategy for the conflict in Syria either.

This shift of attention inwards, toward Trump, became noticeable already in the weeks before Trump took office. To illustrate, the absence of the United States at the negotiation table on Syria in December 2016, with Russia, Iran, and Turkey being major players, raised significant concerns that the United States was being left on the sidelines and that the vacuum in the conflict would be filled by other powers (Hubbard & Sanger, 2016). As the authors sadly admit, "President Obama's reluctance to engage directly in the conflict and President-elect Trump's lack of clear policy intentions have made the United States less relevant in the discussions." While not naming Russia as the major power left in the conflict, it is clear that the disapproval of the government's action, even at a time when the country's leadership was at a transitional stage, suggests a growing concern about Russia's strengthened position in the region. This concern sounds stronger after Trump announced the US withdrawal from Syria. Trump's announcement of the planned withdrawal, "dreaded by America's regional allies and cheered by Russia" (Victor, 2018), was discussed intensively by American journalists. It is worth mentioning that Russia does not always feature in such reports, even if references are made to the anti-ISIS coalition to which Russia presumably also belonged, so it is not surprising that the White House, in order to justify "full and rapid" withdrawal, took full credit for defeating ISIS (Starr et al., 2018). The withdrawal was much criticized by the liberal US press that portrayed Trump in a negative light by emphasizing that

> the withdrawal left Kurdish fighters who fought for several years alongside American troops against [the] Islamic State exposed to attack from the Turkish military. Trump . . . stood by his decision, rejecting criticism from key GOP supporters in Congress that he abandoned Kurdish allies and allowed Russia to fill the void. (Sink, 2019).

Again, by turning their attention against their own president, American reporters may have left Russia out of their immediate focus. Yet, by criticizing Trump's position on Syria and mentioning how that position may strengthen Russia's power, they achieve two goals: They deliver a message to their targeted audiences that the failed foreign policy of Donald Trump emboldens Russia and makes America look weak. Turning their weapons against their own president, they also reenact an old and powerful enemy. Understandably, not always is Russia discussed within the context of the Syrian conflict by the US media; sometimes reporters turn their criticism against their own government that supports and arms multiple rebel groups in Syria. As Carden (2017) pointedly argues in his article "Why Does the US Continue to Arm Terrorists in Syria?" the Central Intelligence Agency (CIA) continues to use its "train and equip" program in Syria, which ultimately is believed to fund ISIS. However, such publications, not involving Russia, have not been the focus of this analysis.

The headlines of most of the news stories, as is expected of reports on military actions, can be considered unbiased and non-sensational. However, the language and the content of most texts are highly biased in presenting the entire country of Russia with the figure of the fearsome and menacing Putin. Here, reporters do not shy away from portraying Putin as an aggressor who increases "the human suffering" in the region, a monstrous but powerful leader, and from describing Russia as an "information-based dictatorship." Moreover, the sentiment that becomes prominent in these texts is the fear that the United States is presented with the dangerous and scary situation of confronting Russia in a military conflict. Clearly, 4 years after the takeover of Crimea, the US media acknowledge the power of resurgent Russia and solidify the image of the old/new enemy that the United States has to deal with, if not in direct combat, then in an information war.

The publication "The Real Reason Russia Is 'Helping' Syria" (Snyder, 2015), which was chosen for a more detailed analysis, already in its headline, with the word *helping* enclosed in quotation marks, suggests a negative attitude toward Russia's involvement in Syria. The author opens his argument by putting the current event—Russia's move into a conflict in Syria—within a more recent event that probably is still fresh in the mind of the reader, the takeover of Crimea a year before, and throughout the article shows similarities between Putin's goals in both affairs.

By deploying forces and military resources from Ukraine to Syria, Snyder (2015) suggests, Russia aims to project power across the Middle East. But more important than just projecting power is what Russia's end goal is. As the author explains, Russia, more likely than not, will try to accomplish two things: hinder democratic or extremist movements so they do not spread to Russia and weaken the European Union. First, Russia's actions in both Ukraine and Syria were similar in that they were designed to prevent movements from spreading to Russia. In Ukraine, the democratic movement toward Western ideology posed a serious risk not only of weakening Russia's strength, due to its influence in Ukraine, but also of such ideology spreading to Moscow, which could, in theory, lead to a revolution. As Snyder illustrates his point, "From Moscow's perspective, there is not much difference between *university students* protesting in Kiev for closer ties with the European Union and Islamicist terrorists gaining ground in Syria." By presenting protests in Kiev as an innocent student demonstration, the author refrains from mentioning another large group of protesters at Maiden, the ultranationalist fascist group under the banner of their national hero, Stepan Bandera. Incidentally, the reference to fascists comes up in a different context, when the author dismisses Putin's call for a revival of an "anti-Nazi coalition" by injecting an unsubstantiated claim that "Putin's friends in Europe include fascists." In order to keep Ukraine in focus, Snyder repeatedly uses phrases such as "Russia invaded Ukraine" or "Russia's intervention in Ukraine." The connotation of the verb "invade" does assume a large-scale insertion of enemy troops into a sovereign state. However, because Crimea held a referendum and by popular vote chose to join Russia and no significant numbers of Russian troops—apart from the Russian Navy that remained in Sevastopol after the collapse of the Soviet Union and a small contingent of security forces, later admitted by Putin—entered Crimea, we may see a populist move to distort facts on the author's part.

Second, as Snyder (2015) asserts, Russia continues to work toward a weaker, or even separated, European Union because with that Russia becomes one of the most dominant powers in Europe. He maintains that Russian interference in Syria will only increase the number of refugees, thus causing a much heavier burden on European countries and reinforcing the right-wing movements in Europe. Thus, Putin's goal, according to the article, is nothing less than "the destruction of the European Union" and "Russian policy in Syria is aimed toward the transformation of the country into a refugee factory." It is noteworthy that the refugee crisis in Europe started well before Russia entered the military conflict in Syria and partly can be blamed on the United States, which enthusiastically promoted the Arab Spring and the change of governments in the Middle East—something that the author chooses not to mention. However, when Putin's remarks—although taken out of context and never presented to the reader—get too close to home, the author engages in a game of tit-for-tat. By agreeing with Putin's comment about failed American policy in Iraq, he still retaliates against such statements as "belief in one's exceptionality" or "tragic consequences of exporting one's own social model," supposedly pointing toward US foreign policies, and turns these statements against Putin and his actions in Ukraine.

As discussed in Chapter 2, reporters often write on a news topic that they do not have much time to familiarize themselves with. We can see examples of such poor journalism throughout these media-based chapters. However, I argue that experts on political topics also can produce highly biased—albeit well-written—pieces. The previously discussed article authored by a reputable history professor presents a clear example of how facts can be distorted—even by historians. Twisting words and way too passionate delivery of the content could serve only one goal and one message sent to the audience: The reader can never trust Russia, even if the author agrees that "President Putin's claim to oppose Islamic terrorism is true *enough*" (Snyder, 2015).

The analysis of the US media on Syria has shown a more defined, by now, image of Russia as a power to be reckoned with, even with Putin's real goals in Syria questioned and his alleged involvement in chemical attacks not proven. With the withdrawal of US troops from Syria that left a void in the conflict expected to be filled by Russia, the US media both acknowledge Russia as a major power and use the resurgent enemy as a tool against their highly unfavored president who allows such a change in a proxy war between Russia and the United States to happen.

Russian Media

In order to be consistent with the analysis of the US media on Syria, Russian publications related to the same three themes—the beginning of Russian engagement in Syria, chemical attacks in 2017 and 2018, and the US withdrawal from Syria—were selected for the analysis. Moreover, as in the analysis of all events, this data set contained reports from the state-controlled media outlets as well as independent media sources.

In the two types of media—state-controlled and independent—there is a sharp contrast between the representation of Russian involvement in Syria's conflict. If an article in the leading government-sponsored outlet,

Pravda[4] (analyzed in more detail later), sounds like an ideological pamphlet depicting Russia as a savior of the Middle East and the United States as an aggressor creating chaos in the region, an article from a relatively independent media source, *Vedomosti* (Apple, 2015), offers a more in-depth look into the role of war in the modern world and in the psyche of Russians in particular. According to the survey conducted by the Levada Center prior to the Russian military operation in Syria, 40% of Russians approved of the government's support for Syrian president Assad and 69% of Russians were against a military conflict in the region. The author raises the important question of why Russians, so greatly impacted by the losses and destruction from World War II, still support the war in Syria. As he suggests, "The militarization of consciousness and the exploitation of the image of the enemy in today's media make the possibility of solving problems by force attractive." In line with the majority of the US reports, the article presents the Russian government as having an ulterior motive behind the conflict in Syria: In addition to fighting terrorism, it hopes to mobilize the population and switch public attention from the conflict in Eastern Ukraine to Syria: Faraway war is perceived as less dangerous, more like a picture rather than reality. The author states, "Such wars allow for the release of aggression and dissatisfaction, reinforcement of national pride, and the possibility of not thinking about consequences."

Yet, the coverage of both of the chemical attacks and the blame game between the United States and Russia do not necessarily present opposite views expressed by the state-controlled and independent media. If we look at an article reporting the 2017 attack in an independent outlet (Zelenski, 2017), the author lists the facts related to the attack that were known officially at the time, including a suggestion made by Moscow that Syria hit warehouses used by the rebels. Apart from pointing out that Moscow's position on the incident has some inconsistencies, the text is not biased in taking a side about the reported event. When a few days later the United States conducted a retaliatory attack on Syrian forces, the same independent outlet released an article[5] presenting the Syrian stance on the US-led attack that killed hundreds of people. Moreover, the article notes that because of the United States'

[4] "Rossija v Sirii Spasaet Ves' Blizhnij Vostok" ["Russia Is Saving the Entire Middle East in Syria"]. (2015, August 10). *Pravda*. Retrieved May 8, 2020, from https://www.pravda.ru/world/1276696-stepanyan.

[5] "Damask: Zapad Nanes Udar po Skladu Himoruzhija IG, Pogibli Sotni Ljudej" ["Damascus: The West Struck a Weapons Warehouse, Killing Hundreds of People"]. (2017, April 13). *Meduza*. Retrieved from https://meduza.io/news/2017/04/13/damask-zapad-nanes-udar-po-skladu-himoruzhiya-ig-pogibli-sotni-chelovek.

retaliatory attack, Russia and the United States have stopped cooperating to prevent accidents in Syrian airspace. Conversely, a state-controlled media outlet, *Izvestia*, presented the well-substantiated opinion of a Russian senator on the alleged 2017 chemical attack and the US response (Pushkov, 2017). Senator Pushkov starts his argument by citing verbatim an excerpt from an article in the British newspaper *Daily Mail* that suddenly was removed from the website after the US retaliatory strike on the Syrian forces. Published in 2013, the article speculated that the United States would conduct a chemical attack in Syria in order to blame Assad for the incident. The author outlines four major reasons why the US statement can be viewed as untrustworthy. Starting with the immediate blame assigned to Assad by the United States without any investigation of the incident and giving examples of six other cases in which chemical weapons were used by the opposition forces in 2016, the author brings in his main point: Why would Assad need such a major distraction from the ongoing peace negotiations that would secure his role as a Syrian leader? If we remember, a similar question was posed by at least one US text (see Barnard & Gordon, 2017). To undermine the US version of events further, he lands a blow that Americans would find difficult to respond to: the infamous test tube presumably containing proof of Saddam Hussein's possession of chemical weapons that justified the US incursion into Iraq and an unsuccessful decade-long war. "The history of U.S. foreign policy" he writes, "is rich with accusations that are very important for Washington in order to start military actions, although later those turned out to be a lie and falsification." So he concludes his argument by saying that whoever was implicated in the chemical attack, Americans or opposition forces, it was not Assad himself.

The media reaction, at least in state-controlled outlets, was not different when a second chemical attack took place a year later. By discrediting the key assumption that the Assad regime was responsible for the attack, one of the reports[6] from the state press questions what "enormous amount of evidence" (quote is original and repeated a few times in quotation marks, hinting at its illegitimacy) the US possesses. Putin's statement that the US-led strike is an act of aggression against a sovereign state concludes the report. What is interesting here is that the Russian side does not provide any evidence to contradict the United States' "assumption," thereby making its own argument quite

[6] "Pentagon Nastaivaet, Chto v Sirii Proizoshla Himicheskaja Ataka" ["Pentagon Insists That a Chemical Attack Happened in Syria"]. (2018, April 17). RIA. Retrieved March 19, 2019, from https://ria.ru/20180417/1518790611.html.

unsubstantiated. The chemical attack of 2018 and the US airstrike against a few sites linked to the chemical weapons in Syria also were covered by the independent media sources.[7] Ironically, the coverage of the alleged chemical attack and the US retaliatory strike did not differ from how a similar attack had been covered a year before. What makes this last publication different from those in official state outlets, however, is the absence of any bias—against the US or the Russian government—in presenting dry facts known about a military incident. A few days later, the same independent press released an article titled "'Russia Creates a Cover' for Chemical Attacks in Syria" (Safronov, 2018), which right away may suggest that the author's position on the event will be different. However, the placement of "Russia Creates a Cover" in quotation marks alerts the reader to the possibility that the author might be challenging someone else's position. Indeed, the author undermines the credibility of the report released by the French Foreign Ministry regarding the alleged chemical attacks in Syria. According to the article, there are several holes and flaws in the report that do not really inspire confidence in it upon review. In addition to the language used in the report (i.e., qualifying language), which leaves some doubt that the Syrian regime is responsible for the attack, the author's critical analysis of the report demonstrates how certain facts simply could be fabricated by the French intelligence agencies. It is noteworthy that the headline in the article promises more focus on Russia as the party indirectly accused of the chemical attack; however, there is little, if any, discussion of Russia in the content of the coverage itself, thereby making the headline irrelevant to the content of the report. Although Russian independent media remain a strong opponent of Putin and his domestic policies, it is intriguing to see how their coverage of the Syrian conflict—within those few selected themes—lacks any bias toward Russia's alleged role in covering up the evil deeds of Assad. Neither supporting nor criticizing the Kremlin, these reports are focused on presenting factual information that pertains to the chemical attacks in Syria, with some even presenting constructive criticism of the information offered by the West.

The US withdrawal from Syria and the diplomacy preceding it found their place in Russian media, too. As discussed previously, the US reports (e.g., Hubbard & Sanger, 2016) noticed the apparent absence of the United States

[7] "SShA Nanesli Aviaudary po Sirii v Otvet na Himicheskuju Ataku v Gorode Duma" ["The United States Launched Air Strikes on Syria in Response to a Chemical Attack in the City of Douma"]. (2018, April 14). *Novaya Gazeta*. Retrieved March 19, 2019, from https://www.novayagazeta.ru/news/2018/04/14/140988-ssha-nanesli-aviaudary-po-sirii-v-otvet-na-himicheskuyu-ataku-v-gorode-duma.

at the peace negotiation talks, which clearly sidelined the United States in the conflict and caused frustration among journalists. A similar article in an independent media outlet (*Novaya Gazeta*[8]) from the Russian side, however, does not make any mention of the US absence and proceeds with the coverage of the talks as though one of the major players in the conflict should not even be there in the first place, thereby, indeed downplaying the importance of the US involvement in Syria and presenting Russia as a power broker in the region. The same style of reporting on the last days of the US military presence in Syria is found in the state media, too (Atasuntzev, 2019), with a slight hint at the obvious power that Moscow has over Turkey ("The Turkish leader discussed his plan with Moscow and Moscow was not against it"), despite the White House claiming that "Turkey agreed" to the proposed plan by the United States. In other words, the question of who is the boss in the region and with whom Turkey should consult finds a rather indirect reflection in what otherwise could be considered unbiased news coverage. The withdrawal of American troops from Syria has been met with a grain of skepticism by a Russian political analyst whose words feature in the headline of another article: "Americans Say Goodbye for a Long Time But Do Not Leave."[9] Based on the example of the prolonged US presence in Afghanistan and on Trump's claim that ISIS was defeated by the US-led coalition while his press secretary soon afterward announced that the coalition continued to fight terrorists in Syria, the text delivers a clear message to the reader: Do not trust Americans and their officially stated intentions.

Except for the article discussed next, the language of most publications in this set remained rather reserved, and the authors, regardless of the agency they represented, could be considered professional in the delivery of the military news. Whether it is the nature of war coverage that requires better control of personal emotions and feelings or something else, the reports on Syria by Russian journalists lacked direct attacks on or harsh criticism of the United States. The role of the *other* in Syria's proxy war where the United States and Russia supported opposite camps while fighting one common enemy, ISIS, was more complicated than in other events despite Russia's awareness of the

[8] "Lavrov Obsudil Peremirie v Sirii s Glavoj MID Turcii" ["Lavrov Discussed the Truce in Syria with Turkish Foreign Minister"]. (2016, December 30). *Novaya Gazeta*. Retrieved May 7, 2020, from https://www.gazeta.ru/politics/news/2016/12/30/n_9521405.shtml.

[9] "Amerikancy Dolgo Proshhajutsja—i ne Uhodjat. Politolog o Vojskah SShA v Sirii" ["Americans Say Goodbye for a Long Time But Do Not Leave. Political Analyst on U.S. Forces in Syria"]. (2018, December 25). RIA. Retrieved March 21, 2019, from https://ria.ru/20181225/1548700286.html.

United States' accusations of Russia's real goals in the military conflict and its alleged involvement in the chemical attacks in Syria.

The article chosen for a more detailed analysis (*Pravda*)[10] was based on an interview with a Russian political analyst. Not incidentally did I choose this particular text: For the US part, we have looked at a publication authored by a historian and—supposedly—expert on Russia (Snyder, 2015). The aim of that article was to show the real goal Putin pursued in Syria. Similarly, the theme of this Russian article is to show the real goal of the US presence in Syria and to whitewash Putin's decision to enter the conflict, as it is seen by the Russian side. Two experts, two opposite camps, two differing opinions, with one shared purpose: To re-create an ominous image of the real enemy—the *other*.

The headline, "Russia Is Saving the Entire Middle East" would sound almost childish and ridiculous if it were not reflecting the words of a political analyst interviewed for this piece, which makes such a headline troubling. The lead that follows the headline outlines the direction in which the entire interview will go: "Clearly, Moscow's decision is not beneficial for Washington: it prevents the Middle East from turning into a chaos zone." In other words, the frame for the interview has been established from the beginning: to present the United States as a major destructive force bringing chaos to the region and Russia as the only savior that braces itself to help its little brothers. One could stop reading this article right there, as there is really no new information to process other than what the headline and the lead promised. However, for the sake of the analysis and remembering that headlines may not be relevant to the content of the report, we proceed further.

In order to frame the argument into a script familiar to the reader, Stepanjan—an analyst on whose interview the text is based—brings up a topic that Russian readers can relate to: the unsuccessful Soviet war in Afghanistan and the US role in creating mujahedeen and, by extension, Bin Laden. Both facts are well known, and mentioning them in this interview serves two goals: to assure the reader that the Russian military incursion in Syria will not turn into another Afghanistan for Russia and to reinforce an image of the United States as a state that once created Islamic terrorists and only can bring more destabilization to the region. To discount the United States further, he notes that times have changed, Russia has good allies in the Middle East, and

[10] "Rossija v Sirii Spasaet Ves' Blizhnij Vostok" ["Russia Is Saving the Entire Middle East in Syria"]. (2015, August 10). *Pravda*. Retrieved May 8, 2020, from https://www.pravda.ru/world/1276696-stepanyan.

the United States no longer is popular in the region or in Europe. To support the latter, he invokes the issue of Germany being divided after World War II but now, after the collapse of the Soviet Union, is "ruled" singlehandedly by America, which makes Germans hate Americans but leaves them unable to do anything: Germans would be happy to get help from Russia but they cannot. Neither the alleged German hatred of America nor the unspecified "help" that Russia can offer to Germany are substantiated by the analyst. The rant against the United States goes on with projecting major chaos that America plans to bring to the Middle East. And if the reader was about to ask the question of why the United States would do so, the answer is right there: to divert the refugee flood to China in order to destroy the Chinese economy, which did not happen due to Syria having stood up to interfere with the American plans. Moreover, it turns out that the United States has a long-term goal of bringing fascist elements to power in Europe in order to create another Hitler and direct those fascist forces against Russia, thereby making America's ultimate goals to destroy China and Russia. Similar to Snyder (2015), who dismisses the real purpose of Russia's entering the conflict in Syria to fight ISIS, Stepanjan ridicules the alleged goal that the United States pursues in Syria: If it were really about fighting ISIS, why were only three out of more than 100 strikes done against ISIS? Having created a monstrous image of the enemy, the political analyst turns to another important angle of his presentation: to show the righteous goals that Russia pursues (nothing but helping old allies, which had agreed with Russia's help offered within the scope of international law) and the new "wise" politics that finally have returned to Russia. "When Russia showed its independence, Americans were surprised. They thought we practically were destroyed and could not do anything. But Russia again has taken primary roles." With this patriotic slogan, he wraps up the interview. The entire rhetoric in this text reminds us of how the Soviet media covered the Soviet war in Afghanistan and the Cuban missile crisis: It always has been about being a Big Brother helping those who had to be defended against the West and the United States, specifically (Isurin, 2017).

Summary

A 3-year-long conflict between the Russian and American militaries in the proxy war in Syria ended with the withdrawal of US troops. The civil war in Syria presented a new scenario in which both countries—albeit not involved directly in military combat—unleashed ideological warfare against one another. Through the analysis of both sets of media, the US and Russian—and through looking separately into a possible difference in how state-controlled versus independent Russian media covered the events—a few interesting findings emerged. First, both sides openly questioned the real goals of their rival's entrance of the conflict, and both offered their own speculations—as absurd as some of those were—of the real motive behind such a political move. Second, the blame game in the US media continued through a series of chemical attacks that immediately were blamed on the Syrian forces and Assad's regime supported by Russia. Here, the unsubstantiated claims and the retaliatory military attacks by the United States were disputed by the Russian side. Although Russia's denial of any involvement in the attacks and its support of Assad's claims were reported by both sets of media, the US media seemed to be more aggressive in promoting their confident belief in *what* really happened and *who* was behind the attack. Russian journalists, however, regardless of the outlet, seemed to be more cautious and reported the known facts while also keeping their emotions in check or trying to find inconsistencies in the claims made both by the Russian and the US governments, as far as the independent media. Third, the image of resurgent Russia and feelings of fear that Russia happened to be on the winning side of the conflict with the United States leaving the scene, as reflected in the US media, have illustrated a new power relationship between the two rivals and a new background against which the *other* was re-created. Finally, what is more important to observe is how unexpectedly similar the reports released by Russian state and liberal media were. Knowing how much Russian independent media are in disagreement with Putin's government and how objectively critical their investigations into criminal or discriminatory acts usually are, we may ask a legitimate question: Can we trust all the facts reported and accusations made in the US media with regard to this conflict?

Our close look into two articles reporting on a similar issue has provided more insight into how media serve the ideological goals of their respective governments. The similarity of how the two pieces [the *Pravda* article and that by Snyder (2015)] are written—apart from better prose in Snyder's (2015) text—is obvious, in my view. Ideological rants against the *other* and unsubstantiated claims found in both publications aim at discrediting the other side, reenacting an old enemy, and promoting the sense of one's own superiority. Ironically, both publications invoked the concept of fascism or Islamic terrorism, as they apply to the opposite side; both presented the ultimate goals that the two countries presumably pursued in Syria as diametrically opposite to the officially stated goals, and both projected that Europe will be destroyed by the *other*. Unfortunately, both pieces are authored not by ordinary reporters who may not have had the time to familiarize themselves with the topic of their coverage but, rather, by presumptuous "experts." Because Snyder represents a reputable academic institution (Yale University), it reminds me of a recent concern expressed by Freedman (2017) that academic writers often politicize their discourse instead of providing a productive interaction between academia and policymakers. "It is not that the encounter with power turns the academic away from truth, but those with a particular interpretation of the truth are more likely to get a hearing" (cited in Fridman, 2018, p. 122). This makes one wonder whether the intellectual thought in American history studies is overtaken by political ideologies and whether Russian political analysts are incapable of articulating their opinions without turning them into an awkwardly written ideological pamphlet. If the answer to these questions is yes, we may suggest that the entire confrontation between the United States and Russia, as evidenced in the Syrian conflict, has reached the point of no return.

Russia's Alleged Interference in the 2016 US Presidential Election

While the civil wars—both in Syria and in Ukraine—were still raging, the investigation into the downing of Malaysia Airlines flight MH17 was not yet complete, and the Russian people stoically continued to carry the heavy burden of economic sanctions imposed on them as a punishment for the actions of their government, another major event took place. The 2016 US presidential election was won by the Republican candidate, Donald Trump, with the Democratic rival, Hillary Clinton, winning the popular vote. This unexpected turn of events stunned the American Democratic Party's base and brought open excitement and celebration of Trump's victory in Russia. Although already in early 2016 there were rumors that Russia may have been meddling in the US election campaign, they were not taken seriously until an official investigation into this issue was launched. Trump blamed Democrats and the media for igniting the fervor in order to justify Clinton's loss, whereas the US media started their own campaign to plant seeds of doubt about the legitimacy of Trump's win. The most unpopular president in the eyes of American journalists has become a major target of the media, whereas Russia and its alleged interference in the election provided the means for the media's attack. Thus, just for once, the media were not trying to reenact Russia as the enemy—its image as the *other* had been well established in American minds by now—they simply used Russia in the attempt to bring down an American president.

US Media

The US publications related to Russia's interference in the 2016 election roughly can be broken into three groups: (1) early reports prior to the election that warned about the possibility of Russia's interference, (2) articles that raised concerns about the interference soon after the election, and (3) the coverage of the relatively long and tedious process of the investigation that resulted in multiple officials being fired and new allegations rising to the surface.

Already in the summer of 2016, Sanger reported that the Senate's minority leader requested that the Federal Bureau of Investigation (FBI) investigate the *rumors* suggesting that Russia *may try* to manipulate voting results. Recent classified briefings from senior intelligence officials "have left him *fearful* that President Vladimir Putin's goal is tampering with this election." Moreover, he asserted that "the *threat* of Russian interference is more extensive than is widely known and *may* include the intent to falsify official election results." Two states, Arizona and Illinois, reportedly were hacked and "the FBI had told state officials that Russians were behind the Arizona *attack*." Later, the author reinforces the "rumor" of Russia's threat to tamper with the election results by referring to the fact that two Russian intelligence agencies "*were believed* to be responsible for the hacking of the networks of the Democratic National Committee" and that intelligence agencies have "*high confidence*" that Russians were behind the hacking. In other words, the report provides so far unverified facts and uses much epistemic language that is not easily noticeable behind the sensationalized information. A few weeks before the elections, the same author (Sanger & Savage, 2016) returned to the topic of Russia's potential threat to hack the US elections. This time it was no longer about a rumor that Russia may present the threat of a cyberattack; it had become official: The White House "formally accused the Russian government of stealing and disclosing emails from the Democratic National Committee . . . that are *intended* to interfere with the U.S. election process."

As the authors note, the statement "did not name President Vladimir Putin of Russia, but that *appeared* to be the intention." Although the report "stopped short of alleging the Russian government was responsible for those probes" and Trump, the candidate, maintained it could have been anyone, not necessarily Russia, such acts were ascribed to Russians, whereas Clinton's campaign chairman directly stated that he is "not happy about being hacked by the Russians in their attempt to throw the election to Donald Trump." As we can see, the narrative that Russia would help Trump win the election had been established prior to the day voting took place, but no efforts were made to prove these allegations before the election, which Donald Trump pointedly would mention later, asking why the Obama administration did not do anything about such suspicious acts at that time. Some may wonder if the long and politically charged investigation would ever have happened had Hillary Clinton won the 2016 presidential election.

In order to tamp down the emerging hysteria that the election system might be rigged, a few weeks before the election CNN delivered much-needed reassurance of the integrity of the US voting system to the American reader (Kopan, 2016). The self-explanatory title, "No, the Presidential Election Can't Be Hacked" provides a detailed explanation of why voters should not lose confidence in the democratic system. In responding to the question of whether voters should be worried, the author clearly says no: "Experts say rather than the hacks, it's the reaction from the public that scares them," which can play into the hand of one of the candidates. Later, he adds that the "Republican presidential nominee Donald Trump has frequently questioned whether the election results can be trusted." However, a few weeks after this report, Trump would become the president-elect and such concerns, still worrying Democrats, no longer would bother him or his hawkish Republican base.

In the next 2 months, a campaign of blaming Russia for interference in the 2016 election unfolded. A *Washington Post* article reports on the final agreement within the Senate's Intelligence Committee (IC)—the FBI and the CIA, to be precise—that Russia was behind the interference in the 2016 election. Entous and Nakashima (2016) discuss the consensus between FBI Director James Comey and the Director of National Intelligence, James R. Clapper, that Russia interfered in the 2016 presidential election to help Donald Trump get elected. Speculation had been going around the IC that Russia was responsible for the hack and the leaking of emails that belonged to Hillary Clinton and the Democratic National Committee in an attempt to help Trump. President-elect Trump denied the allegations against Russia, saying he did not believe them, but multiple reports, still classified, from the IC *strongly suggested* that Trump being elected was one of Russia's goals. However, because Obama officially was still in office, it was up to him to decide how to react to the rumor. As the authors note, "Obama did not directly point the finger at the Russian president. But he came close to doing so by saying: 'Not much happens in Russia without Vladimir Putin' " and vowed to "send a clear message to Russia." With just a few weeks left in office, Obama admitted that "the relationship between [the United States] and Russia has deteriorated, sadly, significantly over the last several years." Although those "last several years" fell into Obama's presidency, it is clear that none of the blame for this dramatic deterioration of the relationship between the two countries ever was taken by the United States. The united stance behind the IC conviction that Russia hacked the election was reinforced further by the determination "that 'only the senior most officials' in Russia *could* have authorized recent hacks into Democratic National Committee and Clinton official emails during the presidential election," and the director of the National Intelligence affirmed that "the Russian government directed the election interference." These statements led to a direct warning by Republican Senator John McCain that "every American should be alarmed by *Russia's attacks* on our nation" (Naylor, 2017). Although the speculation that "Russia was trying to get Donald Trump elected" "has been widely reported" without any concrete findings revealed (note: "*speculation* widely reported" can become a strong persuasion mechanism) and there was "no evidence the Russian hacking changed vote tallies," McCain's premature warning might sound like the familiar title of a comedy from the Cold War era, "The Russians Are Coming, the Russians Are Coming," which perfectly fits the newly ignited information war launched by the US government and media.

The previously discussed *Washington Post* report mentions Obama's intention to punish Russia for its interference in the election, whereas the next one (Ryan et al., 2016) covers the measures taken by Obama's administration a few weeks prior to its departure from the White House. The actions were considered "the most far-reaching U.S. response to Russian activities since the end of the Cold War"—albeit still considered inadequate and not strong enough by some senators, John McCain included—but Russia appeared to disregard any long-lasting damage inflicted by such measures. Meanwhile, Trump continued to call on the Obama administration to present proof and solid evidence of Russian hacking, which at that time the United States seemed not to have.

What followed in the next 3 years after Trump took office was a tedious investigation into Russia's alleged interference in the 2016 election, with much focus placed on Trump and his potential involvement in Russia's meddling. Without boring the reader with all the details pertaining to this event, involving changes of actors in the ongoing investigation, multiple testimonies, and the final report on the results, we discuss just a few news reports from those years.

At the early stages of the investigation, the focus was on determining if there were any links tying Trump to Russia in a joint attempt to shift the 2016 election in his favor. Although the investigation still was going on, the FBI Director, James Comey, "confirmed the intelligence agencies' findings that the goal of Russian interference in the election was to hurt Mrs. Clinton, a particular target of the ire of Russian President Vladimir V. Putin," and then "stated what he suggested was obvious: 'Putin hated Secretary Clinton so much, that the flip side of that coin was he had a clear preference for the person running against the person he hated so much'" (Shane, 2017). In the meantime, Trump continued to downplay any Russian interference in the election and adamantly stated that it could have been other countries, not just Russia. In order to justify his reluctance to accept the findings on Russia's interference, he reminded reporters that the intelligence committee had been 100% certain that Iraq had weapons of mass destruction, which led to the prolonged US-led war in Iraq (Todd et al., 2017). It is noteworthy that such an embarrassing fact from recent US history rarely is brought up by American reporters, whereas it often resurfaces in Russian media and now in Trump's counterargument.

However, a few months later, Trump had to concede publicly that Russia indeed had interfered in the election. It came after "he caused a stir by suggesting to reporters that he believed Putin's denials more than the conclusions of US intelligence officials that Russia did in fact intervene in the election" (Jackson, 2017). Nevertheless, he maintained strongly that Putin was not involved and such accusations by the United States were insulting to the Russian president, which was not good for the United States (Jackson, 2017), and that he personally asked Putin about this matter repeatedly and Putin denied his involvement (Sheth, 2017). As the investigation was going on, the media focus shifted more to Trump's possible collusion with Russia in the election than to Russia itself. The US media have turned Russia's alleged meddling in the election into a pure weapon against President Trump. Finally, when in 2019 the conclusions of the investigation report became public, the accusations against Russia were confirmed; however, the report did not substantiate claims that Trump himself colluded with Russia in order to win the election and cleared him of obstruction of justice. Such findings represented a major victory for Trump but were not comforting to Democrats, who doubted the validity of the report and "appear[ed] eager to enter a protracted legal fight to lift the curtain further on the . . . investigation" (Samuelsohn & Gerstein, 2019). Not surprisingly, in the midst of all these back-and-forth exchanges between Republicans and Democrats, Hillary Clinton called Trump "Putin's puppet" (Seipel, 2020).

By the time the report was released, the next US election of 2020 loomed large and new concerns about Russian potential interference in the election were raised. The self-explanatory and quite biased headline of the CNN article "Russian Meddling Was Out of a Spy Novel in 2016. It's Turning 2020 Into a Horror Movie" reports that intelligence officials allegedly told Senator Bernie Sanders (the front runner in the Democratic presidential primary at the time) that "Russians are actively trying to help him in an effort to split the party." And then the author sarcastically adds that "they're also meddling generally on behalf of President Trump, although *we knew that already*" (Wolf, 2020). Despite the investigation report that did not provide any evidence of Trump's collusion with Russians, the phrase "meddling on behalf of someone" can have an ambiguous meaning, indicating both an outside party acting for someone or directly representing someone. It is up to the reader with an unbiased mind to interpret this particular choice of words. Conversely, the coverage of this claim in *Politico* presented the point of view of the national security adviser who dismissed such a claim (Dugyala, 2020).

I was writing this chapter 5 months before the 2020 US election. The global COVID-19 pandemic overshadowed and/or suspended all political rallies related to the election campaigns; also, for a few months it took Russia and its "obvious and well expected" interference in the next election off the U.S political stage. However, from the analysis of the US media related to Russia's interference in the 2016 US election, it appeared that the vicious attack of American media majorly was directed at Trump rather than at Russia, which makes the image of the *other* in this particular event rather blurry. In the context of this infamous event, we either can reconstruct two *others*—American President Donald Trump and Russian President Vladimir Putin—or see Russia as a means to get at and overturn the most unpopular US president in recent history. Clearly, the 2016 US presidential election is the only political event selected for this project that does not show a clear-cut standoff between the two ideologies—the United States' and Russia's, respectively.

Russian Media

The analysis of Russian media related to the 2016 US election found little difference between the reports released by the government-controlled and independent media outlets. The early accusations against Russia and Putin in particular for their involvement in hacking the Democratic National Committee were rejected aggressively by the state media.[11] The article "Obama and the C.I.A. Are Afraid That Putin Has Become a Hacker," accompanied by an openly biased picture of the American flag eroding over the White House and the flag's red stripes almost bleeding into the iconic architectural symbol, provides a counterattack of the US statement that it was Russian hackers who broke into the server and stole compromising emails. The article argues that no evidence was presented, and Obama's explanation that Trump's campaign is covered in Russia positively is insufficient to justify such serious allegations. The Kremlin commented on the United States' "maniac attempts" to exploit the Russian theme during the election campaign. At the same time, an independent media outlet, *Vedomosti*, chose to refrain from any premature comments or from taking a stance on the issue. Instead, it published a full translation of the earlier publication on this topic from *The Wall Street Journal* that presents the American position on the scandalous hacking and Putin's denial of any involvement in the incident. The authors of the original text mention that the Russian state media point out the compromising nature of the hacked documents demonstrating the flaws of the US democratic system, which, in the eyes of the Kremlin, makes any further criticism of Putin hypocritical.[12]

Already in the summer of 2016, when Donald Trump had won the nomination of the Republican Party, one of the leading state presses, RIA, published an article outlining the reasons why Trump was likely to win the presidential

[11] "Obama i CRU Bojatsja, Chto Putin Stal Hakerom" "Obama and the C.I.A. Are Afraid That Putin Has Become a Hacker"]. (2016, July 27). *Pravda*. Retrieved June 15, 2020, from https://www.pravda.ru/news/world/1308014-obama_putin.

[12] "Hakery Prevrashhajutsja v Oruzhie Politicheskoj Bor'by" ["Hackers Are Becoming a Weapon in the Political Fight"]. (2016, October 20). *Vedomosti*. Retrieved June 15, 2020, from https://www.vedomosti.ru/technology/articles/2016/10/21/661862-hakeri-fancy-cozy.

election (Kosyrev, 2016). The most important factor, according to the author, is Hillary Clinton's increasing unpopularity, whereas Trump's unpopularity seemed to be decreasing. Through reading this publication, it becomes clear that the author's preference for the next US president leans heavily toward Trump, although he is too cautious to be overly optimistic about whether such a change in the White House would be beneficial for Russia. Certain aspects of the program of the Republican Party, revised by Trump, seem to speak in favor of Russia, such as the termination of arming Ukraine with lethal weapons, or indirectly to appeal to similar conservative values, shared by Republicans and currently promoted in Russia (anti-abortion laws, bans on gay marriage, the participation of female soldiers in combat, etc.). Conversely, Democrats are not viewed positively, which can be illustrated through the author's remark about the entire US media being fully controlled by Democrats. When Trump quite shockingly for many people won the presidency, the same state press released a long celebratory editorial on Trump's biography and his path to becoming "the most extraordinary president in the last 100 years in the US."[13] At the same time, an independent media outlet presented the detailed facts of the election process, including some specific direct quotes aimed at the Russian reader (Prosvirova et al., 2016). To illustrate, the authors quote Putin's adviser, who said that "Americans have two choices: either world war or the agreement to have a multi-polar world. Clinton was a symbol of the world war; Trump has a chance to alter this situation." Also, they cite a political science professor from the University of Maryland who admits that America has not had a president with such isolationist views for quite a while and that now the foreign affairs and military policies are likely to change dramatically.

However, when Obama introduced the final set of sanctions imposed on Russia during his presidency, this time for the alleged interference in the US election, the state media reacted in a very reserved manner by simply stating the facts and, in two instances, referring the reader to specific hyperlinks to documents published on the official White House website (https://www.whitehouse.gov).[14] This move seems to be rather unusual for Russian outlets, yet we may argue that even if the Russian reader does not have the ability to

[13] "Chelovek-Sensacija. Kak Donal'd Tramp Shel k Pobede" ["Man-Sensation. How Donald Trump Arrived at Victory"]. (2016, November 9). RIA. Retrieved June 15, 2020, from https://ria.ru/20161109/1480963636.html.

[14] "Obama Ob'jasnil Prichinu Vvoda Novyh Sankcij Protiv Rossii" ["Obama Explained the Reason for the Introduction of New Sanctions Against Russia"]. (2016, December 29). *Lenta*. Retrieved February 25, 2019, from https://lenta.ru/news/2016/12/29/obama_explanation.

read and comprehend the text written in English, the original source is available to check for any possible distortion of the information. The independent media's response was not different from that in the state media. One such article presents Obama's statement in which the outgoing president promised to have more actions in response to Russia's aggressive behavior, some of which would not be shared with the public, as well as the Kremlin's statement that Russia would not leave such evil actions of the outgoing US administration without a response (Smirnov, 2016). Similar to the state media press, this one also uses modifiers, such as "alleged" and "attempted," as they were used in the US statement, without emphasizing the so far unverified information on which the accusations were based. Similarly, a different independent outlet recounted the report released by a US intelligence agency that assures with a "high level of confidence"—the original phrase used twice in the text—that "the Russian President aimed at 'undermining the belief of the American people in democracy, at tarnishing the image of Hillary Clinton, damaging her campaign and interfering with her potential win in the election." The article wraps up by stating that such accusations of Russia's alleged interference have been repeatedly made by Hillary Clinton, intelligence agencies, and the Obama administration, yet Moscow denies all accusations (Bondarenko, 2017). When Trump finally agreed with the findings of the intelligence committee that indeed there was an interference in the 2016 US election but argued that it could be Russia or any other country that had done so, the Russian state press published almost identical brief reports that started exactly with those words of doubt expressed by Trump, which further boosted Russia's repeated denial of such accusations.[15,16]

Interestingly, an independent media outlet chose to focus on one particular event that hardly made any headlines in the US press. The Treasury Secretary, Steve Mnuchin, during an interview with CBS on the proposed tax reform, briefly mentioned that it was time for the American public to move on from the issue of Russia's interference in the election and added that "the president was focused on very important issues, such as North Korea and Syria, where [the US] has to get along with and have common

[15] "Tramp Priznal Vmeshatel'stvo Rossii ili Kogo-to Eshhe v Amerikanskie Vybory" ["Trump Recognized the Intervention of Russia or Someone Else in the American Election"]. (2017, July 6). *Lenta*. Retrieved February 27, 2019, from https://lenta.ru/news/2017/07/06/election_meddling.

[16] "Tramp Zajavil, Chto v Vybory v SShA Mogla Vmeshat'sja ne Tol'ko Rossija" ["Trump Said That Not Only Russia Could Intervene in Elections in the United States"]. (2017, July 6). RIA. Retrieved February 27, 2019, from https://ria.ru/20170706/1497941853.html.

goals with Russia." Also, he said that "nobody thinks Russian interference has had any impact on the election. So whatever occurred, there was no impact" and "the American public is ready to move on to more important issues: tax reform and foreign policy and national security" (Tillett, 2017). It is noteworthy that the CBS coverage of the interview did not focus on Russia or the election, so this particular US text was recovered only in order to verify the facts reported in the corresponding Russian article released by the liberal outlet *Gazeta*. Here, the headline "There Was No Impact on Election" (cf.: the headline in the original CBS report, "Treasury Secretary on Reducing Gov't Spending: 'Not an issue we're focused on right now' ") and the lead referring to Steve Mnuchin's exact remarks that in the Russian publication take up the entire article rather than being a side note, as in the CBS interview, suggest much focus on, if not a need for, concentrating on and emphasizing some good news for Russia, even if its name is not cleared completely (Zhukovsky, 2017). The fact that such a report was released by the independent media indicates much alliance between the two types of Russian press on this particular issue.

For the next 2 years, until the report prepared by the Special Counsel, Robert Mueller, was released, Russian media periodically produced brief updates on the ongoing investigation, which by now probably has become another tedious political affair, important more for political struggles in Washington than for regular readers on either side of the Atlantic. The release of the report was acknowledged by the state media coverage, as brief as most Russian state media publications usually are, and the main focus was on the lack of any evidence of Trump's collusion with Russia during the 2016 US election. However, the headline of one such article, "Mueller's Report Is Recognized as a Bestseller,"[17] undermines the seriousness of the produced document, despite the authors' reference to the Associated Press and "journalists' opinion" that indeed the report has become a top seller among nonfiction publications. Conversely, the independent media provided a more detailed overview of the report in which they emphasized a few of the more important statements (i.e., with the use of bigger fonts), such as the one mentioned previously (i.e., no collusion between Trump and Russia) and

[17] "Doklad Mjullera Priznali Bestsellerom" ["Mueller's Report Is Recognized as a Bestseller"]. (May 2, 2019). *Pravda*. Retrieved June 17, 2020, from https://www.pravda.ru/news/world/1415391-muller/?utm_source=yxnews&utm_medium=desktop&utm_referrer=https%3A%2F%2Fyandex.ru%2Fnews.

the Kremlin's reluctance to spend more time on or pay more attention to the entire investigation (Milchenko, 2019). The article ends with Putin's positive assessment of Mueller's "objective investigation" and his acknowledgment that all the accusations against Russia and the entire investigation have damaged the relationship between the two countries, which, he hopes, now will change for the better.

Similar to the US news reports that Russia is attempting to interfere again in the upcoming 2020 election, state-controlled and independent media reacted to the new accusation in slightly different ways. The state media rejected such absurd accusations as American psychosis and the desire to see a trace of Russia everywhere.[18] Similarly—albeit in a more expanded form and without outright labeling anyone or anything—the independent media discussed Hillary Clinton's warning that Russia may again interfere in the election to help Trump get reelected (Filipenok, 2020). Clinton's rhetorical question, "Will Russians again help us choose the president?" echoed the quoted statement of the Democratic Majority Leader that "Russians are right there again. And again they are trying to help Trump." Also, the author brings up the case of Burisma, a Ukrainian gas company at which a son of the Democratic presidential candidate Joe Biden worked for some time and was suspected of corruption. American intelligence agencies reportedly were investigating a possible connection between the hackers'—presumably Russian—attempt to break into the company's server and the possibility of their interference in the 2020 US election. Of note, the author concludes his report by reminding the reader about the outcome of Mueller's investigation, Moscow's denial of its involvement in any interference, and the fact that no collusion between Trump and Russia was established. The same neutral discussion with similar concluding remarks can be found in other independent media publications related to this new accusation (e.g., *Novaya Gazeta*[19]).

[18] "V Gosdume Prokommentirovali Obvinenija vo Vmeshatel'stve v Vybory SSha" ["The State Duma Commented on Allegations of Interference in U.S. Elections"]. (2020, February 22). RIA. Retrieved February 22, 2020, from https://ria.ru/20200222/1565097324.html.

[19] "Amerikanskie Chinovniki Predupredili Senatora Sandersa o Popytkah Rossii Vmeshat'sja v Ego Predvybornuju Kampaniju" ["U.S. Officials Warn Senator Sanders of Russia's Attempts to Interfere in His Election Campaign"]. (2020, February 22). *Novaya Gazeta*. Retrieved June 17, 2020, from https://novayagazeta.ru/news/2020/02/22/159286-wp-amerikanskie-chinovniki-predupredili-senatora-sandersa-o-popytke-rossii-vmeshatsya-v-ego-predvybornuyu-kampaniyu.

Throughout the analysis of Russian media pertaining to Russia's alleged meddling in the 2016 US election and new concerns that Russia once again may meddle in the 2020 US election, there was almost no difference detected in how state-controlled and independent media outlets covered this incident. The only differences were in the greater breadth of coverage that the independent media provided—that often stayed close to the facts available in US publications—and in the absence of any biased headlines, visuals, statements, or expressed preference of one US presidential candidate over another. Regardless of the source, however, the reporters tend to remind the reader that the Mueller investigation did not find any evidence of Trump's collusion with Russia and that the Kremlin repeatedly denied any accusations of interference.

Summary

As Benkler et al. (2018), in one of their chapters pointedly titled "Are the Russians Coming?" concluded, "One would have to be willfully blind or complicit to deny the fact that there has been a sustained Russian attack on the American media ecosystem aimed at sowing division and disinformation" (p. 254). Without denying this conclusion, in this book I aimed to analyze media in both countries in order to see how the story was reflected and how it was reported in Russian media using the Russian language and targeting the Russian reader; whereas Benkler et al. chose two Russian outlets, *RT* and *Sputnik*, that target Western audiences and broadcast in the languages of those audiences, English included.

Russia's interference in the 2016 US election was the longest and most discussed event in the US press compared to any other event analyzed in this book. However, it also turned out to be the least interesting for the analysis. Having started as a rumor that Russia might be meddling in the election during the summer of 2016, it has blown up into one of the biggest scandals in the highest echelons of American politics. In the process, the focus has shifted to President Trump, who was suspected of colluding with Russia to win the election, and the entire investigation has become another highly partisan political game in Washington. In the meantime, Russia denied all accusations. Because the entire campaign started in the United States and all information was released by American media, the Russian side could only reproduce this information in their state media and repeatedly deny the Kremlin's involvement. Furthermore, in the absence of first-hand access to the evidence, Russian independent media—albeit critical of their government in many other instances—basically reported what the US press released, though in a more detailed way than the state media, and acknowledged Moscow's denial of the accusations. Thus, we do not see a standoff between the two countries in this particular event; rather, there is a monotonous reiteration of facts that often do not sound like convincing evidence, which unsurprisingly may lose the reader's interest after a while. Despite now-late Senator John McCain's calls for Americans to be on alert for Russia's attack on democracy, one clearly can see that the entire investigation remained politically charged, with media unrelentingly going after Donald Trump rather than after an old Cold War foe, Russia.

Whether the readers on both sides were following closely the investigation, the persuasion mechanism obviously was in place. The wide use of qualifying/epistemic language in the US press may go unnoticed in the context of the reinforced image of Russia as an inferior *other*. Moreover, when the same name constantly is being used in relation to the investigation, even those who do not follow the news easily may believe the information fed to them by media. After all, we do not deal here with the complex process of updating the information in the reader's mind: The picture of Russia as an ominous enemy easily has been reenacted in American minds through the coverage of other events preceding the 2016 US election. As for Russian media, the reiteration of Moscow's noninvolvement in the alleged interference promotes persuasion too. Besides, strong anti-American sentiments in Russia are boosted further by the presentation of Russia as a country surrounded by Russophobes and enemies who want to see its faults in everything. Also, to undermine the credibility of the accusations, the Russian reader is reminded of another infamous fact from recent US history when American intelligence agencies with "high confidence"—the same phrase used in the interference allegations—and presenting a test tube that presumably contained the evidence of chemicals, convinced the US government that Iraq possessed weapons of mass destruction, which justified the beginning of the prolonged and unsuccessful US-led coalition war in Iraq.

By the time this book was published, the 2020 US election had become part of history. Donald Trump lost the White House bid to his Democratic rival, Joe Biden. The suspicion that Russia once again *may attempt* to intervene in the democratic process to bring victory to Trump did not materialize.

Yet, soon after the election, there were reports that Russia may again interfere, this time in the US congressional midtem election of 2022 (Herman, 2021). It is hoped that readers will not be too weary to follow the news by then, and journalists will be less biased in their apparent need to ignite more hatred of another country in the minds of their intended audience.

9

The 2014 Sochi Olympics and the 2018 Poisoning of the Skripals

The final chapter devoted to the media analysis examines two less significant events selected for this project—the Sochi Olympics and the poisoning of the Skripals. These two events, incidentally, occupy opposite ends on the temporal continuum of the more important international affairs discussed in this book: The Sochi Olympics happened a month before the takeover of Crimea, and the case of the Skripals' poisoning in the United Kingdom fell on the rich soil of the accumulated anti-Russian and anti-American propaganda in the respective countries. From this point of view, it will be interesting to see how the ideological information war between the two countries had changed over the 4 years that separate these two events.

Sochi Olympic Games

The Olympic Games in Sochi took place in February 2014, a month before the takeover of Crimea. However, the escalated tension between the United States and Russia clearly is visible in the US media at the time of the Games and even prior to the sporting event. Already in 2013, the Olympic Games became a focal point for American journalists who raised concerns about the possible discrimination against competing athletes and their fans who were members of the lesbian, gay, bisexual, and transgender (LGBT) community. That concern was triggered by a controversial law passed in Russia and heavily criticized in the West. Known as the law against gay propaganda, it banned any public discussions of homosexuality as well as holding organized events, such as gay pride parades, that could influence the minds of Russian minors.

Reenacting the Enemy. Ludmila Isurin, Oxford University Press. © Oxford University Press 2022.
DOI: 10.1093/oso/9780197605462.003.0010

US Media

The media publications chosen for the analysis represent a few trends: (1) criticism of the upcoming event in light of the anti-gay law passed before the Games (Lally, 2013; *The New York Times* editorial[1]) and during the Games, in reaction to the unsanctioned performance of the Russian group Pussy Riot (Alyokhina, 2014; CBS News[2]); (2) criticism of the poor preparation for the Games, the dysfunctional construction of the Olympic complex, and the corruption overshadowing the Games (Berman, 2014; Lyall, 2014; Paramagura, 2014; Wharton, 2014); and (3) a much later publication (Ioffe, 2017) that puts the Sochi Olympics into a historical perspective, connecting it with humiliating Russian losses at the previous winter Olympics in 2010 and showing how Vladimir Putin, emboldened by the success in Sochi, took over Crimea and later interfered in the 2016 US presidential election, thereby ascribing to the Olympics a much larger role than merely as an athletic competition.

All but one (Svrluga, 2014) of the headlines in the analyzed texts provide an upfront bias by using phrases such as discrimination, corruption, siege, rigging the Olympics, circus, and so forth. However, such headlines reflect the tone and content of the reports and thereby cannot be considered misleading to the reader. Likewise, the only unbiased headline represents the unbiased text discussing the future of Sochi once the Olympics end (Svrluga, 2014). The discussion of the Olympic Games is contextualized within certain scripts that remind the reader of the relatively recent socioeconomic crash that followed the collapse of the USSR; Russia's corrosive corruption culture; past despotic leaders, such as Stalin; and the current authoritarian leader, Vladimir Putin, who is compared to a pharaoh or tsar. Even the tight security provided by Russians at the Games is labeled a "ring of steel," undoubtedly alluding to the Iron Curtain and the Cold War era. Such contextualization—often done with the help of linguistic means—not only evokes old scripts familiar to the American reader but also enacts the image of Russia as the old *other*. The latter is reinforced through a direct reference to Russia's "increasingly belligerent stance toward the United States" (Berman, 2014) as well as by portraying it as a backwater country that undertook such a major

[1] "Discrimination in Sochi." (2013, December 16). *The New York Times*. Retrieved February 17, 2020, from https://www.nytimes.com/2013/12/17/opinion/discrimination-in-sochi.html?searchResultPosition=2.

[2] "Russian Militia Attacks Pussy Riot Members in Sochi." (2014, February 19). *CBS News*. Retrieved February 29, 2020, from https://www.cbsnews.com/news/pussy-riot-attacked-at-winter-olympics-2014-by-cossacks-in-sochi.

event or "Putin's pet project," as it is called by a few journalists in reference to Putin's attempt to increase patriotism among Russians and erase the memory of prior humiliation and embarrassing losses at the 2010 Olympics. The infrastructure in Sochi, and by extension in the entire country, is described as "rotten at its core," the victories of Russian athletes are downplayed as "pyrrhic," and the entire grand scale of the event is compared to a "circus" by at least two reporters. Even when acknowledging that "by the end, things even seemed not just to be working, but also to be working well" and that Russia "had held an Olympics that were safe and secure and that, thrillingly to the home fans, demonstrated the restoration of Russia's athletic might" (Lyall, 2014), the reporter does not shy away from mocking a technical glitch during the opening ceremony and nodding at the assumed corruption of a Russian figure skating judge (due to her marriage to the head of the figure skating federation) or comparing the tight security to a "ring of steel," as mentioned previously.

Surprisingly, despite highly biased headlines as well as the content of the reports, most visuals accompanying the publications present a rather neutral image of the Olympic Games. Conversely, the choice of quotations and interviewees support the main idea behind each report, where Putin's words often are drowned out by those of his critics, whereas regular people interviewed by journalists always deliver a message in line with the report.

For the closer analysis, we look at a *USA Today* article titled "Putin's Olympic Corruption" (Berman, 2014). In addition to the title suggesting the report will have a negative tone, there is a lead summarizing the three main ideas of the text: the opening ceremony of the Games came under *unflattering* scrutiny; *corruption* has far more to say about Russia's *troubled future*; and Russia's *international role* in places such as Syria and Ukraine has turned *increasingly destructive*. A picture of Putin proudly holding the Olympic torch and Russian athletes standing closely behind him separates the headline from the lead (Figure 9.1). Also, there are subheadings throughout the article, such as "Giant Waste," "Black Market," and "Global Problem." Although these subheadings are explicitly negative, they also predispose the reader to have a negative mindset to information later on in the article that likely will increase those feelings. The headline, the lead, and the subheadings hardly can be considered unbiased. From the start, the reader is exposed to the negative tone of the publication, and even if the reader chooses not to continue reading the entire text, the main message seems to be getting through: Russia is corrupt; there are more troubles to expect in the future; and there is again

Figure 9.1 Russian President Vladimir Putin lights the Olympic flame with a torch, at the Red Square, Moscow, Sunday, October 6, 2013. Associated Press.
Credit: Ivan Sekretarev.

a hint at Russia's aggression and meddling in international affairs, even if at the time of the Olympics Ukraine was not heavily on the minds of American readers. The opening line, "The high-speed *downhill drama* of the Winter Olympic Games wraps up in Sochi," stands in contrast to the previously cited testimony (Lyall, 2014) that at the end things were really working well at the event. The author does not acknowledge a single positive achievement by Russian athletes (33 medals total, more than any other country, although later many athletes were stripped of their medals due to a doping scandal, which was not known yet at the time of this particular publication) but mentions "Russia's *embarrassing* hockey loss to neighboring Finland." The latter is used as an illustration of Russia's shameful performance at the Games—even if it is an entirely distorted fact—as well as a subtle reminder of the glorious victory that the American hockey team had against the Soviet team at the 1980 Winter Olympics, which became known in the United States as the "miracle on ice." Such preparatory work to evoke the script familiar to American readers is done in a somewhat clumsy and ideologically biased manner. Surprisingly, the introduction part of the text refers to Russian corruption in passing without providing any facts other than referring to "myriad mishaps that accompanied the games—from bizarre toilets to brown water to malfunctioning door locks" and then adding that "now those issues have *disappeared*." It is quite likely that the problems were simply fixed; however, the author chooses a different word, implying underhandedness to the problems being solved. Later, a reference to Russia's underground economy, including drug smuggling, arms trafficking, and human trafficking—probably true facts but unsupported by any concrete evidence in the text—reinforces the image of a monster that also has an "increasingly belligerent stance toward the United States" and could bring "a tragedy to the world." Then the author brings in Russia's international role in places such as Syria and Ukraine, without specifying what that role was at the time of the Olympic Games in Sochi, and does not miss the chance to use a very clichéd reference to contemporary Russia as "Putin's Russia."[3] All in all, this publication can be viewed as very biased, unsubstantiated, and hardly relevant to the theme of the athletic event. In my view, it also can be considered an example of poor journalism.[4] The author's sole goal to re-create a devious enemy out of the old one could be achieved only if such a report reached the minds of rather naïve readers, although I might be wrong here.

Despite being the most nonpolitical event chosen for this project, the Olympic Games in Sochi turned out to be as politicized by American media as any other event in the data set. For many people, both in Russia and in the United States, the ongoing crisis in the relationship between Russia and the West—and the United States in particular—may be linked to Putin's takeover of Crimea a month after the Olympic Games. However, the analysis of the US media reports on the Olympic Games preceding the events in Crimea illustrated the increasing negativity on the American side in its attitude toward Russia and the steady portrayal of Russia as a reemerging—if not fully resurfaced by then—old enemy: dangerous, rotten, corrupted, and regaining its prior might, as the victories at the Sochi Olympics indicate.

[3] In my intense reading of both Russian and American media during the Trump administration, never have I come across a reference to "Trump's America," which I believe many American journalists would find problematic.

[4] According to *USA Today*, Ilan Berman is vice president of the American Foreign Policy Council.

Russian Media

The Olympics Games in Sochi were perceived by Russians as an unjustifiably costly project as well as an event that much contributed to the Russian sense of national pride. Therefore, most publications related to the Games involved either the criticism of their own government and corruption or praise for the success of the event. According to a survey conducted by the Levada Center soon after the Olympics, many Russians believed that the money should have been spent on different needs (57%), although they agreed that it was important for the prestige of their country (71%), that the Olympics was a success (77%), and that it contributed to the Russian sense of patriotism (81%) (Sinitzin, 2014). As the author concludes, "What Russian person would say no to a festivity even if he knows about the consequences of a heavy hangover?" The Games showed the world that Russian might was returning, and this is the only context within which the West and the United States are mentioned.

The data set for this event consisted of an equal number of articles released by state-controlled media outlets and articles from the independent press. The preparation for the Olympics in Russia was surrounded by public debates of whether hosting the event justified its cost. This debate was reflected widely in Russian media, with more criticism shown by independent outlets (Rosbalt[5]; Sinitzin, 2014), yet percolating into the state-controlled media as well. The latter attempted to show the profitable side of the Games (*Lenta*[6]) at the end of the Olympics while also questioning if the event was worth the expenditure (Shabanov, 2010). Note, however, that the corruption involved in the building of the Olympics project was rightly acknowledged by both types of media. The concerns about the possible discrimination against homosexuals also are acknowledged by liberal media that reported on the government's decision to reserve special areas for possible protests (*RBC*[7]). Similar to the US report about the future of Sochi once the Olympics were

[5] "Antikorrupcioner: Pri podgotovke k Olimpiade Milliardy Ushli na Postoronnie Ob'ekty" ["Anti-Corruption: In Preparation for the Olympics, Billions Went to Side Projects"]. (2015, December 15). *Rosbalt*. Retrieved February 23, 2020, from https://www.rosbalt.ru/russia/2015/12/16/1472159.html.

[6] "Pravitel'stvo Podschitalo Pribyl' ot Olimpiady v Sochi" ["The Government Calculated the Profit from the Olympics in Sochi"]. (2014, April 16). *Lenta*. Retrieved February 21, 2020, from https://lenta.ru/news/2014/04/16/profit.

[7] "V Olimpijskom Sochi Opredelili Mesto dlja Protesta" ["A Place for Protest Was Determined at Sochi Olympics"]. (2014, January 10). *RBC*. Retrieved February 22, 2020, from https://www.rbc.ru/society/21/02/2020/5e501b479a7947022c679c88.

over (Svrluga, 2014), two publications from different independent Russian sites presented opposite opinions on the state of affairs in the city that hosted the Olympics, one being very critical and painting a dark picture of Sochi a few months after the event (Titov, 2014) and the other, published a few years later, projecting a more optimistic picture of how the city should move forward (Rosbalt[8]).

When we think about collective memory and the way it is constructed by the group, we tend to think that some historical distance is needed to reevaluate the past in light of the group's present goals. From this point of view, it is intriguing to see that at the end of the Games, there was an unfolding public debate of whether the Olympics and Russia's success in the event should be incorporated into a new history textbook (Runkevich & Malay, 2014). The authors argue that the Sochi Olympics were the biggest victory in Russia's history of Olympic Games and equate it with the Soviet Olympics in Moscow in the summer of 1980. By framing the recent event in the context of a similar one that happened in the USSR, the authors distort very important information: The 1980 Summer Olympics were boycotted by the United States along with some other Western countries in protest of the Soviet invasion in Afghanistan, which allowed Russians to claim more victories than they would have otherwise. Moreover, the publication references Putin's suggestion to include the "reunification" of Crimea—which also happened a few months prior to the publication—into the textbook as a justification for adding the Olympics too, so that the young generation of Russians would remember the glory of the Russian victory.

While celebrating Russia's success or questioning the worthiness of its cost, Russian media seem to be looking inwards rather than outwards. Therefore, the next two publications are of more interest for this project because they clearly turn to and directly criticize the obvious *other*, the West and the United States. An article with the unambiguous title "The American NBC TV Channel 'Edited' the Broadcast of the Olympics in Sochi" (R93[9]) criticizes the shortened, "edited" version of the Olympic opening ceremony broadcast to the American audience. The article opens with the claim that "another *negative trolling*" took place, meaning this is not the first circumstance in which

[8] "V Sochi Obsuzhdali, Kak Razvivat' Gorod v Garmonii s Prirodoj" ["Sochi Discussed How to Develop a City in Harmony with Nature"]. (2016, June 3). *Rosbalt*. Retrieved February 23, 2020, from https://www.rosbalt.ru/main/2016/06/03/1520357.html.

[9] "Amerikanskij Telekanal NBC 'Otredaktiroval' Transljaciju Otkrytija Olimpiady v Sochi" ["The American NBC TV Channel 'Edited' the Broadcast of the Opening of the Olympics in Sochi"]. (2014, February 10). *R93*. Retrieved February 22, 2020, from http://www.r93.ru/news/2926.html.

American media have portrayed Russia wrongly. Later, the author mentions the "indignation of the American audience," meaning that the Americans unfairly misrepresented the Sochi Games to spite the Russian people. The worst offense by NBC, according to the author, was not showing the full version of the opening speech made by the Chairman of the International Olympic Committee. He was quoted speaking of the ability of the athletes to compete and strive for victory with respect for the dignity of rivals and mutual understanding. The author believes that this was intentionally left out to encourage the perceived idea regarding the mistreatment of the LGBT community in Russia. Overall, the author believes the editing of the speech was a calculated move by the American press to further the idea that Russians and the state are liable for committing acts of discrimination. To add even more bias to the report, there is an accompanying image of an NBC studio that looks dilapidated—a far cry from its main office in Rockefeller Plaza, Manhattan—which supports the author's rhetoric that NBC is a seedy organization.

Yet another publication, comparable to the one from the US side (Berman, 2014) in terms of its bias as well as the exemplification of bad journalism, was selected for a closer analysis. Bukker's (2014a) report, "Russia's Victory at the Games Is Only the Beginning," was published in the sub-outlet (*Nasledie Pravda*) of the leading state-controlled outlet *Pravda* the day after the closing ceremony. The jubilatory (toward Russia) and insulting (toward the West) tone of this report sets it apart from other articles in this outlet, where the language mostly remains reserved, reporters' emotions are well-controlled, and the facts are presented formally. The title of the article insinuates a rise in Russian dominance and declares that the performance and spectacle of the Games are only the beginning of a resurgence of nationalism. By praising the overall performance of Russian athletes in different sports events, the author attempts to showcase Russia as a leader in the international arena. He further proclaims that the Sochi facilities were built in 4 years, whereas Europeans take decades to build such facilities. By using Europeans, the author separates himself and the reader from the rest of Europe, underlining the solidarity and uniqueness of Russia. Then he discusses the lack of discrimination that skeptics believed would take place during the Games, mentions that more world leaders attended the Sochi Games than the past three Olympics, and claims that the opening performance was the best in decades. It is noteworthy that in declaring such outstanding facts, there is not a single reference to any available evidence. Clearly, the author plays on the reader's patriotic feelings to emphasize his point of Russia surpassing the rest of the world. By doing so, he contextualizes the event within those past victories that still are fresh in Russian collective memory, such as the launch of the first man into space soon after World War II "when the country was still bleeding," thereby inferring another major Russian victory. The reporter does not shy away from thanking those who were behind the success of the Olympics; however, it is not an accident that he places Russian athletes third in line after crediting Putin and his government first. Moreover, in his words, the Olympics in Sochi will enter the nation's history as "Putin's Olympics." The article is strewn with nationalistic ideas calling critics of the country "presumptuous" and referring to Americans as "growing fat and complacent."

The linguistic means in delivering the message deserve additional attention. The main idea of the text is not just to praise Russia but also to make mockery of Russia's "haters" and the Western "scum" that anticipated Russia's failure and were "ranting" about possible discrimination against sexual minorities. Furthermore, the author specifically mocks the American idiomatic expression "we did it," which would have been used in such a proclamation of victory had it happened in the United States, by bringing in a sexual connotation of the phrase to indicate that Russia indeed "did" those enemies and showed how "stupid" they are and how "their pseudo-democratic media" are helpless to damage Russia's image. The reporter states that "the West and the U.S. lost their fight against Russia and now are trying to gain their losses back on the international arena, in our southern low belly," apparently hinting at the beginning of the conflict in Ukraine and the United States' role in it. As though the previously mentioned negativity in the description of "Russia's haters" was not enough, the author continues his verbal rampage by suggesting that those "ugly ones have lost their brain, honor and conscience along with the circumcised flesh," apparently hinting at the West versus Russia, with the latter not exercising male circumcision.

Summary

As can be seen, the media in both countries used the only nonpolitical event analyzed in this project in an attempt to escalate the tension between the United States and Russia and re-create the old enemy within specific scripts that their intended audience would understand. For the American reader, it was done through the contextualization of the Sochi Olympics within the picture of corrupted authoritarian power that was not different from that in the former USSR. By the repeated mention of corruption—both in the construction of the Olympic complex and possible unfair judgments of the athletes' performance—the reporters aim to question the very success of Russians in the Games. The pre-Olympics agony about possible discrimination against sexual minorities somewhat subsided by the end of the event, with only the performance of the notorious Pussy Riot group reigniting the discrimination theme. The reference to Stalin and the labeling of the tightened security provided at the Games as a "steel ring" clearly hinting at the "iron curtain" during the Cold War, further solidified an image of the old, rather than new, *other* for the reader. In order to remind Americans about the aggressive side of the old foe, references both to Ukraine and to Syria are made in passing, prior to those countries becoming hot spots on the international stage.

On the Russian side, however, the success of the Games was placed within a bigger picture both by connecting it with the historical past, such as its victory in World War II and the launch of the first man into space—two events that heavily are used by the current government to increase patriotism in post-Soviet Russia—and negotiating its success against the previous Olympics that happened in the Soviet Union. Here, some equate the importance of the recent Games for Russia with that of the 1980 Summer Olympics in Moscow for the Soviet Union (Runkevich & Malay, 2014), whereas others try to show the significance of Vladimir Putin in the success of the Olympics, something that the 1980s event could not claim due to the unfavorable assessment of the legacy of the Soviet leader at the time of the Olympics, Leonid Brezhnev, in Russian collective memory (Bukker, 2014a). However, the contextualization of the Olympics would not be complete without bringing in the *other*, the United States along with the West, as "Russia's haters." This is supposed to re-create an old narrative of Russia's uniqueness, which makes the rest of the world despise, loathe, and fear it. By noting that the success in the Games is only the beginning, the Russian reader, fueled by the nationalistic rhetoric, is getting ready to applaud upcoming new victories, the first of which will happen a month later with the takeover of Crimea. In other words, the contextualization of the Olympics and putting it into a familiar script serves two goals for Russian and American media: to make the reports more accessible for the intended audiences and to reenact an old enemy.

The macroanalysis of the selected media reports also showed the biased presentation of the information. This was more notable in the US media than in the Russian media, with the latter mostly basking in the glow of the Olympics' success or criticizing the cost of the event and the corruption involved in the preparation for it. The bias was demonstrated mostly through the headlines and the leads of the American publications; yet, as mentioned previously, the biased headlines always reflected the content of the reports, which was not less biased. Moreover, there was factual distortion detected in both sets of media, whether the facts were entirely omitted or the quotes were given without a concrete reference. The use of linguistic means in the attempt to insult the *other* verged on unprofessionalism and was found in both media camps.

The Olympic Games in Sochi is the only nonpolitical event—or as I want to believe, it should not be a politicized event—that found much reflection both in Russian and in American media. It also exemplified how the tug of war between the two countries was going on even before the takeover of Crimea, the downing of Malaysia Airlines flight MH17, and the conflict in Eastern Ukraine. The largest competition in the athletic world in winter 2014—for better or for worse—took place in Russia. It revealed the returning might of Russian sport, which is believed to have emboldened Vladimir Putin for his next move of bringing Crimea back to Russia and the subsequent rise of national patriotism among Russians. However, it also demonstrated the irreconcilable ideological differences between Russia and the United States. The obvious refusal to acknowledge Russia's success in the Games and the sole focus on Russia's inefficiencies and drawbacks seem to have blinded the US reporters in their attempt to bring back home an image still familiar to the older generation of Americans—that is, an image of a corrupted and aggressive enemy that is raising its head and threatening America.

The Poisoning of the Skripals in the United Kingdom

Sergei Skripal, a former Russian intelligence colonel and a double agent—Russia and the United Kingdom—was arrested in 2006 for passing state secrets to Britain's MI6 and later released in 2010 as part of a spy swap between Russia and the United States. Since then, he has been living in Britain. In March 2018, he and his daughter, Yulia, were found unconscious on a park bench in Salisbury, England. It was found that the two were poisoned with a nerve agent. The attack immediately was linked to the Russian government, although the latter denied involvement and blamed the British intelligence for framing Russia in order to ignite more Russophobia in the West. Although the would-be assassins never were found and no hard evidence linking the attack to Russia ever was presented, the story received much coverage both in the United Kingdom and in the United States. Once again, an incident that took place on foreign soil brought Russia and the United States into a new upsurge of the ongoing information war and brought the relationship between the two countries to its newest low since the end of the Cold War.

US Media

The US reports surrounding the Skripals' poisoning follow a few distinctive themes. The earlier ones break the scandalous news of a Russian ex-spy poisoned most likely by the Russian government (CBS[10]; Erickson, 2018). As the story develops, the suspicious nerve agent used in the attempted assassination is identified as Novichok, first developed by "Kremlin scientists" and therefore undeniably linking the poisoning to the Russian government. Later, the name of the agent acquires a menacing new modifier, "military-grade nerve agent," that is used repeatedly in all subsequent publications (Melville, 2018). Moreover, two suspected assassins were found, charged by a British judge, but not extradited from Russia where the two appeared on national TV targeting the Western audience with their story of being just tourists and having nothing to do with the poisoning of the Russian ex-spy (Higgins, 2018). To add more layers to the already mysterious incident, a third suspect was identified as a possible coordinator of the attack (Barry, 2019), but in the absence of any hard evidence linking him to the poisoning, the story quickly was dropped by reporters. The Skripals' story has resurfaced a few more times in recent years, as a reminder of the incident that revealed once again the dangerous "defiant face" of the Kremlin. At that point, the evidence indicating Moscow's involvement was presented as proven facts (Schwirtz, 2019), and the story mostly was brought back to the reader in the context of the worsened relationship between the United Kingdom and Russia (Rodgers, 2020).

The sensational nature of this political event and its presentation by media easily could fit the plot of a detective story. As in an Agatha Christie story, there is a crime scene and there are victims and a dead body (a British

10 "New Details in Suspicious Spy Poisoning After U.K. Officials Meet." (2018, March 10). *CBS*. Retrieved February 8, 2020, from https://www.cbsnews.com/news/sergei-yulia-skripal-spy-poisoning-latest-string-suspicious-cases-uk.

woman who accidentally picked up the perfume bottle containing the nerve agent), a weapon, an immediate suspect—although in our case represented by an entire country—and much mystery surrounding the attempted assassination (Figure 9.2). In the absence of a skilled detective such as the fictional character Poirot, reference is made to the "investigative group," "police," or "some" officials. One important thing missing in this story is a clear motive: Why would Russia need to eliminate an ex-spy who already had served his sentence in a Russian prison and was swapped by Russia for its own spies caught in the United States? This makes the report by Shuster (2018) somewhat different from other texts, in which any discussion of a possible motive simply is dismissed. Published in the days immediately following the attack, the report does not question Russia's involvement but suggests that Russia's rules of espionage probably have changed: "If Russia's spy agencies were involved, the poisoning would go against some basic rules of espionage." The author further notes that "the Russian state had no more grudge against [Skripal] . . . which is partly what makes his poisoning so bizarre." The haphazardness of the assassins' strategy and their inability to cover their trail puzzle some other journalists (e.g., Barry, 2019), who nevertheless

Figure 9.2 The forensic tent, covering the bench where Sergei Skripal and his daughter Yulia were found, is repositioned by officials in protective suits in the center of Salisbury. March 8, 2018. Reuters.
Credit: Peter Nicholls.

refrain from noting that the clumsy execution of the attack does not fit the profile of the government headed for two decades now by a former KGB colonel. However, despite bringing in some doubts about Russia's involvement in the attack and using obscuring phrases, such as "whoever organized the attack," Shuster shifts the reader's attention to the 10 sleeper agents that Skripal was swapped for and paints a sinister picture of "sleeper agents who pose as normal members of American society, complete with fake identities, perfect English, regular jobs and, in some cases, children who have no idea their parents are spies." Such contextualization of an attack in Salisbury within a bigger picture of how Russia infiltrates the daily life of unsuspecting Americans by planting its spies among them serves no other purpose but to ignite a sense of hysteria among the readers.

The further fate of the Skripals is surrounded by mystery as well. The media reports do mention in passing that the British government considered moving both victims under new identities to an undisclosed location. However, it is only mentioned in connection with the Russian authorities demanding a meeting with their citizens and the British officials claiming that the Skripals have declined such requests (Wolgelenter & Pérez-Peña, 2018).

Throughout all analyzed media texts, it is clear that American reporters have no doubt in their minds that the Russian state—repeatedly referred to as "the Kremlin"—was behind the attempted assassination. In order to make this main message believable, the Skripals' story is framed in such a way that constant reminders about previous events, likened to the attack on the Skripals, solidify the reporter's point. Among such events, the most commonly mentioned is the poisoning of another ex-KGB agent, Alexander Litvinenko, or the alleged elimination of a Russian oligarch, Boris Berezovsky, with both deaths also happening on British soil (CBS[11]; Melville, 2018; Wolgelenter & Pérez-Peña, 2018). In both death cases, the victims are claimed to be Putin's critics, which undeniably makes them soft targets for assassination. Although, as in the Skripals' case, both deaths were "contended" by Britain as attacks directed by Moscow, this was never proven. According to the CBS report,

[11] "New Details in Suspicious Spy Poisoning After U.K. Officials Meet." (2018, March 10). CBS. Retrieved February 8, 2020, from https://www.cbsnews.com/news/sergei-yulia-skripal-spy-poisoning-latest-string-suspicious-cases-uk.

> *Some* in Britain say the nerve agent attack fits a pattern of suspicious Russian-related deaths in the U.K. and in the United States, and are calling for a high-level investigation into whether Britain has become a *killing ground* for the state-sanctioned elimination of foes of the Russian government.

Such strong language presenting Britain as a killing ground for the Russian government stands in sharp contrast with how the same report describes Britain as a paradise for super-rich Russians, known as New Russians: "Britain offers wealthy Russians many attractions: the great city of London, the bucolic countryside, exclusive schools, and a global financial hub." But for some critics of President Vladimir Putin, according to the author, it has become lethal. None of the reports, however, explains why it is the United Kingdom, and London in particular, that has been harboring so many super-rich Russians who often have fled Russia due to criminal charges against them and whom Britain refuses to extradite. Instead, the same CBS report acknowledges that "Britain happens to be one of the central places where Russians"—I would add, wealthy Russians—"flee," but the only explanation that the author offers is that "it's the gateway to the West, the seat of the language, the seat of the empire, the seat of major finance." The latter, "the seat of major finance," is referenced in another of the analyzed texts, this one an inquiry into money-laundering, sanctions, and economic crimes committed by Russians in Britain (Melville, 2018; Wolgelenter & Pérez-Peña, 2018). We may wonder who would be involved in such economic crimes if not those Russians who fled Russia to enjoy "the bucolic countryside" and "exclusive schools." The author, however, does not provide such information, which leaves the reader with the solid impression that such crimes again are directed by the Russian government.

Note that through all these media reports, the reader also learns about Russia's denial of any involvement in the attempted assassination at the state level. However, Russia's objection to the crime immediately is dismissed by the journalists, who bring in examples about previous—albeit unresolved—cases of alleged assassinations; note that Russia blames the United Kingdom and the United States for framing Russia to distract attention from the Brexit situation and to ignite Russophobia; cite Putin's words taken out of context, such as that "treason is the gravest crime possible, and traitors must be punished" (Barry, 2019)—a statement that any state official would agree with; or say that "Russian officials have sought to exploit *holes* in the complicated narrative of the poisoning to suggest an anti-Russian conspiracy," indirectly admitting that the investigation is far from being conclusive (Schwirtz, 2019). The mention of the existent holes in the investigation may suggest that the involvement of the Russian government beyond a reasonable doubt was not established and that forensic evidence did not provide indisputable proof of the Russian government's involvement. However, despite the original CBS report suggesting that Russia should be punished if such *indisputable* evidence is obtained, the reader learns from all subsequent texts that such punishment indeed arrived in the form of new sanctions imposed on Russia and the booting out of numerous Russian diplomats, both from Britain and the United States, even in the absence of such *indisputable* evidence.

The headlines accompanying the reports can be considered sensation-driven calls for the reader's attention: "The Kremlin Poisoned Sergei Skripal," "Skripal Attack Was Linked to Moscow," "Russia Offers Defiant Face to Britain and the West," "Britain Meets Resurgent Russia," just to highlight a few. However, note that given many unknown facts and much speculation around the incident, the language of the reports lacks certainty in supporting their main message, something that an average reader probably would not notice. Starting with a vague reference to "*some* in Britain," "*one* official," or "*several* politicians" whose words or exact quotations are provided without giving any specific information about who they are, to referring to the masterminds behind the attack as "*whoever*," the wide use of qualifying language such as "highly likely," "it is thought to be," "seemed," "maybe," "probably," "could be," and "may have been," or asking "why Russian officials—or *anyone else*—would have targeted [Skripal]" (Wolgelenter & Pérez-Peña, 2018) and admitting that "a lot of this stuff is really difficult to prove" (CBS[12]), the presentation of the information does lack convincing clarity. The latter fully is compensated for by attacking Russia as a "swashbuckling maverick, ruthless, dangerous and decisive" (Schwirtz, 2019) or upgrading the assassination attempt to the level of the "first known offensive use of a chemical weapon on European soil since WWII" (Melville, 2018) and "a reckless use of chemical weapons and a brazen attempt to murder innocent people on U.K. soil" (Prime Minister Johnson, as cited in Rodgers, 2020).

[12] "New Details in Suspicious Spy Poisoning After U.K. Officials Meet." (2018, March 10). CBS. Retrieved February 8, 2020, from https://www.cbsnews.com/news/sergei-yulia-skripal-spy-poisoning-latest-string-suspicious-cases-uk.

If we take a closer look at one of the media publications (Applebaum, 2018) with the strongly worded title, "First Russia Unleashed a Nerve Agent. Now It's Unleashing Its Lie Machine," the headline itself prepares the reader to learn how Russia is using both chemical and information weapons against its enemies. Although digital information has become a common mechanism of brainwashing in all countries, including the United States, the use of the phrase "lie machine" and later referring to whatever Russian media produce as disinformation set the tone of an ideologically biased narrative from the start. A picture of daffodils placed in between a pole and police tape stands in sharp contrast with the headline and automatically makes the reader sympathize with the victims of the crime, thereby damning whoever was behind the attack. The article opens with what represents a few of Russia's numerous—21, according to the author—explanations of who may be behind the attack. Besides the origin of the nerve agent having been linked to Russia by the British government—a claim parried by the Russian government, which insisted that the Czechs, Slovaks, and Swedes had it too and that Russia had destroyed all of its chemical weapons—the text provides almost no additional information about the attempted assassination in Britain. Rather, it shifts the reader's attention to the malicious lie machine widely used by Russians. To make this claim more convincing, the author references the information war that raged after a Malaysia Airlines flight MH17 was shot down by Russian-backed troops in Eastern Ukraine in 2014 and during the 2016 US presidential election. Both claims, Russian interference in the election and its involvement in the downing of flight MH17, are presented as well-established facts "*quite* convincingly" proven by the West and serve as the script within which the ruthless enemy is framed.

The report continues by mentioning the British foreign office response (according to *one* unnamed official)—a short video mocking the multiple Russian explanations and a statement accusing Russia of offering "denial, distraction, and threats" instead of explanations. Note that the next sentence informs the reader that "[the British foreign office] sent samples of the Skripals' blood to a neutral international institution, the Organization for the Prohibition of Chemical Weapons (OPCW), for testing to *confirm their conclusions*." The bizarre choice of words in that quote—should not conclusions follow some confirmation of a theory and not the other way around?—may go unnoticed by the average reader. Although at the time of the publication such test results were not obtained yet and, as we know from another report (Wolgelenter & Pérez-Peña, 2018), the findings from the test are limited to identifying the poison but not its source, the reader is left with the impression that Britain has rebutted all Russian claims and supported its premature conclusions with scientific evidence from a reputable international body. The repeated use of the terms "Russian trolls" and "disinformation" is intended to solidify an image of the dangerous enemy that threatens the West. The author concludes by calling for a broader version of Britain's "expose the methodology" campaign in the United States and predicts a dark future unless such efforts are made: "We're doomed to live in a world where truth is defined by those who have the least respect for it." In other words, both the title and the last statement support the intended message sent to American readers: Beware of your enemy, whose effort to provide disinformation and infiltrate your social networks is not limited to the election campaigns but "goes on all the time" and "will be repeated again and again."

As can be seen through the analyzed media texts, American journalists sensationalized the Skripals' story, and despite multiple unknowns still surrounding the case that are evident in the use of qualifying language, the misrepresentation of some facts, and the obvious bias from the start in presenting the information, they succeeded in one thing—sending a strong message to their audience at home that what happened in faraway Salisbury, England, can happen and did happen in the United States, since we are dealing with a resurgent, defiant, deceitful, and dangerous enemy—that is, Russia.

Russian Media

American media fully relied on the reports published in the British press and without questioning any facts presented in those reports unleashed their attack on Russia, whereas Russian journalists had a more difficult job to do. Because Russian officials were denied any involvement in the investigation and access to the evidence as well as to their citizens (Sergei Skripal has dual citizenship, whereas his daughter has only Russian citizenship) and the Russian government was accused blatantly of the attempted assassination, the Russian press was left with nothing but the evidence that they could obtain through the same British media. Here, Russian media followed a few distinctive trends in reacting to the poisoning incident in Britain.

Following the strategy of "the best defense is a good offense," they tried to discredit the British stories often by relying on anecdotal evidence, such as posts on social media. To illustrate, a publication in the leading state-controlled outlet *Pravda*[13] sarcastically suggests that the British Prime Minister Theresa May apparently enjoys watching a British TV crime show in which the nerve agent used in the Skripals' poisoning was created by a fictional character, a Russian—later revealed to be Chechen—scientist. The lead of the article unequivocally states that "Russians *came to the conclusion* that the story of the Skripals' poisoning with the nerve agent Novichok is the plot of a British TV show." It is noteworthy that by using the collective term "Russians," the author presents the ridiculous conclusion as something that the entire nation must have believed. To entertain this version even further, the text suggests that Britain has not reached any conclusion in the Skripals' case because the TV show is still running and the country has yet to watch the end. Moreover, a nod to Chechens is not accidental either because Russia was involved in two recent wars with Chechnya and suffered from terrorist acts committed by Chechens. In other words, who knows who tried to kill the Skripals—it could be Chechens! No less unprofessionally, a few tried to sensationalize the unknown post-incident fate of the Skripals soon after their poisoning (Belokonova, 2018) and a year later (Karpitzkaja, 2019; Koroleva, 2019; Zuevsky, 2019). Here, they exclusively relied on the words of Sergei Skripal's niece, who allegedly got some vague information from her relatives and blew out of proportion her suspicions that the lives of her uncle and cousin were in danger and that they could be eliminated by the British government. Such unsubstantiated suggestions based on the words of a single interviewee—who probably sought the media's attention—show how journalists attempt to resurrect an old story even if they have no new material on which they can base such stories. These bizarre reports aside, other publications maintained more professionalism in covering the incident.

Some referred to reports in British media, especially if those aligned with the Russian point of view, such as a reference to *The Guardian*, a reputable British newspaper, that proclaimed that the British authorities had no proof of Russian involvement in the attacks (Filippov, 2019). According to the author, the British newspaper interviewed the Deputy Director of Scotland Yard, who stated that policemen need solid evidence and "all the theories made so far were based on the suggestions by experts on Russia."

[13] "Istoriju s Otravleniem Skripalja Nashli v Britanskom Seriale" ["The Skripals' Poisoning Was Found in a British TV Show"]. (2018, March 13). *Pravda*. Retrieved April 29, 2020, from https://www.pravda.ru/news/world/1375324-britaine.

As we know already, the US media acknowledged that there were holes in the investigation and that Russians tried to exploit those holes (Schwirtz, 2019). Such holes, indeed, were questioned by Russian media (Kornilov, 2019; RIA): Why was the name of the second policeman allegedly exposed to the nerve agent classified? If the powerful nerve agent created to destroy entire battalions of the enemy indeed was used, why did the policeman have no symptoms? If the Skripals were poisoned in their house, as the traces of the agent found on the doorknob indicate, how could they go to the downtown area, have lunch, walk in the park, and only then collapse on a park bench? Why was the body of a British woman allegedly poisoned by the same chemical in a different city quickly cremated, thereby eliminating the possibility of examining it? By questioning such obvious facts, Russian media aimed at undermining the credibility of the British investigation. To bring more credibility to their own stories, however, Russian journalists turn to authorities from the Russian Ministry of Foreign Affairs (the equivalent of the US State Department), who call the British investigation the "London fake-based anti-Russian campaign" and suggest that "one can write a textbook on anti-Russian fakes in London" (*TASS*[14]).

It should be acknowledged that the immediate accusation of the Russian government in the poisoning incident, even before any evidence was found, seems to bother Russian journalists from state-controlled as well as independent media outlets. As a reporter from one of the most liberal presses, *Novaya Gazeta*, admits, although the source of the nerve agent has not been officially established, all unanimously pointed a finger to Russia (Mineev, 2018). Contrary to the US media that contextualized the Skripals' poisoning within the script of a similar assassination of a former Russian spy in Britain, Russian reports do not bring up those stories. Instead, one mentioned another scandalous incident in the same city of Salisbury that made the front page of British newspapers (Kornilov, 2019). Under the headline "Putin Tried to Kill Me with Rat Poison," there was a story about a Russian photo model and her "orgies' king" boyfriend who later was sentenced to 11 years in prison (the latter did not make headlines in the British press), which supposedly was meant to discredit the British press in the eyes of the Russian audience.

[14] "Zaharova Zajavila, Chto po Antirossijskim Fejkam Londona Mozhno Napisat' Uchebnik" ["Zakharova Said That One Can Write a Textbook on Anti-Russian Fakes in London"]. (2019, June 7). *TASS*. Retrieved February 8, 2020, from https://tass.ru/politika/6525128.

Probably the most interesting finding in the analysis of Russian media was how journalists handled the issue of the nerve agent Novichok that, at least in the minds of British authorities, linked the attempted assassination to Moscow. From calling it simply "a chemical" or "unknown substance" even 5 months after the incident (Belokonova, 2018) to referring to it by its technical identification number "A34" (Tabak, 2020) or simply putting the name "Novichok" in quotation marks, for only the British authorities claimed it was the poison used in the incident, clearly there was an uneasy feeling about repeating the name of the agent that by its uniquely Russian origin would suggest that Russia indeed was behind the attack. To further discredit Britain's accusation that the Skripals were poisoned by a state-produced chemical, Russian media referenced the results of the OPCW's investigation that only could identify the substance but not its origin. Or they dismissed a possible connection to a state lab by emphasizing the weak effect of what should have been a deadly chemical weapon.

The US media unanimously side with Britain and clearly target Russia in their reports on the Skripals' poisoning by reenacting the old enemy in a less than subtle way, whereas Russian media focus on painting Britain as the one that tries to make a scapegoat out of Russia. In other words, the United Kingdom embodies the proverbial *other* in the analyzed texts and the United States is mentioned in passing, if at all. Because the incident in Salisbury led to a scandal at the international level and resulted in the expulsion of Russian diplomats from many Western countries, including the United States, the further harsh measures taken by Washington are acknowledged in some reports.[15] However, the insignificant attention directed at the United States in this set of reports does not diminish the already well-established image of the "real enemy."

The use of headlines in the analyzed texts can be considered less biased than in the US set, as Russian media are reacting to the wrongful, in their view, accusations, whereas the US media sensationalize the incident. However, there were a few openly biased headlines, such as "Dirty English Murderer: British Can Eliminate the Skripals" (Zuevsky, 2019) or "Calculation of Silent Liquidation" (Latynina, 2018). Similar to American media, the accompanying visuals can be considered unbiased, except for a

[15] "Zaharova Zajavila, Chto po Antirossijskim Fejkam Londona Mozhno Napisat' Uhebnik" ["Zakharova Said That One Can Write a Textbook on Anti-Russian Fakes in London"]. (2019, June 7). *TASS*. Retrieved February 8, 2020, from https://tass.ru/politika/6525128.

political cartoon depicting Sherlock Holmes and Watson in their living room as a British news anchor floods out of their TV with water that contains the words "fake news" and "gossip" (Filippov, 2019).

The US media use much of the qualifying language due to numerous unknowns surrounding the case, while Russian media, in response, mock that language, especially the phrase "highly likely," often spelled in Russian, and they tend to place such words in quotation marks to accentuate the lack of any convincing evidence that would tie Moscow to the attempted assassination (e.g., "overwhelming" evidence of Moscow's involvement; Tabak, 2020). There are two particular words, however, that deserve some attention. First, the word motherland, representing a sacred concept for Russians, is used in reference to Yulia Skripal, who "desperately" tries to get back to her *motherland* (Koroleva, 2019). The use of this word that resonates deeply with any Russian may refute Russia's involvement in the incident in the eyes of the reader: Why would a recent victim of an attempted assassination want to return to her assassin? Another linguistic mechanism employed by journalists is the use of the word spy in describing Skripal. In Russian, as in English, there are two words describing this profession—intelligence agent and spy. However, the word spy (*shpion* in Russian) has a highly negative connotation, which does not leave any sympathy for a person who committed treason against their *motherland* and who deserved severe punishment.

The Skripals' story concludes the set of events chosen for analysis in this book. It also represents one of the most controversial news pieces in which the confrontation between Russia and the West reaches a tipping point that has left little hope for reconciliation. From this point of view, it was interesting to take a closer look at how Russian independent—not state-controlled and state-censored—media reflect on this event. The article titled "Effect of the Trust Collapse: The Manufacturer of the Poisonous Substance Is Not Specified, But All Together Point to Russia" (Mineev, 2018) came out in one of the independent media outlets a month after the Skripals were poisoned. It opens with a lead stating that due to its high purity, the nerve agent used in the poisoning incident could be manufactured only under specific conditions by very qualified specialists. Remarkably, the statement is a step away from saying that such an agent could be produced only by a state-sponsored lab, something that the US media persistently claimed. However, already in the first paragraph, the author contends that the results of the investigations by OPCW and four independent toxicology labs *speak in favor* of a state being the source of the agent. Having admitted that the previously mentioned organizations did not aim at identifying the origin of the agent—a fact mentioned in numerous media publications—and did not name the agent explicitly as being "Novichok," the author sadly adds that in the current international atmosphere, it makes no difference for Russia because everyone in unison points a finger toward the country. As previously discussed, the name Novichok and the assertion that OPCW's investigation supported the conclusion made by the British authorities that the Kremlin was involved in the attack have been all over British and, by extension, American media. However, as the author of this article notes, "Dilettantes and journalists can try to figure out suspicious inconsistencies in the story of the Skripals' poisoning as long as they want, yet the OPCW's conclusion weighs more." The article continues by showing how Boris Johnson, "as expected," welcomed the results of the investigation as definite proof of Moscow being behind the attack. In response, the press secretary of the Russian Foreign ministry, "as expected," refuted all the accusations and called them an open provocation against Russia. The deliberate use of the repetitive phrase "as expected" in the presentation of the previous details posits the reporter as a neutral—if not objective—observer who is caught in a confrontation between the two powers. In order to illustrate the escalation of the negative campaign, the article reports on a few other details related to the Skripals by presenting the official stance taken by both sides. Compared to many other publications in which the Skripals' poisoning is either framed within a script of similar assassinations allegedly committed by Russia (US media) or treated out of context (Russian media), this particular report contextualizes the Skripals incident, as well as the escalation of tension between Russia and the West, within the events that preceded the Salisbury attack, such as the takeover of Crimea, the downing of Malaysia Airlines flight MH17, and Russia's engagement in Syria. The author does not take sides; instead, he calls for more diplomacy at what looks like a point of no return: "It is impossible to resolve international confrontations following the principle of who will outsmart another. The biggest conflicts of the second half of the last century were resolved when both sides chose to trust one another." Later, he concludes that trust is at the zero level but assures the reader that all is not really that dark by giving an example of some slight improvement in the relationship between Russia and Europe.

All in all, this particular article can serve as an example of solid journalism in which the reporter's emotions do not overshadow the very essence of what the news coverage is about and where the journalist tries to find a healthy balance in presenting the facts without necessarily showing where his allegiance lies or sensationalizing a story based on poorly substantiated facts just to boost the ideologically biased image of the *other* and potentially increase readership at home.

Summary

The mysterious story of the Skripals' poisoning on UK soil and the immediate accusation of Moscow as the only possible player that had the motive and the means to commit such a crime conclude a series of events that led to the flare-up of tension between the United States and Russia in the second decade of the 21st century. Incidentally, I had started the analysis of media for this project with two events that, I believed, were the least significant: the Sochi Olympics and the attack in Salisbury. Since my reading into the media related to the Olympics and the Skripals' case was done in close proximity to one another, I have observed the increased attacks, often unjustified, that the US press was making against Russia. If the Olympics presented American reporters with just a few reasons to criticize their old foe, such as the expected but not materialized discrimination against sexual minorities during the Games, the Skripals' poisoning fell on the rich soil of the accumulated mistrust and hatred that resulted from the other five events that happened between 2014 and 2018. As for Russian media, the Olympics ignited a sense of patriotism—a feeling long lost in Russians after the collapse of the USSR—and the media's initial attacks against those who were vaguely described as "Russia's haters" now have become more definite with a more crystallized image of the enemy and a deepened sense of Russia being a scapegoat for the West. In the case of the Skripals' poisoning, Britain has embodied the *other* for Russians, whereas the US media, unquestionably relying on the information spread by their closest ally, the United Kingdom, sent a barrage of attacks against Russia, a clearly defined enemy at that point. Ironically, in the US media, Sergei Skripal, a former Russian intelligence colonel and a double agent for Russia and Britain, has been raised to the pedestal of an innocent victim maliciously assassinated (almost) by the evil Russian government. Two years later, Russians may still wonder what happened to that ex-spy, as Russian authorities have been denied any access to him or his daughter since the incident, and they may still firmly believe that Moscow was not behind the attack. American readers, on the other hand, must have all forgotten about the poisoning scandal, as it was something insignificant at that time anyway and did not even happen in their country. Regardless, as the saying goes, there is no smoke without fire, and the smoke from a short-lived fire in the faraway city of Salisbury has reached Americans through their supposedly *unbiased* and *highly trustworthy* media.

10

How the Mind Constructs a Memory of Recent Political Events

In the previous four chapters, we investigated how media—in Russia and the United States—reflected on seven events that happened in the second decade of the 21st century. No matter how ideologically biased and differing in the interpretation of the same event the media in the two countries seem to be, their ultimate goal is to reach the minds of their respective audiences. The question we address in this chapter is how the minds of individuals in those two countries constructed their memory and whether the *producers*' efforts to portray the stories in such a way that they are consumed by people as believable and accurate were successful. Also, we attempt to determine to what extent the stereotypes existent in the sociocognitive constructs of each group contribute to the reconstruction and reenactment of the *other*. Because the two countries represent the proverbial *other* to one another, the construction of memory related to these seven events might reveal the existent bias in the individual minds representing each country.

Due to the extensive analysis of media that is spread over four chapters in this book and in order to remind the reader of the main findings that emerged from the media analysis, I provide a brief recap for each of the events and summarize how it was discussed in Russian and US media before we examine the empirical data on that event gathered through the survey. After we discuss the major findings as they pertain to each of the seven events, I share more general findings on this part of the project.

Although all political events were arranged chronologically in the survey, in order to keep the presentation of the results consistent with how media analysis was discussed in the previous chapters, here we follow the same order, by first looking into a few major events (the takeover of Crimea, the conflict in Eastern Ukraine, and the downing of Malaysia Airlines flight MH17), followed by the conflict in Syria, the 2016 US presidential election, the 2014 Sochi Olympics, and the poisoning of the Skripals.

Reenacting the Enemy. Ludmila Isurin, Oxford University Press. © Oxford University Press 2022.
DOI: 10.1093/oso/9780197605462.003.0011

Table 10.1 How Well Americans Remembered the Events

	Strength of Memory (%)			
Event/Memory Strength	**Very Well**	**Relatively Well**	**Vaguely**	**No Memory**
The takeover of Crimea	5.7	37.5	26	30.8
The conflict in Eastern Ukraine	0.9	12.5	49.1	37.5
The downing of Flight MH17	16.5	40.8	33	9.7
The conflict in Syria	3.9	39.8	46.6	9.7
The 2014 Sochi Olympics	1	25.2	56.3	17.5
The Skripals' case	2.9	28.2	38.8	30.1

As mentioned in Chapter 5, only American respondents were offered the option to self-assess the strength of their memory for a particular event and to skip answering any further questions related to the event if they could not recall it at all (Table 10.1). Moreover, there was a special focus on respondents who retained a very vague memory of the event, as those may exhibit the strongest effect of stereotypes and ideological bias by selecting the responses that would be the most salient with the ideology existent in their group.

Memory of Political Events

Takeover of Crimea

Media Recap

The narratives surrounding the takeover of Crimea drastically differed between the two sets of media. Also, the analysis of numerous reports revealed how those narratives developed over the years, overemphasizing certain aspects of the takeover and deliberately discarding some previously reported facts. Russian media have created a narrative in which the Ukrainian president was removed from his post in violation of constitutional laws, thereby making the decisions of the new government illegitimate. The role of the referendum in which people of Crimea overwhelmingly expressed their free will to join Russia has been a constant reminder to the reader that the takeover was not a forced action on the part of the Russian government. Moreover, the presence of the limited contingent of the Russian military in Crimea during the period of the referendum first was not mentioned by Russian media and only a year later was acknowledged publicly by Vladimir Putin; this fact rarely was repeated in any subsequent reports. Instead, a reminder that the United States orchestrated a change of power in Kiev—a claim supported by audio evidence posted on Twitter and later on YouTube—cemented the message sent to the reader: Americans were involved in installing an illegitimate government in Ukraine and punished Russians with sanctions for letting the free will of the people in Crimea be heard and acted upon.

Conversely, the American press first acknowledged the referendum in Crimea, the fact that military personnel in unmarked uniforms were present in Crimea but were not exhibiting any force or being impolite, and that the event on the ground looked like a "low key invasion." The media later completely changed the narrative by not mentioning the referendum, referring to the takeover as a forceful occupation or invasion (e.g., "Crimea was taken by force"), and, without denying this fact, attacked Russians for posting the evidence that suggested the US State Department's involvement in the change of power in Kiev—unsurprisingly, such evidence never was mentioned later.

The Mind

Most of the American respondents reported either no memory of the takeover (30.8%) or a very vague recollection thereof (26%), with 43.2% still remembering it relatively well or very well (see Table 10.1). Of those who remembered the event, 34.2% had not heard of Crimea prior to 2014. When asked whether Crimea was taken by force, 67% of Americans agreed, whereas almost as many Russians (60%) disagreed. It is noteworthy that 100% of Americans who vaguely remembered the event agreed that Crimea was taken by force. Also, whereas half of Russians (53.4%) admitted that there was a Russian military presence in Crimea, the rest either rejected this fact (12.6%) or resorted to the "I do not know" response (34%). The latter is surprising given Putin's open acknowledgment a year later that a limited contingent of military personnel indeed was on the ground to provide security during the referendum.

When the question of the referendum was brought up, 44.2% of Americans said that they did not know if people in Crimea voted on the referendum, with 39% completely rejecting that fact. Russians, however, were presented with a choice of factors that they believed were the most decisive in justifying the takeover of Crimea, with the referendum, the illegitimacy of the Ukrainian government, the autonomous status of Crimea—main selling points to justify the takeover that were promoted by the Russian government—being among those.[1] Unsurprisingly, 59.6% of the participants found the referendum to be the most important factor that decided the takeover. One of the participants (M: 40)[2] stated that he did not justify the takeover but acknowledged that it was what most people in Crimea wanted. The fact that Crimea always has been Russian in its essence was the second biggest factor, with half the participants selecting that answer (50.5%). Whether such a factor can justify the legality of taking over the peninsula, this trend, nevertheless, shows that the emotional side of the affair—much ignited by the Russian government and the media—played a major role in how Russians think about this event. The next biggest factor, in line with the previous one, was the fact that Crimea predominantly is populated by ethnic Russians (34.3%). The illegitimacy of the new Ukrainian government, despite being much stressed in all media reports after the takeover, did not feature largely in the participants' responses, with only 8% listing it among other factors. Likewise, the autonomous status of Crimea, which was discussed heavily in Russian media only in the first days after the referendum when the Russian government was drafting a bill to add Crimea legally to Russia and the status of the region was one of the key factors used to justify such legality, was listed by only 12% of Russians as a decisive factor.

One of the most sensitive questions in this set concerned the alleged involvement of the US government in the change of power in Kiev. Whereas 35% of Americans and 20.2% of Russians said that they did not know whether the US was involved, there were almost as many Russians (49%) who agreed as Americans (42.9%) who disagreed with this statement, which further supports the opposite views promoted by the media of the two respective countries. To be more precise, the US media did not reflect on the alleged involvement of the US government in the power change apart from a brief comment after Russians posted evidence on Twitter and later YouTube site, which may explain why American respondents were not informed on that particular issue.

[1] Because the question allowed for multiple answers, the cumulative result does not equal 100%.
[2] "M" stands for male and "F" for female, followed by age in years.

Conflict in Eastern Ukraine

Media Recap

The coverage of the civil war in Ukraine has been tightly intertwined with the takeover of Crimea by both countries' media. Russian media framed the conflict within the narrative of the illegitimacy of the Ukrainian government and the legality of adding Crimea to Russia, whereas American media continued their attacks on Russia for "invading" Ukraine and taking Crimea by force. Thus, whatever stories were reported during the years of the conflict, they fit those narrative frames. Russian media also have been reinforcing the theme that Russia is surrounded by Russophobes that are trying to bring NATO bases closer to its borders. Moreover, the overt Russian military involvement in the conflict has been denied by Russian state media and unequivocally not questioned by American media. Also, the latter referred to Ukrainian separatists as "Russian separatists" or simply "Russians," which easily could mislead the American reader. In addition, a rare bipartisan decision by the US government to arm Ukraine with lethal weapons received opposite reactions in the two countries, with the US media supporting it and Russian media, including the liberal press, criticizing this move. As a result of Russia's alleged involvement in the conflict, more sanctions were imposed on Russia—this act, again, receiving opposite reactions in the two sets of media.

These main issues, some overlapping across the two media sets and some unique to only one of the sides, laid the foundation for the questions the two groups of participants were asked.

The Mind

The American group showed a weaker memory for the conflict than that for Crimea, with 37.5% having no memory at all and 49.1% reporting a vague memory. A deliberate confusion of the terms defining separatists in Eastern Ukraine in the US media is reflected in how the American group identified the opposition forces: There were almost as many American participants who chose the correct name of "Russian-speaking separatists" (27.6%) as those who chose a term that is more commonly used in the US media, such as Russian separatists (26.2%). However, almost half the group went for a more biased response by choosing the Russian military (24.6%), militia (15.4%), or simply "Russians" (6.2%). Note that the majority of those who chose the most biased and inaccurate definitions, such as militia (80%), Russians (50%), and the Russian military (62.5%), come from the group of respondents with a vague memory of the conflict.

Russians, on the other hand, seemed not to accept the idea imposed on them by the government that their country is surrounded by Russophobes that are trying to bring NATO closer to its borders. More than half the participants did not agree (55.3%), with the remaining half either agreeing (33%) or providing a more detailed take on the situation (11.7%). The involvement of the Russian military in the conflict, despite the continuous denial of it by the Kremlin, was acknowledged by half the respondents (52.4%), some of whom added that the involvement was not open, whereas others noted that they had first-hand evidence of the involvement. Yet, 27.2% adamantly persisted in their belief that Russians were not present militarily in Eastern Ukraine, with one participant bluntly saying that "the Russian military was not involved in the conflict at all; yet, the American military is more likely to have been involved in this conflict, both overtly and covertly!" (M: 34). When Americans were asked the same question, 77% agreed, with 73% of those with a vague memory providing a positive response as well. As expected, the question of the lethal weapons to be provided by the United States to Ukraine was met with drastically opposite reactions on both sides, with 83.5% of Russians saying the decision was wrong and the majority of Americans supporting it (62.9%). In line with the notorious Russian dark humor, a Russian participant contemplated, "Russians and Ukrainians will be killing each other with this weapon. Hmmm . . ., it might be the right decision, as far as America is concerned" (M: 33).

Approaching the issue of sanctions and how people in both countries view them, we have to remember that we deal here with a very delicate opposition between the "punisher" (US government) and the "punished" (Russia and, more precisely, the Russian people). Although there was the same number of respondents in both groups that considered the sanctions severe (2.9%), the majority of Americans thought of them as insufficient (53.4%), with almost as many Russians viewing them as unnecessary (52.4%). There was only one elaborated response in the US sample: A participant expressed her disappointment by saying that "sometimes sanctions resulted in being more annoying to Americans than Russians: for example, Russians not being able to enter National Labs" (F: 30). More disgruntled voices were heard, however, on the Russian side, from pointing out that the "sanctions were meaningless, as ordinary Russians and not their elite have suffered from them" (M: 29) or that "it is understandable when sanctions are imposed to impact the country;

but they hurt ordinary people who had nothing to do with the actions of their government" (F: 41) to another person further suggesting that "sanctions were an extremely dangerous act that benefitted Putin's power and hurt Russians, all of Europe, and even Ukraine" (F: 65). As one participant pointedly noted, "Sanctions hurt ordinary Russians more than the government and, as a result, the fury of those Russians targets the world that imposed those sanctions on them rather than their own government" (30[3]). The question also caused a few very angry and defensive remarks intended to offend the country that imposed sanctions (i.e., the United States):

> Sanctions make Russia stronger. We are not afraid of America or anyone else. This is RUSSIA! [capitalization in original]. Russia that won a few world wars. Russian spirit cannot be destroyed! Sanctions for us are like a mosquito for an elephant. Beware of us, America, as you will never be as strong as we are!" (M: 34)

Whether the sanctions were an adequate or insufficient measure to punish Russia for its actions in Ukraine, the previous remarks illustrate the growing anti-American feelings among ordinary Russians who carry the burden of the punishment for the actions of their government.

Downing of Malaysia Airlines Flight MH17

Media Recap

The downing of the passenger airliner MH17 in the war zone in Eastern Ukraine in the summer of 2014 and the investigation that followed the crash have been discussed in Russian and American media for almost 5 years. The question of who is responsible for the crash has led to finger-pointing, with the United States—minutes after the crash and not changing the story over the following years—accusing Russia and its support of the rebels, and with Russia denying such accusations by offering new theories of who might be behind the crash. The inconclusive results of the Dutch-led investigation of the crash that identified *what* downed the plane but not *who* pulled the trigger and from *where* the weapon was fired boosted the position taken by Russian media. Conversely, such conclusions, although acknowledged by

[3] The participant chose not to reveal their gender.

some American reporters, did not fit well into the firmly established narrative frame on the US side, where the reporters continued to repeat the original version of the story that flight MH17 was shot by Russian separatists supported by Russia, which often merged into an image of a single villain—Russia and its military.

The Mind

Compared to the takeover of Crimea and the conflict in Eastern Ukraine, the majority of American participants (57.3%) seemed to have a good memory of the MH17 crash (see Table 10.1). Because the coverage of the MH17 crash revolved around the same few issues—as opposite as the presentation of those issues in the two media was—the same three questions were asked of the two groups in relation to this event. First, when asked who shot down the plane, 38.7% of Americans responded that it was downed by the Russian military and 29% responded that it was shot down by Russian separatists. However, 32.3% admitted that it was not clear who was behind the crash. Nobody in that sample chose "Ukrainian government forces" as an answer. On the other hand, the picture on the Russian side is different. The majority of the respondents (54.4%) stated that it was unclear who downed flight MH17, followed by those who blamed the Ukrainian forces (20.4%), separatists (13.6%), or the Russian military (11.6%). Although there were some Russians who agreed with the Americans' conviction that flight MH17 was shot down either by the separatists or by the Russian military, there are 2.7 times more Americans than Russians who believed so (cf.: United States, 67.7%; Russia, 25.2%).

Second, 46.2% of Americans believed that the Dutch-led investigation provided evidence that the separatists downed the plane, with 30% rejecting this statement and the rest stating that they did not know or did not recall. Among Russians, more people said that they did not know (37.9%) than agreed (28%) or disagreed (35%) with the statement. Given the drastically differing coverage of this event in Russian and American media, it may be surprising to see that the two groups did not diverge more in their responses to this question—while still supporting the main lines promoted by their respective media. However, I suggest that individuals' memory of who downed flight MH17—as the first question in this set illustrates—could be constructed by both media and preconceived assumptions existent in the minds of the group members, whereas the concrete conclusions of the investigation might not be remembered well. If the narrative surrounding the crash in both countries has not changed much in the years following the tragedy, the investigation may not change what people have come to believe, whether it produced any evidence or not. After all, apart from the families that lost their loved ones in the horrific crash, who would closely follow the course of the investigation over 5 years?

Finally, an issue much discussed and emphasized in Russian media—and only marginally in American media (as in reports on how Russia tries to whitewash itself by putting blame on Ukraine)—that Ukraine should be held responsible for not closing its airspace over the war zone to commercial flights was addressed. The majority of Russians (54.4%) and just a few Americans (16%) agreed that Ukraine should be held accountable, whereas the reverse was true for those who disagreed (United States, 37.6%; Russia, 12.6%), which again aligns with how this question was presented in the media and how much emphasis was placed on this particular issue.

Civil War in Syria

Media Recap

A recent conflict in Syria that brought much turmoil to the Middle East and resulted in a flood of refugees into Europe also provided a territory for Russian and American military forces to test their power, which set off a new wave of battles in the information war between the two countries. A few key points related to this conflict were identified in the media analysis. First, both sides disputed the real goals of one another's entering the conflict, with Russia claiming that the fight against ISIS—specifically to prevent numerous ISIS fighters who happen to be Russian citizens from returning to Russia and causing more terror on its land—was the major goal, and the United States dismissing that goal and presenting itself as a power that promotes justice and democracy in the region. Second, a few chemical attacks that happened during the war and were blamed immediately by the United States on the Assad regime supported by Russia were presented in Russian media as unverified or most likely staged by the United States and the West to incriminate Assad and, by extension, Russia. Finally, the last moment in the conflict concerns the United States more than Russia: President Trump's decision to withdraw US troops from Syria was much criticized in the US media, which claimed that by leaving Syria, the United States was creating a potential void in the region that quickly would be filled by Russia.

The Mind

Based on the media analysis, only two questions were asked of the Russian group (i.e., the goal of fighting ISIS and who was behind the chemical attacks), whereas an additional question about the US withdrawal from Syria, thereby leaving a void for Russia to claim the region, was addressed to Americans.

Because the Syrian conflict directly involved the United States, it was surprising to find that the number of Americans who had a relatively good or very good memory of the event was lower than that for the flight MH17 crash (43.7% for Syria vs. 57.3% for flight MH17; see Table 10.1).

When asked if the two countries had a shared goal of fighting ISIS in Syria, there were more Americans than Russians who agreed (United States, 47.8%; Russia, 30.1%) and more Russians than Americans who disagreed (Russia, 51.5%; United States, 45.7%). Moreover, many Russians (18.4%) chose to offer their opinion outside of the prefabricated responses, such as "Yes, but each country fought for its influence in the region" (F: 65), "The goal probably was the same but not just related to ISIS; rather it was concerned with economic benefits pursued by each country" (F: 32), or

> The shared goal is the same, at least, on paper. But the sides supported in the conflict are different. As a result, the situation has not stabilized yet. I have provided an extensive report on the acting military units in the region—there are hundreds of those there. (M: 29)

Also, there were a few openly anti-American claims on the Russian side, as far as this question: "Yes, Russia had that goal, while the U.S. aimed at helping ISIS" (F: 26) or

> The U.S. has only one goal—to destroy this world. The U.S. and those who head the UN have only dollars on their minds. It is sad; if they take control over the world it will be destroyed. Russia is the world's soul. If America destroys Russia the entire world will die. (F: 32)

Indeed, it is troubling to read such openly aggressive anti-American sentiments coming from the Russian group, and it is even more troubling to find such sentiments expressed by younger participants, as can be seen from the previous quotes.

The question related to the chemical attacks that took place during the conflict was phrased somewhat differently for the two groups in order to reflect better the dominant narrative in the two respective media. For the American participants, it was worded as follows: "During the Syrian conflict there were a few chemical attacks blamed on the Assad regime and on Russia, by extension. Do you believe there was enough evidence to support such accusations?" On the other hand, Russians were asked who was behind those attacks according to the available evidence. The response variants reflected different theories presented by Russian media (i.e., Assad's regime supported by Russia, rebels, the United States, or the attacks were staged by the West). The results revealed that 46.2% of Americans did believe that there was enough evidence to blame Assad and Russia, with two participants unequivocally blaming Assad but uncertain about Russia's involvement. Russians, on the other hand, believed that the attacks were either staged by the West (26.2%) or the United States was behind them (7.7%). However, there was a relatively large number of people in both samples who said that they did not know who was responsible for the attacks (United States, 44.1%; Russia, 38.8%).

When Americans were asked about the US decision to withdraw from Syria, almost half (49.5%) agreed that such a decision had left a void in the region for Russia to fill, and another 18.4% said that the decision was wrong, with 32.1% also believing that the decision was correct (note: 30% of those were Republicans). Due to a much smaller number of Republicans than Democrats or independents in the US sample, it was difficult to determine whether the opinion on this matter was divided along partisan lines. However, given the media argument that aligned with the predominant opinion in the US group (i.e., the combined survey data show that 67.9% of the respondents did not agree with Trump's decision), we may suggest that, again, the narrative promoted by the US media has constructed a memory—if not a firm opinion—about the Syrian conflict.

2016 US Presidential Election

Media Recap

As discussed in Chapter 8, the investigation of Russia's alleged interference in the US presidential election and Trump's alleged colluding with Russia to win the election have occupied the news for almost 4 years following Trump's victory in the 2016 election. The process was majorly covered in the United States and only made sideline news in Russian media. Clearly, it was more about the United States finding evidence to impeach Trump than it was about Russia defending itself. Thus, the news coverage of this event has turned into the US side presenting accusations and the Russian side denying all of them. After a few Russian citizens linked to internet companies were identified as those who potentially influenced the 2016 election in favor of Trump, no more evidence—especially, any linking the Kremlin to Trump's win—was obtained. The impeachment did not get through the Senate floor and a few months later Trump lost his White House bid, although he never conceded or officially recognized the legitimacy of the election process. Not incidentally, Russians were not blamed this time.

Therefore, based on the media analysis, there were only two questions asked of each group, with an additional question related to the 2020 elections posed just to the American group.

The Mind

Contrary to all other events explored in this project, American respondents were not asked about how well, if at all, they remembered the 2016 US presidential election; rather, they were asked if they followed the news regarding the investigation into Russia's alleged interference. Because this event literally was much closer to home, it was assumed that the majority of people retained some memory thereof. Indeed, 71.8% said that they did follow the news coverage of the investigation closely. Because some evidence of Russian citizens influencing the election on social media was confirmed, it was not surprising that the majority of Americans agreed that there was enough evidence of Russia's interference in the 2016 US election (59.2%), with even more Russians disagreeing with this statement (74.8%). When asked if there was enough evidence to accuse Russia of bringing victory to Donald Trump, there were more Americans who disagreed (45.6%)—as really there was no formal evidence presented during the impeachment process—than those who still agreed (35%). Unsurprisingly, the majority of Russians (78.6%) disagreed with the statement implying that Russia brought victory to Donald Trump in his 2016 presidential bid.

In response to the question of whether Americans were concerned about the potential Russia's meddling in the 2020 US election, regardless of how closely they watched the investigation into the 2016 US elections, 70% responded that they were concerned. Although the representation of the Republican cohort in this sample is not large, we still can see that only 11% of Republicans said that they were concerned. Assuming that Russians do favor Trump over any of his Democratic contenders, this finding is not surprising.

2014 Sochi Olympics

Media Recap

Although the 2014 Sochi Olympics preceded all other events in the analyzed set, it was surprising to see the growing—if not recurring—tension between the two countries. Whereas Russian media praised the success of their athletes and rallied under the flag of a newly resurgent Russia and President Putin, the US media, in anticipation of discrimination against sexual minorities and predicting different organizational mishaps, such as poor security, due to Russian corruption, released a barrage of attacks against Russia. The negative coverage of the Olympics in the US media did not subside at the time of the closing ceremony. Some journalists reluctantly admitted that no discrimination or security breaches were reported, yet they still refrained from acknowledging the achievements of Russian athletes. Conversely, the Russian press, despite reporting on corruption that surrounded the construction of the Olympic complex from both the state and independent media, was overjoyed with the success of the Games. The state media launched a highly patriotic campaign promising Russians even bigger victories in the near future. Also, the narrative that Russia is a nation of winners, albeit surrounded by Western haters, has emerged already in the analysis of media related to the 2014 Olympics.

The Mind

Compared to the other events, the Sochi Olympics were remembered vaguely by most of the US participants (56.3%), with only one person remembering it very well (see Table 10.1). The American group was asked only one question: What characterized the Games? Forced choice answers ranged from the great performance of Russian athletes to discrimination against sexual minorities (note: this question allowed for more than one answer). The results revealed that all negative aspects presumably characterizing the Sochi Olympics, although not necessarily supported even by the most biased reports in the US media, received the biggest number of responses. What is even more telling is that people with a vague memory of the event represented the majority in choosing those responses. To illustrate, 48.1% (76.9% of those had a vague memory) responded corruption, 34.6% (60.7% of those had a vague memory) responded discrimination against sexual minorities, 28.4% (69.6% of those had a vague memory) responded poor security, and 12.3% (60% of those had a vague memory) responded the poor performance of Russian athletes. Although corruption rightly was recognized by both sets of media, Russian and American, all other answers showed a highly biased memory of the event in the minds of the American sample. Neither discrimination against sexual minorities nor poor security was registered during the Olympics by either media side.

In the Russian sample, apart from 12.6% of respondents who chose to add their own answers such as the super-fast construction of the Olympic complex, great long-term investments in the infrastructure of the region, or the high level of organization of the event, the rest of the answers presented a picture opposite from that registered in the American group. Russians acknowledged the high level of security provided at the Games (41.1%) and the great performance of Russian athletes (40%), with a few respondents mentioning also a doping scandal that clearly overshadowed the achievements of Russians in the 2014 Winter Olympics soon after the Games concluded. A lack of discrimination against sexual minorities during the Olympics was not high on the agenda of Russian media, neither before nor after the event; thus, it is not surprising that only 20% of Russians chose this response as one of the characteristic features of the Sochi Olympics. What brings the Russian memory of the Sochi Olympics closer to what Americans remember is that corruption, indeed, surrounded the Games (i.e., in the Russian case, corruption in the construction of the Olympic complex is most likely what they think about and what was reported in their media): 42.2% of Russians (cf.: 48.1% in the US sample) chose that response. Now, if we remember that most of the Russian participants were on the liberal side of the political spectrum and did not vote for Putin in the last presidential election (see Chapter 5), it is not surprising that they are rather critical of corruption in the country and their government. Yet, by acknowledging corruption while still praising the great performance of the Russian athletes and the high level of security provided at the Games—with the latter representing an undeniable fact reported by both sets of media—they are less biased than the American group in remembering the event. However, we can provide a counterargument here that the 2014 Sochi Olympics took place in Russia, thereby making Russians feel more defensive, if not entirely objective, about the event and presenting another venue for Americans to discredit Russians as a long-term *other*.

Because the 2014 Sochi Olympics preceded all other events selected for the analysis in this project and because Russian media identified this event as a precursor of much bigger new victories for Russia, the Russian group was asked two more questions. When asked if they believed that the 2014 Sochi Olympics were a great success for Russian athletes, most participants agreed (52.4%). When presented with the question of whether the Olympics contributed to the rise of Russian patriotism, even more participants agreed (65%), with some having rather conflicting feelings (13.6%). As it was expressed by one Russian,

> I would say the answer is yes rather than no. This is just the country where we live. Personally, I think we still need such events to take place in order to establish better relationships between countries, rather than using such events as a tool in the manipulation of attitudes among people in particular countries. (M: 30)

Given the origin of the project and the survey (i.e., the United States), there is no doubt what the individual meant by "particular countries."

The Skripals' Poisoning

Media Recap

The Skripals' case concludes the series of political events selected for the analysis in this book. The attempted assassination of the former Russian spy Sergei Skripal and his daughter took place in the United Kingdom. Most of the American reports relying on the information in British media immediately accused Moscow in the poisoning. If we think about all the events that preceded the 2018 assassination scandal—as a matter of fact, six of those already have been discussed in this chapter—it is clear that the information war between the United States and Russia was raging in full swing at that time. Russia, on the other hand, acted similarly to how it responded to the accusations of responsibility for the flight MH17 crash—first, denying all accusations; then, providing their own theories; and finally, turning defense into offense. Because Russia was not allowed to have any access to the material evidence or meet with the Skripals, who remained Russian citizens, its denial of involvement could not be substantiated by any evidence. The major point in this event was the nature of the nerve agent used in the attempted assassination. Although the reputable international labs could identify only the nature of the agent, allegedly linking it to a family of so-called "Novichok" agents originally developed and produced in the Soviet Union, they could not point with any certainty to the place where it was manufactured (note: the conclusion was rather similar to how the investigation into the downing of flight MH17 could not identify *who* shot the plane or from *where*). However, the narrative frame in which this fact was embedded in the US media clearly portrayed the Kremlin as the major assassin. Russia continued denying its involvement and, in turn, mocked the epistemic language, such as the notorious "highly likely," that was abundant in the US reports due to numerous blank spots in the ongoing investigation.

The Mind

Despite being a much more recent event compared to the six others, 30.1% of Americans did not remember it at all and 38.8% had a vague memory, with the rest having a relatively good (28.2%) or very good (2.9%) memory (see Table 10.1).

There were only two questions asked of the two groups: whether the Kremlin was behind the assassination attack and whether it has been proven that the nerve agent was produced by the Russian government. Regarding the first question, the majority of Americans (51.4%) believed that "it was clear from the start"—this is exactly how the question was worded—that the Kremlin was behind the attack (40% of those having a vague memory of the event), with 34.7% stating that they did not know and 13.9% stating no. There were as many Russians who refrained from giving an assertive answer to the question as those who agreed (36.9% each), and the remaining 26.2% rejected the Kremlin's involvement. When the question of the nerve agent was posed, there were as many Russians (45.6%) as Americans (47.2%) who said that they did not know whether the agent was produced by the Russian government. However, there were twice as many Americans (52.8%) as Russians (28.2%) who agreed, with almost half of those Americans (47.4%) having a vague memory of the attack. Also, although there were no participants in the US sample who disagreed with this statement, 26.2% of Russians did not believe that the nerve agent was produced by state-owned labs. As can be seen, Americans have a much stronger opinion about the role of the Russian government in the attempted assassination, whereas Russians are split in their blame assignment and have reservations about the Kremlin's involvement in the attack. In other words, there was much more assertiveness on the US side that the Kremlin was involved in the attack and that the nerve agent was produced by the Russian government than there was in the Russian sample. This aligns with the storyline presented by the US media on this event. However, based on the fact that there were many people who hardly remembered the attack and still produced such assertive responses, it can be suggested that the opinion of those people could have been formed by the firmly established stereotypes in the mindset of the US group. Regarding the Russian group, which according to the demographic data is being critical of their own government, their responses can be interpreted as partly aligning with the reports presented both by the state and by independent media, where multiple unknowns rightly were acknowledged, and perhaps, partly more critical of the evidence available in the investigation of the Skripals' poisoning. However, another possible interpretation could be that Russia, once again, was put on the defensive in this event, and its citizens, when being surveyed by an American researcher who happens to be a former citizen, could feel a need to be more defensive of their homeland, no matter how much they may criticize their government among themselves. However, this speculation equally can apply to the interpretation of all other responses in the Russian sample, which further indicates the very thin line that a researcher, as a former group member now representing the *other* to her former group, needs to walk when approaching her former "compatriots."

General Issues

Problems of Leadership

Because political events often are associated with who at the time of the happening was the leader of the country, a few general questions were asked of each group. Americans were asked who they think handled the investigated events better, and not surprisingly, 62% acknowledged Barack Obama, 22% Donald Trump, and yet another 16% said neither. Although the responses on this question fell along partisan lines (for the political affiliations of the respondents, see Chapter 5), I suggest that the main portion of the events discussed in this chapter happened under Obama's watch, thereby granting more power to his leadership in the current assessment. However, when the American respondents were asked a direct question, whether the US media turned Russia into a weapon against Donald Trump, 44.1% of the participants agreed, with almost half of those reporting that they voted for Trump in the 2016 election (48.8%).

Because the Russian President, Vladimir Putin, has been the actual or de facto president since 2000, the Russian participants were asked if they considered him a strong leader in the handling of the political affairs investigated in this book. More than half the sample (67%) agreed, and—what is more telling—65.6% of those did not vote for Putin in the last presidential election. Probably the best explanation of this dichotomy can be found in the words of a young Russian participant:

> The President is in charge of issues related to wars and foreign affairs, whereas the Parliament deals with domestic issues. So, I would not blame Putin much for the internal problems in Russia. Yet, I am partly grateful to him for making other countries respect and even fear Russia. (F: 23)

This explanation, along with the discernible support for Putin's handling of the previously discussed political events, may suggest that the participants' predominant choice not to vote for Putin in the last presidential election was not based on how he has handled foreign affairs in the past decade.

Role of Media

When both groups were asked the same question, whether the media played a major role in how one country perceives another (i.e., how Russians view Americans and how Americans view Russians), the overwhelming majority of participants in both groups agreed (United States, 85.4%; Russia, 90%), with some on the American side claiming that "Americans do not think of Russia as much as they used to" (M: 37) or pointedly asking, "How else would Americans perceive Russia?" (M: 59), with the latter, indeed, signifying the role of media in the creation of stereotypes and opinions about the *other*. Conversely, a few participants in the Russian sample offered their own take on the role of media, too, ranging from those attacking Russian media (e.g., "It is hard to assess the role of media. Russian propaganda is at the level of Goebbels,[4] not less," M: 29) to those attacking the US media ("I do not trust

[4] Joseph Goebbels was a German Nazi politician and Reich Minister of Propaganda of Nazi Germany.

the U.S. sellout media," F: 26), with some, however, taking a middle ground ("Like many other people I have known for quite a while what America and the rest of the West are about, but the same partly can be said about Russia too. It's all about power of money, power of wealth, with the rest of the people keeping silent," M: 34).

In light of the repetitive motif in Russian state media that the West tends to accuse Russia of wrongdoing, even before any evidence is found, the Russian group was asked if they agreed with such a statement. Most of the participants (69.9%) agreed, some disagreed (20.4%), and the rest offered their own opinion. As one young Russian said,

> Partly yes, I agree. First, because of Russia's behavior in recent decades: It begins to evade even before any attempts to accuse it are made. Second, because the intelligence services and armies of other countries also need a military budget. And the image of a "strong and dangerous enemy" is an excellent justification for any expenditure. (M: 29)

A few others seconded this opinion by saying that "in the West—as well as in the East—there are powers that sometimes accuse others without having any strong evidence" (M: 36) or that "journalists—and not only from the state media—say that America makes unsubstantiated accusations" (M: 35).

The most interesting and important question for the purpose of this investigation was about the trustworthiness of each respective media—Russian and American—in the coverage of world affairs. In the US group, most of the participants said that US media are not trustworthy (52.4%), with 30% disagreeing and the rest providing their own opinion that largely boiled down to specific outlets that are less trustworthy than others (i.e., there was a clear partisan line here, with liberals pointing to Fox News as the most untrustworthy channel) or noting that world affairs are not as widely covered as local news or that independent outlets are less biased than the state propaganda ones, with one participant bluntly saying that "the U.S. media are not entirely trustworthy but [are] better than Russian media" (M: 42). The limited background information on the participant (e.g., bachelor's degree, composer) does not allow us to know how much access he has to Russian media to make his best educated guess about it without relying mainly on what the US media report. On the Russian side, there were even more people (79.6%) who did not trust media, and a few others clearly indicated that they did not trust the official state media. As one participant noted, "state-owned—no, not at all. Relatively free online media—yes. But, again, through the prism of constant pressure on them from the authorities" (M: 29).

"Putin's Russia"

When Americans were asked whether they agreed with the media's reference to contemporary Russia as "Putin's Russia," the majority (61.2%) responded positively, and a shared argument was that Putin is a dictator who controls the government and his people. Also, the repetitive references to his KGB past as well as to communism and the USSR that Putin seems to represent were identified in those responses. However, there were quite a few people who argued against such sweeping overgeneralization and ideologically biased labeling of the entire country. As one participant noted,

> It is a woefully oversimplified term that merely attempts to paint modern Russia as a simple dictatorship, with no consideration of how much the nation has changed since the fall of the USSR. It makes no allowance for the complexity of the Russian governmental and political system. (M: 27)

Another referred to the definition as "intentionally biased (and probably unhelpful)" (M: 33). In line with the main argument presented in this book, one participant called such a definition a "distracting qualifier used to designate Russia as OTHER [capitalization in original]" (M: 40), and another added that Putin "is perceived as dominant through the media's eyes which influences people's perception" (F: 62). Regardless of whether the Americans in this sample agreed or disagreed with the stereotyping of Russia as Putin's Russia, the immediate reaction registered in the data was to think of the present America as Trump's America. "I would be upset if America was described as Trump's America," said one participant (F: 19), with another adding that " 'Putin's Russia' fits the same definition as 'Trump's America,' people use it to distinguish the actions of the government from the attitudes of the people" (M: 25).

Surprisingly—and quite contrary to my expectations—even more Russians than Americans found the definition "Putin's Russia" accurate (71.3%). Yet, their reasoning was different. Some admitted that Putin has been in power for 20 years, thereby rendering this reference logical. As a young Russian commented, "I was born and grew up under Putin's rule. We are Putin's children; thus, it is not surprising that Russia is called this. I agree with this" (F: 19). I reiterate, however, that most of the participants in the Russian group did not vote for Putin in the last presidential election (see Chapter 5) and arguably do not favor his leadership. This resulted in opposite explanations of why the definition is correct. Those who clearly supported Putin referred to him as "a strong leader that brought Russia up from its knees" (M: 70)—a quite common argument made by Putin's supporters in Russia—as "a strong and wise leader" (F: 38), and even as "the best leader in the entire Russian history" (M: 72). The opponents bitterly agreed with the definition and provided their take on it: "They are right," said one person,

> There is totalitarianism in Russia. That is, all aspects of the country's life are permeated with Putinism. Nevertheless, one must be careful, since Putinism is leaving with generations and its ideological component is gradually beginning to be rejected by the citizens of the country. (M: 39)

Another respondent added that the current Russia is "a country where all issues are decided by one person with a small group of confidants under the silent consent of citizens" (M: 35), with yet another saying that "Russia has signs of an authoritarian state with a personality cult among a large percentage of the country's population" (M: 28). An even more negative attitude to the current situation in Russia can be seen in a very passionate remark made by a young Russian: "Absolutely right. What the Putin regime has done, it has led to the creation of persistent stereotypes about the population—not vodka and balalaika, but poor scum, absolutely brain-washed scum ("hurray-patriots"), chauvinistic scum, and so on. This is Putin's Russia" (M: 29). It is noteworthy that contrary to an argument among Americans that a definition, such as Putin's Russia, does not encompass Russia's rich culture and its people, some Russians provided a different perception by stressing a clear line separating the government from the people, thereby considering such a definition accurate:

> The definition separates Russian citizens as a whole from the government that has been in place for way too long. It allows one to treat the current leader negatively and contemptuously, and at the same time be respectful towards the people. (F: 30)

However, there were people who felt sad and ashamed to hear that their country is labeled like this in the West: "In the Russian Federation, Putin does not have the support of the absolute majority of the population, so the term 'Putin's Russia' offends Putin's opponents inside the Russian Federation" (M: 43). Similar to responses in the American group, a comparison with a likely definition of America as "Trump's America" was invoked by a few Russians, too:

> "Russia is a people's country, like any other. Of course, now Putin is in power, but this does not mean that we have "Putin's Russia." We are not saying that the United States is "Trump's America." There is simply Russia and there is America with their multinational peoples. (F: 25)

As can be seen, an open-ended question on the group's perception of the definition widely used in the West, "Putin's Russia," has received more positive than negative responses among both Russians and Americans, yet a more in-depth look into those responses has revealed a clear difference in how the participants in the two groups view such a definition. Whereas the American support of such a label reflects how the US media present contemporary Russia, with all the long-lasting stereotypes, such as the KGB, communism, a dictator, and the USSR, Russians are split in their opinions. While agreeing with the accuracy of such a definition, they either marched under the flag raised by Putin or bitterly expressed their understanding of why the West labels them like this and showed their clear opposition to the current political situation in their country.

Identifying the *Other*

The issue of the *other* in this set of the survey questions was approached from a few different angles. First, one of the questions in the survey tapped into what the participants consider first when they think about the current relationship between the two countries, with the choice of answers being government or people. As expected, Americans mostly blamed the Russian government (54.4%) or Putin (41.7%), with just a few thinking of Russian people in general (3.9%). This shows a clear trend to separate the actions of the government from the entire nation and not to hold ordinary Russians accountable for the worsened political climate surrounding the relationship between the two countries. Conversely, 23% of Russians put the blame on the

American people (cf.: only 3.9% of Americans blame the Russian people), with the majority, however, blaming the American government (77%).

Second, they were asked a direct question, what country they perceived as the biggest threat at the present time, with the possibility of choosing more than one answer. China was viewed as the biggest threat by the overwhelming majority of Americans (86.6%), followed by Russia (50.5%), Iran (23.7%), and North Korea (7.2%). A few (3.1%) reported that the United States itself was a threat to the nation, with one participant identifying a far-left movement within the United States as the biggest threat. As one American elaborated,

> This depends on how threat is defined. In my opinion, China will supersede the U.S. as the next dominant world power. However, the citizens of the U.S. and their elected representatives are the biggest threat to the U.S. way of life. (M: 41)

On the other hand, when Russians were approached with the same question, the United States was chosen by more people (42.9%) than any other country, yet the number is still lower than that of Americans thinking of Russia as the biggest threat (cf.: 50.5%). China was perceived as the second biggest threat (33.7%), and there were five times more Russians than Americans who thought that their own country and its government represented the biggest destructive force (15.3% of Russians compared to 3.1% of Americans).

Finally, in order to determine to what extent the Cold War stereotypes precipitated the current perceptions of one another, a question of whether people in each country still perceived the other as an enemy after the collapse of the Soviet Union in 1991 was asked. Unfortunately, neither sample had many people who were adults during the Cold War, with the American group having twice as many as the Russian group (United States, 30.1%; Russia, 15.5%). Regardless of the small numbers, there were more Americans than Russians who trusted their respective media at that time (United States, 54.8%; Russia, 37.5%) and who still considered one another as an enemy after the collapse of the USSR (United States, 42%; Russia,12.5%). This may suggest that the trust or distrust of the media during the Cold War impacted how the citizens in the two respective countries perceived one another after the Cold War ended.[5]

[5] As anecdotal evidence, in the mid-1990s on my visit to Russia, a few people asked me what Americans said and thought about Russia, showing much concern for how their country was perceived after the collapse of the USSR; the attitude in Russia drastically has changed in the 2000s.

Summary

Through the in-depth analysis of media reports, both in the United States and in Russia, we have tried to identify distinctive trends—as biased as most of them were—of how the seven political events selected for the analysis were framed in order to become more accessible and believable when they were delivered to the intended audiences. In this chapter, we examined how the individual minds in both countries processed and consumed the information, thereby constructing shared memories. After all, where else would those minds get such information if not from the media outlets in their own country?

Here, I start with one of the findings reported in this chapter: Do people trust their media in the coverage of world affairs? Any scholar working on media bias and having read the burgeoning literature on mind manipulation through the deliberate misrepresentation of information related to political events may rejoice at learning that neither Americans nor Russians find their media trustworthy. However, this finding may violate two main assumptions: (1) American readers are exposed to the most democratic free media in the world, which they unequivocally should trust; and (2) Russian readers are brainwashed by their authoritarian state-controlled media—as was pointed out in at least one American report (Gregory, 2017).

Having established this reference point, that neither group trusts their media, it was intriguing to look at the memory that the individual minds, nevertheless, formed as far as the seven political events selected for this study. Moreover, I have attempted to tap deeper into such memory construction by looking specifically into the minds of those people who retained a very vague remembrance of an event. Indeed, if traces of memory for a particular event are weak, the reconstructed memory may rely heavily on the stereotypes and sociocognitive frames existent in the group.

The analysis across all seven events has demonstrated that most of the memories constructed by individual minds align with how media in the two respective countries have framed narratives surrounding each of those events. To illustrate, both Russians and Americans provided opposite reactions to the takeover of Crimea in 2014: Americans believed that Crimea was taken by force, whereas Russians disagreed with this statement and provided a referendum that showed the free will of the people in Crimea as the main justification for the takeover. Moreover, all participants in the US sample, who agreed that Crimea was taken by force, only vaguely remembered the event. Conversely, the referendum that disappeared from American reports soon after it took place was not remembered by most Americans. Similarly, Americans rejected the fact that the US government was involved in the change of power in Kiev, a fact that appeared only briefly in US media coverage, contrary to greater focus on such evidence in the Russian press, which resulted in more Russians believing in US involvement. Also, the deliberate confusion with the terms defining the opposition forces in Eastern Ukraine, as they loosely varied in the US media, featured into how Americans tended to label them, with people who only vaguely remembered the conflict providing the most biased definitions, such as the Russian military, militia, or simply Russians. The alignment of the constructed memories with how the conflict was discussed in the media can be seen further in the opposite reactions that Russian and Americans expressed toward the US bipartisan decision to send lethal weapons to Ukraine. Unsurprisingly, the attitude to sanctions supported the line found in media, too; although here, as I said, we have to be careful in the interpretation of the result because Russian participants carry the burden of sanctions in their daily lives, whereas Americans want to see the evil punished but not at their own expense. The downing of flight MH17, as expected, was blamed by the majority of Americans on Russian separatists or the Russian military, whereas the Russian participants constructed a different memory, that the investigation did not point to any party responsible for the firing of the missile—a fact repeatedly discussed by Russian media and not as widely by US media. The same alignment with media ideology was found in the analysis of responses related to the alleged Russian interference in the 2016 US presidential election, with Americans claiming Russia's interference in the election but denying any evidence of Trump's colluding with Russians (exactly as it was reported in the US media) and Russians denying either of those alleged involvements, again perfectly aligning with how Russian media covered the investigation.

The most biased memories constructed by the American group came from the 2014 Sochi Olympics, where the participants with a vague memory of the Games produced the most negative and incorrect facts attributed to the event—facts not even reported by American journalists. Similar to the inconclusive results of the investigation into the MH17 crash, the investigation of the attempted assassination of the Skripals could not directly point a finger at the Kremlin, which did not prevent the US media from the creation of a narrative in which from the beginning Moscow was accused of the poisoning. The latter permeated into the minds of the Americans in this sample, with half of those having only a vague memory of the event. At the same time, Russians agreed that most of the time the West, and the United States in particular, tries to accuse Russia before any evidence even is found, which partly is supported by how Russian media promotes this narrative and partly by how, indeed, Russia is being accused by the West minutes after an event with multiple unknowns is reported.

Nevertheless, we cannot say that the media have a 100% effect on how individual minds construct memories of recent political events. There were a few instances in which the participants' responses did not line up with the stories presented to them by the media. It is noteworthy that most, if not all, of such instances were registered in the Russian group. Russians did not agree with the persistent denial by their state media that the Russian military has not been involved in the ongoing civil war in Eastern Ukraine or with the repetitive narrative that their country is surrounded by Russophobes that are trying to bring NATO bases to the Russian border. Also, despite the official Russian media stressing that the goal of Russia's entering the Syrian conflict was to fight the homegrown ISIS fighters on Syrian soil, Russian participants in this sample did not agree with this statement.

How can we explain such a dichotomy, that both Russians and Americans constructed most of their memories of recent political events along the ideological lines presented to them by the media of the two respective countries and, at the same time, only Russians still disputed some of those ideologies? If we remember that the Russian sample in this study is represented mostly by anti-Putin (i.e., not voting for Putin) people and that many of those participants clearly indicated that they trust independent media more than the state media, I suggest that the general distrust of media, not just in terms of pure numbers, as we could see in this chapter, among Russians is much higher than it is among Americans, who, in this study, also happened to be more on the liberal end of the political spectrum. Yet, if both samples represent liberals, one may ask a legitimate question: Why would Americans, while claiming that their media are not trustworthy, still construct memories along the narrative lines presented to them by media, without questioning the accuracy of the delivered information? I suggest two separate scenarios. First, American liberals, while claiming their distrust of media, still realize that most of the American media outlets, including the conservative Fox News that recently has been criticized even by conservatives, are liberal. Second, in the absence of firsthand exposure to Russia or anything Russian, American participants in this group could have relied on the Cold War stereotypes still persistent in the American psyche: There were more Americans than Russians who believed that Russia remained an enemy after the collapse of the Soviet Union. The support for the previous suggestion comes from the individuals who had a very vague memory of an event and who still produced the most biased responses.

As for Russians, their liberal stance extends not just to the distrust of their media but to the distrust of their government in general. Moreover, their open disgruntlement about the sanctions imposed on the Russian people for the actions of their government and about the United States' position on certain issues that ordinary Russians oppose (e.g., the United States being behind a change of power in Kiev or the immediate accusations of Russia in the MH17 crash) could contribute to a more analytical, if not defensive, take on the interpretation of media reports. Also, if we remember that there were more Russians than Americans who perceived the *other* as a threat, I suggest that while being critical of their own government but not fully accepting the interpretations presented by media—whether they be state controlled or independent—Russians may be more sensitive to the issues related to the politics of their country, especially when approached by a researcher whom they no longer view as part of their group, thereby feeling a need to defend their country against the *other*, which in this case, ironically, is represented by the author of this book.

To conclude, most of the findings in this part of the study did provide support for how the ideological, often biased, narratives formed by media contribute to the construction of shared memories in individual minds, despite those minds being consciously aware that their media are not trustworthy. However, the process of memory construction by individual minds does not rely entirely on the information delivered by media. Often, in the absence of a clear memory of the event, the mind falls back on the preexistent stereotypes about the *other* or remains skeptical of the information found in the news due to the general distrust of the leadership in the country and, by extension, media.

PART III

REENACTING THE ENEMY IN MEDIA AND IN THE MIND

11
Memory, Media, and the Mind
Revisiting the Framework

When we think about a relatively brief period in history, such as 5 years in the second decade of the 21st century, it may sound bizarre that the relationship between two major countries in the world would come to a dramatically volatile and seemingly irreconcilable point, as happened between the United States and Russia. I am not a political scientist nor a historian who can present an analysis of which country began the conflict—in my view, this would be like a children's finger-pointing game: "It was him who started the fight, not me." To avoid the blame assignment that already is abundant among politicians and, by extension, journalists, and stick strictly to how media, as the major messenger of all ongoing political events, deliver the information to the intended audiences, thereby igniting and reigniting the fire of hatred, mistrust, and (mis)representation of the *other*, we will attempt to bring together the major findings on how the information was presented, repeated, and often distorted by the news coverage and how ultimately it was consumed by individual minds.

Reenactment of the *Other* in Media

In light of the media analysis presented in Chapters 6–9, we can reconceptualize the proposed framework (see Figures 4.1 and 4.2) by bringing the reenactment of the *other* into primary focus while preserving the original components of the framework. Such reconceptualization of the framework is illustrated schematically in Figure 11.1.

Any presentation of an ongoing political event should fit some script that makes the new information believable and easily accessible to the reader. The more familiar the script is to the viewer/reader, the better new information will be accepted as believable regardless of how inaccurate it might be. This is known as typification in news making, which relies on media templates, such

Reenacting the Enemy. Ludmila Isurin, Oxford University Press. © Oxford University Press 2022.
DOI: 10.1093/oso/9780197605462.003.0012

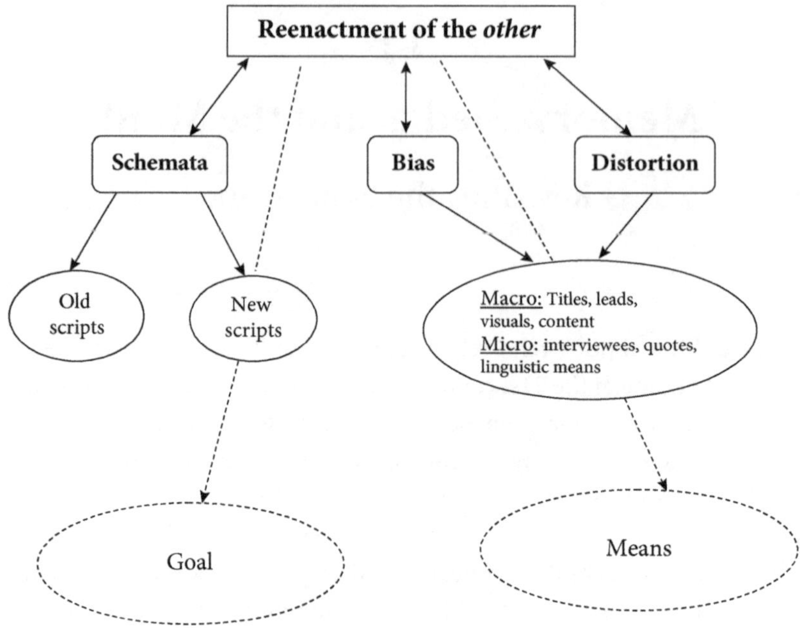

Figure 11.1 Reenactment of the *other* in media.

as frames, headlines, images, and linguistic means, through which all news events are contextualized. Invoking old schemata often entails bringing back an old enemy that is easy to stereotype. As discussed in Chapter 2, the reenactment of the old *other*, already familiar to the reader, makes the news report more publishable than any piece of news that covers an event involving a new *other*, even one perceived as very inferior to the values of the main group. In other words, the evoked schemata will serve the goal of bringing back an existent stereotyped image of the *other* as well as strengthening it. Yet, any new piece of information related to the old foe will create a new script within which subsequent developments may be contextualized. Thus, we can conceptualize schemata as the combination of old and new scripts, both aiming at delivering a clear message of what the reader knows already about an old enemy and what new pieces of information easily can be perceived as believable. Moreover, any new script with time will either be incorporated into the general, much bigger schema related to a particular group as well as a set of events involving that group or may be discarded as insignificant and not useful for any future references.

On the other hand, the reenactment of the *other* would not be possible without some sort of bias in depicting the event, if not distorting the facts related to it. The mechanism of bias operates both at the macro level and at the micro level of the text, bringing titles, leads, visuals, and the content (macro level) as well as the subjective choice of eyewitnesses/interviewees, quotes, and linguistic means (micro level) into the major focus of the news analysis undertaken in this project.

Although the roles of the schemata, bias, and distortion in the reenactment of the *other* were conceptualized within the original framework developed at the onset of the current study, a new component emerged through the process of the media analysis. The question of why the *other* is brought back into the picture seems not to find a straightforward answer. The media analysis suggested that the re-creation of the *other* can be a goal on its own—and here one can find all the textbook rules that apply to such a case—and it also can serve as a means of revealing problems within the group medium, such as a conflict between the media providers and the group's leadership that is embodied by one person, as we have seen in the media analysis of the late stages of the Syrian conflict and of the 2016 US presidential election.

Next, we examine separately each of the components related to the reconceptualized framework based on the results of the media analysis in the previous four chapters. Then, we discuss how the mind reenacts the *other*, after which we return to the main framework within which we discuss the complexity of the mind and media interconnection in the construction of collective memories related to recent political events.

Schemata in Reenactment of the *Other*

Chronologically, the 2014 Winter Olympic Games were the first in the series of events central to this book. The Sochi Games took place a month before the takeover of Crimea, 5 months prior to the downing of Malaysia Airlines flight MH17, and 2 years before the 2016 US presidential election. Therefore, this was the only event that was contextualized within some old scripts, often going back to the Cold War era, by the US media. Moreover, this event did not seep into the framing of any of the events that happened in the next 4 years. On the American side, the humiliating losses that Russia endured in the previous 2010 Olympics, the reminder of the glorious victory of the American hockey team against the Soviet team in 1980 ("miracle on ice," as it lives on in American collective memory), and Russian despotic leaders such as Stalin are used as scripts to depict the old enemy that is reemerging in a new skin, with its "increasingly belligerent stance toward the United States" that could bring "a tragedy to the world" (Berman, 2014). Conversely, Russian media working on the wave of rising patriotism that was boosted by the success of the Olympics evoked scripts from Russia's historic past, such as World War II and the Soviets' launch of the first man in space, that are directed inwards, as well as scripts portraying Russia as a nation surrounded by "Russia's haters" (Bukker, 2014a), which can be viewed as scripts directed outward, toward the West and the United States in particular. However, the dichotomy of these two types of scripts—inward versus outward—should be perceived as the whole, where the internal boost of nationalism and patriotism in a group inevitably rely on the perceived threat of another group, thereby making the headline "Russia's Victory at the Games Is Only the Beginning" a promise of new scripts in the making for the Russian nation as well as a warning to Russia's "haters."

The biggest event that became a turning point in the relationship between Russia and the United States was the takeover of the Crimean Peninsula. In the weeks before the takeover, the United States clearly defined its stance on Ukraine as a country trying to get out of Russia's grip and join the West, thereby providing its full support to the interim government without questioning the legitimacy of such a sudden change of power in the first place. Nevertheless, besides portraying Putin as a villain and drawing sympathy toward Ukraine, the early US reports, prior to the takeover and immediately following it, were in an apparent search for the right script to contextualize what happened as a surprisingly quick and bloodless act of redrawing international borders by Russia. Although initially American reporters acknowledged Russia's claims of NATO's expansion to its borders and the accusation of less than stellar US acts in toppling Libya's government as well as its war in Kosovo, such claims soon were dropped from US media coverage. Instead, the takeover has established a new storyline and a new script that later was referred to as Russian annexation, intervention, invasion, and occupation. What is noteworthy here is that the referendum in Crimea that expressed the "free will of the people" first was acknowledged, then labeled as a "sham," and later completely taken out of the script. The repetitive references to the takeover of Crimea with the use of the previously mentioned descriptive nouns, the deliberate omission of any mention of the referendum, and the overly exaggerated emphasis on the presence of the limited military contingent on the ground—initially recognized as nonthreatening and peaceful and having no identifiable military insignia—established a new frame within which all subsequent events in the next few years would be contextualized. The narrative of Putin seizing Crimea by force—as distorted as the reference to the force is—has become very familiar to the American reader. Moreover, starting with the takeover of Crimea, one can observe a clear tendency in the US media to be on the offensive and blame Russia outright for whatever happened, even before evidence was obtained and facts were verified; Russian media, on the contrary, took the defensive position by firing back at the United States for what they perceived as false accusations, which finally would turn their defense into offense (note: there is a Russian saying, "the best defense is offense").

Russia, alternatively, has created its own discourse on Crimea in which the free will of the Crimean people to join Russia, the ultra-right nationalist groups that brought the turnover of power in Kiev and threatened ethnic Russians in Crimea, the illegitimacy of the new Ukrainian government, as well as the legality of the reunification process were emphasized, whereas the presence of any Russian military on the ground first outrightly was denied and then reluctantly admitted by Putin as an insignificant factor. Having justified the takeover of Crimea in such terms—the narrative that would be repeated all over again when discussing other political events in those years—Russian media have established a portrait of the United States as the notorious *other* that orchestrated the overturning of the Ukrainian government. Using the undeniable facts of such overt interference in the foreign affairs of another state—the facts initially not denied by the US media but quickly dismissed as poorly fitting into the established discourse—and stressing the obvious burden of unjust economic sanctions imposed on Russia as the result of the takeover, Russian media created a new script within which the West and the United States, in particular, were discussed. The image of Russia as a heroic savior of the Crimean people from the danger of ultra-right/"fascist" militant forces and the image of the United States as a puppet master behind the coup in Kiev have entered a new script, deviations from which did not happen in the next few years.

The takeover of Crimea in 2014 created two opposite templates that were used by both media sides for the next few events. The conflict in Eastern Ukraine that came out of the same political unrest—a change of power in Kiev—immediately was incorporated into Crimea's script that by then the

US media firmly had presented as land-grabbing by Putin or a Russian military invasion of Crimea. As the civil war between the separatists and the Ukrainian government forces raged, US reporters had no doubt of a Russian military presence, although this was denied by Russia. The "*widely thought*" Russian military presence was *widely* reported; peaceful demonstrations in a few cities were referred to as crowds calling for their land to be *invaded* by Moscow; and the accurate reference to separatists as "Russian-speaking" soon and most likely deliberately was replaced by the simple, although highly misleading, modifier "Russian." The new information that Russians were fighting the Ukrainian government forces perfectly fit the earlier established script of the Russian military seizing Crimea. Later, the US Senate's decision to arm Ukraine with lethal weapons in order not to let Vladimir Putin get away with invading another sovereign country was an easy sell to the American audience, so was the prospect of adding Russia to the list of terrorism sponsoring states that was enthusiastically blown out of proportion by the US media. As can be seen, Crimea's script has been bolstered tremendously by another political event in the region, a civil war in Ukraine, which has been woven into a narrative of Russia as a military aggressor—a Cold War image extremely familiar and highly believable to the targeted American audience.

Conversely, Russian media have capitalized on the same repetitive theme of the illegitimacy of the Ukrainian government and the legality of Russian actions in Crimea and presented the Kremlin's denial of any Russian military involvement in the conflict. Instead, the emphasis on the increased sanctions imposed on Russia by the West and the United States, first of all, has helped the media bolster the image of the United States as an unjust punisher relentlessly going after Russia for meeting the "free will of the people" in Crimea. The image of "Russia's haters" that initially emerged in the coverage of the Sochi Olympics has been solidified by what all Russians could relate to and sense on a daily basis—economic sanctions with which they were all punished.

When flight MH17 crashed in Eastern Ukraine, the US media immediately delivered the message that the plane was shot down by Russian separatists, which perfectly fit the script created by the preceding events in Ukraine and answered the need of the American audience to know right away what happened and who was to blame. Although the investigation into the crash continued for the next few years and the Dutch-led team did not produce any conclusive evidence of *who* fired the missile or from *where* it came, there was no deviation from the original script in the narrative delivered by most of the US reporters. Moreover, the American reader needed to know right away how the villain would be punished, which quickly was answered with a new set of sanctions imposed on Russia. The defensive stance taken by the Russian side, however, resulted in a series of different theories of what happened to flight MH17. Here, the independent media criticized the Kremlin for playing a game unbefitting a great power. Later, they also showed discrepancies between the Dutch and Russian investigations, without white-washing Russian claims, and presented the reader with the facts. Contrary to the unanimously agreed upon script that was created by the US media on the MH17 crash in which Russian separatists and Russia itself were to blame, one can see two different narratives provided by Russian state media and Russian independent media. Whereas the state-controlled press continued to present different theories of who might be behind the MH17 downing, blamed the United States for not providing satellite images requested by Russia for 2 years, blamed Ukraine for not closing its war-ridden airspace for commercial flights, and stressed the discriminatory attitude that the West and the United States showed toward Russia, the independent media either criticized their own government for its attempt to shift from one theory to another or just presented the known facts for the reader to interpret. The latter characterizes the independent media in Russia that often choose to list the known facts and leave it up to the reader to infer the information from those facts. Whether this indicates a more cautious act on the part of the reporters in light of the tightening state control over media or a better reliance on the readers' intelligence remains to be seen.

A year later, the Russian military entered the conflict in Syria, where US troops already were present. The two countries, once again, happened to take opposite sides in Syria's civil war, and the confrontation between the two powers ignited yet another battle within the information war. In the US media, Russia's entering the conflict was contextualized within the script that by now had become an old one for the American reader: Russia, as an evil aggressor, now intends to show its might in the world arena and flood Europe with more Syrian refugees. So the presentation of all events related to the Syrian conflict by the US media fit the same narrative in which Russia had been reduced to or, should we say, embodied by one person, Putin; the clear danger of meeting the Russian military in direct combat was acknowledged; and any alleged attacks by Syrian forces were blamed on Russia, similar to how Russia was blamed right away for the downing of flight MH17 hours after the crash. Russian state media, however, took another defensive stance and unleashed their offensive by accusing the United States in the fabrication of false evidence of the Syrian forces being behind the chemical attacks as well as reminding their readers about the infamous test tube that presumably contained "hard evidence" to justify the recent war in Iraq or the US role in creating mujahedeen and, by extension, Bin Laden during the Soviet war in Afghanistan. The message sent to the reader was clear: Washington cannot be trusted, as accusations are their main strategy to start a new military action. Although Russian independent media were not different from the state media in their coverage of this event, once again they showed an unbiased presentation of facts that were known at the time of the event.

Whereas the previously discussed events, except for the Sochi Olympics, firmly were framed within a similar script by the US media, with the takeover of Crimea, the conflict in Eastern Ukraine, the MH17 downing, and the conflict in Syria contributing to and reinforcing the image of Russia as the evil *other* for all subsequent events, Russia's alleged interference in the 2016 US presidential election and the accusation of Trump's colluding with Russia to win the election were covered without invoking any specific scheme related to Russia. Through reading and analyzing the media texts pertaining to this event, it seemed like the very name—Russia—had become sufficient to reenact the enemy whose evil intentions and actions would cast no doubt in the reader's mind. Senator John McCain's call for Americans to be on alert for a new Russian attack on their democracy could remind one of the Cold War rhetoric: The old enemy repackaged as Russia is not different from its official, although much bigger in size, predecessor, the Soviet Union. Russian media, on the other hand, reiterated the same denials of Moscow's involvement in the alleged interference and also framed their narrative in a familiar script of Russia being surrounded by haters who try to find it at fault everywhere. Moreover, in order to boost their defense, they produced the same script of the notorious test tube with the alleged evidence of Saddam Hussein's possession of chemical weapons, which supposedly aimed at undermining another instance of the US intelligence agencies' "high confidence" in Russia's alleged role in yet another foreign affair—this time its interference in the 2016 US presidential election. Thus, Russia's defense again turned into another offense.

As for the Skripals' poisoning, chronologically last in the series of seven events analyzed in this book, Britain has embodied the *other* for Russians, whereas the US media sent a barrage of attacks against Russia, a clearly defined enemy at that point. Although the two countries, Russia and the United

States, did not present the proverbial *other* to one another in this particular case, both contextualized the event within familiar scripts. The US reporters brought back home Russia's denial of its involvement in the MH17 crash, of their military support of the separatists in Eastern Ukraine, and of their interference in the 2016 US presidential election and likened it to the same denial by the Kremlin of its alleged involvement in the assassination attempt. By presenting the poisoning of the Skripals within such a context, mentioning another incident of the mysterious assassination of a former Russian spy in the United Kingdom, and reminding the readers about the relatively recent arrest of a few Russian "sleepers" in the United States, American journalists both sensationalized the story and ignited certain hysteria about an ominous and omnipresent enemy that Americans should be aware of. Conversely, Russian media, relying on the information revealed by the British press and having no firsthand access to the evidence, attempted to discredit the accusations that the Kremlin was behind the attack and questioned multiple holes in the investigation. A familiar script of Russia once again becoming a scapegoat for the West and being wrongly accused without any concrete proof was used by Russian media to frame the delivery of the Skripals' poisoning to their audience.

The role of schemata in the reenactment of the *other*, as it was demonstrated in this study, is undeniable. By invoking old scripts and creating new ones—just to use those as old ones for the next event—media agents in both countries have contributed to the promotion of the idea of whom each country should view as an enemy. Furthermore, in order to keep the *other* in focus, the same template and the same storyline were evoked and repeated again and again to update and solidify the delivered information in the minds of their targeted audiences. It can be suggested that once the script within which the image of the other was created and reinforced becomes strong enough, the reader would need just a mention of the name to trigger the right script that would support their belief in the evil intentions and actions of that *other*. This could be seen in American media's coverage of Russia's alleged interference in the 2016 US presidential election or, in Russian media, by the presentation of the West and the United States as Russia's haters that punish Russians with sanctions for what they have not done. At some point, the information hammered into the readers' mind by the media cannot easily be overwritten—hence the power of the right scripts within which the ongoing political events must be discussed by the reporters and which, correspondingly, should be invoked in the mind of the readers.

Bias and Distortion in Reenactment of the *Other*

No schema presenting the *other*, however, can be well established without the use of certain mechanisms, bias and distortion being among them. However, as van Dijk (1988) pointedly argues, the notion of ideologically biased or distorted news coverage

> presupposes that the distorted image can simply be compared to some kind of objective reality or with some kind of neutral or correct image. Yet, this reality represented in or through the news is itself an ideological construct, based on the definitions given by the accredited sources of journalists, such as the government. (p. 11)

From this point of view, our focus on bias and distortion in reenactment of the *other*, as seen through the media analysis, should not be on extracting the absolute truth and deciding the degree of the report's deviation from that truth. Rather, what I tried to illustrate in the four chapters based on the media analysis was how journalists used different techniques to make their texts believable to the reader and aligned with the government ideology. In order to avoid repetition, the discussion of bias is limited to a few major points identified through the media analysis.

First, multiple examples of highly biased headlines and some biased visuals were recorded in both sets of media. Second, epistemic language, especially in the reporting of the events with multiple unknowns (e.g., the downing of flight MH17, the Skripals' case, the chemical attacks in Syria, and Russia's alleged interference in the 2016 US presidential election) widely was used in the analyzed texts. Often initially it appeared in the US media and later was mocked by Russian media, as a suggestion that the US media do not operate on solid facts in their immediate accusation of Russia (e.g., "highly likely," as used in the Skripals' story and later transliterated as "*haili laikli*" by Russian journalists).

Third, the use of linguistic means, besides the qualifying/epistemic language, contributed to a highly biased presentation of the events. To provide just a few examples, the deliberate reference to Russian-speaking separatists who are Ukrainian citizens as Russian separatists or simply referring to the civil war in Ukraine as a war between Russia and Ukraine appeared in most US reports related to events that happened in Ukraine. The reference to Putin/Russia as the new "master" of Crimea or defining the takeover of

Crimea not simply as annexation but as a Russian invasion, intervention, or occupation and later overusing derivatives of the word "terrorist" to label the Ukrainian separatists and Russia as a whole were common for most of the US media. The bizarre adherence to the word "invade" led to an awkwardly written piece in which the author described a pro-Russian demonstration in Eastern Ukraine as people holding signs calling for Russia to *invade* their land. Also, when describing the protests in Eastern Ukraine, pro-Russian demonstrators were labeled as a "crowd" or "militia," whereas the neutral term "pro-Kiev demonstrators" was used to depict the opposite camp. Note that the majority of Russian publications were more restrained in the outright labeling of the *other* and definitely did not sink as low as some US journalists who used derogatory language to refer to the Russian president as a "thug" or a "pharaoh" or made unsubstantiated claims that some of his friends in Europe are fascists. It is intriguing how the concept of fascism has entered media discourse on both sides, with each loosely using the word to blame the other for promoting fascism. Furthermore, to project the clear superiority of the American reader to the Russian reader who supposedly is ideologically brainwashed, a ridiculous statement that American people *instinctively* know the truth made me question where such *healthy instincts* in Americans come from, if not from their press that is equally ideologically biased. Moreover, the misleading use of modifiers to identify the origin of the missile launcher from which flight MH17 allegedly was shot down, such as "Russian Buk" or "Buk from Russia," on the American side, or "Ukrainian Buk" (with Russia or Russian separatists taken out of the equation), on the Russian side, served the ideological goal of identifying the guilty party before—and even after—the investigation was complete. Russian journalists, on the other hand, emphasized a concept sacred to Russian culture, motherland, to present Crimea as returning back home or used the same word to show the Skripals' intention to return home, thereby undermining any accusations that the Kremlin was behind the assassination attempt. Another example of using lexical means to provide bias—if not deliberate distortion—is the incorrect translation of Trump's phrase that "Crimea was *taken* by Russia" as "Crimea was *captured* by Russia" in Russian media, which intended to disillusion the Russian reader about any potential change that the Trump administration might bring for Russia's case.

Fourth, the selective choice of quotes or interviewees to support the main ideological line of the report was recorded in both sets of media. For example, Russian journalists chose to interview two Western political analysts whose opinions coincided with that of the Kremlin and whose Western affiliation gave more credibility to such opinions for the Russian reader and further boosted their belief in the "truth" promoted by the Kremlin. Alternatively, American reporters chose to interview two Tatars who opposed the takeover of Crimea or a few eyewitnesses during the protests in Eastern Ukraine who were suspicious that Russians were behind the protests. It is noteworthy that almost all media publications, regardless of the country or the outlet, provided quotes without giving any direct references or by simply referring to the source as "an official" or "an expert." From this point of view, it was quite surprising to find hyperlinks to the sanction-related documents available on the official White House website in one of the publications by Russian state media. Such cross-checking of facts would be a very welcome move on the part of media, even if the reader often cannot understand the language of the original source.

Finally, bias could be detected through the content analysis of media reports. Here, we can see a rather fuzzy line separating bias from distortion, with the latter greatly contributing to the former and the former relying heavily on the latter. Finger-pointing and mutual accusations, offense versus defense, with the latter turning into offense, characterize the US and Russian news coverage analyzed in this project. Such clearly defined positions and the growing tension between the two countries at the government level clearly translated into the biased and often distorted presentation of the events by media. Distortion could be observed in how the events initially were reported and how the narrative was changed later by omitting or misrepresenting the originally reported facts. It also could be registered if one knows some basic facts (e.g., the boycott of the 1980 Moscow Olympics) or if access to the evidence is provided by the reporter. In other words, while agreeing with van Dijk's (1988) argument presented previously, I maintain that distortion can be identified through the close analysis of the texts even in the absence of direct access to the ground where the event took place. After all, even if we find ourselves as eyewitnesses of what happened, how objective might be our personal interpretation of the event? In this light, distortion can be exemplified by how Crimea-related reports in the US media first acknowledged the referendum and the fact that 97% of people voted to join Russia, then labeled it as sham, and later totally omitted any mention of the "free will of the people" in Crimea. Conversely, the latter became the focal point of all reports on Crimea in Russian media that also provided evidence of international observers who found the referendum legitimate. Next, the

US reference to a Russia that "seized Crimea by force" contradicts all the immediate American reports in which no military force or violence was mentioned and the takeover was described as a bizarre "low-key invasion." Russia, on the other hand, denied any military presence in Crimea until a year later when Putin admitted it. The somewhat overt involvement of the US government in the orchestration of the power change in Ukraine reluctantly was admitted by the US media only after some evidence was presented by Russians (note: the video evidence was still available on the internet at the time of this study). However, it was quickly dropped from any further discussion, and Russia was blamed for another low in posting such compromising documents. The Russian press ridiculed this reaction as the inability of a free democratic society, such as the United States, to face clear evidence of its dirty games. In other words, the omission of facts can be characterized as an example of distortion. Likewise, when the facts are blown out of proportion, they also can illustrate distortion: Russian state media reported on an interview with a US government official who said just a few words about the United States needing to move past the alleged Russian interference in the 2016 US presidential election (the original interview was accessed during the analysis). Those words not only made the headline of a Russian report but also provided the entire content. Moreover, when reporting on the Sochi Olympics, the US media deliberately downplayed any major success that Russians had at the Games, whereas Russian media inaccurately compared the Russian success in Sochi with that in the 1980 Moscow Olympics. As noted previously, the 1980 Summer Games were boycotted by the United States and other Western countries, which made the Russian wins much easier and clearly not comparable to the Sochi Olympics.

Moreover, there was much distortion of the information in the US media related to the flight MH17 investigation and the Skripals' poisoning. Because the Dutch-led investigation could not identify *who* fired the missile or from *where* it was fired, as some American journalists rightly acknowledged, others proceeded with making false, although definitive-sounding, claims that it was fired by Russian separatists or even by the Russian military. In the case of the Skripals, only the nature of the nerve agent used in the attempted assassination was established by reputable international organizations; however, some American reporters quickly stated that the origin of the agent was found and that it was manufactured by the Russian government. On the other hand, Russian journalists refrained from using the Russian name "Novichok" for the nerve agent, which would implicate Russia as far as its origin, and referred to it by its neutral-sounding—rather than Slavic—technical name.

Bias and distortion, as witnessed in the analyses of the media texts in this study, are ideologically driven, they align with the ideology supported by the power group—the government when it comes to foreign affairs—and they serve the goal of presenting the events in such a way that the values, interests, and motives of the *other* group are stressed as inconsonant with the values of the main group. Hence, the media contribute to the promotion of such political ideology and the reinforcement of the *other* in the minds of their audience.

Reenactment of the *Other*: Goal or Means?

If we agree that media are always biased and that news delivery—especially in the case of international affairs—would follow the definitions outlined by the power group (i.e., government, in our case), it is interesting to see how bias featured in the news reports produced by the two countries. Here, we could clearly identify a similarity in how Russian state-controlled media and the majority of the US outlets presented and supported the stance taken by their respective governments on any political event. Yet, if we take a separate look at Russian media, we can see a clear difference in some coverage of news by the independent press. Contrary to a rather firm stereotypical belief that all media in Russia are controlled by Putin and all liberal journalists are being persecuted—if not assassinated—by Putin (I do not argue with some of the truth in these beliefs), one can find quite a few independent media outlets in Russia. The news reports in those often stand in sharp contrast with reports in the US media as well as Russian state media. Journalists in those agencies do not hesitate to criticize their own government and its actions in some political affairs. At the same time, they do not necessarily align with the position taken by the US press. Instead, they often produce a very level-headed analysis of the situation, which may or may not support the stance held by the Russian government, and leave it up to readers to make up their own minds based on the dry facts provided. To illustrate, the US decision to arm Ukraine with lethal weapons was not cheered by the independent press, but neither was it ready to accuse Russia of being involved in chemical attacks in Syria. Nonetheless, they criticized their own government for changing its theories on the MH17 crash and for Putin's decree on classifying military losses in peacetime; the latter was similar to how the US media reflected on this issue.

All in all, I have found the reports published by Russian independent media outlets the least biased and the best written in general among all analyzed texts. The journalists' ability to rise above the ideological lines promoted by their governments, to rely on solid facts in order to avoid immediate accusations of wrongdoing by the other group, and to engage the readers in the negotiation of the event rather than feeding them a prefabricated ideological construct is praiseworthy, in my opinion. Ironically, this type of journalism, in the current data set, was found not in the country boasting its free speech and free media but in Russia, where, contrary to Western convictions, not all media are controlled by Vladimir Putin.

If we think more about the role of the government in dictating ideology to media agents, we have to acknowledge that whereas Russia has had the same leader, Vladimir Putin, for almost two decades now, 5 years of which were under investigation in this study, the United States had a change of power—from Barack Obama, who was on great terms with media, to Donald Trump, who began fighting a no-win war with media as soon as he became the president-elect. Thus, a change of the media's attitude to their new president reflected in how the reenactment of the *other* was unfolding in a few later political events, such as Syria and the 2016 US presidential election. Here, we clearly can see how Russia, as the *other*, has turned from a target of attack and criticism to a means for the US media attacks of Trump. In other words, while reporting on the earlier events that took place when Barack Obama was President—the conflict in Syria included—there was no deviation from the government's stance in how the US media reflected on Russia. Here, one of the goals was to convince the reader that the resurgent Russia that later was embodied in the sole figure of Putin is as ominous, aggressive, untrustworthy, and dangerous as its predecessor, the Soviet Union. The media rallied behind all White House decisions to punish the evil *other* and to alert Americans that "the Russians are coming" again. The change of leadership in the United States first was reflected in reporting on the Syrian conflict, in which the media criticized Trump for withdrawing US troops from the region and leaving a void to be filled by Russia. The attacks became much stronger when Trump's win in the election was allegedly helped by Russia. The reenactment of the *other*—or should I say, the firmly reenacted *other*—now has turned into a means for media to unleash a barrage of attacks on Trump in his alleged colluding with Russia. Hence, we could see how the role of the *other* in media coverage of political news can change from being a goal to becoming a weapon.

Reenactment of the *Other* in the Mind

As discussed in Chapter 10, both Russians and Americans do perceive one another as a threat; however, this feeling of alienation seems to be stronger among Russians, who also tend to extend their attitude to the relationship between the two countries beyond the US government, thinking of American people as the *other*. Incidentally, there were just a few Russians in this study who thought about America as an enemy at the time the Soviet Union disintegrated, compared to more Americans who continued thinking about Russia this way, even after the fall of the Soviet Union. How did it happen that in a relatively short period of time people's perception of another country has changed so dramatically? How did the media representation of another country impact that perception?

In order to address the first question, we can look into general questions that Russians were asked in the survey. Through the analysis of the empirical data, a few distinctive trends emerged. Although the majority of the participants in the Russian sample did not vote for Putin, they support his leadership as far as his handling of international affairs. While bitterly agreeing about why contemporary Russia is referred to as "Putin's Russia" in the West, they nevertheless want to separate ordinary people from the government. Moreover, while not agreeing with the repetitive motif in their state media that poor Russia is surrounded by enemies, they still admit that Russia often is accused by the West and the United States of wrongdoing without any clear evidence being provided thereof. From the participants' responses related to sanctions imposed on Russia, which Americans view as an insufficient punishment, we could see a painful reaction: After all, it is the Russian people and not the Russian government that were penalized for the actions of their leadership. I suggest that it is through the prism of this punishment that Russians now perceive Americans. Americans are no longer merely a proverbial *other*; they are unjust punishers.

If we look at the American side, it is clear that the Cold War stereotypes are more persistent in this group's sociocognitive construct. Thinking about contemporary Russia, the same old scripts are invoked, such as communism, the KGB, and dictatorship. By ascribing all these characteristics to the Russian President, Vladimir Putin, they extend them to the country as well, thereby accepting the label "Putin's Russia" as an accurate characteristic of the *other*.

The second question, to what extent media have affected the perception of one another in Russia and the United States and have contributed to the reenactment of the *other* in the minds of group members, has revealed two rather contradictory findings—one predictable, and the other rather surprising. As expected, both groups agreed that media did contribute significantly to how Americans think about Russians and how Russians think about Americans. Because media remain the major, if not the only, source of information about the *other*, this finding is rather logical. However, the fact that both groups do not find their respective media trustworthy and yet form their perception of one another through the prism of the information delivered by the very media they do not trust presents an intriguing dichotomy. Can the individual mind consciously acknowledge the untrustworthiness of media but subconsciously still process and consume the intended messages delivered by that media? As the results of the current study suggest, it can.

I remind the reader that the human mind has its own bias in how it processes any new information (see Chapter 3). First, any new information should fit the existent sociocognitive script in the minds of group members. Second, the overwriting or updating of the information is not an easy process, and the inaccurate information—or we may say, misinformation—can be implanted into individuals' minds. Finally, the information about the old *other* for which the group has a well-established script will be accepted as more believable and, thus, more accurate than the information about a newly created one.

Further evidence of how the mind consumed the media reports, thereby reenacting the *other*, can be found in those individual, yet shared, memories constructed by each group about the seven political events discussed in this book. In order not to repeat all the results discussed in Chapter 10, I only will reiterate that most of the information presented by the two respective media featured in the group memories, with the American participants having formed a stronger image of the evil *other*—that is, Russia—and not questioning the accuracy of the immediate accusations of Russia by the US media. Russian participants, on the other hand, did not agree with some actions of their government but showed a more critical, if not defensive, take on a few events with multiple unknowns, which again aligned with how Russian media reflected on those events.

Furthermore, one of the most interesting findings, in my view, came from American participants who claimed a very vague recollection of an event.

Those tended to fall back on old stereotypes and reported the most biased and distorted facts that were not even acknowledged by their media. This finding further supports the bias that exists in the human mind; it is through this bias that the memory about the *other* is reconstructed in the absence of a much clearer remembrance of a political event. To illustrate, in line with biased coverage of the 2014 Sochi Olympics by US reporters, where a mention of the "steel ring" referring to the tight security at the Games brought into play the stereotype of the notorious "iron curtain" from the Cold War era, most Americans with a vague memory of the Olympics reported poor security at the Games. The same can be said about the inaccurate information related to the investigation into the MH17 crash and the attempted assassination of the Skripals. The inconclusive findings of both investigations seeped into American minds as the most definitive answers to the burning question: Who did it? The epistemic language surrounding the coverage of these two events and the inaccurate claims made by most of the reporters served to protect the journalists' integrity in delivering the truth—even if that truth often did not sound like one—yet it went unnoticed by the individual minds processing such reports and forming strong beliefs of *who* actually did it. Moreover, I suggest that with every new event that involved the two countries and made headlines in the two respective media, such beliefs could no longer be changed, updated, or deleted. The old script of the *other* was revived and further strengthened by new stories, whether the audience remembered the previous one or not.

However, we may ask a legitimate question: If American participants processed the media information in such a way that they almost unequivocally believed that Russia was behind almost all events where its involvement was recognized from the start by the US media and Russians remained skeptical about some of those—this being perfectly in line with the reports in their media—why were there more Russians who perceived America as a threat (should we say, the *other*?) than Americans who viewed Russia as a threat?

I start with the American side in my attempt to answer this question. No matter how much the US media may be bringing Russia into focus as a resurging old enemy, the American people are more preoccupied with their domestic life, where their economy faces a looming threat from the growing economic power of China. Because much production has moved from the United States to China and many businesses have become increasingly dependent on China, that country occupies more space in national news and political debates. As a result, China was listed as a bigger threat than Russia by most Americans in this study. Russia may be viewed as the *other* by Americans—often due to the habit of having perceived it as such for the decades of the Cold War—but it is not considered a power that is capable of directly affecting the lives of ordinary Americans. Moreover, as some participants in the American sample noted, the US media provide more coverage of national news than foreign affairs, which can make China, with its economic threat, more visible than Russia. After all, if Russia goes after its former spies in the United Kingdom, fights somewhere in Ukraine, or grabs some land, these are not events likely to affect American lives directly.

As to Russians, in addition to the huge impact of sanctions on the daily lives of ordinary Russians and the fact that those sanctions are blamed on the United States, there is in general more coverage of international affairs in Russian media, and, allegedly, there is more focus on immediate accusations of Russia by the United States. Just to illustrate the latter, while I was working on this book in the summer of 2020, a wave of domestic riots and protests took place in American streets, which soon turned into a nationwide movement under the slogan "Black Lives Matter." One of the main Russian state media outlets (*Lenta*)[1] released a report titled "And the Flame Will Break Out" with the most sensation-seeking lead: "After the death of the black man, the United States was engulfed in riots and pogroms. Why is Russia blamed for this?" The report briefly covers what happened in American cities during those few turbulent weeks and only at the very end makes the brief statement that "local anti-fascists and external forces, including Russia, were accused of inciting pogroms." As closely as I have been watching the US news coverage and reading media sites, particularly in light of this project, this article from a Russian state-controlled outlet struck me as deliberately inaccurate, highly biased, and borderline paranoid. However, later I did a search of American sites, which made the Russian report no longer look completely distorted. According to *The Washington Post* (Švedkauskas et al., 2020), Russian disinformation campaigns specifically were targeting African Americans, although the authors refrained from explaining how exactly such campaigns intended to reach the minds of African Americans; instead, the authors shifted the readers' attention to a scenario of how Russians might interfere

[1] "I Vspykhnet Plamya" ["And the Flame Will Break Out"]. (2020, June 2). *Lenta*. Retrieved November 18, 2020, from https://lenta.ru/photo/2020/06/02/usa.

in the 2020 US presidential election. At the same time, the conservative Fox News (Re, 2020) reported that former Obama administration national security adviser, Susan Rice, had "bizarrely suggested . . . that the Russians *could be* [emphasis added] behind the violent nationwide demonstrations . . . although she offered no evidence for the incendiary claim." Regardless which site we are more likely to agree with, the Russian claim that the United States blamed it for the riots unfolding in American streets in the summer of 2020 is not completely unsubstantiated, yet the deliberate shift of attention to such sideline comments on the part of Russian media is not accidental. I also suggest that whatever accusations of Russia's alleged involvement in the US's internal affairs, such as riots following the death of an African American, are made by American reporters, they may go unnoticed by most of the American audience—as happened in my personal case—yet Russians may be more attuned to such claims obediently reported to them by their media that, in turn, strengthen their belief that the United States, indeed, tends to blame Russia for whatever happens in the world, even for racially incited riots in American cities. This may further reinforce the image of the old reemerged Cold War enemy, the United States, that ironically was not perceived as an enemy by most Russians during Soviet times. Whether Russians in this sample would find the previous accusation believable—for they did agree that Russia immediately is blamed by the United States for whatever happens—goes beyond the scope of the current investigation; nevertheless, it adds additional evidence of the ideologically driven attempts on the part of Russian state media to incite hysteria surrounding legitimate as well as false claims that the United States blames Russia for whatever happens in the world.

Returning to the question of why Russians perceive America as the major threat, I only can suggest that Russians—as critical as they tend to be of their government—can feel more defensive about their own country and be more aggressive about America, as they rightly perceive the punishment, in the form of the increased sanctions, as counterproductive and as hurting ordinary Russians rather than their president. If we remember that most of the Russian respondents in the current study did not vote for Putin in the last presidential election and, assumedly, do not support his policies, we can expect an even more negative attitude toward the United States from those Russians who support their president and may be more ideologically biased in their attitude to the old-time rival.

Memory, Media, and the Mind

In the 21st century, all ongoing political events quickly are recorded by media and delivered to the targeted audience so that the audience or group members, as we refer to them, consume and process the information, thereby forming shared memories. The delivery of such information by news reporters is constrained by the ideological interests of power groups standing behind news agencies and is scripted in such a way that the targeted mind will process this information exactly as expected by the news reporter. Often such information processing is made easier for the consumer by the reporter's reference to the already formed collective memories or by the re-creation of an old stereotype of the *other*. Stories about an old enemy are assumed to be more believable and accepted as accurate. The intricate interconnection between shared memories, media, and the targeted mind has been the focus of this book.

In this case study of recent political events that took place in the second decade of the 21st century, we could see how the coverage of political events revolving around Russia and discussed in the media of the two countries—Russia and the United States—has revealed all the elements of biased journalism. From the open distortion of facts to the later omission of previously reported facts, from the biased selection of eyewitnesses and quotes to the repeated attempts to solidify the existent memory about the *other*, from the reenactment of old stereotypes to instilling hysteria and sensation—the media of the two countries contributed to how the individual minds processed such information and formed shared memories. Such memories—especially in the absence of a clear recollection of what happened, as can be seen in the case of the American sample—often were based on old stereotypes and the bias existent in the minds of group members. This brings collective memory of past events, especially those that go back to the decades of the Cold War between Russia and the United States, into focus. Indeed, shared memories about recent events should fit the schemata present in the accumulated shared memories of the group. As was shown in this book, the reference to the Cold War and later—to the takeover of Crimea that seemed to define a starting point in the new phase of the worsened relationship between the two countries—characterized American news coverage. Conversely, Russian media ignited patriotic feelings in their readers by invoking a national memory of Russia's victory in World War II or the groundbreaking achievements in space exploration, on which the current government capitalizes to a great extent, or undermined American claims by reminding the readers about a few shameful events in recent US history, such as the false US claim that Iraq possessed weapons of mass destruction that justified the prolonged war in Iraq.

If we look chronologically at the events covered in this book, the references to the Cold War, on the American side, and to World War II, on the Russian side, that were intended to invoke old collective memories in the two respective groups mostly were made in the coverage of the 2014 Sochi Olympics. Later, all subsequent events, starting with the takeover of Crimea, were framed into a new script of Russia as an aggressive invader and land grabber—on the American side—and America as untrustworthy in its claims of having reliable evidence, as a meddler in the affairs of sovereign states, and as Russia's hater—on the Russian side. In addition to the repetitive narrative that Russia is surrounded by Russophobes that blame it for whatever happens in the world, on the Russian side, and the newly emerged belief that Russians are capable of corrupting US democracy, on the American side, the media in both countries have contributed to the formation of new scripts within which the current relationship between the United States and Russia is negotiated. These new scripts, in turn, have created a foundation for the formation of new collective memories that may still rely on old stereotypes and the old image of the *other* but are reinforced by new notions of the re-created *other* for each group.

One of the major questions addressed in this book concerned the individual minds that are targeted by media: How do they process and consume news stories to form memories shared with their group, and how do these memories fit the collective memories accumulated by that group? A few decades separate us from the time when the USSR collapsed and the Cold War ended. Just a few respondents in each sample were adults during those times, whereas the majority know about the time when their countries were two major superpowers in the Cold War confrontation only from history textbooks, movies, and probably other sources. Through the analysis of the data gathered from Russians and Americans, it was fascinating, yet troubling, to see how Russians progressed from not thinking of Americans as a threat 30 years ago—when the USSR fell apart and most people did not have trust in the official Soviet propaganda and history—to overwhelmingly thinking of it as such now; this hatred of another country was especially evident in the comments provided by younger Russians. In the case of Americans, the news coverage of the events that happened in the second decade of the 21st century and involved Russia seemed not to produce such an eye-opening discovery of Russia as a reemerged enemy; rather, it simply reinforced an old established image of it as the major enemy. At the same time, being focused more on their immediate domestic issues, Americans seemed to maintain the old stereotype of Russia as an evil empire while feeling more threatened by China and, assumedly, its growing economy. Thus, while holding on to old stereotypes and beliefs, including a strong belief that Russians are not punished enough for the deeds of their leader, they seemed to be less attuned to the coverage of news related to Russia and, in the absence of memory of those events, tended to fall back on the ideologically biased stereotypes existent in their collective memory.

If we remember that both Russians and Americans in this study do not trust their respective media yet form their memories of the political events precisely along the ideological lines promoted by that media, we may conclude that media are a powerful factor in how people construct their perception of what is going on around them and whom they should perceive as an enemy. Thus, it is through the permanent flux of old collective memories and old stereotypes shared by the group, the new information delivered by media that inevitably feeds into those memories and stereotypes, and the consumption of that information by individual minds that the *other* or the enemy is reenacted.

Conclusion

In the fall of 2016, a week before the civilized world woke up to the shockingly sobering news that Donald Trump has become the 45th President of the United States, my "home" state of Ohio, as a contested swing state, was in the heat of political rallies, presidential candidates' visits, and continuous news coverage. At that time, I was still finishing my monograph on collective memory, while this current project had not been conceptualized in my mind clearly. Quite unexpectedly, I was contacted by a reporter from the major Russian state-controlled TV, Channel One. He requested an interview with me and when asked whether the interview would be related to the upcoming presidential election, he vaguely replied that he wanted to talk about my work at the university. During the campus interview, however, after a few brief questions related to my teaching—which clearly was not his interest—he did switch to the elections. Two days later, the piece was aired on the Russian Channel One Nightly News. A night before it was released, the journalist emailed me to apologize for the report that probably did not meet my expectations; he also added that it was beyond his control. Indeed, a few phrases taken out of context and accompanied by grim pictures of the city where I live did not reflect what I had hoped to convey in the interview and see in the coverage. I remember how sad it made me feel and how immediately I ascribed this type of distorted presentation of the interview to Russian state-controlled media.

However, the more I delved into this current project, the more I read the scholarship on media, and the more I read news reports, both in American and Russian outlets, this time for the current book project—the more I understood why the Russian journalist apologized to me and why the outcome of my interview disappointed me. Moreover, I realized that it is not just the state-controlled media in "Putin's Russia" that operate this way; this is the state of affairs in the entire news industry.

Yet, my scholarly mind wanted to see what was behind this: How do journalists frame their stories to make them believable and how do they repeat those stories to construct solid memories in people's minds? How do

Reenacting the Enemy. Ludmila Isurin, Oxford University Press. © Oxford University Press 2022.
DOI: 10.1093/oso/9780197605462.003.0013

people, as consumers of news coverage, process and absorb such reports? Do they believe all the information fed to them by their media, and do they even trust that media? How do they construct their shared memories of what happened in the recent past and to what extent do those newly constructed memories rely on the persistent stereotypes and firmly established scripts present in the sociocognitive construct of their group? I launched a large-scale investigation into this issue, and at the end of this book I need to provide some concluding thoughts answering the eternal question that all researchers face at the end of their journey: So what?

I believe, in this book, I have provided support for the major arguments raised by scholars in media research. Also, I have shown how shared memories, media, and the mind can be studied in their entirety and their intertwined complexity. Media are never free of an ideological bias, regardless of what country they represent. The journalists' techniques to deliver the information to the targeted audience in the most believable and acceptable way are grounded in the basic principles shared by the media controlled by authoritarian states, such as Russia, and presumably free democratic states, such as the United States. In order to make new stories believable, reporters turn to the scripts that exist in the sociocognitive frame of their group as well as in the minds of their group members. By invoking those scripts, bringing in old collective memories and old stereotypes of the so-called *other*, and repeatedly updating the old message, they intend to reinforce their point about that proverbial *other* or, simply put, the enemy. Not unexpectedly, the minds of the group members targeted by their respective media reject the trustworthiness of their media yet construct the memories of new political events along the exact ideological lines promoted by that media.

In light of these findings, I wonder whether the two countries that were the focus of investigation in this project—Russia and the United States—will start working more toward *togetherness* rather than *otherness* and whether Russians and Americans will find an alternative way to learn more about one another than through their respective and ideologically biased media.

Although the politics that defines the direction in which international relationships go most likely will remain unaffected by our humble academic attempts to challenge it, I hope our scholarly efforts to elucidate these issues will not stop and/or go in vain. With this, I conclude the project that has been on my mind and on my computer screen for a year and a half, and I leave it for readers to judge. I also welcome other scholars to join me in the pursuit of the most fascinating and complex issues, such as the one involving the interconnected nature of collective memory, media, and the mind.

References

Abel, M., Fairfield, B., Takahashi, M., Roediger III, H., & Wertsch, J. (2019). Collective memories across 11 nations for World War II: Similarities and differences regarding the most important events. *Journal of Applied Research in Memory and Cognition*, *8*, 178–188.

Almasy, S., & Gray, J. (2017, July 6). *Netherlands: We will bring MH17 killers to justice here*. CNN. Retrieved May 15, 2020, from https://edition.cnn.com/2017/07/05/europe/netherlands-mh17/index.html

Alyokhina, M. (2014, February 20). Sochi under siege. *The New York Times*. Retrieved February 17, 2020, from https://www.nytimes.com/2014/02/21/opinion/maria-alyokhina-of-pussy-riot-on-the-olympics-deceptive-face.html?searchResultPosition=6

Andén-Papadopoulos, K. (2014). Journalism, memory and the "crowd-sourced video revolution." In B. Zelizer & K. Tenenboim-Weinblatt (Eds.), *Journalism and memory* (pp. 148–163). Palgrave Macmillan.

Apple, N. (2015, October 1). Komu vojna, a komu slava Rossii [Who needs the war, and who gets the glory of Russia]. *Vedomosti*. Retrieved May 7, 2020, from https://www.vedomosti.ru/opinion/articles/2015/10/02/611178-komu-voina-komu-slava-rossii

Apple, N., & Sinitzyn, A. (2016, September 26). Politika otricanija [Denial policy]. *Vedomosti*. Retrieved April 17, 2020, from https://www.vedomosti.ru/opinion/articles/2016/09/29/658958-politika-otritsaniya

Applebaum, A. (2018, March 23). First Russia unleashed a nerve agent. Now it's unleashed its lie machine. *The Washington Post*. Retrieved January 10, 2020, from https://www.washingtonpost.com/opinions/first-russia-unleashed-a-nerve-agent-now-its-unleashing-its-lie-machine/2018/03/23/5eb85628-2ed4-11e8-8ad6-fbc50284fce8_story.html

Aptekar, P. (2015a, July 28). Pochemu Rossija protiv tribunala po MH17 [Why Russia is against the MH17 tribunal]. *Vedomosti*. Retrieved April 10, 2020, from https://www.vedomosti.ru/opinion/articles/2015/07/29/602545-pochemu-rossiya-protiv-tribunala-po-mh17

Aptekar, P. (2015b, December 8). Pamjati neizvestnogo soldata [In memory of the unknown soldier]. *Vedomosti*. Retrieved June 5, 2020, from https://www.vedomosti.ru/opinion/articles/2015/12/09/620194-pamyati-neizvestnogo-soldata

Artemjev, M. (2015, July 30). *Ni shagu nazad: zachem Rossija zablokirovala provedenie tribunala po Boeing* [Not one step back: Why Russia has blocked the holding of a tribunal for Boeing]. RBC. Retrieved April 17, 2020, from https://www.rbc.ru/opinions/politics/30/07/2015/55ba423c9a79471fbd6366a8

Atasuntzev, A. (2019, October 19). *Jerdogan otvetil Trampu na prizyv ne byt' durakom* [Erdogan responded to Trump's call not to be a fool]. RBC. Retrieved May 7, 2020, from https://www.rbc.ru/politics/19/10/2019/5da98f049a79478f303dd79b

Azar, I. (2014, February 27). Poluraspad poluostrova: Kak Krym soprotivljaetsja ukrainskoj revoljucii [Semicollapse of the peninsula: How Crimea resists Ukrainian revolution]. *Lenta*. Retrieved May 26, 2020, from https://lenta.ru/articles/2014/02/27/crimea

Baklanov, A. (2018, September 17). Ot ukrainskogo Su-25 do "Buka" iz Ternopol'skoj oblasti. Kak menjalis' zajavlenija Rossii o krushenii malajzijskogo "boinga" [From the Ukrainian Su-25 to the "Buk" from the Ternopil region. How Russia's statements about the crash of the Malaysian Boeing have changed]. *Meduza*. Retrieved April 14, 2020, from https://meduza.io/feature/2018/09/17/ot-ukrainskogo-su-25-do-buka-iz-ternopolskoy-oblasti-kak-menyalis-zayavleniya-rossii-o-krushenii-malayziyskogo-boinga

Balandra, A. (2018, June 24). Otpechatki pal'cev Rossii: chto ne tak v otchete po MH17 [Fingerprints of Russia: What is wrong with the MH17 report]. *Gazeta*. Retrieved April 10, 2020, from https://www.gazeta.ru/social/2018/05/24/11762323.shtml

Barnard, A., & Gordon, M. (2017, April 4). Worst chemical attack in years in Syria; U.S. blames Assad. *The New York Times*. Retrieved May 6, 2020, from https://www.nytimes.com/2017/04/04/world/middleeast/syria-gas-attack.html

Barnhurst, K. (2011). The problem of modern time in American journalism. *KronoScope*, *11*(1–2), 98–123.

Barry, E. (2019, June 30). "Third man" in Skripal attack was link to Moscow, investigative group says. *The New York Times*. Retrieved January 10, 2020, from https://www.nytimes.com/2019/06/30/world/europe/uk-skripal-poisoning-russia.html

Bartlett, F. (1932). *Remembering: A study in experimental and social psychology*. Cambridge University Press.

Bartlett, F. (1967). *Remembering. A study in experimental and social psychology*. Cambridge University Press.

Baumeister, R., & Hastings, S. (1997). Distortions of collective memory: How groups flatter and deceive themselves. In J. Pennebaker, D. Paez, & B. Rimé (Eds.), *Collective memory of political events* (pp. 277–293). Erlbaum.

Bella, R., Madsen, R., Sullivan, W. M., Swidler, A., & Tipton, S. M. (1996). *Habits of the heart: Individualism and commitment in American life*. University of California Press.

Belokonova, E. (2018, August 4). Viktorija Skripal': Julija "otchajanno" hochet vernut'sja v Rossiju [Victoria Skripal: Julia "desperately" wants to return to Russia]. *Komsomol'skaya Pravda*. Retrieved January 25, 2020, from https://www.alt.kp.ru/online/news/3076947

Benkler, Y., Faris, R., & Roberts, H. (2018). *Network propaganda: Manipulation, disinformation, and radicalization in American politics*. Oxford University Press.

Berger, S. (2007). Writing national histories in Europe: Reflections on the pasts, presents, and futures of a tradition. In K. H. Jarausch & T. Lindenbereger (Eds.), *Conflicted memories: Europeanizing contemporary histories* (pp. 55–68). Berghahn Books.

Berkowitz, D. (2011). Telling the unknown through the familiar: Collective memory as journalistic device in a changing media environment. In M. Neiger, O. Meyers, & E. Zandberg (Eds.), *On media memory: Collective memory in a new media age* (pp. 201–212). Palgrave Macmillan.

Berman, I. (2014, February 20). Putin's Olympic corruption. *USA Today*. Retrieved February 28, 2020, from https://www.usatoday.com/story/opinion/2014/02/20/putin-olympics-sochi-corruption-russia-column/5655815

Bernstein, D., Laney, C., Morris, E., & Loftus, E. (2005). False memories about food can lead to food avoidance. *Social Cognition*, *23*, 11–14.

Bernstein, D., & Loftus, E. (2009). The consequences of false memories for food preferences and choices. *Perspectives on Psychological Science*, *4*(2), 135–139.

Bird, E. (2011). Reclaiming Asaba: Old media, new media, and the construction of memory. In M. Neiger, O. Meyers, & E. Zandberg (Eds.), *On media memory: Collective memory in a new media age* (pp. 88–103). Palgrave Macmillan.

Birnbaum, M. (2014, November 28). Crimean Tatars say Russian annexation has brought fear and repression all over again. *The Washington Post*. Retrieved May 25, 2020, from https://www.washingtonpost.com/world/europe/crimean-tatars-say-russian-annexation-has-brought-fear-and-repression-all-over-again/2014/11/28/c2a3bcea-73ed-11e4-95a8-fe0b46e8751a_story.html?tid=a_inl&utm_term=.8a01838c58cf

Blake, A. (2017, April 4). Trump's puzzling blame—Obama statement on the Syria tragedy. *The Washingtom Post*. Retrieved December 31, 2021 from https://www.washingtonpost.com/news/the-fix/wp/2017/04/04/trumps-puzzlingly-political-statement-on-the-syria-tragedy/

Blatz, G., & Ross, M. (2009). Historical memories. In P. Boyer & J. Wertsch (Eds.), *Memory in mind and culture* (pp. 223–237). Cambridge University Press.

Blight, D. (2009). The memory boom: Why and why now? In P. Boyer & J. Wertsch (Eds.), *Memory in mind and culture* (pp. 238–251). Cambridge University Press.

Bodnar, J. (1992). *Remaking America: Public memory, commemoration and patriotism in the twentieth century*. Princeton University Press.

Bondarenko, M. (2017, January 7). *Razvedka SShA obnarodovala doklad o «vmeshatel'stve Rossii» v vybory* [US intelligence released a report on "Russian interference" in election]. RBC. Retrieved February 27, 2019, from https://www.rbc.ru/politics/07/01/2017/587007609a794793e714b5bb

Booth, W. (2014, February 22). Ukraine's parliament votes to oust president; former prime minister is freed from prison. *The Washington Post*. Retrieved September 4, 2018, from https://www.washingtonpost.com/world/europe/ukraines-yanukovych-missing-as-protesters-take-control-of-presidential-residence-in-kiev/2014/02/22/802f7c6c-9bd2-11e3-ad71-e03637a299c0_story.html?utm_term=.3f2d78be877a

Bourdon, J. (2011). Media remembering: The contributions of life-story methodology to memory/media research. In M. Neiger, O. Meyers, & E. Zandberg (Eds.), *On media memory: Collective memory in a new media age* (pp. 62–73). Palgrave Macmillan.

Boyer, P. (2009). What are memories for? Functions of recall in cognition and culture. In P. Boyer & J. Wertsch (Eds.), *Memory in mind and culture* (pp. 3–28). Cambridge University Press.

Boyer, P., & Wertsch, J. (2009). How do memories construct our past? In P. Boyer & J. Wertsch (Eds.), *Memory in mind and culture* (pp. 29–32). Cambridge University Press.

Bratersky, A., & Telmanov, D. (2015, November 2). SShA gotovjat oruzhie dlja Ukrainy [The U.S. is preparing weapons for Ukraine]. *Gazeta*. Retrieved June 4, 2020, from https://www.gazeta.ru/politics/2015/02/11_a_6408525.shtml

Britton, B. (2019, June 19). *MH17 crash investigators say four suspects face murder charges*. CNN. Retrieved May 21, 2020, https://amp.cnn.com/cnn/2019/06/19/europe/malaysia-airlines-flight-17-suspects-intl/index.html

Bronstein, M., Pennycook, G., Bear, A., Rand, D., & Cannon, T. (2019). Belief in fake news is associated with delusionality, dogmatism, religious fundamentalism, and reduced analytical thinking. *Journal of Applied Research in Memory and Cognition*, *8*, 108–117.

Brown, A., Kouri, N., & Hirst, W. (2012). Memory's malleability: Its role in shaping collective memory and social identity. *Frontiers in Psychology*, *3*, 1–3.

Brown, R., & Kulick, J. (1977). Flashbulb memories. *Cognition*, *5*, 73–99.

Bukker, I. (2014a, February 24). Pobeda Rossii na igrah - tol'ko nachalo [Russia's victory at the Games is only the beginning]. *Nasledie Pravda*. Retrieved February 20, 2020, from https://nasledie.pravda.ru/1195116-olympiada_sotchi_2014

Bukker, I. (2014b, July 18). Rejs MN17: vmesto istiny – igra specsluzhb [Flight MH17: Instead of the truth—the game of intelligence agencies]. *Pravda*. Retrieved September 27, 2018, from https://www.pravda.ru/world/europe/european/18-07-2014/1216835-boeuing_777-0

Burke, P. (1989). History as social memory. In T. Butler (Ed.), *History, culture, and the mind* (pp. 97–113). Basil Blackwell.

Carden, J. (2017, March 3). Why does the US continue to arm terrorists in Syria? *The Nation*. Retrieved June 14, 2020, from https://www.thenation.com/article/archive/why-does-the-us-continue-to-arm-terrorists-in-syria

Clark, N., & Kramer, A. (2015, October 13). Malaysia Airlines flight 17 most likely hit by Russian-made missile, inquiry says. *The New York Times*. Retrieved May 15, 2020, from https://www.nytimes.com/2015/10/14/world/europe/mh17-malaysia-airlines-dutch-report.html

Cohen, T. (2014, July 19). *Malaysian plane shot down in Ukraine: What happened?* CNN. Retrieved September 11, 2018, from https://www.cnn.com/2014/07/18/world/europe/ukraine-malaysia-plane-questions/index.html

Corcoran, K. (2017, July 5). Any suspects in shooting down of MH17 passenger jet will be put on trial in the Netherlands. *Business Insider*. Retrieved May 15, 2020, from https://www.businessinsider.com/mh-17-trials-held-in-netherlands-2017-7

Davis, J., & Cooper, H. (2017, April 11). White House accuses Russia of cover-up in Syria chemical attack. *The New York Times*. Retrieved May 5, 2020, from https://www.nytimes.com/2017/04/11/world/middleeast/russia-syria-chemical-weapons-white-house.html

Dergachev, V. (2014, September 5). V shest' chasov vechera posle vojny—Zasedanie kontaktnoj gruppy v Minske zakonchilos' resheniem o prekrashhenii ognja na vostoke Ukrainy [At six o'clock in the evening after the war—The contact group meeting in Minsk ended with a ceasefire in eastern Ukraine]. *Gazeta*. Retrieved June 3, 2020, from https://www.gazeta.ru/politics/2014/09/05_a_6204229.shtml

Dergachev, V. (2016, June 6). Malajzijskij Boeing mogli sbit' sluchajno [Malaysian Boeing could have been downed accidentally]. *Gazeta*. Retrieved February 26, 2019, from https://www.gazeta.ru/politics/2016/06/06_a_8288345.shtml#page1

Dergachev, V., & Zinchenko, S. (2014, March 3). Esli Rossija ne zajmet Krym, jeto sdelajut SShA [If Russia does not take up Crimea, the United States will do it]. *Gazeta*. Retrieved September 16, 2018, from https://www.gazeta.ru/politics/2014/03/04_a_5934745.shtml

D'Haenens, L., Jankowski, N., & Heuvelman, A. (2010). News in online and print newspapers: Differences in reader consumption and recall. *New Media & Society*, *16*(3), 363–382.

Dorell, O. (2018, April 13). Russian President Vladimir Putin: Missile strikes on Syria "act of aggression." *USA Today*. Retrieved March 4, 2019, from https://www.usatoday.com/story/news/world/2018/04/13/russia-pledged-counter-any-u-s-missile-strike-syria/516756002

Dugyala, R. (2020, February 23). National security adviser dismisses claim of Russian aid for Trump in 2020 race. *Politico*. Retrieved June 13, 2020, from https://www.politico.com/news/2020/02/23/russia-interference-2020-obrien-trump-116806

Dzhordzhevich, A. (2020, March 9). Россия использует защиту Барта Симпсона [Russia uses the protection of Bart Simpson]. *Novaya Gazeta*. Retrieved April 10, 2020, from https://novayagazeta.ru/articles/2020/03/09/84228-rossiya-ispolzuet-zaschitu-barta-simpsona-ya-etogo-ne-delal-vy-menya-ne-videli-vy-ne-smozhete-etogo-dokazat

Earles, J., Kersten, A., Vernon, L., & Starkings, R. (2016). Memory for positive negative and neutral events in younger and older adults: Does emotion influence binding in event memory? *Cognition and Emotion, 30*(2), 378–388.

Edy, J. (2014). Collective memory in a post-broadcast world. In B. Zelizer & K. Tenenboim-Weinblatt (Eds.), *Journalism and memory* (pp. 66–79). Palgrave Macmillan.

Entous, A., & Nakashima, E. (2016, December 16). FBI in agreement with CIA that Russia aimed to help Trump win White House. *The Washington Post*. Retrieved January 14, 2019, from https://www.washingtonpost.com/politics/clinton-blames-putins-personal-grudge-against-her-forelection-interference/2016/12/16/12f36250-c3be-11e6-8422-eac61c0ef74d_story.html?utm_term=.9c104973db82

Erickson, A. (2018, March 26). The U.S. and Europe say the Kremlin poisoned Sergei Skripal. Russians don't buy it. *The Washington Post*. Retrieved January 10, 2020, from https://www.washingtonpost.com/news/worldviews/wp/2018/03/26/who-poisoned-sergei-skripal-not-russia-russians-say

Etkind, A. (2009). Post-Soviet hauntology: Cultural memory of the Soviet terror. *Constellations, 16*(1), 182–200.

Fahrutdinov, R. (2018, March 26). Prisoedinenie Kryma k Rossii, k sozhaleniju, javljaetsja faktom [The accession of Crimea to Russia, unfortunately, is a fact]. *Gazeta*. Retrieved April 5, 2020, from https://www.gazeta.ru/politics/2018/03/26_a_11696959.shtml

Fasick, K., & Balsamini, D. (2016, May 22). Gorbachev backs Putin's invasion of Crimea. *New York Post*. Retrieved April 16, 2020, from http://nypost.com/2016/05/22/gorbachev-backs-putins-invasion-of-crimea

Filipenok, A. (2020, January 14). *Klinton predupredila o "vmeshatel'stve" Rossii v vybory v pol'zu Trampa* [Clinton warned of Russian "interference" in the election in favor of Trump]. RBC. Retrieved June 17, 2020, from https://www.rbc.ru/politics/14/01/2020/5e1e0e519a7947732ecbcdb5

Filippov, A. (2019, October 1). *London priznal otsutstvie dokazatel'stv prichastnosti Kremlja k delu Skripalja* [London admitted lack of evidence of Kremlin involvement in Skripal case]. RIA Novosti. Retrieved February 2, 2020, from https://ria.ru/20190807/1557258294.html

Fisher, M. (2014, September 3). Everything you need to know about the Ukraine crisis. *Vox*. Retrieved June 1, 2020, from https://www.vox.com/2014/9/3/18088560/ukraine-everything-you-need-to-know

Flammer, A., & Tauber, M. (1982). Changing the reader's perspective. In A. Flammer & W. Kintsch (Series Eds.), *Advances in psychology: Vol. 8. Discourse processing* (pp. 379–391). North-Holland.

Flintoff, C. (2016, May 7). *Russian military involved in shooting down flight MH17, researchers say*. NPR. Retrieved January 15, 2019, from https://www.npr.org/2016/05/07/477168263/russian-military-involved-in-shooting-down-flight-mh17-researchers-say

Freedman, L. (2017). Academics and policy making: Rules of engagement. *Journal of Strategic Studies, 40*(1–2), 263–268.

Frenda, S., Nichols, R., & Loftus, E. (2011). Current issues and advances in misinformation research. *Current Directions in Psychological Science, 20*(1), 20–23.

Fridman, O. (2018). *Russian hybrid warfare*. Oxford University Press.
Galimova, N. (2014, March 11). Krym stanet respublikoj v sostave Rossii [Crimea will become part of Russia as a republic]. *Gazeta*. Retrieved April 7, 2020, from https://www.gazeta.ru/politics/2014/03/11_a_5945605.shtml
Gans, H. (2003). *Democracy and the news*. Oxford University Press.
Gaouette, N., & Roth, R. (2017, February 3). *UN Ambassador Haley hits Russia hard on Ukraine*. CNN. Retrieved January 31, 2019, from https://www.cnn.com/2017/02/02/politics/haley-russia-un/index.html
Garagozov, R. (2002). Collective memory and the Russian "schematic narrative template." Journal of Russian and East European Psychology, 40(5), 55–89.
Garry, M., French, L., Kinzett, T., & Mori, K. (2008). Eyewitness memory following discussion: Using Mori technique with a Western sample. *Applied Cognitive Psychology*, *22*(4), 431–439.
Gorjashko, S. (2015, November 10). Voennye poteri v mirnoe vremja zasekretili okonchatel'no [Peacetime military casualties finally classified]. *Kommersant*. Retrieved June 5, 2020, from https://www.kommersant.ru/doc/2850904
Goscilo, H. (2012). Putin's performance of masculinity: The action hero and macho sex-object. In H. Goscilo (Ed.), *Putin as celebrity and cultural icon* (pp. 180–207). Routledge.
Grabe, M., & Kamhawi, R. (2006). Hard wired for negative news? Gender differences in processing broadcast news. *Communication Research*, *33*(5), 346–369.
Gregory, P. (2017, March 15). Is Putin preparing to admit guilt for MH17? *Forbes*. Retrieved January 30, 2019, from https://www.forbes.com/sites/paulroderickgregory/2017/03/15/is-putin-preparing-to-admit-guilt-for-mh17/#3343ecaf1884
Grever, M., & van der Vlies, T. (2017). Why national narratives are perpetuated: A literature review on new insights from history textbook research. *London Review of Education*, *15*, 286–301.
Griffin, J. (2014, July 18). *Malaysia Airlines crash: Ukraine, Russia point fingers after missile downs plane*. *Fox News*. Retrieved May 14, 2020, from https://www.foxnews.com/world/malaysia-airlines-crash-ukraine-russia-point-fingers-after-missile-downs-plane
Halbwachs, M. (Ed.) (1950). *The collective memory*. Harper & Row.
Halbwachs, M. (1992). *On collective memory*. University of Chicago Press.
Hamilton, K., & Benjamin, A. (2019). The human–machine extended organism: New roles and responsibilities of human cognition in a digital ecology. *Journal of Applied Research in Memory and Cognition*, *8*, 40–45.
Hariman, R., & Lucaites, J. L. (2014). Hands and feet: Photojournalism, the fragmented body politic and collective memory. In B. Zelizer & K. Tenenboim-Weinblatt (Eds.), *Journalism and memory* (pp. 131–147). Palgrave Macmillan.
Harris, C., Peterson, H., & Kemp, R. (2008). Collaborative recall and collective memory: What happens when we remember together? *Memory*, *16*(3), 213–230.
Harris, C., Sutton, J., & Barnier, A. (2010). Autobiographical forgetting, social forgetting, and situated forgetting. In S. Sala (Ed.), *Forgetting* (pp. 253–284). Psychology Press.
Harris, G. (2017, December 7). Tillerson says the U.S. will never accept Crimea annexation. *The New York Times*. Retrieved January 31, 2019, from https://www.nytimes.com/2017/12/07/world/europe/rex-tillerson-russia-trump.html
Hart, B. (2014, July 17). Malaysia airlines flight MH17 shot down over Ukraine, U.S. officials say. *Huffington Post*. Retrieved September 11, 2018, from https://www.huffingtonpost.com/2014/07/17/malaysia-airlines-plane-crash-missile_n_5597014.html

Hauer, N. (2018, January 18). *Chechen and North Caucasian militants in Syria*. Atlantic Council. Retrieved April 16, 2020, from https://www.atlanticcouncil.org/blogs/syriasource/chechen-and-north-caucasian-militants-in-syria

Herman, S. (2021, July 27). Biden accuses Russia of already interfering in 2022 election. *Voice of America*. Retrieved December 21, 2021, from https://www.voanews.com/a/usa_us-politics_biden-accuses-russia-already-interfering-2022-election/6208813.html

Herszenhorn, D. (2013a, November 21). Facing Russian threat, Ukraine halts plans for deals with E.U. *The New York Times*. Retrieved September 4, 2018, from https://www.nytimes.com/2013/11/22/world/europe/ukraine-refuses-to-free-ex-leader-raising-concerns-over-eu-talks.html

Herszenhorn, D. (2013b, November 26). Ukraine in turmoil after leaders reject major E.U. deal. *The New York Times*. Retrieved September 4, 2018, from https://www.nytimes.com/2013/11/27/world/europe/protests-continue-as-ukraine-leader-defends-stance-on-europe.html

Higgins, A. (2018, September 13). We were tourists, not assassins, Novichok attack suspects say. *The New York Times*. Retrieved January 26, 2020, from https://www.nytimes.com/2018/09/13/world/europe/russia-salisbury-skripal-novichok.html

Higgins, A., & Kramer, A. (2015, January 3). Ukraine leader was defeated even before he was ousted. *The New York Times*. Retrieved May 22, 2020, from https://www.nytimes.com/2015/01/04/world/europe/ukraine-leader-was-defeated-even-before-he-was-ousted.html

Hinder, E. (1982). Effects of verbal and pictorial context cues on free recall and clustering of text themes. In A. Flammer & W. Kintsch (Series Eds.), *Advances in psychology: Vol. 8. Discourse processing* (pp. 279–289). North-Holland.

Hirst, W., & Manier, D. (2008). Towards a psychology of collective memory. *Memory, 16*(3), 183–200.

Hodge, N. (2019, March 31). *Ukraine's President is running against—Vladimir Putin*. CNN. Retrieved April 16, 2020, from https://www.cnn.com/2019/03/30/europe/ukraine-elections-putin-intl/index.html

Hofstede, G. (2001). *Culture's consequences: Comparing values, behaviors, and organizations across nations* (2nd ed.). Sage.

Hoskins, A. (2011). Anachronisms of media, anachronisms of memory: From collective memory to a new memory ecology. In M. Neiger, O. Meyers, & E. Zandberg (Eds.), *On media memory: Collective memory in a new media age* (pp. 278–288). Palgrave Macmillan.

Hoskins, A. (2014). A new meory of war. In B. Zelizer & K. Tenenboim-Weinblatt (Eds.), *Journalism and memory* (pp. 179–194). NY, USA: Palgrave MacMillan Memory Studies.

Hrolenko, A. (2015, February 25). *Oruzhie SShA dlja mira na Ukraine* [American weapons for peace in Ukraine]. RIA. Retrieved June 4, 2020, from https://ria.ru/20150225/1049539418.html

Hubbard, B., & Sanger, D. (2016, December 20). Russia, Iran and Turkey meet for Syria talks, excluding U.S. *The New York Times*. Retrieved May 5, 2020, from https://www.nytimes.com/2016/12/20/world/middleeast/russia-iran-and-turkey-meet-for-syria-talks-excluding-us.html

Ilyushina, M., & McKenzie, S. (2020, January 15). Russian government resigns as Putin proposes reforms that could extend his grip on power. *Edition CNN*. Retrieved January

19, 2020, from https://edition.cnn.com/2020/01/15/europe/russian-government-resigns-vladimir-putin-reforms-intl/index.html

Ioffe, J. (2017, December 6). How the Kremlin tried to rig the Olympics and failed. *The Atlantic*. Retrieved February 17, 2020, from https://www.theatlantic.com/international/archive/2017/12/kremlin-doping-scandal-sochi-winter-olympics/547616

Isachenkov, V., & Danilova, M. (2013, December 17). Putin: Russia to buy $15 million in Ukraine bonds. *USA Today*. Retrieved August 28, 2018, from https://www.usatoday.com/story/news/world/2013/12/17/russia-ukraine-bonds-putin/4058059

Isurin, L. (2014). "They call us names, they call us Russians!" Nationality and conceptual non-equivalence. Slavic and East European Journal, *58*(4), 663–685.

Isurin, L. (2017). *Collective remembering: Memory in the world and in the mind*. Cambridge University Press.

Ito, H., Barzykowski, K., Grzesik, M., Gülgöz, S., Gürdere, C., Janssen, S., Khor, J., Rowthorn, H., Wade, K., Luna, K., Albuquerque, P., Kumar, D., Singh, A. D., Cecconello, W., Cadavid, S., Laird, N., Baldassari, M., Lindsay, S., & Mori, K. (2019). Eyewitness memory distortion following co-witness discussion: A replication of Gary, French, Kizett, and Mori (2008) in ten countries. *Journal of Applied Research in Memory and Cognition*, *8*, 68–77.

Jackson, D. (2017, November 11). Trump says he believes intelligence assessment that Russia interfered in election—but Putin does not. *USA Today*. Retrieved January 29, 2019, from https://www.usatoday.com/story/news/politics/2017/11/11/trump-says-he-believes-intelligence-assessment-russia-interfered-eleelect-reeddnent-mcne-kintinettid/855783001

Jalbert, M., Schwarz, N, & Newman, E. (2020). Only half of what I'll tell you is true: Expecting to encounter falsehood reduces illusory truth. *Journal of Applied Research in Memory and Cognition*, *9*(4), 602–613.

Jamieson, A. (2016, October 1). *MH17 investigation: Why justice might still never come for victims' families*. NBC News. Retrieved May 15, 2020, from https://www.nbcnews.com/storyline/ukraine-plane-crash/mh17-investigation-why-justice-might-still-never-come-victims-families-n656721

Jansen, B. (2015, October, 13). Report confirms MH17 shot down—but why? *USA Today*. Retrieved October 29, 2018, from https://www.usatoday.com/story/news/world/2015/10/13/dutch-investigation-malaysia-airlines-17-ukraine-russia-separatists/73873062

Kansteiner, W. (2002). Finding meaning in memory: A methodological critique of collective memory studies. *History and Theory*, *41*, 179–197.

Karpitzkaja, D. (2019, June 23). Sergej Skripal' zhiv i reguljarno zvonit svoej plemjannice Viktorii [Sergei Skripal is alive and regularly calls his niece Victoria]. *Komsomol'skaya Pravda*. Retrieved January 25, 2020, from https://www.kp.ru/daily/26980/4039650

Katkov, K., & Myre, G. (2018, April 13). *U.S., allies hit 3 Syrian sites linked to chemical weapons program*. NPR. Retrieved March 4, 2019, from https://www.npr.org/sections/thetwo-way/2018/04/13/601794830/u-s-launches-attacks-on-syria

Kazanas, S., & Altarriba, J. (2015). The survival advantage: Underlying mechanisms and extant limitations. *Evolutionary Psychology*, *13*(2), 1–54.

Kersten, A., & Earles, J. (2017). Feeling of familiarity and false memory for specific associations resulting from mugshot exposure. *Memory & Cognition*, *45*, 93–104.

Kintsch, W. (1982). Memory for text. In A. Flammer & W. Kintsch (Series Eds.), *Advances in psychology: Vol. 8. Discourse processing* (pp. 186–204). North-Holland.

Kitch, C. (2014). Historical authority and the "potent journalistic reputation": A longer view of legacy-making in American news media. In B. Zelizer & K. Tenenboim-Weinblatt (Eds.), *Journalism and memory* (pp. 227–241). Palgrave Macmillan.

Kitzinger, J. (2000). Media templates: Key events and the (re)construction of meaning. *Media, Culture, & Society, 22*(1), 61–84.

Kopan, T. (2016, October 19). *No, the presidential election can't be hacked*. CNN. Retrieved January 10, 2019, from https://www.cnn.com/2016/10/19/politics/election-day-russia-hacking-explained/index.html

Kornilov, V. (2019, February 10). *Neudobnaja godovshhina. Zabytoe otravlenie v Solsberi* [Inconvenient anniversary. Forgotten Salisbury poisoning]. RIA Novosti. Retrieved February 2, 2020, from https://ria.ru/20191002/1559330322.html?in=t

Koroleva, E. (2019, June 23). Vpervye posle Solsberi: otkrovenija otravlennogo Skripalja [For the first time since Salisbury: The revelations of the poisoned Skripal]. *Gazeta* Retrieved January 25, 2020, from https://www.gazeta.ru/social/2019/05/23/12371863.shtml

Kosyrev, D. (2016, July 20). *Respublikanskuju partiju Donal'd Tramp uzhe pobedil* [Republican Party Donald Trump has already won]. RIA. Retrieved February 25, 2019, from https://ria.ru/20160720/1472423944.html

Kovalyova, A. (2013, November 28). *Is Vladimir Putin rewriting Russia's history books?* NBC News. Retrieved March 6, 2019, from https://www.nbcnews.com/news/other/vladimir-putin-rewriting-russias-history-books-f2D11669160

Kozminsky, E. (1977). Altering comprehension: The effect of biasing titles on text comprehension. *Memory & Cognition, 5*(4), 482–490.

Kramer, A. (2015, May 28). Putin declares soldiers' deaths and wounds secret, in war and peace. *The New York Times*. Retrieved June 5, 2020, from https://www.nytimes.com/2015/05/29/world/europe/putin-russian-soldiers-ukraine.html

Kuvaldin, S. (2013, March 22). New history textbooks may promote conservative values in Russia. *Russia Beyond the Headlines*. Retrieved March 6, 2019, from https://rbth.com/society/2013/03/22/new_history_textbooks_may_promote_conservative_values_in_russia_24163.html

Kuzio, T. (2015, January 25). Ukraine reignites: Why Russia should be added to the state sponsors of terrorism list. *Foreign Affairs*. Retrieved June 5, 2020, from https://www.foreignaffairs.com/articles/russian-federation/2015-01-25/ukraine-reignites

Lally, K. (2013, September 29). Russia anti-gay law casts a shadow over Sochi's 2014 Olympics. *The Washington Post*. Retrieved February 28, 2020, from https://www.washingtonpost.com/world/russia-anti-gay-law-casts-a-shadow-over-sochis-2014-olympics/2013/09/29/3646344c-27a6-11e3-9372-92606241ae9c_story.html

Lally, K., Englund, W., & Booth, W. (2014, March 1). Russian parliament approves use of troops in Ukraine. *The Washington Post*. Retrieved September 3, 2018, from https://www.washingtonpost.com/world/europe/russian-parliament-approves-use-of-troops-in-crimea/2014/03/01/d1775f70-a151-11e3-a050-dc3322a94fa7_story.html?utm_term=.cfbb114572c2

Lambert, A., Scherer, L., Rogers, C., & Jacoby, L. (2009). How does collective memory create a sense of the collective? In P. Boyer & J. Wertsch (Eds.), *Memory in mind and culture* (pp. 194–217). Cambridge University Press.

Landau, E., Magnay, D., & Wedeman, B. (2014, March 3). *In Russia's "low-key" invasion of Crimea, the fight is over information*. CNN. Retrieved May 23, 2020, from http://www.cnn.com/2014/03/03/world/europe/ukraine-crimea/index.html

Larsen, S. (1982). Knowledge updating in text processing. In A. Flammer & W. Kintsch (Series Eds.), *Advances in psychology: Vol. 8. Discourse processing* (pp. 205–218). North-Holland.

Lashov, Y. (2015, October 7). *Crimea under sanctions: What has changed in a year and a half.* RIA. Retrieved March 29, 2020, from https://ria.ru/20151007/1298117202.html

Latynina, Y. (2013, December 19). Zachem Putin dal 15 mlrd dollarov Janukovichu? [Why did Putin give $15 billion to Yanukovich?]. *Novaya Gazeta*. Retrieved May 26, 2020, from https://novayagazeta.ru/articles/2013/12/20/57729-zachem-putin-dal-15-mlrd-dollarov-yanukovichu

Latynina, Y. (2018, September 5). Raschet na tihuju likvidaciju: Otravlenie Skripalej—o tehnicheskoj storone voprosa [Calculation of silent liquidation: Skripal poisoning—on the technical side of the issue]. *Novaya Gazeta*. Retrieved February 2, 2020, from https://novayagazeta.ru/articles/2018/09/05/77721-raschet-na-tihuyu-likvidatsiyu

León, J. (1997). The effects of headlines and summaries on news comprehension and recall. *Reading and Writing*, *9*, 85–106.

Levin, V. (2016, September 28). Rossija oprovergla vyvody gollandskoj komissii [Russia has denied the findings of the Dutch commission]. *Novye Izvestia*. Retrieved April 10, 2020, from https://newizv.ru/news/world/28-09-2016/247390-rossija-oprovergla-vyvody-gollandskoj-komissii

Loewen, J. (1995). *Lies my teacher told me: Everything your American history textbooks got wrong*. Norton.

Loftus, E. (1992). When a lie becomes memory's truth: Memory distortion after exposure to misinformation. *Current Directions in Psychological Science*, *1*(4), 121–123.

Loftus, E. (1993). The reality of repressed memories. *American Psychologist*, *48*, 518–537.

Loftus, E. (2005). Planting misinformation in the human mind: A 30-year investigation of the malleability of memory. *Learning & Memory*, *12*(4), 361–366.

Lyall, S. (2014, February 23). A four-and-a-half-ring circus ends, and a relieved Russia roars. *The New York Times*. Retrieved February 29, 2020, from https://www.nytimes.com/2014/02/24/sports/olympics/with-olympics-closing-ceremony-a-chance-to-exhale.html

MacFarquhar, N. (2015, March 9). Putin contradicts claims on annexation of Crimea. *The New York Times*. Retrieved May 23, 2020, from https://www.nytimes.com/2015/03/10/world/europe/putin-contrary-to-earlier-assertions-suggests-planning-to-seize-crimea-started-in-early-2014.html

Mandl, H., & Ballstaedt, S. P. (1982). Effects of elaboration on recall of texts. In A. Flammer & W. Kintsch (Series Eds.), *Advances in psychology: Vol. 8. Discourse processing* (pp. 482–494). North-Holland.

Mannheim, K. (1952). The problem of generations. In P. Kecskemeti (Ed.), *Essays on the sociology of knowledge* (pp. 276–320). Routledge & Kegan Paul.

Marques, J., Paez, D., & Serra, A. (1997). Social sharing, emotional climate, and the transgenerational transmission of memories: The Portuguese colonial war. In J. Pennebaker, D. Paez, & B. Rimé (Eds.), *Collective memory of political events* (pp. 253–275). Erlbaum.

Marsh, E., & Rajaram, S. (2019). The digital expansion of the mind: Implications of internet usage for memory and cognition. *Journal of Applied Research in Memory and Cognition*, *8*, 1–14.

Martinov, K. (2019, March 16). Plach po Krymu [Crying over Crimea]. *Novaya Gazeta*. Retrieved April 5, 2020, from https://novayagazeta.ru/articles/2019/03/16/79895-plach-po-krymu

McDaniel, C. (2018). Russia's proud past and patriotic identity: A case study of historical accounts in contemporary Russian history textbooks. *Modern Languages Open, 1*, 1–33. https://doi.org/10.3828/mlo.v0i0.239

Melville, T. (2018, March 27). *Former Russian spy poisoned by nerve agent on door of home in England, police say*. CNBC. Retrieved January 10, 2020, from https://www.cnbc.com/2018/03/29/ex-russian-spy-skripal-poisoned-by-nerve-agent-on-door-of-home.html

Milchenko, A. (2019, May 30). "Dostatochno vnimanija:" v Kremle ne hotjat govorit' o Mjullere ["Enough attention": The Kremlin does not want to talk about Mueller]. *Gazeta*. Retrieved June 17, 2020, from https://www.gazeta.ru/politics/2019/05/30_a_12384571.shtml

Mineev, A. (2014, December 20). Ob otmene sankcij zabyli do marta [The lifting of sanctions was forgotten until March]. *Novaya Gazeta*. Retrieved March 29, 2020, from https://novayagazeta.ru/articles/2014/12/20/62445-ob-otmene-sanktsiy-zabyli-do-marta

Mineev, A. (2018, April 12). Jeffekt krushenija doverija: Izgotovitel' otravljajushhego veshhestva ne ukazan, no vse druzhno ukazyvajut na Rossiju [Effect of the trust collapse: The manufacturer of the poisonous substance is not specified, but all together point to Russia]. *Novaya Gazeta*. Retrieved February 2, 2020, from https://novayagazeta.ru/articles/2018/04/12/76158-effekt-krusheniya-doveriya

Mink, L. (1978). Narrative form as a cognitive instrument. In R. Canary & H. Kozicki (Eds.), *The writing of history: Literary form and historical understanding* (pp. 129–149). University of Wisconsin Press.

Misztal, B. (2003). *Theories of social remembering*. Open University Press.

Morello, C., & Constable, P. (2014, March 16). Crimeans vote to break away from Ukraine, join Russia. *The Washington Post*. Retrieved May 25, 2020, from https://www.washingtonpost.com/world/2014/03/16/ccec2132-acd4-11e3-a06a-e3230a43d6cb_story.html?utm_term=.11260d251ac5

Murdock, D. (1962). The serial position effect in free recall. *Journal of Experimental Psychology, 64*, 482–488.

Murphy, B. (2016, November 16). Russia snubs International Criminal Court amid scrutiny of Crimea annexation. *The Washington Post*. Retrieved December 1, 2018, from https://www.washingtonpost.com/world/russia-snubs-international-criminal-court-amid-scrutiny-of-crimea-annexation/2016/11/16/6186d2b0-ac05-11e6-8b45-f8e493f06fcd_story.html?utm_term=.a3d91762c766

Murphy, D. (2014, February 06). Amid US-Russia tussle over Ukraine, a leaked tape of Victoria Nuland. *The Christian Science Monitor*. Retrieved December 23, 2021, https://www.csmonitor.com/World/Security-Watch/Backchannels/2014/0206/Amid-US-Russia-tussle-over-Ukraine-a-leaked-tape-of-Victoria-Nuland

Myersand, S. L., & Barry, E. (2014, March 18). Putin reclaims Crimea for Russia and bitterly denounces the West. *The New York Times*. Retrieved May 25, 2020, from https://www.nytimes.com/2014/03/19/world/europe/ukraine.html

Naylor, B. (2017, January 5). *Intelligence chiefs "stand more resolutely" behind finding of Russia election hacking*. NPR. Retrieved January 28, 2019, from https://www.npr.org/2017/01/05/508355408/intelligence-chiefs-stand-more-resolutely-behind-finding-of-russia-election-hack

Nechepurenko, I. (2016, April 26). Tatar legislature is banned in Crimea. *The New York Times*. Retrieved January 17, 2019, from https://www.nytimes.com/2016/04/27/world/europe/crimea-tatar-mejlis-ban-russia.html

Neiger, M., Meyers, O., & Zandberg, E. (2011). On media memory: Editors' introduction. In M. Neiger, O. Meyers, & E. Zandberg (Eds.), *On media memory: Collective memory in a new media age* (pp. 1–24). Palgrave Macmillan.

Neuman, S., & Ritchie, L. C. (2014, February 22). *Ukrainian President voted out; opposition leader freed*. NPR. Retrieved August 29, 2018, from https://www.npr.org/sections/thetwo-way/2014/02/22/281083380/unkrainian-protesters-uneasy-president-reportedly-leaves-kiev

Niegemann, H. (1982). Influences of titles on the recall of instructional texts. In A. Flammer & W. Kintsch (Series Eds.), *Advances in psychology: Vol. 8. Discourse processing* (pp. 392–399). North-Holland.

Nora, P. (1989). Between memory and history: Les lieux de mémoire. Representations, 26, 7–25.

Novick, P. (1999). *The Holocaust in American life*. Houghton Mifflin.

Olick, J. (2014). Reflections on the underdeveloped relations between journalism and memory studies. In B. Zelizer & K. Tenenboim-Weinblatt (Eds.), *Journalism and memory* (pp. 17–31). Palgrave Macmillan.

Ost, J., Granbag, P., Udell, J., & Hjelmsäter, E. R. (2008). Familiarity breeds distortion: The effects of media exposure on false reports concerning media coverage of the terrorist attacks in London on 7 July 2005. *Memory, 16*, 76–85.

Paez, D., Basabe, N., & Gonzales, J. L. (1998). Social processes and collective memory: A cross-cultural approach to remembering political events. In J. Pennebaker, D. Paez, & B. Rimé (Eds.), *Collective memory of political events* (pp. 175–190). Erlbaum.

Paramagura, K. (2014, January 30). The not so sustainable Sochi Winter Olympics. *TIME*. Retrieved February 17, 2020, from https://time.com/2828/sochi-winter-olympics-environmental-damage

Paschyn, C. (2016, May 19). Russia is trying to wipe out Crimea's Tatars. *The New York Times*. Retrieved May 25, 2020, from https://www.nytimes.com/2016/05/20/opinion/russia-is-trying-to-wipe-out-crimeas-tatars.html

Peleschuk, D. (2015, March 19). What's happening to Crimea a year after Russia annexation. *USA Today*. Retrieved March 28, 2020, from https://www.usatoday.com/story/news/world/2015/03/19/globalpost-russia-crimea/25009393

Pennebaker, J., & Banasik, B. (1997). On the creation and maintenance of collective memories: History and social psychology. In J. Pennebaker, D. Paez, & B. Rimé (Eds.), *Collective memory of political events* (pp. 3–19). Erlbaum.

Pennebaker, J., & Gonzales, A. (2009). Making history: Social and psychological processes underlying collective memory. In P. Boyer & J. Wertsch (Eds.), *Memory in mind and culture* (pp. 171–193). Cambridge University Press.

Petelin, G., & Gromov, A. (2015, October 14). Rosaviacija somnevaetsja v "Buke" [Russia Aviation doubts "Buk"]. *Gazeta*. Retrieved May 19, 2020, from https://www.gazeta.ru/social/2015/10/14/7820465.shtml?updated

Pickard, V. (2020). *Democracy without journalism? Confronting the misinformation society*. Oxford University Press.

Poplavsky, A. (2020, January 31). "Nikogda ne priznaem Krym": kak SShA pomogut Ukraine ["We will never recognize Crimea": How the USA will help Ukraine]. *Gazeta*. Retrieved March 23, 2020, from https://www.gazeta.ru/politics/2020/01/31_a_12937634.shtml

Prosvirova, O., Yrchenko, V., & Mineeva, Y. (2016, November 8). Trump pobedil na vyborah prezidenta SShA. Hronika [Trump won the U.S. presidential election.

Chronicle]. *Novaya Gazeta*. Retrieved June 15, 2020, from https://novayagazeta.ru/articles/2016/11/08/70457-vybory-prezidenta-ssha-onlayn

Pushkov, A. (2017, April 11). Udar SShA po Sirii: chto ostalos' za kadrom? [The U.S. strike on Syria: What was left behind the scenes?]. *Izvestia*. Retrieved May 11, 2020, from https://iz.ru/news/680243

Re, G. (2020, May 31). *Susan Rice makes claim that Russians could be behind violent George Floyd demonstrations*. Fox News. Retrieved December 8, 2020, from https://www.foxnews.com/politics/susan-rice-suggests-russians-behind-violent-george-floyd-demonstrations

Reading, A. (2011). Memory and digital media: Six dynamics of the globital memory field. In M. Neiger, O. Meyers, & E. Zandberg (Eds.), *On media memory: Collective memory in a new media age* (pp. 241–252). Palgrave Macmillan.

Reading, A. (2014). The journalist as memory assembler: Non-memory, the war on terror and the shooting of Osama bin Laden. In B. Zelizer & K. Tenenboim-Weinblatt (Eds.), *Journalism and memory* (pp. 164–178). Palgrave Macmillan.

Rendall, S. (2005, January 1). The fairness doctrine. *Fair*. Retrieved April 16, 2020, from https://fair.org/extra/the-fairness-doctrine

Reynolds, R. E., Taylor, M. A., Steffensen, M. S., Shirey, L. L., & Anderson, R. C. (1982). Cultural schemata and reading comprehension. *Reading Research Quarterly*, *17*(3), 352–366.

Rich, P., & Zaragoza, M. (2020). Correcting misinformation in news stories: An investigation of correction timing and correction durability. *Journal of Applied Research in Memory and Cognition*, *9*(3), 310–322.

Rodgers, J. (2020, January 20). Johnson and Putin: Brexit Britain meets resurgent Russia, and they don't get on. *Forbes*. Retrieved February 8, 2020, from https://www.forbes.com/sites/jamesrodgerseurope/2020/01/20/johnson-and-putin-brexit-britain-meets-resurgent-russia-and-they-dont-get-on/#144a67351847

Roediger, H., Zaromb, F., & Butler, A. (2009). The role of repeated retrieval in shaping collective memory. In P. Boyer & J. Wertsch (Eds.), *Memory in mind and culture* (pp. 138–170). Cambridge University Press.

Romanova, O. (2014, December 16). U kazhdogo svoj Krym. U nas vot takoj [Everyone has their own Crimea. We have this one]. *Novaya Gazeta*. Retrieved March 29, 2020, from https://novayagazeta.ru/articles/2014/12/16/62380-u-kazhdogo-svoy-krym-151-u-nas-vot-takoy

Roth, A. (2014, March 3). From Russia, "tourists" stir the protests. *The New York Times*. Retrieved June 3, 2020, from https://www.nytimes.com/2014/03/04/world/europe/russias-hand-can-be-seen-in-the-protests.html?searchResultPosition=2

Rumelhart, D. (1980). Schemata: The building blocks of cognition. In J. R. Spiro, B. C. Bruce, & W. F. Brewer (Eds.), *Theoretical issues in reading comprehension* (pp. 33–58). Erlbaum.

Runkevich, D., & Malay, E. (2014, June 23). Sochinskaja Olimpiada vojdet v edinyj uchebnik istorii [Sochi Olympics will be included in a single history textbook]. *Izvestia*. Retrieved February 21, 2020, from https://iz.ru/news/572728

Ryan, M., Nakashima, E., & DeYoung, K. (2016, December 29). Obama administration announced measures to punish Russia for 2016 election interference. *The Washington Post*. Retrieved January 10, 2019, from https://www.washingtonpost.com/world/national-security/obama-administration-announces-measures-to-punish-russia-for-2016-election-interference/2016/12/29/311db9d6-cdde-11e6-a87f-b917067331bb_story.html?noredirect=on&utm_term=.f8055baf0786

Safronov, Y. (2018, April 18). Rossija sozdaet prikrytie dlja himicheskih atak v Sirii [Russia creates a cover for chemical attacks in Syria]. *Novaya Gazeta*. Retrieved March 19, 2019, from https://www.novayagazeta.ru/articles/2018/04/14/76183-rossiya-sozdaet-prikrytie-dlya-himicheskih-atak-v-sirii

Sahdra, B., & Ross, M. (2007). Group identification and historical memory. *Personality and Social Psychology Bulletin*, *33*, 384–395.

Samuelsohn, D., & Gerstein, G. (2019, March 24). Mueller finds no Trump–Russia conspiracy. *Politico*. Retrieved June 12, 2020, from https://www.politico.com/story/2019/03/24/breaking-news-barr-to-release-summary-of-mueller-report-1233771

Sanger, D. (2016, August 29). Harry Reid cites evidence of Russian tampering in U.S. vote, and seeks F.B.I inquiry. *The New York Times*. Retrieved January 10, 2019, from https://www.nytimes.com/2016/08/30/us/politics/harry-reid-russia-tampering-election-fbi.html

Sanger, D., & Savage, C. (2016, October 7). U.S. says Russia directed hacks to influence elections. *The New York Times*. Retrieved January 10, 2019, from https://www.nytimes.com/2016/10/08/us/politics/us-formally-accuses-russia-of-stealing-dnc-emails.html

Schacter, D. (1999). The seven sins of memory: Insights from psychology and cognitive neuroscience. *The American Psychologist*, *54*(3), 182–203.

Schoichet, C. (2015, May 28). *Putin makes Russia's peacetime military deaths a state secret*. CNN. Retrieved June 5, 2020, from https://www.cnn.com/2015/05/28/europe/russia-putin-peacetime-military-deaths-state-secret/index.html

Schudson, M. (2011). Journalism as a vehicle of non-commemorative cultural memory. In B. Zelizer & K. Tenenboim-Weinblatt (Eds.), *Journalism and memory* (pp. 85–96). Palgrave Macmillan.

Schwartz, B. (2014). American journalism's conventions and cultures, 1863–2013: Changing representations of the Gettysburg Address. In B. Zelizer & K. Tenenboim-Weinblatt (Eds.), *Journalism and memory* (pp. 211–226). Palgrave Macmillan.

Schwirtz, M. (2019, March 4). A year after Skripal poisoning, Russia offers defiant face to Britain and the West. *The New York Times*. Retrieved January 13, 2020, from https://www.nytimes.com/2019/03/04/world/europe/russia-skripal-poisoning-britain.html

Seipel, B. (2020, February 21). Clinton calls Trump "Putin's puppet" amid reports of Russian interference in 2020 election. *The Hill*. Retrieved June 12, 2020, from https://thehill.com/homenews/news/484105-clinton-calls-trump-putins-puppet-amid-reports-that-russia-is-interfering-in

Shabanov, V. (2010, June 13). Olimpiada v Sochi. Za cenoj ne postoim? [Olympics in Sochi. Do we not stand for the price?]. *Pravda*. Retrieved February 20, 2020, from https://www.pravda.ru/economics/1036093-news

Shane, S. (2017, March 20). Highlights from the House hearing on Russian interference in the U.S. election. *The New York Times*. Retrieved January 29, 2019, from https://www.nytimes.com/2017/03/20/us/politics/takeaways-russia-intelligence-committee-hearing.html

Shapiro, J. (2015, February 3). *Why arming the Ukrainians is a bad idea*. The Brookings Institution. Retrieved June 4, 2020, from https://www.brookings.edu/blog/up-front/2015/02/03/why-arming-the-ukrainians-is-a-bad-idea

Sheth, S. (2017, November 11). CIA splits with Trump following his controversial remarks about Putin and Russia's election meddling. *Business Insider*. Retrieved January 29, 2019, from https://www.businessinsider.com/mike-pompeo-splits-with-trump-putin-on-russian-meddling-2017-11

Shuster, S. (2015, March 20). Putin's confession on Crimea expose Kremlin media. *TIME.* Retrieved October 29, 2018, from http://time.com/3752827/putin-media-kremlin-crimea-ukraine

Shuster, S. (2018, March 8). The poisoning of ex-spy Sergei Skripal suggests Russia's rules have changed. *TIME.* Retrieved January 10, 2020, from https://time.com/5190988/russia-sergei-skripal-poison-fsb-kremlin

Shvejc, M., Galimova, N., & Rustamova, F. (2013, November 21). Progib, shag vpered i dva nazad [Bending down: A step forward, two steps back]. *Gazeta.* Retrieved May 26, 2020, from https://www.gazeta.ru/politics/2013/11/21_a_5763025.shtml

Sidorkova, I. (2017, June 5). *Bellingcat dokazala rossijskoe proishozhdenie "sbivshego MH17 Buka"* [Bellingcat has proven the Russian origin of the "downed MH17 Buk"]. RBC. Retrieved May 19, 2020, from https://www.rbc.ru/politics/05/06/2017/593333359a79474381064c91

Sinitzin, A. (2014, July 3). Ot redakcii: Kak spisat' olimpiadu [Editorial: How to write off the Olympics]. *Vedomosti.* Retrieved February 23, 2020, from https://www.vedomosti.ru/opinion/articles/2014/07/04/prazdnichnye-ubytki

Sink, J. (2019, October 16). *Trump warns Erdogan not to be "tough guy" or "fool," seeks deal. Bloomberg News.* Retrieved May 5, 2020, from https://www.bloomberg.com/news/articles/2019-10-16/trump-warns-erdogan-not-to-be-tough-guy-or-fool-seeks-deal

Smirnov, S. (2016, December 29). Iz SShA vysylajut 35 rossijskih diplomatov [35 Russian diplomats are sent from the US]. *Vedomosti.* Retrieved February 25, 2019, from https://www.vedomosti.ru/politics/articles/2016/12/29/671770-ssha-vveli-sanktsii

Smith, M., & Eshchenko, A. (2014, March 18). *Ukraine cries "robbery" as Russia annexes Crimea.* CNN. Retrieved September 11, 2018, from http://www.cnn.com/2014/03/18/world/europe/ukraine-crisis/index.html

Smith, P. (2019, June 20). *MH17 attack probe accused 4 men of murder—here's why.* NBC News. Retrieved September 29, 2019, from https://www.nbcnews.com/news/world/mh17-attack-probe-accused-4-men-murder-here-s-why-n1019586

Smith-Spark, L. (2015, July 17). *Victims' families wait for justice a year after MH17 shot down in Ukraine.* CNN. Retrieved October 29, 2018, from https://edition.cnn.com/2015/07/17/europe/ukraine-conflict-mh17-up-to-speed/index.html

Smith-Spark, L., Gumuchian, M. L., & Magnay, D. (2014, January 23). *Ukraine, Russia sign economic deal despite protests.* CNN. Retrieved September 4, 2018, from https://www.cnn.com/2013/12/17/world/europe/ukraine-protests/index.html

Smith-Spark, L., & Masters, J. (2018, May 24). *Missile that downed MH17 "owned by Russian brigade."* CNN. Retrieved May 15, 2020, from https://edition.cnn.com/2018/05/24/europe/mh17-plane-netherlands-russia-intl/index.html

Snyder, T. (2015, September 30).The real reason Russia is "helping" Syria. *TIME.* Retrieved October 29, 2018, from http://time.com/4054941/putin-russia-syria

Sokolov, M. (2015, October 13). *Sled babochki: chem Rossija dokazyvaet neprichastnost' k gibeli MH17* [Butterfly trail: How Russia proves its innocence in the death of MH17]. RBC. Retrieved April 10, 2020, from https://www.rbc.ru/politics/13/10/2015/561ce0049a79470879b597bb

Stanley, M., Yang, B., & Marsh, E. (2019). When the unlikely becomes likely: Qualifying language does not influence later truth judgments. *Journal of Applied Research in Memory and Cognition, 8,* 118–129.

Starr, B., Browne, R., & Gaouette, N. (2018, December 19). *Trump orders rapid withdrawal from Syria in apparent reversal.* CNN. Retrieved March 4, 2019, from https://www.cnn.com/2018/12/19/politics/us-syria-withdrawal/index.html

Stelnbuch, Y. (2016, July 1). One-armed Chechen warlord named as Istanbul attack mastermind. *New York Post*. Retrieved April 16, 2020, from http://nypost.com/2016/07/01/one-armed-chechen-warlord-mastermind-behind-istanbul-attack

Storm, B. (2019). Thoughts on the digital expansion of the mind and the effects of using the internet on memory and cognition. *Journal of Applied Research in Memory and Cognition*, *8*, 29–32.

Švedkauskas, Ž., Sirikupt, C., & Salzer, M. (2020, July 24). Russia's disinformation campaigns are targeting African Americans. *The Washington Post*. Retrieved December 8, 2020, from https://www.washingtonpost.com/politics/2020/07/24/russias-disinformation-campaigns-are-targeting-african-americans

Svrluga. B. (2014, February 21). When the Olympics end, what will become of Sochi? *The Washington Post*. Retrieved February 26, 2020, from https://www.washingtonpost.com/sports/olympics/when-the-olympics-end-what-will-become-of-sochi/2014/02/21/d05bc8ca-9a4d-11e3-80ac-63a8ba7f7942_story.html

Sychev, V. (2014, July 18). Vne zony otvetstvennosti [Beyond the responsibility zone]. *Lenta*. Retrieved October 1, 2018, from https://lenta.ru/articles/2014/07/18/buk

Tabak, M. (2020, January 19). *Prem'er Britanii nazval Putinu uslovie normalizacii otnoshenij* [British Prime Minister called Putin a condition for normalizing relations]. RIA Novosti. Retrieved January 26, 2020, from https://ria.ru/20200119/1563608122.html

Tillett, E. (2017, November 12). *Treasury secretary on reducing gov't spending: "Not an issue we're focused on right now."* CBS. Retrieved June 16, 2020, from https://www.cbsnews.com/news/treasury-secretary-mnuchin-on-reducing-govt-spending-not-an-issue-were-focused-on-right-now/

Titov, E. (2014, October 21). Ogon', voda i kanalizacionnye truby: Zakonchilas' Olimpiada, otshumeli fanfary «Formuly-1», a gorod po-prezhnemu sbrasyvaet nechistoty v Chernoe more [Fire, water and sewer pipes: The Olympics has ended, the "Formula 1" fanfare has made a noise, and the city is still dumping sewage into the Black Sea]. *Novaya Gazeta*. Retrieved February 21, 2020, from https://novayagazeta.ru/articles/2014/10/22/61651-ogon-voda-i-kanalizatsionnye-truby

Todd, C., Murray, M., & Dann, C. (2017, July 6). *Trump downplays Russian election meddling yet again*. NBC News. Retrieved January 29, 2019, from https://www.nbcnews.com/politics/first-read/trump-downplays-russian-election-meddling-yet-again-n780031

Tousignant, J., Hall, D., & Loftus, E. (1986). Discrepancy detection and vulnerability to misleading postevent information. *Memory & Cognition, 14*(4), 329–338.

Tuchman, G. (1980). *Making news: A study in the construction of reality*. Free Press.

Turchinov, A. (2014). Ukraina obvinila Rossiju v popytke anneksii Kryma [Ukraine accuses Russia of trying to annex Crimea]. *Lenta*. Retrieved May 27, 2020, from https://lenta.ru/news/2014/03/01/scenario

van Cauwenberge, A., Schaap, G., & van Roy, R. (2014). "TV no longer commands our full attention": Effects of second screen viewing and task relevance on cognitive load and learning from news. *Computers in Human Behavior*, *38*, 100–109.

van Dijk, T. (1988). *News as discourse*. Erlbaum.

van Dijk, T. (2018). Socio-cognitive discourse studies. In J. Flowerdew & J. E. Richardson (Eds.), *The Routledge handbook of critical discourse studies* (pp. 25–43). Routledge, Taylor & Francis.

van Dijk, T., & Kintsch, W. (1983). *Strategies of discourse comprehension*. Academic Press.

Vaschenko, V., Bratersky, A., & Dergachev, V. (2015, October 13). MH17: itogovyj doklad o krushenii Boeing v Donbasse [MH17: Final report on the crash of Boeing in Donbass]. *Gazeta*. Retrieved October 31, 2018, from https://www.gazeta.ru/politics/2015/10/13_a_7818707.shtml

Vernitzky, A. (2014, August 27). *Po itogam peregovorov v Minske Vladimir Putin sdelal rjad vazhnyh zajavlenij* [Following the talks in Minsk, Vladimir Putin made a number of important statements]. 1 TV. Retrieved June 4, 2020, from https://www.ru/news/2014-08-27/40448-po_itogam_peregovorov_v_minske_vladimir_putin_sdelal_ryad_vazhnyh_zayavleniy https://www.1tv.ru/news/2014-08-27/40448-po_itogam_peregovorov_v_minske_vladimir_putin_sdelal_ryad_vazhnyh_zayavleniy

Victor, D. (2018, April 11). Suspected chemical attack in Syria: What we know and don't know. *The New York Times*. Retrieved March 4, 2019, from https://www.nytimes.com/2018/04/11/world/middleeast/syria-chemical-attack.html

Wang, Q. (2019). The individual mind in the active construction of its digital niche. *Journal of Applied Research in Memory and Cognition*, *8*, 25–28.

Wang, Q., Conway, M., Kulkofsky, S., Hou, Y., Mueller-Johnson, K., Aydin, C., & Williams, H. (2009). The "egocentric" Americans? Long-term memory for public events in five countries. *Cognitive Sciences*, *4*(2), 111–120.

Ward, K. (2006). *History in the making: An absorbing look at how American history has changed in the telling over the last 200 years*. The New Press.

Wender, K. (1982). Influence processes in discourse comprehension measured by sentence reading times. In A. Flammer & W. Kintsch (Series Eds.), *Advances in psychology: Vol. 8. Discourse processing* (pp. 166–171). North-Holland.

Wertsch, J. (2002). *Voices of collective remembering*. Cambridge University Press.

Wertsch, J. (2009). Collective memory. In P. Boyer & J. Wertsch (Eds.), *Memory in mind and culture* (pp. 117–137). Cambridge University Press.

Wertsch, J., & Roediger, H. (2008). Collective memory: Conceptual foundations and theoretical approaches. *Memory*, *16*(3), 318–326.

Wharton, D. (2014, February 2). Sochi Olympics tainted by corruption? *Chicago Tribune*. Retrieved February 28, 2020, from https://www.chicagotribune.com/sports/ct-xpm-2014-02-02-ct-sochi-corruption-spt-0203-20140203-story.html

White, H. (1987). *The concept of the form: Narrative discourse and historical representation*. Johns Hopkins University Press.

Winter, J. (2009). Historians and sites of memory. In P. Boyer & J. Wertsch (Eds.), *Memory in mind and culture* (pp. 252–268). Cambridge University Press.

Wolf, Z. (2020, February 22). *Russian meddling was out of a spy novel in 2016. It's turning 2020 into a horror movie*. CNN. Retrieved February 22, 2020, from https://edition.cnn.com/2020/02/22/politics/what-matters-february-21/index.html

Wolgelenter, M., & Pérez-Peña, R. (2018, April 10). Yulia Skripal released from U.K. hospital after poisoning. *The New York Times*. Retrieved January 10, 2020, from https://www.nytimes.com/2018/04/10/world/europe/yulia-skripal-released-hospital.html

Wong, K. (2015, February 2). Lawmakers to Obama: Arm Ukraine now. *The Hill*. Retrieved June 4, 2020, from https://thehill.com/policy/defense/231874-senators-to-obama-arm-ukraine-now

Yamashiro, J., & Roediger, H., III. (2019). Expanding cognition: A brief consideration of technological advances over the past 4000 years. *Journal of Applied Research in Memory and Cognition*, *8*, 15–19.

Yavlinsky, G. (2014, July 18). Jeta voenno-politicheskaja avantjura beskonechno opasna i strategicheski bessmyslenna [This military–political adventure is infinitely dangerous and strategically meaningless]. *Novaya Gazeta*. Retrieved April 10, 2020, from https://novayagazeta.ru/articles/2014/07/18/60398-eta-voenno-politicheskaya-avantyura-beskonechno-opasna-i-strategicheski-bessmyslenna

Zelenski, M. (2017, April 5). Siriju obvinili v himicheskoj atake, iz-za kotoroj pogibli 72 cheloveka. Moskva zashhishhaet Damask [Syria blamed for chemical attack which killed 72 people. Moscow defends Damascus]. *Meduza*. Retrieved May 7, 2020, from https://meduza.io/feature/2017/04/05/siriyu-obvinili-v-himicheskoy-atake-iz-za-kotoroy-pogibli-72-cheloveka-moskva-zaschischaet-damask-glavnoe

Zelizer, B. (1992). *Covering the body: The Kennedy assassination, the media, and the shaping of collective memory*. University of Chicago Press.

Zelizer, B. (2011). Memory as foreground, journalism as background. In B. Zelizer & K. Tenenboim-Weinblatt (Eds.), *Journalism and memory* (pp. 66–79). Palgrave Macmillan.

Zelizer, B. (2014). Memory as foreground, journalism as backround. In B. Zelizer & K. Tenenboim-Weinblatt (Eds.), *Journalism and memory* (pp. 32–49). NY, USA: Palgrave MacMillan Memory Studies.

Zhukovsky, I. (2017, November 13). Vozdejstvija na vybory ne bylo [There was no impact on the election]. *Gazeta*. Retrieved February 27, 2019, from https://www.gazeta.ru/politics/2017/11/12_a_10982474.shtml

Zuevsky, V. (2019, December 1). Grjazno anglijskoe ubijstvo: britancy mogut likvidirovat' Skripalej [Dirty English killing: British can eliminate the Skripals]. *Izvestia*. Retrieved February 8, 2020, from https://iz.ru/947854/vladislav-zuevskii-nikolai-pozdniakov/griazno-angliiskoe-ubiistvo-britantcy-mogut-likvidirovat-skripalei

Index

For the benefit of digital users, indexed terms that span two pages (e.g., 52–53) may, on occasion, appear on only one of those pages.

Tables and figures are indicated by *t* and *f* following the page number.